ON SUBJECT AND THEME

AMSTERDAM STUDIES IN THE THEORY AND HISTORY OF LINGUISTIC SCIENCE

General Editor

E. F. KONRAD KOERNER

(University of Ottawa)

Series IV - CURRENT ISSUES IN LINGUISTIC THEORY

Advisory Editorial Board

Volume 118

Ruqaiya Hasan and Peter H. Fries (eds)

On Subject and Theme

ON SUBJECT AND THEME

A DISCOURSE FUNCTIONAL PERSPECTIVE

Edited by

RUQAIYA HASAN
Macquarie University

PETER H. FRIES
Central Michigan University

JOHN BENJAMINS PUBLISHING COMPANY
AMSTERDAM/PHILADELPHIA

™ The paper used in this publication meets the minimum requirements of American National Standard for Information Sciences — Permanence of Paper for Printed Library Materials, ANSI Z39.48-1984.

Library of Congress Cataloging-in-Publication Data

On subject and theme : a discourse functional perspective / edited by Ruqaiya Hasan, Peter H. Fries.

    p.   cm. -- (Amsterdam studies in the theory and history of linguistic science. Series IV, Current issues in linguistic theory, ISSN 0304-0763 ; v. 118)

   Includes bibliographical references and index.

   Contents: Approaching the French clause as a move in dialogue / Alice Caffarel -- Mood and the ecosocial dynamics of semiotic exchange / Paul J. Thibault -- The English "tag question" / Bill McGregor -- "Nothing" makes sense in Weri / Maurice Boxwell -- Subjectlessness and honorifics in Japanese / Motoko Hori -- A dynamic perspective / L.J. Ravelli -- Subject and theme in Chinese / Fang Yan, Edward McDonald, Cheng Musheng -- A systemic-functional approach to the thematic structure of the Old English clause / Michael Cummings -- Themes, methods of development, and texts / Peter H. Fries -- Defining and relating text segments / Carmel Cloran.

   1. Grammar, Comparative and general--Topic and comment. 2. Discourse analysis. I. Hasan, Ruqaiya. II. Fries, Peter Howard. III. Series.

P298.05   1995

415--dc20   95-8905

ISBN 90 272 3621 6 (Eur.) / 1-55619-572-9 (US) (alk. paper)   CIP

John Benjamins Publishing Co. • P.O.Box 75577 • 1070 AN Amsterdam • The Netherlands
John Benjamins North America • P.O.Box 27519 • Philadelphia PA 19118-0519 • USA

Acknowledgments

Many people have helped in bringing this book about, and we would like to take this opportunity to thank them. First and foremost are, of course, the contributors to the volume: without them there would have been no book! This is reason enough for thanking, but we wish to give special thanks to them for so willingly attending to the many calls we have made on them. Our thanks are due to the anonymous referees who were generous with their time and permitted us to benefit from their expertise. Nancy Fries helped in many ways, giving a good deal of practical assistance and good counsel. We are indebted to Neil Halliday for his generosity in "donating" not only his Apple Macintosh but also his time, troubleshooting when the machines felt mismanaged! We thank Michael Halliday for so readily coming to our assistance in many ways. Professor Konrad Koerner, the General Editor of the Series, saved us valuable hours by giving helpful advice during a very busy lecture tour in Australia; we remember his visit with pleasure and thank him for his kindness. Our especial thanks are due to Yola de Lusenet, of Benjamins. It has been a real pleasure working with her on this volume: we have greatly appreciated her readiness to help, her expert guidance and her unfailingly positive approach.

Behind this volume lies also the work of the Organising Committee of the 19th ISFC92, which was the occasion for the production of the papers in this volume. We thank Macquarie University, the School of English and Linguistics and especially the discipline of Linguistics for their generous support of the Congress, and although it is not possible to name the many good friends, students and colleagues who helped make the Congress a success, their help is gratefully remembered and warmly appreciated.

Ruqaiya Hasan
Peter H. Fries

Contents

Contents

About the authors

Maurice BOXWELL has been a member of the Summer Institute of Linguistics (SIL) since 1961, working for much of that time amongst the Weri people of Papua New Guinea. His main interest lies in the area of Papuan languages and he has published a number of papers on the phonology and grammar of Weri. His doctoral dissertation (Macquarie University) was based on a study of the co-referential relations established through nominal elements in Weri. He is currently working in Australia, teaching a cross-cultural communications course, and may be contacted at *4 Pleasant Court, Carlingford, NSW 2118, Australia.*

Alice CAFFAREL's main research interests are the grammar and semantics of spoken and written French, register variation, and computational linguistics. She is currently developing a systemic functional description of some aspects of the grammar of French for her doctoral research at Sydney University, while also working towards the implementation of a register specific grammar of French in the context of the multilingual text generation project (director: Christian Matthiessen). For an example of register specific grammatical description see her 'Interacting between a generalised tense semantics and register-specific semantic tense systems: A bi-stratal exploration of the semantics of French tense', *Language Sciences* 14.4, 1992. Contact: *The Department of Linguistics, University of Sydney, NSW 2006, Australia.*

CHENG Musheng is Professor of English and Chair of the Department of Foreign Languages, Tsinghua University. Her research areas have been general and historical linguistics, lexicology, foreign language teaching and the description of Chinese. She is one of the Chief Editors of *An English-Chinese Dictionary of Science and Technology* and one of the main compilers of the *English-Chinese Word-Ocean Dictionary*, both published by the National Defence Publishers. Professor Cheng can be contacted at the *Department of Foreign Languages, Tsinghua University, Beijing, PRC, 100084.*

Carmel CLORAN's research interests include context and language, language and socialisation, language and cognitive development, and lexis as delicate grammar. She has played a major investigative role in the sociolinguistic research project The Role of Language in Establishing Ways of Learning Phases 1-3 (director: Ruqaiya Hasan), and is currently engaged in research on Reasoning in Everyday Talk (with Ruqaiya Hasan) and Lexis as Delicate Grammar (with Colin Yallop and Ruqaiya Hasan). She is the author of *Rhetorical Units and Decontextualisation: An enquiry into some relations of grammar, meaning and context* – her doctoral dissertation – published 1994 by the Department of English Studies, Birmingham University in the series Monographs in Systemic Linguistics. Contact: *School of English, Linguistics, and Media, Macquarie University, NSW 2109, Australia.*

Michael CUMMINGS has research interests which include Old English, modern synchronic linguistics and logic programming. He is the co-author of *The Language of Literature: A linguistic introduction to the study of literature* (with R Simmons, published by Pergamon Press, 1983) and co-editor of *Linguistics in a Systemic Perspective* (with J Benson and William Greaves, published by John Benjamins 1988). He chairs the *Department of English, Glendon College, York University, 2275 Bayview Avenue, Toronto, Ont M4N 3M6, Canada.* [e-mail: <GL250004@Venus.YorkU.Ca>]

FANG Yan is Professor of English at Tsinghua University. Her research interests include the description of Chinese grammar in the framework of systemic functional linguistics, linguistic schools, and linguistics and foreign language teaching. Her publications include 'A tentative study of the theme and rheme structure in Chinese', *Journal of Tsinghua University: Philosophy & Social Science*, 2.1989, 'On Subject in Chinese – 'Subject', 'Actor' and 'Theme' in *Language System and Function,* edited by Hu Zhuanglin (Peking University Press, 1990), and 'Applications of functional grammar to the teaching of the advanced reading course' in *Language, Text and Context*, edited by Zhu Yongsheng (Tsinghua University Press, 1993). Professor Fang may be contacted at the *Department of Foreign Languages, Tsinghua University, Beijing, PRC. 100084.*

Peter H FRIES is Professor of English and Linguistics at Central Michigan University (Mount Pleasant, Michigan 48859, USA.) and an Honorary

Professor of Hangzhou University (China). His research interests include linguistic theories, grammatical description of English, discourse analysis and lately corpus linguistics. He has published widely in linguistics; in particular his work on thematic structures, method of development and discourse is widely known. Currently he is engaged in writing *The Cambridge Grammar of English* with Rodney Huddleston, Keith Brown, Peter Collins, David Lee, Pam Peters, and Peter Peterson. He has co-edited *Discourse in Society: Systemic functional perspectives* (with Michael Gregory, to be published shortly by Ablex). Contact : *Box 310 Mount Pleasant, MI 48804, USA.* [e-mail <343i2tw@cmuvm.csv.cmich.edu>].

Ruqaiya HASAN is Professor Emerita of Linguistics at Macquarie University. Her research interests include stylistics, discourse analysis, lexis as delicate grammar, semantic networks, and socio-semantic variation, and she has published in all of these areas. Her recent major research concerned the investigation of socio-semantic variation in and around Sydney. Contact: *School of English, Linguistics and media, Macquarie University, NSW 2109, Australia.* [e-mail: <rhasan@pip.engl.mq.edu.au>].

Motoko HORI currently works in the area of functional and pragmatic analysis of Japanese. She has been associated with a sociolinguistic research on the language of Japanese women, and has focussed particularly on honorific expressions in Japanese. Her publications (in English) include 'A sociolinguistic analysis of the Japanese honorifics', *Journal of Pragmatics* 10.3, 1986, 'Politeness strategy on the morphological level: A case study of Japanese', *The Tsuda Review,* 33, 1988, and 'Language forms reflecting social hierarchy and psychological attitude', *ERIC Microfiche* 1988. Contact: *Tokai Women's College, Kakamigahara City, Gifu Prefecture, Japan 504.*

Edward McDONALD's research interests include Chinese grammar and text analysis, application of systemic functional theory to the teaching of grammar, and the ideological status of the Chinese language among Chinese intellectuals and Western Sinologists. For his doctoral research, he is developing aspects of the grammar of Chinese in textual contexts. Apart from producing a text-based grammar of Chinese for foreign students learning the Chinese language at the tertiary level, he has published 'Outline of a functional grammar of Chinese for teaching purposes', *Language Sciences,* 14.4,

1992, and 'The complement in Chinese grammar' (to appear in *Functional Descriptions*, edited by Ruqaiya Hasan, Carmel Cloran & David G. Butt, to be published shortly by Benjamins). Contact: *Department of Linguistics, University of Sydney, NSW 2006, Australia.*

William McGREGOR holds an Australian Research Council Fellowship at the University of Melbourne. He has made an in-depth study of Gooniyandi, reported in his *A Functional Grammar of Gooniyandi* (Benjamins, 1990). Currently he is engaged in writing an encyclopaedic grammar and dictionary of Nyulnyul, and shorter sketch grammars of Warrwa, Ungummi, Yawiji-baya, Umiida, Unggarrangu and Gunin (to appear in *Languages of the World/Materials*, Lincom Europa). McGregor is co-editor (with Hilary Chappell) of *The Grammar of Inalienability: A typological perspective on the part-whole relation and body-part terms*, (to be published by Mouton de Gruyter). Contact: *Linguistics Department, University of Melbourne, Parkville, Victoria 3052, Australia.* [Phone: (03) 344 5195].

Louise RAVELLI currently teaches linguistics at the University of Wollongong with a strong focus on systemic functional linguistics and its educational applications at a variety of levels. She is exploring literacy at the tertiary level, as well as working with the State Education Departments on the teaching of systemic functional linguistics at the secondary level, and with the Australian Museum on the production of exhibition texts in the context of workplace practices. She is the co-editor of *Advances in Systemic Linguistics: Recent theory and practice* (with Martin Davies, published by Pinter 1992). Contact: *Department of English, University of Wollongong, Wollongong, NSW 2522, Australia.*

Paul J. THIBAULT is Associate Professor in English Language and Linguistics, at the University of Padova, Italy. His interests include functional grammar and semantics, discourse analysis, genre theory, semiotics, literary and social theory, and increasingly, child language, educational linguistics and literacy. Major publications include *Text, Discourse, and Context: A social semiotic perspective* (Toronto Semiotic Circle, 1986), and *Social Semiotic as Praxis* (Minnesota University press 1991). He is currently completing a book for Routledge entitled *Reading Saussure*. Contact: *Dipartimento di Linguistica, Università di Padova, via Beatto Pellegrino 1, 35137 Padova, Italy.*

Reflections on Subject and Theme:
An introduction

Ruqaiya Hasan
Macquarie University

Peter H Fries
Central Michigan University

1. Ideas about language

The papers in this volume represent a selection from amongst those heard at the 19th International Systemic Functional Congress 1992 which was held at Macquarie University in July of that year. They are concerned with two descriptive categories – subject and theme – both of which have attracted much attention in modern linguistics, and both are surrounded by questions which are still in search of answers. For example: is subject a universal category? Is theme? If so, what definition of these categories will hold universally, and how can the categories be recognised across languages? Is there any specific relation between subject and theme? For example, are there some languages which are best described as "subject-predicate languages", and others which are really "theme-rheme languages"? Linguists do recognise that sometimes in a language a clause constituent may not only be a subject but also an agent/actor. Does a comparable situation exist with respect to subject and theme, with the same clause constituent having both these functions? And what difference, if any, does it make for the same constituent to have both these functions as opposed to simply one or the other? Given that agency, long-recognised as a grammatical category (see, for example, Lyons 1968: 295 ff), is granted a semantic value, could the grammatical categories of subject and theme be said to have some semantic value as well? If so, what is this value and is it the same across languages?

If it is suggested that the categories of subject and theme do not have any semantic value, it seems pertinent to ask why this should be so, and whether as linguists we are able to recommend any criteria for differentiating those grammatical categories that have a semantic value from the others that do not enjoy this privilege?

Reflection on such issues leads us to suggest that in the last resort these and other such questions derive from a more fundamental one the answer to which is grounded in the linguists' conception of language. This fundamental question may be phrased as follows: is everything in the linguistic system – its words, phrases, its elements of structure, the sequential order of these elements and their conflation which, according to the systemic functional model, derives from the simultaneous operation of distinct metafunctions – necessarily meaning-construing? Linguists have answered this question differently depending on their ideas about language. If they think of language as a mirror which simply reflects a pre-existing (material) reality, they are bound to attach a different and privileged status to just those categories which correspond to what they perceive as reality. In such a view, the concept of "meaning" is naturally limited to that of correspondence to pre-existing reality: the categories of language, being grounded in some language-independent reality, are thus taken to mirror the categories of nature. This approach denies the meaning creating power inherent in language – the potential of language to construe meanings so that the meanings are essentially an artefact of the linguistic system. So, not surprisingly, in this perspective the term *meaning construal* is devoid of meaning. We will refer to this view as the *correspondence* perspective on language. If, on the other hand, one thinks of language not as a mirroring device but as a potential for creating a semiotic reality which stands in some systematic relation to material reality without actually mirroring it, then language becomes a powerhouse for construing meaning, and the concept of meaning itself bursts the bonds of representation, extending to include both interpersonal and textual meanings which are largely, if not entirely, linguistically created. This perspective, which we shall refer to as *constructivist*, grants an equal status to all formal devices, including those whereby the so called "non-referential" meanings are construed. We need to emphasise that these "non-referential" meanings – the interpersonal and the textual – do relate to important aspects of reality: in fact, we can claim with confidence that this order of reality concerns phenomena that are specifically human, viz., an intersubjectivity which is based not on instinct but on social interaction, and modes of social interaction which are based not on pre-programmed communicative devices but on an open ended, socially sensitive verbal system for the exchange of meaning. The reality to which interpersonal and textual meanings relate is, thus, very real to human beings, even if it is not material.

The interpretation of functionalism in the systemic functional model suggests an acceptance of the *constructivist* view; the adoption of this point of view in its turn creates an object of study for the SF linguist which looks remarkably different from any that the *correspondence* perspective has given rise to. Failure to appreciate these fundamental differences has resulted in a good deal of mis-reading of the SF position; its descriptive categories have often been judged by reference to a view of language which from the point of view of the SF model would be rejected as entirely untenable. We will draw attention here to three points fundamental to the SF approach, pursuing their implications which appear most relevant for our purposes.

(i)   Since language is a potential for creating meanings which bear a system-
      atic relation to the conditions of human existence, the primary goal of
      linguistics is to explain not only how meanings are construed but also
      how they maintain a systematic relation to the already linguistically
      construed socially defined world. Reflection shows that in the construal
      of this world, all meanings – experiential, logical, interpersonal and
      textual – are equally important, and all are first and foremost semiotic
      in nature. This removes all justification for treating logical and experi-
      ential meanings – ie., those traditionally known as referential – as the
      only/primary meanings relevant to linguistic form. Human language
      evolves only as its speakers use it for the living of their life, and speak-
      ers live just as much by the semiotically created interpersonal and
      textual meanings as they do by the referential ones.

(ii) Since language is seen as a powerhouse for the creation of these differ-
      ent sorts of meaning, the description of language logically demands
      attention to what a lexicogrammatical device does, ie., the meaning(s)
      it construes for some speakers, somewhere, under some conditions. The
      observation that a given lexicogrammatical device might construe
      different meanings for different (groups of) speakers is not an argument

against viewing language as a meaning potential; it is simply an argument against monolithic descriptions that ignore variation. It follows
that inquiry into the (semantic) value(s) of a category is an essential
aspect of the sf approach, and attention to this aspect is not something
peripheral. From this point of view there are no descriptive categories
which are purely "notional" or "teleological", just as there are none
which are purely "formal". It follows from this discussion that in a
truly functional model the forms of a language do not exist simply as
form; they have some function, some semantic value, and it is this
semantic value of a category such as subject or theme that is viewed as
its *definition criteria* (Halliday 1985).

(iii) Equally important, and in no way in opposition to the former view, is
the need to focus on the formal properties of a lexicogrammatical
category, ie., what identifies it as that type of descriptive category. This
is an essential step without which we cannot hope to establish which
formal patterns have the potential for construing which meanings. It is
these formal properties that furnish what Halliday (1985) refers to as
the *recognition criteria* of a lexicogrammatical category. The identification of formal criteria by which some category type is recognised often
constitutes the only preoccupation of formal grammars, and, perhaps
somewhat unthinkingly, this limited concern with form is sometimes
pitted against a concern with meaning. Clearly, from the point of view
of the sf model the relation between meaning and form is not that of
mutual exclusion – either this or that; rather, it is a relation between the
manifested and the manifesting, the construed and the construing,
where one without the other is either an impossibility or an absurdity,
and both are essential for the description of the whole. The grammatical
description produced within the framework of the sf model is, thus,
REQUIRED to be both functional AND formal; it cannot be just the one
or the other. This has the significant consequence that whereas for some
linguistic approaches being "purely formal" is a desirable goal, for the
systemic functional model being purely formal is something to be
avoided.

Taking these three points together it is obvious that in the sf model the
linguist's object of study, language, is viewed as a highly complex phenome-

non. By the same token the definition of "linguistics proper" current in many of the formal approaches begins to appear quite inadequate. So far as the SF linguist is concerned, the job of linguistics is to describe the entire complex phenomenon of language, not just some specific aspect eg., its formal syntax, to which a privileged status has been ascribed on grounds the validity of which remains far from proven. It may appear a practical convenience at a first glance to relegate specific components of the study of language to distinct (sub-)fields, such as sociolinguistics, psycholinguistics, and/or pragmatics; but this step, far from creating out of the residue an objective and scientific linguistics, in fact poses a serious problem: where, when, and how do we "synthesise" the aspects of language – its social cognitive basis; its active power – which have been "analysed out" in order to create a "pure" science of language? We believe that the catholic view of the goals of linguistics accepted in the SF model is necessary if we are to avoid an undesirable fragmentation of the object of study in linguistics. If linguistics is the study of language, then the goal of linguistics has to be the description of language in its entirety. To describe this requirement as a form of "linguistic imperialism" (cf Leech 1983) seems to miss the real point. Each of the three issues discussed above is relevant to theory and practice in linguistics; as such it should be relevant to the discussion of subject and theme as conceptualized in the SF model.

1.1 Ideas about language and the definition of a linguistic category

It is notable that the categories of subject and theme have been interpreted in the SF model as relating to interpersonal and textual meanings respectively. This already poses a problem for linguistic models with a correspondence perspective; such models only recognise representational meaning, with the obvious consequence that there is nothing comparable to the interpersonal and/or textual meaning in these models. But the situation is made even more problematic because of the peculiar nature of these latter categories of meanings. What these meanings relate to in the social conditions of human existence is far more abstract than is the case with either the logical or the experiential meanings – the mainstay of the correspondence approach. For example, in prototypical cases, the situational referent of most entities with the representational/ experiential role of Agent can, at least in principle, be physically observed by someone somewhere as the agency acting to bring about some process. By contrast, it is not very easy to physically apprehend a "resting point of the argument" which is how Halliday (1985: 77) glosses the meaning of the grammatical category Subject. Nor is it easy to figure out, as Fries points out in his contribution to this volume, what "the point of departure" or "the starting point of a message" looks like, which is the offered meaning of the category of Theme by Halliday (1985: 39); the same applies to Mathesius' gloss of theme (1939) as "that which is known or at least obvious in the given situation and from which the speaker proceeds". We suggest that the source of the problem lies in the nature of interpersonal and textual meanings. The "reality" to which such meanings relate "exists" itself only by virtue of semiotic activity – the question of correspondence to something in the extra-linguistic world cannot be raised very sensibly. However we doubt if it helps to reject the very possibility of the existence of such abstract meanings simply because their "referents/correlates" are not easy to point to; nor does it seem to be a sufficient reason for rejecting the postulated semantic value of these descriptive categories for some language such as English. What might help in this situation is to establish somehow, if we can, what actually happens *in* the language as it gets used. It is this kind of inquiry that might be capable of creating a more tangible sense of what these abstract semantic characterisations mean. In other words, while for reasons to which Halliday (1984) drew attention, it may be problematic to provide an easily intelligible gloss for the semantic characterisations of a category, it may yet be possible to show what one means through apt illustrations of how the category works in use.

To provide an example of this process we turn to Halliday, who has shown what he means by semanticising the Subject in English as "the resting point of the argument" (1985) or "the modally responsible element" (1992). He does this by illustrating the central role that Subject plays in an English dialogic exchange (Halliday 1985: 71ff; see also comparable discussion both in Caffarel and Hori, this volume). So long as the experiential meaning of the (declarative) clause initiating a dialogic exchange remains constant, any subsequent dialogic move eg., acknowledging, contradicting, accepting, rejecting, or enquiring into the why, how, when of the case, if realised by a major clause, will involve invoking the same entity as Subject. This can be seen by comparing the appropriateness of (a) and (b) as rejoinders to the initial clause in example (1):

(1)   Mum, my teddy wants another scone.
    (a) oh, does he (want...)?   (b) oh, is it (wanted by him)?
    (a) no, he doesn't (want...).   (b) no, it isn't (wanted...).
    (a) why does he (want...)?   (b) why is it (wanted...)?

In this example the (b) rejoinders appear 'suspect'; they are definitely not typical of how exchanges go in English, and yet note that the referential/experiential meanings of the (b) response – its "content" – is not different from that of the (a) response. We note then that to describe the Subject as "modally responsible" is to say that its choice is "interactionally central". Note also that the semantic value accorded to Subject is made tangible not by considering single isolated clauses on their own but by examining snatches of dialogic exchange. Similarly, the semantic description of Theme as the "point of departure" can be understood only in the context of textual organisation, for it is this aspect of language use to which the patterns of thematic selection bear some non-random relation, as pointed out in this volume by Fang, McDonald and Cheng for Chinese, Cummings for Old English, Fries for mostly monologic discourse and Cloran for dialogues in modern English. What this aspect of the present discussion clearly draws attention to is the fact that the semantic value of categories such as Subject and Theme cannot become available if one's scope for evidence is limited to single, simple sentences. And focus on such inadequate evidence tends to be the norm rather than the exception in most formal linguistic models, whether or not they are also inspired by the *correspondence* perspective. Whatever the impetus, whatever the motivation, that such linguistic models have for remaining imprisoned in single often simple sentences while deliberating on the deep universal features of human language, this artificially limited example of "language in use" cannot provide the environment for checking out the validity of the sort of semantic phenomena to which SF draws attention in defining the categories of Subject and Theme in English. Note also that the commitment of SF to discourse has a motivation that harks back once again to its constructivist perspective. Our insistence on appeal to discourse as furnishing the necessary environment for apprehending the semantic value of Subject and Theme is not fortuitous: what is largely semiotically created must be investigated in a semiotic environment, which is, properly speaking, discourse. This explains the subtitle in the title of this volume *On Subject and Theme: A discourse functional perspective*.

1.2 Ideas about language and linguistic universals

Linguists often debate whether or not a category such as subject or theme is universal. This formulation renders invisible the fact that someone somewhere actually *postulated* this or that descriptive category as a means of 'accounting for' some aspect of some specific language; it objectifies the category, giving it a spurious quality of existence while hiding the history of its genesis. The resulting reification of grammatical categories divorces them from the sort of languages with which speakers and hearers live their lives, which, in its turn, has the effect of catapulting the categories into a qualitatively different universe of discourse. Instead of being seen as having their genesis in some specific language or language group, the categories of grammar begin to be seen as deriving from some other system, some other structure – a *lingua mentalis*, perhaps. And yet, it is notable that no convincing evidence for the existence of a lingua mentalis can be adduced at all without recourse to *lingua vocalis*.

We are of course not suggesting that comparison across languages is either invalid or impossible – simply that the nature and basis of this comparison needs to be better understood. If it is accepted that every descriptive category has a (semantic) value and a (formal) identity, then comparison across languages is a complex operation rather than simply a matter of matching morphemes or seeking the similarity of suffixes, though these may be important too! In any event, we do need to be aware which aspect of the category is at issue in the comparison. Are we concerned with locating the category across languages simply in terms of what it does for the speaker/hearer of the languages being compared – ie., in terms of the definition criteria – or are we attempting to find equivalent formal properties – ie., in terms of the category's recognition criteria? The results of our inquiries are likely to be different depending on which of these goals is adopted. And, irrespective of which goal is targeted, it is highly unlikely that the categories being compared across two (or more) languages will be identical in either their meaning or their form: at best, one operates on the basis of similarity, with the implication that some sort of compromise is inevitable in the decision to call by the same name a pair of formal patterns identified as the "same" in two different languages. These points may be briefly exemplified by reference to Subject in English and French.

2. The category Subject: A cross-linguistic comparison

Let us ask first if both English and French can claim to "have" the formal category Subject; that is to say, our concern is with the recognition criteria for Subject in these two languages. Since in any comparison one has to begin somewhere, we will honour the dominant (though dubious) tradition in linguistics by using English as the starting point. The five major features of the constituent typically regarded as Subject in English can be listed as follows:

(i) The English Subject is a nominal group or nominalisation;
(ii) it is anaphorically presupposed by the pronoun in the Mood-Tag; if the latter occurs, its pronoun will be co–referential with Subject (on Mood-Tag, see Halliday 1985 and McGregor this volume for further discussion; the latter does not treat the co-referentiality of Subject and Mood-Tag pronominal as a necessary feature);
(iii) Subject occurs in close contiguity with the element Finite; if an intervening element occurs at all, it will prototypically be a Modal Adjunct eg., *usually, normally, surely* ... (on Finite and Modal Adjunct as clausal elements, see Halliday 1985: 68ff);
(vi) when Subject is instantiated by a pronoun, in some cases the pronoun will be marked for case (nominative); and
(v) under certain conditions, the Subject nominal will display person and number concord with the primary tense, ie., with the Finite element.

2.1 Comparing recognition criteria across languages

Is there a category in French that "has" all the above formal features? We gather from Caffarel's account of the interpersonal organization of the French clause in this volume that the only truly IDENTICAL feature shared by what is traditionally known as Subject in the two languages is the first one: Subject in English as in French is a nominal group or a nominalisation. However it should be noted that this feature is hardly criterial: a nominal group/nominalisation clearly does not have to be Subject. The position concerning feature (ii) is just as clear-cut: it is a feature that is entirely irrelevant to French, since a formal pattern having the properties of Mood-Tag cannot be found in the language. So far as features (iii–v) are concerned, we may offer one generalisation: they display similarity but not identity. For example, with respect to (iii), although the two elements, Subject and Finite, typically occur in close contiguity in French as in English, what may intervene between the two in French is rather different as shown by the clause *je le lui ai donné* – something that would be totally untenable in any dialect of English. Feature (iv) like (iii) is similar without being identical: Subject if instantiated by a pronoun will under certain conditions display the nominative case; but the conditions are not identical with those in English (cf *it, you* in English and *nous, vous* in French). Finally so far as feature (v) is concerned it goes far beyond anything we find in English, the concord in French being far more regular and wide spread than it is in English. Speaking literally, then, the features which constitute the recognition criteria for Subject in English are replicated so far in French and no further. The categories are not formally identical in every respect, and from the point of view of formal criteria alone, the decision to label *je* in *je le lui ai donné* and *I* in *I gave it to him* as Subject is, strictly speaking, a kind of compromise. Further, underlying this compromise there is an unspoken assumption that the formal differences we have observed across the two languages with regard to features (ii–v) are immaterial, or at least less material to the Subject status of a constituent. We would claim that, irrespective of the myths perpetuated by formal linguistics about formal categories that share the "same" formal criteria across the languages of the world, the type of compromise we have noted here is not at all unusual: in fact, every time we look closely into the formal properties of the "same" category across languages, we are likely to find evidence of some compromise. Given the nature of human language, it could hardly be otherwise.

Clearly, then, we intend no criticism in saying that the labelling of two formally non-identical categories by the same name, as for example Subject in English and French, is a compromise; in fact we applaud this compromise. But at the same time we would like to understand what makes it a good compromise; why it is "intuitively satisfying". And an equally relevant question is: on what grounds do we decide that formal differences of the kind that exist between the English and French Subject can be safely ignored, or treated as immaterial to their status as formal equivalents? To explore these issues, we will turn to the definition criteria for the category Subject.

2.2 Comparing definition criteria

Let us begin once again with English. According to Halliday (1985; 1992) the category Subject in English specifies that which functions as the "resting point of an argument"; as we have illustrated above (cf example 1), it is modally responsible, ie., interactionally crucial and together with the Finite it functions as the interactional nub in a dialogic exchange (we offer the term *interactional nub* as the semantic value of the clausal element Mood in English, which as Halliday (1985) points out is the element that is typically tossed back and forth in any dialogic exchange). It should perhaps be asserted quite clearly that the fact that the English language "has" such meanings for the grammatical categories Subject and Mood is no argument for supposing that all languages must have such meanings too, or that if they do have such meaning, these must be realised by grammatical categories having the formal properties of the English Subject and Mood. Observation shows, however, that speakers everywhere do conduct dialogic negotiations; this raises the expectation that something comparable in function to an interactional nub might be present in all languages, irrespective of how it is realised. We may ask then: how is dialogic exchange effected in French, if it is? Is there something comparable to the interactional nub? If so, how is it realised? What part, if any, does the category called Subject in French play in this realisation?

Turning to Caffarel again, her suggestion is that the function of interactional nub in French is realised by the grammatical category that she refers to as Negotiator: it is the Negotiator that acts as the interactional nub in the French dialogic exchange and functionally, ie., from the point of view of the definition criteria it is comparable to the Mood element in English. Caffarel claims that although the internal formal structure of the French grammatical category Negotiator differs considerably from that of the element Mood in English, nonetheless the elements, Subject and Finite, form part of the former as they do of the latter: in both languages, the formal category having the function of interactional nub "has" Subject and Finite as its important constituents.

2.3 Cross-linguistic comparison: The basis for compromise

If we accept Caffarel's analysis, then the critical and primary fact would seem to be that in both languages there is a "bonding" of the two elements, viz, Subject and Finite; further, this bonding is significant both formally and functionally. In English this bonding is formally construed by a strong sequential contiguity criterion (cf formal features ii-iii above); in French, it is construed by the extensive concord between the elements Subject and Finite. In both languages the two bonded elements play an important role as (part of) the interactional nub, and we would claim that the formal means of realising this bonding in the two languages are, in fact, formal equivalents. The justification for making this claim is quite obvious: in general terms, human languages have but limited means for identifying their formal categories. These are: (i) syntagmatic means, ie., sequential ordering; (ii) morphological means eg., inflection and concord; and (iii) phonological prosodic means, eg., rhythm and intonation (for *phonological prosodic* realisation of grammatical categories, see Halliday 1967a; 1985). It is simply different configurations of these same three realisational means that constitute the recognition criteria for formal categories in languages all over the world. From this point of view, the recognition criterion (ii) for English formally does the same job which is done in French by means of extensive and regular concord: both achieve the same result of bonding the Subject to the Finite element. Note that underlying this observation there is a powerful principle for deciding which of the formal differences are criterial: what is important is not the actual realisational means but the relation established between categories. Thus the means by which the bonding between Subject and Finite is effected – by syntagmatic means or by morphological ones – is a secondary matter; the fact of both formal bonding and functional similarity is criterial. This is, of course, not to say that the meaning of the French and English Subject or Mood is identical: in fact, the meaning of grammatical categories, being highly abstract, is not easy to "pin down" or "gloss" effectively (on the ineffability of grammatical categories, see Halliday 1984); it is however possible to observe points of similarity. And so far as the English and French categories of Subject and Mood are concerned, there does seem to exist reasonable similarity between them.

If these arguments are accepted then it would seem that there is good formal and functional reason for the compromise we have applauded. Moreover, we do not need to make a mystery out of our intuitive satisfaction with this compromise as if this intuition is an inexplicable phenomenon that lies beyond the reaches of linguistic analysis, forcing us to recognise divine intervention. To say that on occasions we are intuitively satisfied with the compromise of calling non-identical but similar formal patterns by the same name is simply to say that as speakers of the language we have an unconscious sensitivity to the prehension between form and meaning which, due to our adherence to received ideas about language, often fails to get recognised in our conscious analyses. The possession of such sensitivity is obviously beyond dispute, for in its absence, we would be just as hopeless at using language as most grammars are at explaining how we do it. Let us also add in passing that we do not find it useful to suggest, as some linguists have done (see, for example, Huddleston 1984), that cross-linguistic comparison might typically be "notional". In the first place, we recognize no "notions" in the description of language, which are not construed by the form of language; thus there can be no notional comparison without some (overt or covert) formal comparison. Secondly, unless the grammar of each language already recognizes the dialectics of function and form, meaning and lexicogrammar, it is rather difficult to imagine how a notional ie., meaning-based comparison of grammatical categories could be effectively carried out across different languages. In our view, it would be misleading to suggest that any valid semantic comparison of languages is possible where as a matter of principle intra-linguistic grammatical categories are seen as devoid of semantic value. Nor is it helpful to be told that a category in some language merits the label of Subject more or less depending on the place it occupies on some imaginary scale of quintessential, idealised "Subjecthood", which is itself described in terms of a large number of formal features (Keenan 1976). Notably, these features appear to bear no necessary logical relation to each other; but amazingly, they are still treated as if together they were capable of defining some absolute quality of "subjecthood" towards which each language is striving with greater or lesser success! To set up universal categories along these lines is to practice a dangerously reductive linguistics which is incapable of shedding any light on what is truly universal to human language. Our discussion of Subject in English and French shows that underlying the allocation of the same nomenclature is a complex process of comparison and of compromise both in terms of form and of meaning, and the ways in which, say, French differs from English are at least as important to the semantic potential of that language as the ways in which it resembles English; and what is common to both languages – thus a possible candidate as a universal – is very much deeper than morphological marking or syntagmatic order. For these reasons, we question the value of current ideas about universality; we believe that a theoretically more viable approach to language universals is needed, which respects the humanity of the human species without disregarding its most outstanding characteristic, viz, its infinite capacity for variation.

3. Theme

In our discussion so far, we have focussed mainly on the category of Subject, but our approach to the concept of Theme across languages and in any specific language would be along similar lines. Although like Subject, Theme is not a new concept – in fact, if anything, it is an older concept than Subject (see for example Halliday 1977a) – its discussion in modern linguistics is still surrounded by unresolved problems. In this section, we will draw attention to certain problems specific to the description of Theme in the SF model, which revolve around its definition and its recognition criteria. Like Subject, the semantic characterisation of Theme in the SF model is highly abstract. It therefore stands in need of similar clarification. The formal identification of the category, at least so far as English is concerned, is primarily syntagmatic viz. Theme is that which occupies a specific position in the sequence of elements in some unit type(s); unlike the English Subject, here we find no "associated" features with morphological markings, such as case and concord.

3.1 Theme: Definition criteria

Let us begin with the definition criteria for Theme – what Theme does. As pointed out in the last paragraph, Theme is realised in English by means of syntagmatic ordering. So taking English as our point of reference once again, we may ask less metaphorically: what is the speaker of English doing by putting certain constituents in one order as opposed to another? (cf Halliday 1967a; 1977b). As Fries (1981) has pointed out, the answer to this question is itself a matter of dispute. Mathesius (1939) assigns two distinct functions to Theme by describing it as (i) "that which is known or at least obvious in the given situation" and (ii) that "from which the speaker proceeds". Fries refers to Mathesius view of Theme's function as the "combining approach", which he contrasts with Halliday's definition of the concept as "the point of departure for what the speaker is going to say," (1985: 36). Halliday's formulation abstracts out Mathesius' second function for Theme, separating it from the first. In the SF framework, Mathesius' first function is ascribed not to Theme but to the element Given. Most SF linguists adopt these views, using as their justification the fact that the two functions identified by Mathesius as the functions of Theme can, in fact, be dissociated from each other. A constituent with the function of Theme does not necessarily have the function Given as well; instead, under certain conditions, Theme might be conflated with New, thus no longer functioning as "that which is known or .. obvious" (cf Mathesius, ibid.).

While the issue of the choice between the "combining" and the "separating" approaches appears to have been resolved easily, this is not to say that, as a result, the semantic characterisation of Theme in the separating approach of the SF model has become clearer. The abstract semantic characterisation of Theme as "the point of departure" – and its other equivalent glosses not only by Halliday but also by other SF linguists eg., Matthiessen (*in press*) who talks of Theme as "the resource for manipulating the local **contextualization** of the clause .. for setting up a local context for each clause in a text" still stand in need of clarification. And notwithstanding the principle of ineffability (cf Halliday 1984), this abstract semantic value ascribed to Theme in the SF literature does need to be made concrete at least to the same extent as in the case of the element, Subject. This seems to be a reasonable demand, whose satisfaction is however beset with serious problems. To render concrete the thrust of the abstract semantic characterisation of Subject – to show what happens in the language as it gets used – we were able to use illustrations which extended over a mere adjacency pair (see example 1). Subject, let it be recalled, is concerned with interactional exchange, and while examining the interactional function of Subject by considering a single adjacency pair is not an ideal procedure, at least it suffices for the purpose. Theme, on the other hand, is said to construe some variety of textual meaning – a point that Halliday (1977b) demonstrated by an exercise in "theme scrambling" and Fries (1981) elaborated on by examining Theme in relation to a text's method of development. To adduce an illustration of the operation of Theme, the efficacy of which might be at least comparable to that of the adjacency pair for Subject, the textual segment that needs to be used has to be very much more extensive than just an adjacency pair: Fries (1981), for example, used two medium length paragraphs from a naturally occurring text. The need for a more extensive stretch of language as example arises because the nature of textual meanings can be appreciated only when enough of the textual environment is taken into account to demonstrate the contribution, if any, that Theme might make to textual organisation. The practical difficulty of having to use extensive snatches of text is serious enough – as all editors and publishers of discourse oriented linguistics are painfully aware!! – but here one encounters a much more fundamental problem, which itself arises due to the state of the art in text analysis: it is to be doubted if linguists really know what counts as "enough of the textual environment".

    Even though much progress has been made in the field of text linguistics since the appearance of the first few studies in the late 60s (Labov and Waletzky 1967; Hasan 1967; van Dijk 1972; Grimes 1975; Halliday and Hasan 1976; Schank and Abelson 1977; Halliday 1977b; Hasan 1978), we are still far from having a powerful framework for the analysis of text, and while our framework for the analysis of clause is far from perfect, that for text analysis lags even further behind. This has the consequence that we cannot be very certain what that unit and/or aspect of textual analysis is, if there is one, to which the pattern of Theme selection is primarily relevant. Does Theme choice construe method of development in a text, as Fries (1981) suggests? Does it play a part in identifying elements of text structure? Fries (this volume) explores aspects of this issue among others, bringing positive evidence from a number of studies. Fang, McDonald and Cheng suggest that the patterns of thematic progression could be systematically related to a textual unit they refer to as the paragraph (see Appendices to their contribution). We may pause at this point to ask: what relation, if any, is there between elements of structure and such thematically identified paragraphs? Cummings' paper suggests that the patterning of Theme selection non-randomly correlates with register variation in Old English. Cloran shows that a text can be segmented into constituents each having a specific character of its own while playing a part in conjunction with other such constituents within the structure of the text. She refers to this textual unit as "rhetorical unit". The theoretical question in text analysis is: what is the relation of her rhetorical unit to Fang *et al*'s paragraph, to text, to text structure, to genre and finally to register? Notably, each of these is an area as yet not certain of its own identity. Cloran goes on to suggest that the different patterns of Theme-Rheme selection at the boundaries of rhetorical units "signal" various kinds of relations between such textual units. The functions of (the patterns of) Theme selection thus provide us on the one hand with an *embarras de richesse*, and on the other hand they reveal our uncertainties in text analysis. The rich results claimed by the scholars researching Theme inevitably raise the question: are all of these indicative of the semantic value of Theme? If so, how might we conceptualize and formulate that value so that it accurately reflects these varied findings? At present, at least, it is not easy to see how the rather varied functions of Theme selection in the economy of the text may be logically related to a Theme's being the point of departure for what the speaker is going to say (cf Halliday 1985) or its being a resource for setting up the local context of each clause in a text (cf Matthiessen *in press*).

These issues concern the SF linguists deeply, as the constructivist interpretation of language necessarily predisposes them to the understanding and description of discourse. By the same token, these SF concerns are almost impossible to 'translate' in the metalanguage (cf Martin *in press*) of those frameworks which do not accept the assumption basic to SF, namely that explaining the property of textuality is a legitimate and proper concern of linguistics. If being limited to isolated simple sentences is a handicap in appreciating the meaning of Subject, it is a much worse handicap where an understanding of the semantic value of Theme is concerned. It is obvious that SF linguists lack clarity in their discourse on theme; but it seems to us equally clear that the credentials of formal linguistics for understanding these problems or for criticising their solutions are not exactly impressive. Sometimes the notion of Theme in SF has been equated with that of topic in formal models. However, because in a formal model meanings are typically constrained to be referential, the concept of topic has been assimilated to an aspect of representational meaning. If the initial constituent of a sentence is about the referential meaning "x" then within the limits of the formal model it can be easily treated as the topic of that sentence; if reference to "x" occurs in subsequent sentences, it is, again, viable to talk of topic continuity. But items such as *anyway, still, however..* in sentence initial position can hardly be regarded as topic, since according to these models topic must have "content" and, of course, cohesive conjunctives have no referential meaning. It follows that the textual organisation that is indicated by the thematic status of much of what SF linguists refer to as textual or interpersonal Theme bears no relation to what is known as topic. This seems to suggest that the SF concept of Theme and the formal model's notion of topic differ significantly, and no useful purpose is served by equating the two. This is not to say that work being carried out at present in formal models on the description of the clause initial position occupied by contentful items is irrelevant to scholarship on Theme; simply that there is no direct "translatability" across these notions.

3.2 Theme: Recognition criteria

Turning to the recognition criteria for Theme in English, the position is again not as settled as, for example, in respect to Subject. The recognition criterion for the English Theme appears very simple at first glance: Theme equals clause initial constituent(s). But the meaning of this simple-seeming criterion is not as straightforward as one might expect. The problems arise because the SF framework recognises (i) distinct sub–categories of Theme, which may co-occur within the same clause, thus putting the familiar lay meaning of *initial* under stress; and (ii) the system of THEME is relevant to units of different ranks, thus suggesting that the recognition criteria might be complex. Let us take each of these in turn.

Theme is classified by reference to the different metafunctions in the SF model. Since all metafunctions operate simultaneously, this opens up the possibility of more than one Theme occurring in the same clause, as in (2) *well but then Anne surely wouldn't the best idea be to join the group?* (Halliday 1985: 55); the Theme elements are italicized and only the onset of Rheme is shown:

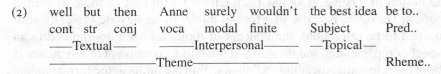

(2)   well but then   Anne   surely   wouldn't   the best idea be to..
        cont str conj   voca   modal   finite   Subject   Pred..
        ——Textual——   ——Interpersonal——   —Topical—
        ————————————————————Theme————————————   Rheme..

The clause here has multiple Themes: *well but then* are Continuative, Structural and Conjunctive themes respectively; they derive from the textual and the logical metafunctions, and are together referred to as Textual Theme; *Anne surely wouldn't* are Vocative, Modal Adjunct and Finite Themes respectively; these derive from the interpersonal metafunction, and are known as Interpersonal Theme; *the best idea* is Topical Theme which is said to derive from the experiential metafunction. A topical Theme always conflates with both an interpersonal and an experiential role: for example, *the best idea* in (2) is Theme/Subject/Value.

The formal behaviour of textual and interpersonal Themes differs markedly from that of the topical Theme. Two possibilities are open to interpersonal and textual Theme: (i) that the occurrence of either and/or both in a clause is optional; clauses are not constrained to have an interpersonal and/or a textual Theme (though there are certain exceptions, eg., structural Theme in a finite hypotactic clause, and finite Theme in a polar interrogative clause is very likely to occur); and (ii) that with certain restrictions, the same clause may have an iterative choice of Theme from either or both subcategories – the textual and the interpersonal (cf example 2). This is in contrast to the situation regarding topical Theme where (i) every major non-hypotactic and some specific hypotactic clause types must have at least one topical Theme; and (ii) iterative selection of topical Theme is possible only under certain conditions, and only if Theme is marked. This point is discussed later in this section; (3i) provides an example of a non-iterative single marked Theme:

(3)　i　Last year　I bought those same shoes for eighty dollars in LA.
　　　　Top:mkd　——————————————Rheme——————————

Note that all Theme elements in the preceding discussion are realised by a group/phrase rank constituent. However, some categories of clausal Theme may be realised by an embedded clause as illustrated by examples (4i) and (4ii), both taken from Halliday (1985: 42):

(4)　i　*What the duke gave to my aunt* was that teapot.
　　ii　*This teapot* is what the duke gave to my aunt.

Here in (4i) the Theme is a marked equative, while in (4ii) it is unmarked equative. Another parameter for Theme categorisation is the possibility of its predication. Compare (5i) and (5ii):

(5)　i　*John* blamed Leonie.
　　ii　*It was John* who blamed Leonie.

In (5i) *John* is unmarked topical Theme that is also unpredicated, whereas in (5ii) *it was John* is an unmarked topical Theme that is predicated. (See Halliday 1985: 59ff for further discussion of predicated Theme).

The distinct sub-categories of Theme we have referred to in the last few paragraphs can be summarised briefly as follows:

I: metafunctional basis:
      a: interpersonal   vocative; finite; modal; comment
      b: textual   continuative; conjunctive
      c: logical   structural eg., *if, since,... and, but...*
      d: experiential   topical

II: expectancy basis:
      a: unmarked   S/Th in indicative; Pred/Th in imperative
      b: marked   anything else (see Halliday 1985: 44ff)

III: equation basis:
      a: non-equative   as I; II
      b: equative   with 'psuedo-cleft' clause embedding

IV: predication basis:
      a: non-predicated   as I; II
      b: predicated   with 'cleft' clause embedding

V: co-occurrence basis:
      a: simple   (Theme must be topical)
      b: multiple   (topical and textual and/or interpersonal)

The postulate of these distinct categories (which are not presented here
in terms of systemic choices, but clearly systemicity is implied) raises two
interesting issues, which are briefly examined before turning to the question
of its effects on the interpretation of the term "initial". The first of these
issues seems to be relevant to the definition rather than the recognition of
Theme: it seems reasonable to ask whether the semantic value of all these
various categories of theme is the same so far as their function in the economy of textual organisation is concerned? While there is a discussion of the
local meaning of equative and predicated Themes, and remarks will also be
found on the local meaning of marked Theme (as for example in Halliday
1985; see also Cloran, this volume for some comments), the question of
whether or not they function variably within the economy of discourse has,
to the best of our knowledge, not been addressed by SF linguists. As for the
Themes metafunctionally classified, only sporadic remarks (eg Christie *in
press*; Fries and Francis 1992) have been made about the relevance of some

category of Theme (logical and topical respectively) to some specific aspect of textual organization. There are some fairly obvious grounds for suggesting that the patterns of thematic progression (on thematic progression, see Fries and also Cloran, this volume) concern only topical theme, and that these may be primarily relevant to some aspect of the field of discourse. This is in fact an issue discussed by several SF linguists, though without any conclusive results (see for some details Fries, this volume). Textual theme, especially its sub-category structural, on the other hand appears to be systematically related to what has been referred to as the "rhetorical structure" of the text in Rhetorical Structure Theory (RST), for which a better name might have been "logical Structure Theory" (for details, see Thompson and Mann 1987; Matthiessen and Thompson 1989; Mann, Matthiessen and Thompson 1992). These studies are, in fact, simply indicative not providing any firm hypotheses about the role of the metafunctionally differentiated subcategories of Theme in textual organisation. Again, one might ask if multiple theme selection is systematically different in its textual function from simple theme selection? For example, is there a textually significant location where the choice of multiple Theme is at risk? All of these issues are relevant to the clarification of the semantic value of Theme. The second issue to which attention is drawn here is more general in nature: note that hypotactic and paratactic conjunctions eg., *if, since, but, and* ... etc. which pertain to the logical metafunction have been grouped together with conjunctives such as *well, anyhow, anyway* ... etc. which pertain to the textual metafunction. Together, they realise a textual Theme (see the analysis and discussion of example (2) above). This grouping for the purposes of the analysis of Theme, dissociates the logical metafunction from its usual grouping with the experiential one, but in so doing, it raises a question about the significance of this step: why are logical and textual items grouped together here? What principle guides such re-alignments?

In view of the possibility of multiple themes occurring in a clause, the question about initial position merges into that of where this position ends. We, then, have two questions: what counts as an initial position, and what is the principle for determining the boundary between Theme and Rheme. In our understanding of Halliday's position, topical Theme plays a significant part in providing the answer to both these questions. As pointed out before, this category of Theme pertains to the experiential metafunction. The concept of initial position can be stated very clearly by reference to the experiential structuring of the clause: initial position in the clause is defined as the very first constituent of the clause with some experiential function. In clauses that are said to have simple Theme, it is this initial constituent that will function as topical Theme; everything else – ie., all that follows this initial constituent in such clauses – will automatically fall into Rheme. What this means is that topical Theme will always conflate with some TRANSITI-VITY element – a position not applicable to any other category of Theme, as can be checked by a quick look at the textual and interpersonal Themes in example (2). Note two relevant points here: first, the exact experiential function of the initial constituent is completely immaterial to the identity of topical Theme as a topical Theme; ie., the constituent may be a Participant, or a Circumstance or a Process, without having any repercussions for topical Theme as such. Secondly, every clausal constituent having an experiential function is bound to conflate with an interpersonal function as well – the reverse is not true eg., consider the interpersonal Themes in example (2) none of which have any TRANSITIVITY function. And it is the specific nature of this interpersonal – ie., MOOD – function of the initial constituent that plays a crucial role in determining the status of the topical Theme. For the systemic option [marked] versus [unmarked] is directly related to what MOOD function conflates with topical Theme. To elaborate on this point let us take the declarative clause as the prototypic case since it is this clause type which is the most hospitable to the co-occurrence of different categories of Theme. Typically, in this clause type, the initial constituent has the MOOD function of Subject, which is conflated with some participant role in TRAN-SITIVITY. To say that a constituent is a topical Theme in a declarative clause is to say that Theme is realised by a clause initial constituent which has *both* a TRANSITIVITY *and* a MOOD function in the clause; to say that a topical Theme in a declarative clause has the feature [unmarked] is to say that it occupies a clause initial position where it conflates with the MOOD function of Subject and the TRANSITIVITY function of some Participant role. The implication is that if the initial constituent has a MOOD function other than that of Subject, then the topical Theme would be [marked], a position illustrated by (3i) where *Last year* has the textual functions of marked topical Theme, the interpersonal function of Adjunct and the experiential function of temporal Circumstance. One position taken in the SF model was that under certain conditions a marked Theme of this type – ie., where Theme conflates with Adjunct/Circumstance – could be iterative, which is to say that more than one marked topical Themes could occur in the clause so long as they all conflated with Adjunct/Circumstance. This is exemplified in (3ii):

(3)   ii   *last year*   *in* LA   I   bought....
           Adjunct   Adjunct   Subj   F Pred.....
           Circ:temp   Circ:loc   Ac   Process
           Th:top:mkd   Th:top:mkd   ——Rheme——

It is, however, not difficult to imagine cases where more than one marked topical Themes occur such that they conflate with distinct MOOD functions. An imaginary example is given below in (3iii):

(3)   iii   *last year*   *in* LA   *those same shoes*   I..
            Adjunct   Adjunct   Complement   Subj
            Circ:temp   Circ:loc   Goal   Ac
            Th:top:mkd   Th:top:mkd   Th:top:mkd   ..
            ———————————Theme———————————   Rheme..

In example (3iii) two Adjuncts followed by a Complement occur in the clause initial ie., pre-Subject, position. These are analysed as three marked topical Themes; the first two are conflated with Adjunct, while the third is conflated with Complement. (3iii) is an imaginary example and it is an open question whether the clause type instantiated by this example actually does occur in English, a matter that can now be, perhaps, more easily settled since large size corpora of naturally occurring discourse are now more readily available. Based on his personal observation of English, Halliday (1967b; 1968) has suggested that this configuration of marked Themes is not very likely in English; in other words, it was expected that multiple marked Themes in a clause would either conflate with Adjuncts or with Complement, but not with both.

Be that as it may, what matters to our discussion here is the fact that in the context of the recognition criteria for topical Theme the element Subject is relevant at least in the indicative clause type for stating the meaning of the term *clause initial position*, since as our analysis shows in all these cases marked topical Theme precedes the element Subject. If we assume that marked Themes exhaust the thematic potential of the clause, and additionally, that textual and/or interpersonal Themes in such a clause will ONLY precede the element Subject, not follow it (consider *Well but Tom last year in* LA *those same shoes I bought*...by analogy with (2)), then the criterion for determining the extent of Theme may be expressed in two steps:

(i)   Everything up to and *including* the element Subject is Theme so long
      as there is no marked Topical Theme (cf example 2);
(ii) Everything up to and excluding Subject is Theme so long as there is a
      marked Topical Theme (cf examples 3i-iii, and variant in last para-
      graph).

Note that in conformity with these generalisations, in example (2) the
Subject *the best idea* is analysed as Theme while in (3i-iii) the Subject *I* is
not analysed as Theme, but forms part of Rheme. It would seem that this is
a perfectly clear view of how Theme is to be recognised in the English
clause, what the term "initial position" means in this context, and what the
extent of Theme in the case of multiple Theme selection is.

But as Ravelli in this volume points out there are alternative views to
those presented above on both issues: what counts as Theme and on where
the element Theme stops and Rheme begins. Some scholars (eg., Berry 1987,
1992a, 1992b) have treated the especial status of the element Subject in the
context of Theme in indicative clauses as the ground for arguing that Subject
should always be treated as thematic, whether or not preceded by marked
Theme. If this principle is followed, then the two steps stated above would
have to be revised as: *everything up to and including the element Subject is
Theme*. In the majority of cases, this alternative recognition criterion for
Theme in English does not lead to very different analyses. And all else being
equal, different analyses will be offered only for clauses with marked Theme
such as exemplified by (3i) through to (3iii): in all these cases, whereas in
the position ascribed to Halliday, Subject would fall into Rheme, in this
alternative position it would form part of Theme, functioning, presumably,
as an unmarked topical Theme. However, all else is seldom equal, and there
is some indication that scholars such as Berry do not accept the proviso
about textual and interpersonal Themes always and only occurring prior to
the element Subject. Ravelli, in this volume, quotes Berry's example (Berry
1992a) which is itself taken from VandeKopple:

(6)   *The alternative to dogmatic realism, fortunately,* is not...

Here, Ravelli points out, Berry's recommendation would be that the entire
italicised portion should be treated as Theme, with *fortunately*, presumably

analysed as interpersonal Theme. It seems to us that both these recommenda-
tions raise some questions to which, at least, we ourselves have not encountered clear answers. For example, what is gained by claiming that Subject
is *ipso facto* also Theme? What can the constituent in question "do" as a
result of being Theme which it is prevented from doing simply as Subject?
And in any event how can an answer to this question be validated since in
this position the dissociation of Subject and Theme becomes logically
impossible? Again, how does the status of Subject as unmarked topical
Theme in (3i-iii), where it follows marked topical Themes, differ from the
status it has in clauses such as *John left before lunch* where again *John*
would be unmarked topical Theme, but this time not preceded by any
marked Themes? It seems also that in this view the concept of initial position
as a relevant recognition criterion for Theme must be abandoned; it seems
rather that one is being asked to assume the existence of some "basic" or
"typical" order of sequence for clausal constituents, any departure from
which has to be viewed as thematic. As our discussion shows, the postulate
of multiple Themes – especially the textual and the interpersonal Themes –
complicates the statement of recognition criteria, both for Theme and Theme
extent. The presence of alternative views is an indication of the problematic
nature of these recognition criteria; and, these alternative views themselves,
further complicate the picture. We leave this debate with two observations.
The first concerns a significant comment made by Halliday (1967b; 1979;
1985) that the Theme-Rheme structure, like other textual structures, is
"periodic" or wave-like. Therefore, the entire debate of where Theme
"stops" and where Rheme "begins" is itself perhaps an artefact of how
analysis is represented. This brings to the fore one of the biggest challenges
for SF linguists – to devise some mode of representation for wave-like
structures which does not assimilate them to the segmental/particulate ones
that characterise experiential structures. Secondly, in an interesting way, this
entire debate and the disagreements emphasise the importance of being clear
about the semantic value of Theme: the order of sequence of the constituents
of primary unit types is seldom, if ever, entirely fixed, in any language. In
English Comment Adjuncts eg., *fortunately, surprisingly, luckily*... can
"move around" in the clause apparently quite freely, but of course in a
functional model there is no such thing as "free word order," and all these
variations would be taken to make some difference to the construal of
meanings (see discussion in Halliday 1994: 83). If order of sequence is being

invoked as a recognition criterion for Theme, as it is in English, then we need to be clear which cases of the variation in order of sequence should be treated as Theme? And if Theme is what Theme does, then naturally we have to be clear about what this function is. For a discussion of some of these same issues, see Ravelli in this volume, who attempts to give us an explication in terms of her dynamic framework.

We turn now to the second source of complexity in the recognition criteria for Theme, viz., what unit type acts as the entry point to the system of THEME? According to Halliday, at least three different unit types enjoy this privilege: the clause complex, the clause, and the group/phrase. It is however, hardly likely to be the case that the terms of the system in all three cases remain the same. We would expect that choices in the system for one unit would be critically different from those at another rank. This raises the question: what are the details of these differences? For example, does Theme at the clause complex rank show the systemic contrast of [marked] versus [unmarked]? And again is it the case that at this rank, the distinction between textual, interpersonal, and topical is neutralized? If not, how are these distinctions realised? And if the distinction is neutralised, what arguments support the postulate of this neutralisation? We believe these questions have not yet been addressed in SF. Turning to Theme selections at the group rank, it is probably not an exaggeration to say that, apart from some initial exploratory studies (eg., see Fries and Francis 1992), very few SF linguists have analysed these. An exception is Cloran's work, who found such an analysis fruitful in her hypotheses about the rhetorical unit, as her contribution to this volume indicates. Clearly, however, so far as recognition criteria are concerned, these will have to be different for Theme in clause complex, from Theme in clause, from Theme in groups.

Theme is not a new concept: in fact, Halliday (1977a) traces it back to the Sophists. Its revival first in Prague School linguistics and then in Halliday's work on English in the 60s (Halliday 1967a; 1968) has resulted in a good deal of attention to the concept. But it is clear from the above discussion that both its definition and its recognition criteria stand in need of further clarification. It is significant that there is an uncertainty about both sorts of criteria: it is, in fact, not easy to figure out what some device does without some idea of what the device actually looks like; and there is little reason for singling out something as a formal device unless it at least promises to reveal some regularity in significance. We believe that enough indication has been provided of the textual relevance of the notion of Theme as conceptualized in the SF model not only in the seminal work of Halliday (eg 1967a; 1968; 1977) but in later studies such as by Fries (1981; 1992; 1993), Berry (1987; 1992a; 1992b), Martin (1992a; 1992b; 1995), and others (see for other useful references, chapters 7-10 this volume) to suggest that attention to the problems highlighted in our discussion would make a useful contribution. It is perhaps true to say that at least partial answers to many of the questions we have raised here are already implicit in the practices of SF linguists. What is needed is to develop these underlying assumptions and to make them explicit. This represnts a major research agenda.

4.   About the chapters in this volume

The foregoing sections conclude our reflections on subject and theme, the discussion of which is offered here as background material relating to the studies presented in this volume. These studies themselves are largely descriptive, and they concern not simply English but other languages. As a concluding move to this introduction, we will add a few words about each of the ten chapters in the volume.

Caffarel's paper, as earlier references to it show, examines the interpersonal organization of the French clause, attempting to highlight the respects in which the interpersonal grammar of the French and the English clause converge and diverge. Thibault's treatment of the English MOOD system uses the semantic level as its point of reference, arguing that the grammar of MOOD must faithfully represent each significant semantic fact as a step in the construal of the subjectivity of the speaker and the addressee. McGregor's chapter is concerned with "Tag Questions"; his use of the term "Tag" is somewhat wider than what is referred to as Mood-Tag in the discussion of Subject above. McGregor provides examples to support his case that the semantic value of "Tag Questions" is not invariant; this value differs according to the varying MOOD choice in the main clause to which it is related in a "whole–whole" relation. Boxwell's contribution moves away from a consideration of the MOOD system as such: it is concerned, instead, with exploring how the absence (and presence) of the element Subject is textually deployed in the Weri language. In formal linguistics Weri would be described as a "pro-drop" language; so would, of course, Japanese, which is discussed by Hori in this volume. Interestingly, to describe Weri,

Japanese and a host of other languages as "pro-drop" tells us very little about these languages themselves; it simply draws attention to the fact that they differ from a small handful of Indo-European languages, notably English and French, where Subject does not simply have to be selected, it has also to be heard/seen to have been selected. In Weri, as in Urdu (Hasan 1984) or Italian (Piccioli 1988), the situation is comparable to that described by Hori for Japanese: "Subject appears on the surface in a Japanese clause only when it is marked." Boxwell argues that Subject-ellipsis in Weri establishes the textual relation of co-referentiality, whereby the absence of an overt Subject comes to have the textual meaning "identity of referent" across the Subject elements presupposed by ellipsis. Hori's contribution too focuses on "Subjectless" clauses; however, she is concerned with showing how certain morphological devices permit the speakers of Japanese to deduce the specific characteristics of the underlying Subject even in the absence of an overt Subject selection. The bonding of the element Subject by morphological means to some other element of the clause – typically a verbal constituent or a particle – opens up a resource for language to construe meanings out of both the presence and absence of that element. This meaning is over and above the semantic value of that element *per se*. Thus in Urdu the modal responsibility of the Subject is "there" even in the case of clauses with Subject-ellipsis; the ellipsis itself is a means for indicating the textual function Given on the one hand and on the other hand for pointing to the relevance of the "same, specific identical referent" as that which is also referred to by the presupposed Subject (see Hasan 1984). As Boxwell concludes "*Nothing* makes sense in Weri"; and, one might add, it does this in most languages of the world.

While Subject-ellipsis points us into the direction of the textual metafunction, with Ravelli's chapter we move into a somewhat different domain. Ravelli brings a dynamic perspective to the examination of some of the problems in establishing the recognition criteria for Theme. She suggests that the synoptic approach which is typical of mainstream SF linguistics is incapable of producing the description of language as process, and attempts to show that some of the problems in the description of Theme can be better understood with the help of the dynamic approach. Fang, McDonald and Cheng provide a somewhat condensed picture of the grammar of the clause in Chinese, attempting to relate the concepts of Theme, Subject and Actor. They suggest that the interpersonal organization of the Chinese clause is not brought about by syntagmatic or morphological means, the rhetorical choices being realised phonologically. According to these authors both the semantic characterisation of Theme in Chinese and its recognition criteria approximate those in English: Theme, they claim, "normally comes first in the clause, and may be marked off from the Rheme by a pause and/or textual particle such as *a, ba, me, ne*." They go on to explore the relevance of patterns of thematic progression to the clustering of clauses in a text, suggesting that most probably a unit intermediate between the clause complex and the text could be established by reference to patterns of thematic selection. Cummings is concerned with the comparability of descriptive categories across distinct diachronic stages of the same language, English. To this end he applies the SF framework for the analysis of Theme to the Old English clause. He concludes that in general the categories designed to describe today's English also serve Old English well, permitting some interesting generalizations about patterns of Theme selection in relation to register variation in Old English. As Cummings himself points out, conclusions such as these based on fairly limited data size have to be treated cautiously; nonetheless, such explorations are valuable not only for their indicative results but also for the questions which they raise about the description of Theme, for example: is the frequent conflation of topical Theme with Predicator in OE declarative clauses to be regarded as a case of marked Theme as it would be in contemporary English? In effect, Cummings' questions too call for further explication of the concepts relevant to Theme analysis to which we have already drawn attention in section 3. Fries in his chapter examines Thematic patterns and patterns of thematic progression (ie., where did the information in a subsequent Theme come from). He continues to explore the usefulness of Theme in accounting for the nature of texts, demonstrating both through the summary of the work of others and by adding his own data that texts of different genre tend to use different patterns of thematic development, and that they also tend to place different sorts of information in the Themes of the clauses. The latter point cannot be simply explained by saying that certain sorts of texts contain more instances of, say, temporal information than do other texts: this is of course one of his findings. However, in addition, his data show that the different genres display shifting percentages of thematic and non-thematic uses of locative and temporal information. His results predict that a greater percentage of the locatives in the text will function as Theme if that text describes a scene than will be the case if that text describes a series of events. This is precisely what we meant by saying earlier that topical Themes are typically field-sensitive. The central concern of this volume with Subject and Theme is brought together in Cloran's contribution, through her examination of their role in discourse. Her analysis makes contact with many of the points in the earlier chapters. For example, the notion of Central Entity – a semantic concept – bears a realisational relation to the concept of Subject as the modally responsible element. The rhetorical identity of chunks of discourse – ie., what the speakers are trying to achieve eg., an account, a recount, a commentary etc. – according to Cloran is largely recognised by properties of Subject and Finite in the clauses realizing these rhetorical units. Theme comes into play in her examination of how some specific rhetorical units may form part of the larger ongoing discourse through the relation of expansion and/or embedding. Cloran's analysis demonstrates that the specific nature of this relation is typically indicated by the patterns of theme-rheme selection at the boundaries of the relevant units. To Daneš's three thematic progression patterns, she adds a fourth one, which is in effect based on the regularity of Rheme-Rheme relation.

The ten papers in this book are offered on the one hand as a contribution to the study of the concepts of Subject – or perhaps, more accurately of MOOD – and THEME, and on the other hand they form an example of the growing literature in linguistics which attempts to see language as a meaning potential the meanings-wordings of which are instantiated daily in our verbal give and take – that is to say, in our discourse. And it is in the discourse of its speakers that language has its origin, its evolution, the source of its control over the speakers' social universe, and thus over the speakers' ideas about what is real.

References

Berry, Margaret. 1987. The functions of place names. *Leeds Studies in English: New Series XVIII: Studies in Honour of Kenneth Cameron,* edited by Thorlak Tur-ville-Petre and Margaret Gelling, 71-88. Leeds: School of English, University of Leeds.

Berry, Margaret. 1992a. Theme and variation. Plenary address to the 1992 Conference of the Applied Linguistics Association of Australia, University of Sydney.

Berry, Margaret. 1992b. Bringing systems back into a discussion of Theme. Keynote speech to the 19th International Systemic Functional Congress, Macquarie University.

Christie, Francis. *in press.* Negotiating school learning. *Literacy in Society,* edited by Ruqaiya Hasan and Geoff Williams. London: Longman.

van Dijk, Teun A. 1972. *Some Aspects of Text Grammars.* The Hague: Mouton.

Fries, Peter H. 1981. On the status of Theme in English: Arguments from discourse. *Forum Linguisticum* 6.1: 1–38.

Fries, Peter H. 1992. The structuring of written English text. *Current Research in Functional Grammar, Discourse, and Computational Linguistics with a Foundation in Systemic Theory,* edited by M.A.K. Halliday and Fred C. Peng. Special Issue of *Language Sciences,* 14.4: 1-28.

Fries, Peter H. 1993. Information flow in written advertising. *Language, Communication and Social Meaning,* edited by James Alatis, 336-352. Georgetown University Round Table on Language and linguistics, 1992. Washington, DC: Georgetown University Press.

Fries, Peter H. and G. Francis. 1992. Exploring Themes: Problems for research. *Occasional Papers in Systemic Linguistics.* 6: 45-60. Reprinted 1992 in *Systemic Functional Linguistic Forum.* 1.1: 51-63.

Grimes, Joseph. 1975. *The Thread of Discourse.* The Hague: Mouton.

Halliday, M.A.K. 1967a. *Intonation and Grammar in British English.* The Hague: Mouton.

Halliday. M.A.K. 1967b. Notes on transitivity and theme in English. Parts 1-2, *Journal of Linguistics,* 3.1: 37-81 & 3.2: 199-244.

Halliday. M.A.K. 1968. Notes on transitivity and theme in English. Part 3, *Journal of Linguistics,* 4.2: 179-215.

Halliday. M.A.K. 1977a. Ideas about language. *Aims and Perspectives in Linguistics.* Series Occasional Paper No 1 by Applied Linguistics Association of Australia.

Halliday. M.A.K. 1977b. Text as semantic choice in social contexts, *Grammars and Descriptions,* edited by Teun A. van Dijk & Janos Petofi. Berlin: Mouton de Gruyter.

Halliday, M.A.K. 1979. Modes of meaning and modes of expression: types of grammatical structure, and their determination by different semantic functions. *Function and Context in Linguistic Analysis,* edited by D. J. Allerton, Edward Carney and David Holdcroft. Cambridge: Cambridge University Press.

Halliday, M.A.K. 1984. On the ineffability of grammatical categories. *The Tenth LACUS Forum,* edited by Alan Manning, Pierre Martin and Kim McCalla. Columbia, South Carolina: Hornbeam Press. (Reprinted in *Linguistics in a Systemic Perspective,* edited by James D. Benson, Michael J. Cummings and William S. Greaves. 1988. Amsterdam: Benjamins.)

Halliday, M.A.K. 1985. *Introduction to Functional Grammar.* London: Arnold.

Halliday, M.A.K. 1992. Systemic grammar and the concept of a science of language. *Waiguoyu* 2, 1–9. (Reprinted in *Network* 19.1992: 55-64.)

Halliday, M.A.K. 1994. *Introduction to Functional Grammar*. 2nd ed. London: Arnold.

Halliday, M.A.K. & Ruqaiya Hasan. 1976. *Cohesion in English*. London: Longman.

Hasan, Ruqaiya. 1967. *Grammatical Cohesion in Spoken & Written English*. Programme in Linguistics and English Teaching: Paper 7. London: Longman.

Hasan, Ruqaiya. 1978. Text in the systemic functional model. *Current Trends in Textlinguistics*, edited by W.U. Dressler. Berlin: Mouton de Gruyter.

Hasan, Ruqaiya. 1984. Ways of saying, ways of meaning, *The Semiotics of Language and Culture. Volume 1: Language as social semiotic,* edited by Robin P. Fawcett, M.A.K. Halliday, Sydney M. Lamb and Adam Makkai. London: Francis Pinter.

Huddleston, Rodney. 1984. *Introduction to the Grammar of English*. Cambridge: Cambridge University Press.

Keenan, Edward L. 1976. Towards a universal definition of "Subject". *Subject and Topic,* edited by Charles N. Li. New York: Academic Press.

Labov, William & Joshua Waletzky. 1967. Narrative analysis: Oral versions of personal experience. *Essays on the Verbal and Visual Arts* edited by June Helm. Seattle: University of Washington Pres.

Leech, Geoffrey N. 1983. *Principles of Pragmatics*. London: Longman.

Lyons, John. 1968. *Introduction to Theoretical Linguistics*. Cambridge: Cambridge University Press.

Mann, William C., Christian M.I.M. Matthiessen, & Sandra A. Thompson. 1992. Rhetorical structure theory and text analysis, *Discourse Description: Diverse linguistic analyses of a fund-raising text,* edited by William C. Mann & Sandra A. Thompson. Amsterdam: Benjamins.

Martin, James R. 1992a. Theme, methods of development and existentiality: The price of a reply. *Occasional Papers in Systemic Linguistics* 6, 147-186.

Martin, James R. 1992b. *English Text: System and structure*. Amsterdam: Benjamins.

Martin, James R. 1995. More than what the message is about: English Theme. *Thematic Development in English Text*, edited by Mohsen Ghadessy. London: Francis Pinter.

Martin, James R. in press. Metalinguistic diversity: The case from case. *Functional Descriptions,* edited by Ruqaiya Hasan, Carmel Cloran & David Butt. Amsterdam: Benjamins.

Mathesius, Vilém. 1939. O tak zvanem aktualnim cleneni vetnem [On the so called Functional Sentence Perspective]. *Slovo a Slovestnost* 5, 171-174.

Matthiessen, C.I.M.M. *in press. Lexicogrammatical Cartography.* Tokyo: International Language Sciences Publishers.

Matthiessen, Christian, & Sandra A. Thompson 1989. The structure of discourse and "subordination", *Clause Combining in Grammar and Discourse,* edited by John Haiman & Sandra A. Thompson. Amsterdam: Benjamins.

Piccioli, Maria Theresa. 1988. S-ellipsis in Italian: a systemic interpretation. *Rassegna Italiana di Linguistica Applicata* 2, 43-54.

Schank, Roger and Robert Abelson. 1977. *Scripts Plans Goals and Understanding: An inquiry into human knowledge structures.* Hillsdale, NJ: Lawrence Erlbaum.

Thompson, Sandra A. & William C. Mann. 1987. Antithesis: A study in clause combining and discourse structure, *Language Topics: Essays in Honour of Michael Halliday,* edited by Ross Steele and Terry Threadgold. Amsterdam: Benjamins.

1

Approaching the French Clause as a Move in Dialogue: Interpersonal Organisation*

Alice Caffarel
University of Sydney

1. Introduction

From the point of view of systemic functional theory, a clause in any language is multifunctional. It is a simultaneous representation of different types of meaning: textual, experiential and interpersonal (Halliday 1985), organised at once as a message (textual), as a process configuration (experiential), and as an interactive move in speech exchange (interpersonal). It follows that the grammar of any language may be approached from any or all three of these metafunctional view points. In this paper, I will focus on the French clause primarily from the point of view of the interpersonal metafunction. More specifically, I will be concerned with an examination of the clause as the realisation of an interactive move in dialogue.

The descriptive orientation of the paper will be guided by a number of assumptions based both on insights into the nature of language in general and into the particularities of a specific language under examination – here French. Interpersonally, every language constructs dialogue for exchanging meaning, for at the most abstract level the exchange of meaning consists precisely in giving or demanding information [propositions] or goods & services [proposals] (Halliday 1984; 1985). The interaction of the primary speech roles – those of giving or demanding – with the commodities to be exchanged – namely, information or goods & services – makes up the four primary speech functions of statement, question, offer and command. If the

* I am greatly indebted to Peter Fries, Ruqaiya Hasan and Christian Matthiessen for their many comments and suggestions on earlier drafts of this paper. I owe a special debt of gratitude to Ruqaiya Hasan for her in-depth comments, which have made a significant contribution to this final version. Of course, I alone am responsible for the errors and shortcomings.

lexicogrammatical systems which realise the semantics of exchange, or speech functional semantics in the languages of the world, are referred to as MOOD systems, then it will be true by definition that the grammar of all languages will have MOOD systems. But we can go beyond the trivial issue of similarity by nomenclature, and point to more specific similarities which are functional in nature: because of the universality of the primary speech functions that are essential to the process of dialogue, we can assume that the primary MOOD options will be similar across languages (see Matthiessen 1992 for a typological outlook on MOOD across languages). In keeping with this claim, it will be found that the grammar of MOOD in French resembles that of English and other languages in terms of its primary MOOD options, differentiating between indicative and imperative as well as between the indicative subtypes, declarative and interrogative.

It, however, does not necessarily follow from this claim that there exists a complete identity of MOOD systems across languages; far from this, as our description of the interpersonal grammar of the French clause becomes more delicate, the MOOD options in the systems will be found to be more specific to French. Further, the similarity of primary systemic choices does not entail that the structural realisation of these primary features will be the same in French as it is in English, displaying a Mood-Residue structure (Halliday 1985). Rather than implying a similarity of structural elements and/or their configuration, what the theory predicts is that the mode of expression for MOOD choices will be prosodic rather than segmental in all languages (Halliday 1979; Matthiessen 1990). So the interpersonal organisation of the French clause presented here begins with phenomena that are assumed to be congruent across languages, such as the primary categories of speech functional semantics, MOOD systems and the mode of expression or structure type, to arrive at a particular description which, in terms of both systemic options and their structural realisation, will on the whole, be specific to the French clause as interaction, respecting the particularities of the French language.

With this goal in mind, in section 2 I will examine how the French clause is organised structurally as an interactive move[1] in an exchange, how

---

1. Following Sinclair and Coulthard (1975), move is the rank below that of the exchange. These are seen as belonging within the discourse semantics stratum (Martin 1992). The SPEECH FUNCTION system is located at move rank. A move is realised in the grammar by a clause selecting independently for MOOD.

exchanges are initiated and responded to, which part of the clause is typically replayed, and how propositions and proposals are realised lexicogrammatically at the primary degree of delicacy. Section 3 will be concerned with the MOOD structure of French. Here I will account for the various structural patterns, characterising the most important structural features of the interpersonal organisation of the French clause. This will pave the way for an examination of the MOOD system in section 4, where the syntagmatic phenomena already outlined in section 3 will be examined from a systemic or paradigmatic perspective. Attention will be drawn in section 5 of the paper, to certain aspects of the textual organisation of the French clause in a dialogic context. This will allow us to indicate the typical pattern of conflation for the textual and interpersonal elements in the French clause. Hopefully these discussions will have provided sufficient details of the French clause as interaction to permit in section 6, a general comparison of the modal structure of the French and English clause. As according to the systemic functional descriptions, Subject plays an important function in this structure, at this point we will also compare the role of Subject in French and in English. The paper will close with some general remarks.

2. The French clause as a move in an exchange

Let us begin by asking how statements, questions, offers and commands are initiated and responded to in French dialogic texts since an understanding of this will enable us to determine which part of the clause is crucially involved in the process of exchange and how interpersonal choices are lexicogrammatically realised in French.

2.1 A preliminary exploration of French exchanges

Consider the text in (1), taken from Simone de Beauvoir's *Les Bouches Inutiles* (1945). In text 1, each individual clause is numbered in lower case Roman numerals; the first line of each clause provides the French wording; the second gives an inter-linear gloss, while the third represents an idiomatic translation in English:

Text 1:

[*Une femme à une autre* =a woman to another woman]

(i)   *Hâte-toi!*   (ii)   *Les cloches   sonnent.*
       Hurry-you   the bells   ring
       Hurry up!   The bells are ringing.

[*Une autre femme* = Another woman]

(iii) *Est- ce   commencé?*
       Is   it   started
       Has it started?

[*Un vieillard* = An old man]

(iv)   *C' est   commencé ?*
       It   is   started
       Has it?

[*Un homme* = A man]

(v)   *C' est   commencé.*
       It   is   started
       It has.

[*Voix* = Voices]

(vi)   *C' est   commencé!   C'   est   commencé!*
       It   is   started   It   is   started
       It has!

(vii) *[Ils   sortent   en courant..]*
       [They   go out   running]
       [They run outside.]

Semantically this short exchange may be characterised as a macro-proposal, which starts with a command in (i) followed by a justifying statement in (ii) and ends with a non-verbal response described in (vii) to the initial command issued in (i). The resolution of the exchange is interrupted by four dynamic moves (Martin 1992). Move (iii) demands clarification by means of a question as to why 'they should hurry up'. Move (iv) echoes this preceding question, while move (v) is a statement in response to the clarification question and move (vi) is an exclamation. Because the text is congruently realised, with MOOD options harmonising with the SPEECH FUNCTION ones, we note that command is realised by an imperative, the justifying statement and response statement by a declarative, the clarification question and echo question by an interrogative and the exclamation by the exclamative. But how is this negotiation carried forward? How are the mood options such as interrogative, declarative etc. realised?

As pointed out above, the resolution of the exchange in (1) is prolonged by four moves (iii-vi) which play an important role in negotiating the exchange. An analysis of their modal structure is presented in (2) where these moves are freshly re-numbered as individual clauses (i-iv). In the analysis presented here, function labels have initial capital letter e.g. Subject, Finite etc., while names of systems are capitalised throughout. Thus Mood is the name of a function in a structure, while MOOD is the name of a system of options. The key to function labels is located at the end of the paper:

(2) i   *Est-* *ce*   *commencé?*
          Fin   Subj   Pred
     ii   *C'*   *est* *commencé?*
          Subj   Fin   Pred
     iii *C'*   *est* *commencé.*
          Subj   Fin   Pred
     iv   *C'*   *est* *commencé!*
          Subj   Fin   Pred

The modal structure and the speech functions of (2i-iv) in this dialogue show that negotiating the resolution of the exchange involves the replaying of the interpersonal functions of Subject (Subj), Finite (Fin) and Predicator (Pred). It is suggested here that these three functions are, as a general rule, crucial both to the negotiation process in French and to the realisation of MOOD options. In view of this, I will refer to that part of the clause as **Negotiator** which is comprised of these three crucial functions. The Negotiator is the most salient part of the interpersonal structure of the French clause, thus implying the same status to the three functions which comprise it. Ignoring the difference in the ordering of Subject and Finite between 2i and 2ii, as irrelevant to the present discussion, Figure 1 summarises graphically the structural relation between the Negotiator and the three crucial MOOD functions which comprise it in (2i-iv).

Note further that the realisation of the MOOD options instantiated in the clauses of (1-2) employs the prosodic mode of expression. Intonation is quite obviously the prototypical means for prosodic expression; and it is notable that this may be the only resource used to indicate the systemic MOOD contrasts in French, as is obvious from a consideration of (2i-iv). The

C'	est	commencé
Subject	Finite	Predicator
Negotiator ———————————————————————————→		

Figure 1: The 'Minimal' Negotiator

different tones associated with these clauses are indicated by the conventional punctuation marks (please see section 2 on the different tones in French). In clause (2ii) the sole realisation of a yes-no interrogative is by intonation, while (2i) shows that in addition to tone, this MOOD option can also be realised by ordering Finite before Subject (F^s). This latter type of realisation is called grammatical prosody (Matthiessen 1992: 398). It is prosodic in the sense that the systemic option interrogative is realised by the ordering of the two functions, so that the realisation spreads over more than one constituent of the clause. From this point of view, the concatenations s^F and F^s indicate a contrast analogous to falling versus rising tone.

The structure of the Negotiator as outlined here pertained to the indicative mood types. How does this compare with the analysis of the imperative clause? There are some differences as the analysis in (3) shows:

(3)   *Hâte toi*
       Pred C-clitic

So far as the modal structure of the imperative is concerned, it appears to consist simply of Predicator followed by a Complement-clitic (C-clitic). The clitic in (3) is coreferential with the Subject; and the function Subject is always implicit in the French imperative mood. (For greater detail, see sub-section 3.2). The verb *se hâter* (to hurry up), like many other such verbs in French, is constructed with a pronominal clitic and therefore the *toi* in *hâte-toi* must be treated as an obligatory element. With the analysis of this imperative clause as an exemplar, we can postulate that the Negotiator in imperative clauses consists of an obligatory function, Predicator; and in addition, a C-clitic must occur if the verb in the Predicator is 'reflexive', as in (3). Though these represent some of the most crucial functions in the Negotiator, there is more to this element than is pointed out here; later I shall identify certain optional functions such as polarity and modal Adjuncts, in addition to functions, which, depending on their textual status, might either occur inside or outside the Negotiator.

3. Modal Structure in French: the Negotiator and Remainder

Hopefully, my account of clauses from dialogue (1) has highlighted two important facts about the French clause as interaction. First, the replay of Subject, Finite and Predicator is one means of resolving an exchange in French. Secondly, the MOOD options have a prosodic mode of expression, which either solely employs the phonological means or a combination of both phonological and grammatical ones. I will now probe the interpersonal structure of the French clause further in delicacy by focussing on a range of exchanges which highlight the recurrent linguistic patterns central to negotiation. Sub-section 3.1 examines a series of adjacency pairs concerned with giving and demanding information. This will be followed in 3.2 by an account of adjacency pairs concerned with giving and demanding goods and services. A word should be added here about the conventions used in the presentation and analysis of these examples. As in (1) and (2) each clause in the adjacency pair is numbered individually. The second line presents an interlinear translation for every newly introduced French example; the third line provides the linguistic analysis, where those functions are shown in bold which are relevant to the structure of the Negotiator. The idiomatic translation of the entire adjacency pair is given only after both members of the pair have been analysed. The analysis of the adjacency pair is followed by comments on the lexicogrammatical means used to realise the speech functional semantics of exchange. A summary of this discussion is then tabulated (see for example Figure 2 in 3.1.1).

3.1 The clause as exchange of information: the structure of French propositions

This section is concerned with the description of the structure of clauses functioning in question-response adjacency pairs. Questions can be further classified as **confirmation question** or **information question**. The realisation of these speech functions is distinct; the former are realised by a polar interrogative, the latter by a non-polar interrogative. Further, the element picked up in the response varies depending on whether the initiating question is a confirmation one or an information one. Typically it is the Negotiator that is replayed in a response to confirmation question, and the Remainder in response to the information question. I will begin by examining the type of adjacency pair which is initiated by a confirmation question as exemplified in the initiating move of (4) to (12). These questions and their responses are discussed in 3.1.1, while subsection 3.1.2 is concerned with those adjacency pairs which are initiated by an information question as in examples (13) to (17).

3.1.1 Confirmation questions and their responses

In section 2.1 we noted two means of realising polar interrogatives, intonation and the ordering of Finite^Subject (cf examples 2i-ii). A third means of realising polar interrogatives is exemplified in the initiating move of (4):

(4)   i   *Est-ce que tu*   *vois*   *la lune?*
          is it that   you   see   the moon
          M-int   **Subj Fin/Pred**   Comp
                 —**Negotiator**—   Remainder
     ii   *Oui*   *je*   *la*   *vois*
          Yes   I   it   see
          P-mrkr **Subj C-clitic Fin/pred**
              ——**Negotiator**——
      (i) Do you see the moon? (ii) Yes, I do.

The feature polar interrogative in the initiating move of example (4) is realised by the Mood interrogator *est-ce que*. Matthiessen (1992: 398) refers to this type of grammatical prosody as juncture prosody, since the element Mood-interrogator (M-int) can only occur at the boundary of the clause. Although clearly a part of the interpersonal organisation of the clause, this element falls outside the negotiatory structure: certainly, M-interrogator is associated with the presence of the option polar interrogative; however, it is by no means crucial to the realisation of that option, since the rising tone is by itself sufficient for the purpose. M-interrogator has the status of Theme, pointing to the interpersonal role of the clause as a yes/no question; unlike other interpersonal functions such as Subject or Complement, it does not conflate with any experiential function. The nominal group *la lune* in example (4i) realising the element Complement (Comp), forms the **Remain-**

der of the clause. I am thus identifying three categories of interpersonal functions: (i) those which enter into the Negotiator, e.g., Subject, Finite, Predicator, and the various clitics; (ii) those which enter into the Remainder, namely, Complement(s) and/or Adjuncts; and (iii) functions that remain peripheral to both the Negotiator and the Remainder. So far as the French clause as an interactive move is concerned, it is the first two categories of interpersonal functions – those which enter into the Negotiator and the Remainder – that are of special interest to us. The Negotiator and the Remainder together form a structure, which should, in fact, be viewed as the modal structure of the French clause in the sense that it is the immediate components of this modal structure that are relevant to negotiation in speech exchange. For this reason it seems appropriate to refer to it as the **negotiatory structure** of the French clause. By implication, then, I am suggesting four layers of interpersonal structure as shown in Figure 2.

Est-ce que	tu	vois	la lune
M-marker	Subject	Fin/Pred	Complement
	Negotiator ⟶		Remainder
	negotiatory structure ⟶		
interpersonal structure ⟶			

Figure 2: The Interpersonal structure

I claimed earlier (see section 2.1) that the resolution of an exchange in French often revolves around the replay of the Negotiator. This claim is further supported by the responding move in (4ii). The response statement here is expressed by means of the Polarity-marker (P-mrkr) *oui* followed by the replay of all the interpersonal functions of the initiating move; only the latter – *je la vois* – enters into the negotiatory structure. Note that in this replay cohesive relations become central; thus the complement of (4i), *la lune*, reappears in (4ii) simply as *la* acting as a Complement-clitic. As a cohesive device (Halliday and Hasan 1985), *la* is given and recoverable. What can be recovered by both interactants from context and stays a constant in the exchange is realised by a pronominal in the form of a clitic, which in the indicative is prefixed to the verbal group functioning as Fin/Pred, as it is in (4ii). However, given and recoverable entities may be indicated in other ways. So, in (5ii), it is full clausal ellipsis that marks this shared aspect of the dialogue. The textual resources of both REFERENCE and ELLIPSIS are quite commonly employed in the type of exchange, where the initial move is realised by a polar interrogative, and the following response by a declarative (see also 18 and 19 in section 3.1.3).

(5) i *Pierre* *vois*   *tu*   *la lune?*
        Pierre   see   you   the moon
        Fin/Pred **S-clitic** Comp
        ——**Negotiator**—— Remainder

     ii *Non*
         no
         P-mrkr
         (i) Pierre, do you see the moon? (ii) No.

Example (5i) resembles (2i); both realise the polar interrogative by ordering the Finite before Subject (F^s), and in addition, the Subject in both is realised by a pronominal clitic. In (5i), the Subject-clitic (S-clitic) is coreferential with the nominal *Pierre*, which occurs in a thematic position. This nominal segment is separate from the rest of the clause as an interactive move and plays no role in its transitivity structure. It performs only a textual function. Such themes, which neither enter in the interpersonal nor the experiential structure of the clause, are referred to as **absolute Theme** (Th-abs). Nominals, such as *Pierre* here, are not limited to having just this function; for example, *Pierre* could also have been assigned the function of New, realised phonologically. In that case, it would have had a contrastive meaning (Pierre and not the others). Rothemberg (1989: 153) points out that "orally the organisation of the clause as message is not dependent on word order alone. Intonation can assign the role of rheme[2] even to a term which is not in final position" (translation mine, AC). She goes on to say that "graphically, to convey the information that the one at whom the question is directed is Paul, not others, the solution is to add a tonic pronominal following the absolute Theme, as in *Paul, lui, je l'ai vu*" (translation mine, AC), where she would interpret *Paul* as Theme and *lui* as Rheme. However, following Halliday's

2. What Rothemberg calls 'Rheme' is very much like Halliday's notion of 'New' in the sense that it is listener-oriented rather than speaker-oriented (see Halliday, 1985).

distinction between Theme-Rheme and Given-New structures, I interpret both *Paul* and *lui* as absolute Theme in Rothemberg's examples, treating *Paul* as Given and *lui* as New. (For further discussion of some aspects of the textual organisation of the French clause specifically from a dialogic point of view, see section 5).

Example (5) also shows that, unlike English, the Finite is not always discretely realised in an interrogative clause, but can be fused in the Predicator depending on tense selection, in which case the Subject is ordered in relation to that Predicator with which the Finite is fused. Thus the generalisation holds true that Subject is always ordered in relation to the verbal constituent which specifies direct temporal reference to the speech event, that is, the Finite. This constituent is discrete when the realisation of temporal relations is complex, and fused when the tense is simple, i.e., when the tense selection is either simple past, imperfect past or present. From this it follows that whenever Finite is discretely expressed, and the interrogative mood is partly/wholly realised by ordering Finite before Subject, the latter would intervene between Finite and Predicator in the Negotiator of the clause; otherwise, it follows the Predicator.

Exchange (6) is a follow up to exchange (5). This time the interrogative is realised by intonation alone rather than by the juncture particle *est-ce que* as in (4i) or by ordering Finite before Subject-clitic as in (5i).

(6) i *Tu*   *la*   *vois*   *Paul?*
        you   it   see   Paul
        S-clitic C-clitic Fin/Pred
     ii *Oui*
        yes
        P-mrkr
        (i) Do you see it, Paul? (ii) Yes.

Here the shift in Subjecthood is emphasised by the nominal *Paul,* which in this example follows the Negotiator. Like the nominal *Pierre* in (5i), *Paul* too is **absolute Theme**, having simply a textual function and not conflating with any interpersonal or experiential function in the clause. Such a Theme, when clause final, is referred to as **reprise Theme**. In example (6), the reprise Theme conflates with the function Given, in the sense that it is not contrastive. If instead of *Paul,* we had the tonic pronominal *toi* as in *tu la vois, toi* (which would contrast the addressee of this move with Pierre), then *toi* would be analysed as both reprise Theme (Th-rep) and New (see section 5 for more detailed discussion on absolute Themes). The important role played by absolute Themes in spoken discourse is further exemplified by (7):

(7)   i   *L'   as   tu   vu?*
          it   have you   seen
          C-clitic Fin Subj Pred

     ii   *Moi,   oui*
          I   yes
          Th-abs P-mrkr
          (i) Have **you** seen her? (ii) Yes, **I have.**

The resolution of an exchange may revolve around the two textual functions of absolute Theme and Polarity-marker as in (7). When the absolute Theme is coreferential with the Subject it serves to emphasise 'modal responsibility'[3]. The addressee may decide to validate the speaker's information (as in example 7) or may assign modal responsibility to someone else. When the absolute Theme is coreferential with a Complement as in *elle, je l'ai vu (I saw her)*, it gives the interactant an opening to challenge the information given by the preceding speaker. A possible follow up to move (i) of example (7) would be *elle, non; une autre (her, no, someone else)*.

If, as proposed here, the Negotiator realises MOOD selections, then clearly this realisation is prosodic. According to Halliday (1979) the prosodic mode of expression is not restricted to MOOD selections alone; it extends to all the interpersonal resources, as can be seen from the patterns exemplified in (8). Here negative polarity is realised as a prosody *ne..pas* , the items occurring in different places in the clause. Negation occurs first following *tu* as a negative clitic Adjunct (A-neg-clitic), *ne*, then it occurs after the Finite as a negative non-clitic Adjunct (A-neg) *pas*. *Pas* may be replaced by other negative Adjuncts e.g., *plus* (any more), *jamais* (never), or by a negated Complement or one that is itself negative e.g., *personne* (nobody). With negative Subject, *pas* is not present as in *personne n'ai venu* (nobody came). (See Battye and Hintze 1992: 268). Note in passing that the polarity marker

3. Halliday (1985) defines the Subject as the one modally responsible. In a proposal, the modally responsible participant is the one 'responsible for carrying out the offer or command. In a proposition this means the one on which the validity of the information is made to rest.'

in (8ii) also shows that a polarity positive response to a negative question is *si* rather than *oui*.

(8) i | *Tu* | *ne* | | *l'* | | *as* | *pas* | *vu?* |
|------|------|------|------|------|------|------|------|
| you | not | | it | | have | not | seen |
| Subj | A-neg-clitic | | C-clitic | | Fin | A-neg | Pred |

　　ii *Si*
　　　　yes
　　　　P-mrkr
　　　　(i) Didn't you see it? (ii) Yes, I did.

The lexicogrammatical realisation of negative polarity may vary depending on tenor and mode. Battye and Hintze (1992: 268) note that in "less formal styles of spoken French, it is common for the first element *ne* not to appear..", citing the following examples in support of their claim:

(9) *Je vois pas Marie*
　　　I see not Marie
　　　I don't see Marie.

(10) *Je vois plus Marie*
　　　I see any more Marie
　　　I can't see Marie any more.

(11) *J' ai mangé aucune tarte*
　　　I have eaten no pie
　　　I didn't eat any pie.

On the other hand, "in written French there is a small class of verbs which permit negative structures to be formed by the use of *ne* alone. These are *pouvoir* [be able to], *savoir* [to know], *cesser* [to stop] and *oser* [to dare]" (Battye & Hintze 1992).

It is obvious from these examples that, in addition to Subject, Finite and Predicator, the Negotiator may have a Complement clitic and/or negative clitic and/or non-clitic Adjuncts. The responding move in Example (12) below illustrates that more than one Complement clitic may be attached to the Finite:

(12) i | *As-* | *tu* | *donné* | *le livre* | *à Paul?* |
|------|------|------|------|------|
| have | you | given | the book | to Paul |
| **Fin** | **Subj** | **Pred** | Comp | Comp |
| **—Negotiator—** | | | ——Remainder—— | |

ii *Oui je   le   lui   ai   donné.*
    yes   I   it   to him   have   given
         S-clitic C-clitic C-clitic Fin   Pred
         ————————————Negotiator————————--
    (i) Did you give the book to Paul? (ii) Yes, I did.

The relative ordering of Complement clitics is governed by a number of semantic variables, which cannot be discussed within the scope of this paper. Interpersonally the Complement clitics with interactant roles e.g., *me*, *te* precede non-interactant Complement clitics e.g., *le*, *la*. If there are two third person non-interactant clitics as in (12), then the accusative pronominals e.g., *le* always precede dative pronominals e.g., *lui*, whatever the MOOD choice. Thus they follow the ordering of the nominals they cohere with. This is in contrast with the clitics referring to the interactant roles: here the accusative pronominal clitic does not necessarily have to precede the dative one, as can be seen from *Paul me le donne* (Paul gives it to me), where the dative *me* precedes the accusative *le* .

3.1.2 Information questions and their responses

Turning to adjacency pairs where the initiating move constitutes a demand for information rather than for confirmation, such questions are congruently realised by nonpolar interrogatives. In (13i) the focus is not on polarity, but on a missing element of information; this is what the Q-element stands for.

(13) i   *Quand   est-ce-que tu   arrives?*
          when   is it that you   arrive
          Q-Adj   M-int   **S-clitic Fin/Pred**
          Remainder   ——Negotiator——
      ii *Demain.*
          tomorrow
          Adj
          Remainder
          (i) When are you arriving? (ii) Tomorrow.

The Q-element may conflate with the interpersonal functions Subject, Complement or Adjunct. In (13i) it is conflated with the Adjunct function, and followed by the Mood-interrogator *est-ce que* . In discussing the structure of the polar interrogative, we identified three different means of realisation: presence of Mood-interrogator, tone, and the ordering of the Finite before the Subject. These three means are available to nonpolar interrogatives, as well. However, when Q-element is conflated with Subject, the possibility of inversion does not exist, and the conflated Q-Subject, together with the Finite, functions within the Negotiator, as (14) illustrates.

(14) i   *Qui   est   arrivé?*
          who   is   arrived
          Q-Subj Fin   Pred
          ——**Negotiator**——
      ii *Ton cousin.*
          your cousin
          Subj
          Negotiator
      (i) Who has arrived? (ii) Your cousin.

In spoken French, when the Q-element conflates with either an Adjunct or a Complement which refers to a non-human, then it may occur in Rheme as (15) and (16) illustrate. In this environment, Subject always precedes Finite. Note that in French this type of interrogative is not limited to simply realising echo questions; it can also realise an initiating question, at least in the spoken mode.

(15) *Tu   arrives   quand?*
      you   arrive   when
      Subj Pred/Fin   Q-Adj
      —**Negotiator**— Remainder
      When do you arrive?
(16) *Tu   parles   quoi?*
      you   speak   what
      Subj Pred-Fin   Q-Comp
      —**Negotiator**— Remainder
      What (language) do you speak?

In (16), *quoi* is the tonic form of *que*, the latter being used only in initial position, as in (17):

(17)   *Que*   *veux-*   *tu?*
       what   want   you
       Q-Comp   **Pred/Fin**   **Subj**
       Remainder   —**Negotiator**—
       What do you want?

Hopefully, the preceding examples have served (a) to illustrate how exchanges of information progress in French and (b) to exemplify the various prosodic structural patternings that realise MOOD selections. In presenting the linguistic analysis, I have highlighted in bold, those interpersonal functions which constitute the Negotiator. This, it is hoped, has further emphasised the crucial role that is played by the Negotiator in argumentation. Before turning to a discussion of the French proposals, it might be helpful to add a few more words in section 3.1.3 about the Negotiator.

3.1.3 Negotiator, clitics and cohesion

In section 2.1 where the Negotiator was first introduced, it was pointed out that this component of the French clause consists of the functions Subject, Finite and Predicator (see Figure 1). During the discussion of the adjacency pairs, attention was drawn to the fact that where Complement and Adjunct are realised by a clitic, these form part of the Negotiator, while the same functions, when realised by nominals and prepositional phrases respectively, enter into the make up of the element we have referred to as Remainder. The clitics – whether they realise polarity, Complements and/or Adjunct – are thus integral to the Negotiator: whenever they occur, they are crucial to negotiation, so that it is not simply Subject, Finite and Predicator but the entire complex consisting of Subject, Finite, Predicator **and** the clitics that is involved in the negotiation. The Negotiator is, thus, crucial to the arguability status of the French clause. In dialogues it is this part of the clause which is tossed back and forth. If ellipsis occurs, it is defined in relation to the Negotiator or the Remainder. Thus with full ellipsis, both Negotiator and Remainder are ellipsed, and the clause 'has' only textual functions e.g. polarity marker and/or absolute Themes. Partial ellipsis involves either the whole of the Negotiator or whole or part of the Remainder. Further, exchanges of information, initiated by a confirmation question tend to be carried forward by the Negotiator, displaying ellipsis of whole or part of the

Remainder, while information exchanges initiated by an information question tend to progress around the Remainder and thus display ellipsis of the whole of the Negotiator. Examples (18) and (19) illustrate how the textual systems of ELLIPSIS and REFERENCE are used in negotiation:

(18) i *est-ce-que tu pars en vacances demain?*
          is it that you part in holidays tomorrow
          M-int **Subj Pred/Fin** Adj   Adj
          —**Negotiator**— ———Remainder———

      ii *Oui j' y   pars.*
          yes I   there part
          P-mrkr **Subj Adj-clitic Fin/Pred**
          ————**Negotiator**————

(i) Are you going on holidays tomorrow? (ii) Yes, I am.

Here the initiating question in (18i) is a confirmation question. Its interpersonal structure is Mood-interrogator^Negotiator^Remainder as shown in the analysis. Note that the Negotiator consists of Subject^Finite/Predicator expressed by *tu pars*. The response in (ii) is a declarative, in whose structure the polarity marker is followed by the Negotiator. This Negotiator is related cohesively to the elements of the Remainder in (18i). Thus *y* refers anaphorically to *en vacances*; and there is ellipsis of *demain*. Both these cohesive relations are with elements that form part of the Remainder in (18i). Compare this with (19) which is initiated by a demand for information, realised by a nonpolar interrogative:

(19) i *Qu'   est-ce-que tu parles?*
          what   is it that you speak
          Q-Comp   M-int   **Subj Pred/fin**
          Remainder   —**Negotiator**—

      ii *Franglais.*
          Franglish
          Comp
          Remainder

(i) What (language) do you speak? (ii) Franglish.

In the negotiatory structure of the initiating clause in (19), Remainder consists of Q-Comp; this is followed by M-int *est-ce que* which in turn is followed by the Negotiator. The latter is realised by *tu parles*, consisting of

Subject *tu* and Finite/Predicator *parles*. The response to this in (19ii) is a declarative, which consists simply of the element Remainder, displaying the ellipsis of the Negotiator which would be expanded as Subject^Predicator/ Finite *tu parles*. These functions are presumed from the first pair part of the adjacency pair i.e. from (19i). A possible continuation of this exchange is shown in (19 iii) and (iv), where (iii) is another question, and (iv) its response. Here, the elliptical clauses consist solely of the Remainder; nonetheless, the Negotiator still plays an important part in carrying the exchange forward, being presumed by ellipsis. The Negotiator is, thus, a constant throughout the dialogue; it is always relevant and recoverable from the cotext.

(19)   iii   *Francais et Anglais ?*
              French and English
              Comp
              ——Remainder——
        iv   *Non,   Franglais*
              no   Franglish
              P-mrkr   Comp
              Remainder
              (iii) French and English? (iv) No, Franglish.

The fact that interpersonal prosodies, other than those indicating MOOD, have the Negotiator as their domain of realisation further supports the interpretation of this element as interpersonally salient. An example of this has already been given above in (8), where we drew attention to the negative prosody. A further example of this is found in the modal prosodies within the Negotiator. As is evident from example (20), modality[4] can be expressed repeatedly in the Negotiator appearing in the Finite and/or the Predicator as well as in a modal Adjunct:

(20)   *Jean pourrait   peut-être faire   ça.*
        Jean   could   maybe   do   this
        Subj Fin-mod   A-mod   Pred   Comp
        ————————Negotiator———————   Remainder
        Jean could maybe do this.

---

4. The term modality here refers to both modalisation and modulation, which correspond more or less to epistemic and deontic modality, respectively.

Here, the meaning of probability is expressed three times. First by a form of the modal verb, *pouvoir*, secondly, in the Finite (Fin-mod) which makes modal rather than temporal reference to the speech event in *pourrait* , and third by the modal Adjunct (Adj-mod), *peut-être*. Modal Adjuncts do not just realise modality but also 'presumption, time, degree and intensity' (Halliday 1985: 82). Thus the postulate of the Negotiator appears justified, both by its function in the speech exchange and by the fact that its mode of expression is prosodic, as I have attempted to show through the discussion of various examples. It is that part of the clause which must be replayed in the negotiation of speech exchange. Not surprisingly, it is "always there", either overtly or by cohesive presumption.

We turn now to a fuller structural account of the Negotiator. If the analysis of the examples discussed so far is examined, it will be seen that the functions Subject, Finite and Predicator are obligatory: there is no indicative clause where the Negotiator does not include these functions either explicitly or implicitly. In addition to these, we find certain other functions that are optional. These include a negative Adjunct clitic and/or a negative Adjunct, both exemplified in (8), and/or modal Adjuncts, as shown in (20), Complement clitics illustrated in the various examples, and/or an Adjunct clitic (see 18ii). The unmarked order in which these functions may occur in the Negotiator varies somewhat depending on whether the Finite is discrete or fused. By unmarked order, I mean Subject before Finite, which is always the case with declaratives, often also with the interrogatives, though in some cases they may be reversed, as for example in (2i) of section 2.1. The unmarked order of the various functions in the Negotiator is as shown in (a) and (b) below. The key to the symbols is presented at the end of the paper.

(a)   **Subj^(A-neg-clitic^)(C-clitic^)(A-clitic^)Fin^(A-mod•)(A-neg^)Pred.**

(b)   **Subj^(A-neg-clitic^)(C-clitic^)(A-clitic^)Fin/Pred^(A-mod•)(A-neg).**

Examples (21) and (22) illustrate the maximal structures (a) and (b) respectively:

(21)	*Je*	*ne*	*le*	*lui*	*ai*	*probablement*	*pas*	*donné*
	I	not	it	him	have	probably	not	given
	Subj	**A-neg-clitic**	**C-clitic**	**C-clitic**	**Fin**	**A-mod**	**A-neg**	**Pred**

————————————————Negotiator————————————————

I probably didn't give it to him.

Compare the structure of (21) with the structure potential of the (a) variant
of the Negotiator shown above. With respect to English, Matthiessen (1992:
335) points out that in a negative clause, it is the Subject that is outside the
negative prosody in the unmarked case precisely because it is the element
on which the argument rests: with respect to Subject, the proposition or
proposal is negative rather than positive. The same observation appears to
apply to the French Subject in (21) which too falls outside negative prosody.
This is however not true of example (22):

(22)	*Ne*	*le*	*lui*	*a-(t) il*	*pas*	*encore*	*donné?*
	not	it	him	have he	not	yet	given
	A-neg-clitic	**C-clitic**	**C-clitic**	**Fin**	**S-clitic**	**A-neg**	**A-mod** **Pred**

————————————————————Negotiator————————————————————

Hasn't he given it to him yet?

Examples (21) and (22) show quite clearly that the Negotiator has the
potential of functioning as a complete clause on its own which has the verbal
group as its domain of realisation. Note that when the Subject is realised as
a nominal rather than a clitic it is not attached to the verbal group, but it still
remains part of the Negotiator. It is the only participant of the Negotiator
which may be realised as either a pronominal clitic or a nominal. The shift
from pronominal clitic Subject to nominal Subject correlates with the
assignment of modal responsibility to some other function. This other
function is usually a Complement, and it is secondary to the negotiation
process. The status of the Complement is variable. When non-clitic, the
Complement is part of the Remainder (compare, for example, (4) and (5) in
section 3.1.1), and typically has the textual status of New. The clitic status
of the Complement shows that it is at the center of the negotiation; and once
this happens, then quite predictably it becomes Given.

Our statement of the structure potential of the unmarked Negotiator has
shown that its minimal structure consists of Subject, Finite, and Predicator.
A minimal Negotiator is still capable of functioning as a complete clause.
When the Subject in a minimal Negotiator is a clitic, with the Negotiator
functioning as a complete clause, the latter presents itself as a kind of Clause
nucleus, in experiential terms. To elaborate, the minimal Negotiator with S-
clitic consists of constituents which are in themselves sufficient to support
the realisation of an experiential structure. In this respect the Negotiator is
quite different from the Mood element in English, which by itself cannot be

assigned an experiential structure. This raises interesting issues in relation to the typological location of the French language which arguably has characteristics of both polysynthetic and analytic languages. Also, it suggests that in French the labour of transitivity is shared between the clause and the verbal group. However, these issues must await another occasion. With this general discussion of the Negotiator in French, we turn to the giving and demanding of goods and services.

3.2 The clause as exchange of goods and services: the structure of proposals

As in English, so in French, there does not seem to be a lexicogrammatical structure dedicated specifically to the realisation of offers. We turn therefore to the demand for goods and services, i.e. the command type, grammatically realised as imperative. The structure of the imperative was briefly visited in section 2.1 (see example (5)). In this section we ask how the Negotiator in the imperative compares with that of the indicative (see (a) and (b) previous section).The first point to note is that imperatives do not have a Finite element. They specify neither modal nor temporal reference to the speech situation. Secondly, although the Subject does not appear overtly, its person, number and social distance (formal vs informal) are realised syncretically in the verb which functions as Predicator. Thus the only obligatory function to appear discretely in the Negotiator of an imperative is the Predicator, as illustrated by (23-26):

(23) i *Dites-*   *moi*   *la vérité!*
        tell   me   the truth
        Pred-2-sing-form C-clitic Comp
        ——**Negotiator**——   Remainder

     ii *Non*   *je*   *ne*   *vous*   *le*   *dirai*   *pas*
        no   I   not   you   it   will tell   not
        P-mrkr **S-clitic A-neg-clitic C-clitic C-clitic P/F   A-neg**
        ——————————————————**Negotiator**——————————

     (i) Tell me the truth! (ii) No, I won't.

(24) i *Toi,*   *dis-*   *moi*   *la vérité!*
        you   tell   me   the truth
        Th/New   **Pred-2-sing-inf. C-clitic** Comp
        ——**Negotiator**——   Remainder

	ii	C'	est	quoi?
		it	is	what
		S-clitic Fin		**Q-Comp**
		Negotiator		**Remainder**

(i) You, tell me the truth! (ii) What's truth?

(25)	i	Allons	á la plage!
		go	to the beach
		Pred-1-S+	**Adj**
		Negotiator	**Remainder**
	ii	Allons-	y
		go	there
		Pred-1-S+	**A-clitic**
		–Negotiator–	

(i) Let's go to the beach! (ii) Yes, let's!

The first move of (23-25) enacts a command which is realised as an imperative. The responding move in each case consists of the Negotiator alone. In (24), the responding move is a challenge, rather than a compliance or an initiating question. These examples highlight the respects in which the interpersonal organisation of the imperative differs from that of the indicative. To reiterate, the imperative has no Finite; nor does it have an explicit Subject. Rather, the person and number of the implicit Subject of each clause is marked on the Predicator, and predictably the implicit Subject of a French imperative is either a second person or 'first person plus', the latter being different from first person plural. The marking of these as well as of formality is indicated clearly in the above analysis. A further feature of imperatives should be noted: clitics, whenever they occur in a French imperative, follow the Predicator, except where the clause has a negative prosody. In the latter case, the order of clitics vis a vis the Predicator is reversed as illustrated in (26):

(26)	Ne	le	lui	donnes	pas!
	not	it	him	give	not
	A-neg	**C-clitic**	**C-clitic**	**Pred-2-sing**	**A-neg**

Don't give it to him!

This closes the discussion of the structure of the French clause as an interactive move in an exchange. The description offered here has highlighted the specific interpersonal functions which occur in the Negotiator. The Negotiator and the Remainder form what I have called the negotiatory structure, which constitutes the essence of the modal structure in French (see the graphic representation in Figure 2 in section 3.1.1). We have also encountered some functions that are outside the negotiatory structure e.g. the Mood-interrogator, absolute Theme and Polarity marker. I suggested that the Mood-interrogator is part of the interpersonal structure but falls outside the Negotiatory structure; the textual function of absolute Theme, whether initial or reprise, as well as Polarity markers, were seen to have an important role in dialogue. One strong motivation for dividing the clause into Negotiator and Remainder was provided from a consideration of the behaviour of ellipsis, which is defined in relation to these two parts. Thus, ellipsis may either be of the entire Negotiator, or Remainder or of both, when simply a Polarity marker e.g. *oui* or *non* might occur. If there is an ellipsis of the Negotiator, all of its functional parts must be ellipsed. Thus, unlike English, a move cannot be expressed by a replay of just Subject and Finite (Halliday and Hasan 1976; 1985; Martin 1992). The fact that Finite and Predicator must always function together in French indicative clauses, whether the two are fused or not, in addition to the fact that both Finite and Predicator may realise modality (see example (20) in section 3.1.3) suggests that both elements in conjunction with the Subject make the clause arguable. So far this description has been provided in terms of functions in the syntagm – what elements must occur in a structure, and in what order. In the following section, we attempt an examination of the system 'behind' the syntagmatic organisation of the French clause as a move.

4. MOOD potential in French: Options and their realisations

As pointed out in the introduction, the SF model predicts that the primary semantics of the exchange of information and goods & services will reflect similarities across languages. This follows from the more general assumption that 'commonalities across languages are primarily functional rather than structural or realisational' (Matthiessen, Nanri and Licheng 1991: 966). On the other hand it can be predicted that the structural output of the systemic options as well as the secondary more delicate options will tend to differ from one language to that of another. My account of the interpersonal structure of the French clause is true to this prediction. But, at the same time, at a more abstract level, we note also that MOOD options and interpersonal resources in French have a prosodic type of structure, as they do in English. As far as specific realisations of MOOD selections are concerned, we saw that French makes use of all three types of realisation encountered across languages: tone, MOOD Marker and Subject Finite ordering. The system itself will have to reflect these realisational differences through more delicate features. The lexicogrammatical network presented below will attempt to balance the semantic 'facts' of French with the structural ones. The key to system network notations is provided at the end of this paper.

4.1 The primary MOOD options

We saw in text I, that the three indicative clause types, i.e. declarative, exclamative, and interrogative may have the same interpersonal organisation with the Subject preceding the Finite, differing in terms of tone contours which are indicated in writing by the use of different punctuation marks. The unmarked intonation of French polar interrogatives is a rising tone, and of the non-polar interrogatives, a falling one. A declarative may have a falling or rising-falling tone depending on how many information units it realises, but it will always end with a falling tone. Exclamatives too have a falling tone. Battye and Hintze (1992: 144) point out that

> for declaratives the last syllable of the tone will be on a low pitch falling below the normal speaking range. For non-polar interrogatives and exclamatives, the first syllable will start off on a note which is slightly above that of a normal speaking range.

Thus, both tone and pitch are crucial to the realisation of MOOD features in French, as they may be the only means of manifesting systemic distinctions. Secondary options are distinguished by means of different modes of prosodic expression and thematic organisation. Since I have approached the MOOD grammar of French from dialogue, the options systemised in the networks presented here are representative of spoken language. Some of the resources in the interrogative and exclamative systems are not found in the written mode.

Figure 3a presents the primary options of the MOOD system, those which are expected to be applicable to most languages. Note the slanting arrow below the option [indicative]; such arrows point to the realisational patterns, which themselves are shown in italics. Thus in Figure 3a, this arrow claims

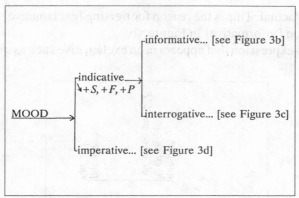

Figure 3a: Primary MOOD options

that the option [indicative] is realised by the insertion of functions Subject, Finite and Predicator into the structure, so that any clause with the feature [indicative] must have these functions. In Figure 3a, the other three options are followed by information, which is a guide to the development of the network. For example, following the option [informative] there appear the words *Figure 3b*, which is to say that the options dependent on [informative] are developed in Figure 3b. The term [informative] is used in preference to the term affirmative to avoid connotations of positive polarity (Martin 1992). The options dependent on [interrogative] and [imperative] are presented in figures 3c and 3d, respectively.

4.2 Options of the informative feature

The option [informative] permits a choice between [declarative] and [exclamative]. In French the crucial properties of the structure of the declarative clause are very easily stated. All French declaratives must 'have' Subject, Finite, and Predicator, in that order. These functions are inserted as a response to the feature [indicative] (See Figure 3a); the criterial ordering of Subject vis a vis Finite is indicated in Figure 3b.

As Figure 3b shows the term contrasting with [declarative] is [exclamative]. Grammatically exclamative clauses may sometimes be similar to interrogatives, but semantically they are closer to declaratives in the sense that they give rather than demand information, which is primarily attitudinal

rather than factual. This is the reason for treating [exclamative] as an option
dependent on [informative] in Figure 3b.

The *qu*-expression that appears in an exclamative such as *qu'il est sage!*

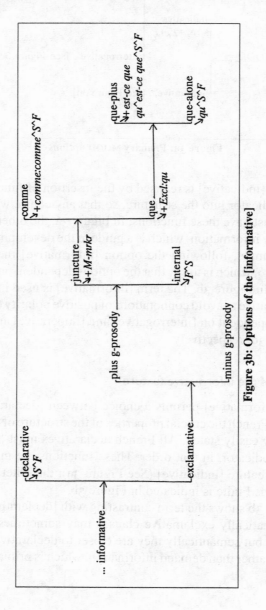

Figure 3b: Options of the [informative]

or *qu'est-ce qu'il est sage!* superficially resembles the Q-element in non-polar interrogatives. However, the two are significantly different. The non-polar interrogative Q-element has the realisational resource of a full paradigm consisting of such items as *que, qui, quand, quoi,* etc. Further, each of these when it occurs in a clause conflates with some interpersonal and experiential function as can be seen from examples 13-17 in section 3.1.2. The *que* which functions as an exclamator in the exclamative, contrasts only with *comme*; and neither of these exclamators – *que* or *comme* – conflate with any experiential function in the clause. The exclamators, *que* or *comme*, are not like Q-items; their function is comparable to *est-ce-que* in polar interrogative (see section 3.1.2): both function simply as MOOD markers. The situation is further confounded by the fact that the expression *est-ce que* may also occur in exclamatives as in the example *qu'est-ce qu'il est sage!* When the *est-ce que* expression occurs in an exclamative, it no longer has the function of MOOD marker, for there is no "interrogativeness" about the exclamative. Rather, the choice of *est-ce qu* in an exclamative is indicative of certain register variables. Instantiations for each possible selection expression applicable to the feature exclamative are presented in Table 1:

Table 1: Exclamative clauses: some examples

il est sage!	minus g-prosody
est-il sage!	plus g-prosody: internal
comme il est sage!	plus g-prosody: juncture:comme
qu'il est sage!	plus g-prosody: juncture:que:que alone
qu'est-ce qu'il est sage!	plus g-prosody: juncture:que:que plus

The left column in Table 1 provides examples of the exclamative clause type, while the systemic features relevant to that type are presented in the right column. The five instances of French exclamatives could be translated by the English clause *How nice he is.* Note that the Subject of a French exclamative clause may be brought into prominence indirectly through its cohesive relation to a nominal functioning as absolute initial or absolute reprise Theme, and/or as New as illustrated in (27-29).

(27)	*Cet enfant,*	*qu'*	*il*	*est*	*sage!*
	This child,	how	he	is	nice
	Th-abs	M-mrkr	**Subj Fin**		Comp
			Negotiator		Remainder

How well behaved is this child!

(28) *Qu'est-ce qu'* il   *est*   *sage,*   *cet enfant*
      How   he   is   nice,   this child
      M-mrkr   **Subj Fin**   Comp Th-rep
                    Negotiator Remainder
      How well behaved is this child!

(29) *Qu'* il   *est*   *sage,* *lui*
      How   he   is   nice,   him
      M-mrkr **Subj Fin** Comp Th-rep
             Negotiator Remainder
      How well behaved he is!

In (27) and (28), the nominal *cet enfant* functions as the absolute Theme; it is initial Theme in (27) and reprise Theme in (28), and in both cases it is related cohesively to the Subject *il* – anaphorically in (27), cataphorically in (28). In (29), *lui* is both the absolute reprise Theme and New; further, it is anaphorically related to the Subject *il*.

4.3 Options of the interrogative feature

The interrogative network presented in Figure 3c, starts with two simultaneous systems: the INTERROGATIVE TYPE system, shown in the network as I-TYPE acting as the entry condition to the options [polar] versus [non-polar], and MOOD MARKER system, shown as M-MARKER leading to the options [minus g-prosody] versus [plus g-prosody], where *g-prosody* stands for 'grammatical prosody'. The option [minus g-prosody] implies that phonological prosody – i.e. intonation – is the only mode of realisation; by contrast, the option [plus g-prosody] means that, in addition to intonation, a grammatical prosodic expression will occur in the clause. This grammatical prosody may occur either at clause [juncture] or it may be clause [internal]. With [juncture], the M-marker *est-ce que* is chosen as the clause-initial element, whereas with the choice [internal], the prosody takes the form of inversion whereby Finite is ordered before Subject. If a clause 'is' both [polar] and also [minus g-prosody], then this conjunction permits a choice between [tagged] and [untagged].

The realisation of the option [non-polar] calls for the insertion of Q-element, which typically occurs clause initially. Q-element may conflate with Subject or other function, as reflected in the systemic options [qu-Subject]

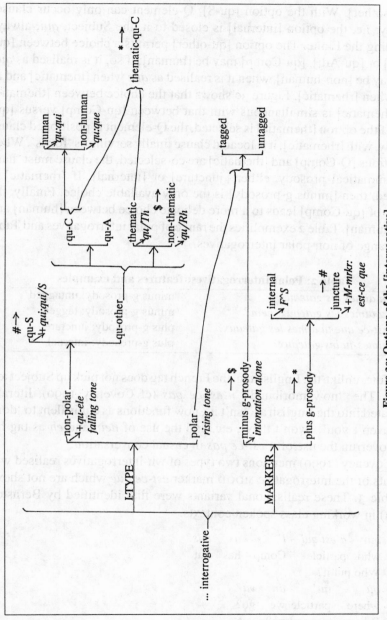

Figure 3c: Options of the [interrogative]

or [qu-other]. With the option [qu-S], Q-element can only occur clause-initially; i.e. the option [internal] is closed to it, the Subject, *qui*, always preceding the Finite. The option [qu-other] permits a choice between [qu-Comp] or [qu-Adj]. [qu-Comp] may be [human]; if so, it is realised as *qui*, or it may be [non-human], when it is realised as *que* when [thematic] and as *quoi* when [rhematic]. Figure 3c shows that the choice between [thematic] and [rhematic] is simultaneous with that between [qu-Comp] versus [qu-Adj]. If the option [thematic] is selected, the Q-element is positioned clause initially, with [rhematic], it is located clause finally serving as 'focus'. When the options [Q-Comp] and [thematic] are co-selected, the clause must 'have a' grammatical prosody, either [juncture] or [internal]. If [rhematic] is selected, then [minus g-prosody] is the only available choice. Finally, the choice of [qu-Comp] leads to a more delicate choice between [human] and [non-human]. Table 2 exemplifies the range of polar interrogatives and Table 3 the range of non-polar interrogatives.

Table 2: Polar interrogatives: features and examples

tu aimes les gateaux?	minus g-prosody: untagged
tu aimes les gateaux, hein?	minus g-prosody: tagged
est-ce que tu aimes les gateaux?	plus g-prosody: juncture
aimes-tu les gateaux?	plus g-prosody: internal

Note, unlike the English tag, the French tag does not pick up Subject and Finite. The "now moribund" *n'est-ce pas* (cf Coveney 1990), literally translated into the English as 'isn't it', now functions as equivalent to 'don't I', 'haven't you', 'won't they', etc. and the use of *hein* and *eh* as tag has quite overrun the use of *n'est-ce pas* in casual conversation.

Coveney (1990) mentions two types of wh-interrogatives realised with variants of the interrogative MOOD marker *est-ce que* which are not shown in Table 3. These realisational variants were first identified by Bernstedt (1973) in working class spoken contexts.

(30)   *qui*   *c'est qui*   *l'*   *a*   *mis?*
      who   particle   Comp   has   put
      Who put it?

(31)   *où*   *qu'*   *on*   *va?*
      where   particle   we   go?
      Where are we going?

Table 3: Non-polar interrogatives: examples and features

qui a mangé ce gateau?	qu-Subject; minus g-prosody
qui est-ce qui a mangé ce gateau?	qu-Subj; plus g-prosody: juncture
que vois-tu?	qu-Comp: non-human; thematic; plus g-prosody: internal
qui vois-tu?	qu-Comp: human; thematic; plus g-prosody: internal
tu vois quoi?	qu-Comp: non-human; rhematic: minus g-prosody
tu vois qui?	qu-Comp: human; rhematic: minus g-prosody
qu'est-ce que tu vois?	qu-Comp: non-human; thematic; plus g-prosody: juncture
qui est-ce que tu vois?	qu-Comp: human; thematic; plus g-prosody: juncture
òu tu vas?	qu-Adj; thematic; minus g-prosody
tu vas òu?	qu-Adj; rhematic; minus g-prosody
òu vas-tu?	qu-Adj; thematic; plus g-prosody: internal
òu est-ce que tu vas?	qu-Adj; thematic; plus g-prosody: juncture

This sub-section has highlighted the various modes of prosodic expression that serve to realise the options dependent on [interrogative] MOOD. It should be noted that the various options in the MOOD MARKING system not only indicate variable ways of expressing the same interrogative types, they also embody different *valeurs* as a result of their use in differing environments (cf the *valeur* of *est-ce que*, as well as of *que-* and *comme*).

4.4 The options of the imperative

From the realisational point of view, the imperative MOOD differs from the indicative by virtue of the absence of the elements Subject and Finite. However, in the imperative the features of person and number relevant to Subject are marked on the Predicator, while in the indicative they are marked on the Finite. This marking within the verbal group thus becomes a means of recognising which nominal has the function of Subject; and the principle applies both in propositions where Subject and Finite are in agreement and in proposals where it is Subject and Predicator that agree in number and person. I shall return to this issue in Section 6. The absence of Finite in the imperative is explained by the fact that this clause type does not specify temporal reference to the speech event. The imperative system represented in Figure 3d distinguishes between the [exclusive] and the [inclusive]. The former is oriented towards the addressee(s), held responsible for complying, whilst the latter is oriented towards both the speaker and the addressee.

Note that the realisation of the systemic options in each case implicates the Predicator; this is because such distinctions as that between [exclusive] versus [inclusive] are marked on that element, and this marking is always indicative of the implied Subject. Table 4 gives some examples and their systemic features:

Table 4: the imperative mood: examples and options	
mangeons!	inclusive
mange, Paul	exclusive: singular: informal
mangez, monsieur	exclusive: singular: formal
mangez, les enfant	exclusive: plural

The imperative differs from the indicative in that it neither has a Finite nor an explicit Subject. Further, in an indicative clause clitics precede the Predicator, while in an imperative clause they follow it so long as the polarity is positive. Thus in (32) which is [indicative:informative:declarative] the clitics precede the Predicator *donne*; in (33) which is an imperative, they follow it:

(32)   *je le lui donne*
      I it him give
      I give it to him

(33)   *Donne-le-moi*
      Give it to me
      Give it to me.

When the final clitic of an imperative is first or second person it is realised in its tonic form, i.e. as *moi* or *toi*. In some dialects of French, (34) functions as a variant of (33):

(34)   *Donne-me-le*
      Give me it
      Give it to me.

Declarative clauses differ lexicogrammatically from exclamative and inter-rogative clauses in that their MOOD is never realised by a juncture particle, such as *comme* or *que* in exclamatives and *est-ce que* in interrogatives. The increase in the use of *est-ce que* in both spoken and written discourse to realise interrogative correlates with a lessening of the order Fin/Pred^S or Fin^S as a means of its realisation. Although the relative order of Subject to either Finite and/or Predicator may serve to realise MOOD selections, in the

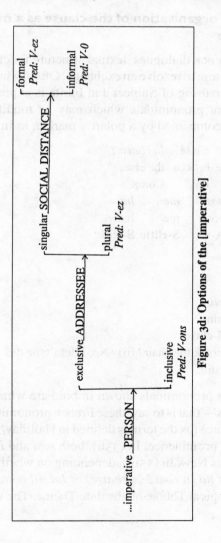

Figure 3d: Options of the [imperative]

majority of cases the Subject will precede the Finite whatever the MOOD. It is this ordering that has been referred to as the unmarked one. Thus, obviously, we cannot generalise quite as we can in English, that the order of Subject and Finite realises MOOD options. The dominant variables which distinguish the mood features are the realisational resources of intonation and the presence or absence of the MOOD markers.

5. The textual organisation of the clause as a move in an exchange

It seems that in French dialogues, textual structure functions together with interpersonal structure to resolve an exchange. Often, what in English would be realised as the pairing of Subject and Finite is expressed in French by textually prominent pronominals which may be modified by a negative Adjunct and/or accompanied by a polarity marker, as in (35):

(35)   i   *Tu   as   cassé   la chaise?*
           you   have   broken   the chair
           Subj Fin   Pred   Comp

       ii *–Non   pas   **moi,   lui.***
           No   not   me   him
           P-mrkr A-neg **S-clitic S-clitic**

       iii *–Lui?*
           him
           S-clitic

       iv *–Oui,   **lui.***
           Yes   **him**
           P-mrkr **S-clitic**

       (i) Did you break the chair? (ii) –No, I didn't; he did. (iii) –He did?
       (iv) –Yes, he did.

In (35ii-iv), all the pronominals shown in bold are what I shall refer to as 'tonic pronominals' – that is to say, these French pronominals typically carry phonological salience (as the term is defined in Halliday 1985); as such they all express textual prominence. In (35ii), both *moi* and *lui* are New, but *lui* is marked as well as New. In (35iii), depending on whether we interpret the elliptical clause as *lui (a cassé la chaise)* or *lui, (il a cassé la chaise),* it is either unmarked topical Theme or absolute Theme. The same interpretation applies to (35iv). Thus Theme appears to have a special status in maintaining exchange coherence, and among the various types of themes, the absolute Theme seems to be most relevant to exchange.

5.1 Absolute Theme: a type of prominence specific to French dialogic texts

Absolute Themes, whether reprise or not, are Themes that do not play a role either in the interpersonal or experiential structure of the clause. A reprise Theme is always in a cohesive relationship with the Subject, while a non-reprise absolute Theme may be in a cohesive relationship with any of the (pro)nominals that form part of the Negotiator. This type of thematic organisation, where a textual function is in cohesive relation to a function in the Negotiator is specific to spoken language and particularly to dialogic texts. Such Themes, although they fall outside the negotiatory structure, play an important role in the resolution of an exchange as example (35iii and iv) above illustrate. Hagège (1990: 177-178) interprets these Theme patterns as follows:

> French distinguishes between two types of Themes in conversation: the Theme as old information or reprise of known material tends to be postposed, while the Theme as supporting material is generally preposed. Thus we find, on the one hand, sentences like *ça s'élève tout seul, les enfants* ("it raises itself, children", i.e. "children raise themselves"), or *il n'est pas là, papa* ("he isn't here, papa", i.e. "papa isn't here") in which *les enfants* and *papa* are contrastive postposed Themes representing information already given. On the other hand, we have *les chiens mordent quand on les provoque* ("dogs bite when provoked") in formal style, with weak thematisation of *chiens*; or *les chiens, ça mord quand on les provoque* in spoken style, with strong thematisation of *chiens*, recapitulated as Subject through the resumptive pronoun *ça*.

Hagège interprets all reprise Themes as contrastive. This is because he combines information and thematic structures. However, his claim does not seem to be supported by the existence of such examples as (6) *Tu la vois, Paul* (see section 3.1.1) where Paul is coreferential with the unmarked topical Theme. It functions as an absolute reprise Theme, but is not presented as contrastive; it is simply Given. The possibility of this sort of selection argues for a distinction between the Theme Rheme structure and the Given New one. To quote Halliday (1985: 278):

> although related, Given + New and Theme + Rheme are not the same thing. The

Theme is what I, the speaker, choose to take as my point of departure. The Given
is what you, the listener, already know about or have accessible to you. Theme
+ Rheme is speaker oriented, while Given + New is listener oriented.

It would seem that either or both of Hagège's preposed and postposed
Themes may be either New or Given depending on their phonological
marking which is what construes their contrastive meaning. Halliday (1985:
277) points out that "One form of 'newness' that is frequent in dialogue is
contrastive emphasis such as that on *you* and *I* in ..//**you** can go /if you /like
//**I**'m not/ going//". It is relevant to note here, however, that in French, there
are two possible translations of Halliday's clause, with the meaning of '**I**'
being either realised as initial absolute Theme or reprise absolute Theme:

(36)   *Tu peux t'en aller si tu veux,* **moi,** *je reste.*
(37)   *Tu peux t'en aller si tu veux, je reste,* **moi.**

In both instances **moi** is absolute Theme and New but it is only in the second
case (37), that it is absolute reprise Theme. Both these absolute Themes are
tonic pronominals,[5] contrasting with the preceding Subject *tu.* In Hagège's
examples, (cf above quote) the Themes are nominal and, contrary to his suggestion, do not seem to have contrastive emphasis. In the present model, both
would be analysed as both Theme and Given. Since the examples have to be
interpreted out of context, we cannot be sure that they are not contrastive.
However, the point to note is that pronominal absolute Themes are not
necessarily New and nominal absolute Themes are not always Given. Thus
depending on intonation, *'Paul, je l'ai vu'* could mean either *Paul,* [as for
him], *I saw him,* where *Paul* is Theme and Given or *Paul* [him but not the
others] *I saw him,* where *Paul* is Theme and New (see Rothemberg 1989).
In those displaced dialogic texts which are accessed entirely via the graphic
channel and therefore provide no direct intonational clue, tonic pronominals
are typically New, whilst nominals are typically given as (38) and (39) illustrate:

---

5. Tonic pronominals as opposed to the pronominals which function within the negotiatory
element cannot be cliticized. Tonic and non-tonic pronouns, ie clitics, have different
realisations.

(38)

Je	l'	ai	vu	Pierre.
I	him	have	seen	Pierre
Th-unmkd	Rheme————			Th-rep
Given	New			Given

As for Pierre, I have seen him.

(39)

Je	l'	ai	vu,	lui
I	him	have	seen	him
Th:unmkd	Rheme————			Th-rep
Given————				New

Him, I have seen.

In (38), *Pierre*, an absolute reprise Theme, is also Given; the function New conflates with Predicator, which is of course part of the Negotiator. In (39), on the other hand, the reprise Theme is presented as New information, and to convey the contrastive meaning the tonic pronominal *lui* is used.

Typically, tonic pronominals do not play a role in the Negotiator of the clause. The sole exception to this generalisation is the third person tonic pronominal referring to the non-interactant **and** functioning as Subject. In such contexts of use, predictably, they are always contrastive as exemplified by (40):

(40)

Lui	est	venu	[pas sa femme]
he	is	come	[not his wife]
Subj	Fin	Pred	
Th	Rheme——		
New	Given——		

He came (not his wife).

In (40), *lui* which is Theme/New also plays the role of Subject within the Negotiator of the clause, as opposed to the Themes in (34) and (35) which are only in a cohesive relationship to some negotiatory functions. Let me now take a brief look at the typical patterns of conflation between the interpersonal and the textual functions in the organisation of the French clause.

5.2 Negotiatory structure and textual organisation in the French Clause

In section 3.1.1 it was suggested that the negotiatory structure of the French clause consists of two parts – the Negotiator and (optionally) the Remainder in that order (see Figure 2). Of the MOOD functions identified as capable of occurring in the Negotiator, Complements and two types of Adjunct have a special status, in that they may function either within the Negotiator or in the Remainder. (See for example the discussion of 4i-ii in section 3.1.1). When Complement or Adjunct form part of the Negotiator, they are cliticised; and to say that they are cliticised is to say that they are Given; they are identifiable and non-prominent. When these functions form part of the Remainder, they are New, identifiable or non-identifiable and prominent. The Subject function is typically conflated with Theme and therefore unmarked. Thus the unmarked textual organisation of the negotiatory structure can be characterised as having initial prominence (Subject), a non-prominent median phase (Negotiator minus Subject) and a prominent final phase (Remainder), as shown in Figure 4.

The textual organisation schematised in Figure 4, can be elaborated through an examination of (41):

(41) *Jean*   *lui*   *a acheté*   *une glace*   *à la plage*
      Jean   to him   has bought   an ice   at the beach
      Subj **C-clitic Fin Pred**   Complement   Adjunct
      ————**Negotiator**————   ————Remainder————
      Theme   Rheme ————————————————————————————
      Given   ————————————————————————————————————New
      Jean bought him an ice cream on the beach.

Note the negotiatory structure in line four of (41); the functions that form part of the Negotiator and the Remainder are identified in line three. The last two lines of analysis provide information about the textual organisation of the clause. *Jean* is both Theme and Given; it is a topical Theme since it also

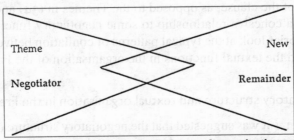

Figure 4: The unmarked textual organization of the negotiatory structure

has an experiential function (the details of which need not concern us here). It is an unmarked Theme, being Given and Subject. The rest of (41) falls within the ambience of Rheme; thus the 'boundary' of Rheme is not isomorphic with that of the Negotiator; it penetrates the latter, as Figure 4 shows. In terms of the Given-New structure, the function New extends right up to the C-clitic *lui*, thus embracing all of the Remainder and most of the Negotiator, simply leaving the Subject *Jean* out of its ambience, which conflates with the textual function Given. This does not mean that Subject must always be Given and unmarked. Thus in (40) Subject is New. Elements of the Remainder, and especially Adjuncts with the experiential function of temporal Circumstance may sometimes function as marked Theme as exemplified in (42):

(42)
Demain	*je*	*ne*	*suis*	*pas*	*là*
tomorrow	I	not	am	not	here
Adj	**Subj**	**A-neg**	**Fin**	**A-neg**	Adj
Th-mkd	Rheme ————————————————————
Given	————————————————————New

Tomorrow I won't be there.

It would seem that from the textual point of view, the French clause, as an interpersonal move, may have two textual layers, one realised by absolute Themes which fall just outside the boundaries of the interpersonal structure and the other realised by Themes conflated with Subject, Adjunct; the latter fall inside the interpersonal structure. Typically, the outer textual layer is marked, the inner unmarked. This organisation of the French clause is graphically represented in Figure 5.

In Figure 5, I have conflated the unmarked textual layer with the interpersonal structure rather than the negotiatory structure because *est-ce que* which is typically the unmarked Theme of a polar interrogative does not have a function in the negotiatory structure but does play a role in the interpersonal structure, as shown in (43):

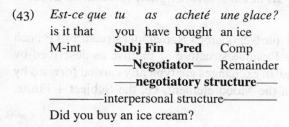

(43)
Est-ce que	*tu*	*as*	*acheté*	*une glace?*
is it that	you	have	bought	an ice
M-int	**Subj**	**Fin**	**Pred**	Comp
	——Negotiator——		Remainder
	——negotiatory structure——
————interpersonal structure————

Did you buy an ice cream?

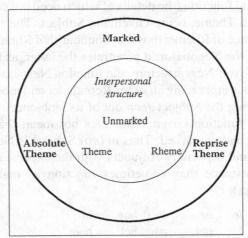

**Figure 5: The two potential textual layers
of the clause as a move**

In (43), the functions shown in bold comprise the Negotiator; the Remainder has only the function Complement in it. These two together form the negotiatory structure of the clause. However, Mood-interrogator is an important element of the interpersonal organisation of the clause, and together with the negotiatory structure it makes up what I have called the 'interpersonal structure' of the French clause. These remarks on the interaction between the interpersonal and the textual structures of the French clause as a move conclude my exploration of the process of exchange in French. Partial though this account is, it furnishes sufficient basis for examining how the interpersonal organisation of the French clause compares with that of English and, particularly, what the element Subject means in French. Can it be interpreted in terms of modal responsibility as in the case of English Subject? If so, on what basis?

6. French negotiatory structure and English modal structure: some comparisons

From a functional view point, the Negotiator + Remainder structure of French is analogous to the Mood + Residue structure of English as described by Halliday (1985). Whilst English exchanges are typically carried forward by means of adjustment within the Mood element, i.e. the Subject + Finite,

French exchanges revolve around the Negotiator, involving at least its minimal components, i.e. Subject + Finite + Predicator. Moves consisting of just Finite and Subject are not possible in French. 'One cannot answer *je l'ai* (I have) to the question *est-ce que vous l'avez vu?* (have you seen it)' (Spence 1976) but rather *je l'ai vu*. In French , the arguability status of a proposition depends on the Subject, Finite and Predicator functions whilst in English it rests on the Subject and Finite alone. The resources that make the clause arguable, i.e. options in the systems of POLARITY and MODALITY are realised within the Negotiator in French as they are in English. In French, negative POLARITY is realised as the prosody *ne–pas*, which surrounds the Finite or the Predicator depending on whether the two are fused or not. MODALITY options may be realised in different ways: only as an Adjunct that typically follows the Finite or Predicator; it may also be expressed in the Finite; it may be expressed in the Predicator; or all three preceding means of realisation might co-occur. Examples of these modes of realisation were provided in section 3. In a French imperative clause, negative POLARITY is realised on the Predicator, whilst in the English imperative negation is realised in the Finite, as in *don't cry*. Furthermore, In a French dependent non-Finite clause, negative POLARITY and MODALITY are both realised in the Predicator as in (44):

(44)

Il	a	peur //	de	ne	pas	pouvoir	partir
he	has	fear	of	not	not	to-be-able	to part
Subj	Fin	Comp		A-neg	A-neg	Pred-Mod	Pred

(i) he's afraid he won't be able to go; OR   (ii) he's afraid he can't go

Note that *pouvoir* functions as Predicator in the French interpersonal structure, whilst *can* functions as Finite in the English interpersonal structure in idiomatic translation (ii). The difference lies in the fact that French modal verbs are involved in expansions within the verbal group, while the favoured construction in English is to express modality as a function of the finite auxiliary. Another point of divergence between the two languages concerns the deployment of order as specific means of realisation. In English, the more delicate options of the indicative, are realised by the 'order of Subject and Finite which is significant in realising mood features' (Halliday 1985). In French, the means employed primarily is the presence or absence of MOOD marker and/or intonation. However, looking at structure from a more abstract point of view, both languages are alike: both realise MOOD selections prosodically.

Keeping these differences and similarities in view, we will now turn to the notion of Subject. It is useful to carry out this comparison, from the two perspectives identified by Halliday (1985) as 'recognition criteria' and 'definition criteria.' The former specify characteristics whereby one may recognise the segment carrying a function in some clause type; the latter – the definition criteria – specify the semantic value of the function under examination. I will consider Subject in French from the point of view of recognition criteria in section 6.1; and then, from the point of view of definition criteria in section 6.2.

6.1 French Subjecthood: recognition criteria

In English, the specific character of the Mood-tag and its cohesive relation to Subject act as a reliable means of recognising the segment with the function of Subject. However, French tags are quite unlike the English one; here no nominal is picked up as it is in English. How, then, can we recognise the Subject of the French clause? Although tagging cannot be used as a criterion to establish Subjecthood of a nominal in French, there are some resemblances between English and French that are worthy of attention. For example, both in English and in French, a polar-interrogative may be realised by ordering Finite before Subject. Thus one may probe the validity of the statement, *elle est malade* (she is sick) by the confirmation question *l'est-elle?* (is she?). The Subject is always the clitic suffixed to the Finite in a polar interrogative of this type, the Subject being the element "by reference to which the proposition can be affirmed or denied" (Halliday 1985). Another criterion for identifying the Subject, is person and number agreement with the verbal group. Thus the Subject is the function which is marked in person and number in the Finite or Predicator depending on whether the MOOD is indicative or imperative, as the following comparisons will show:

(45) *Les cloches   sonnent*
      the bells   ring
      Subj-3-pl   Fin/Pred-3-pl
      The bells are ringing.

(46) *Sonnez   les cloches*
      ring   the bells
      Pred-2-sing-formal   Comp
      Ring the bells!

Here (45) is a declarative with *les cloches* as its Subject; the Finite/Pred agrees with it in person and number. In (46), which is an imperative, *les cloches* is Complement, but since the marking on the Pred in an imperative relates to the Subject, the person and number marked on the Predicator signal addressee attributes of person (2nd), number (singular), and social distance from the speaker (formal).

When the verbal group realising the Finite and Predicator of a Negotiator has a secondary tense choice with the auxiliary *être,* the agreement spreads from the Finite to the Predicator. Thus, the realisation of the Subject is itself prosodic. It can be repeated throughout the Negotiator as in (47) below:

(47) *Les fourmis   sont   parties*
      the ants   are   gone
      Subj-3-pl   Fin-3-pl   Pred-pl
      The ants are gone.

Note that in addition to person and number, the Predicator also marks the gender of the Subject. This adds further support to the analysis of the Predicator as a Function of the Negotiator rather than of the Remainder. While in French, intonation is a primary realisational resource for MOOD options, the Subject together with the Finite and the Predicator are at least equally crucial to this realisation, since it is the fall or rise of the tone on the Predicator which is criterial to MOOD choice recognition. Note in passing that the Predicator is the last function in the Negotiator. These are then fairly substantial recognition criteria for the function Subject in French. But what does the function Subject "do" in French? This is the question I address below.

6.2 French Subjecthood: definition criteria

As pointed out before, the Subject of a proposal is responsible for complying with or rejecting a command, whereas a proposition is affirmed or denied in relation to the Subject. Thus in both types of speech functions, Subject has what Halliday (1985) has called 'modal responsibility'. In both French and English, this interpretation is reinforced by several features of Negotiator and the Mood, respectively. For example, the location of Subject outside the negative prosody (see discussion of example 8) is significant. The modal responsibility of Subject is also made manifest in modulated indicative clauses, where the realisation of Subject spreads prosodically over the modal process through the devices of person and number marking. This clearly highlights that what is at issue is the inclination, willingness, ability etc of the Subject, not of any other nominal in the clause. French modal verbs are lexical and as such may function both as Finite and Predicator in the interpersonal structure of the clause as in:

(48) *Nous*   *devons*   *partir.*
      we-1-pl   must-1-pl   to leave
      Subj   Pred-mod   Pred
      We must leave!

Here it is the Subject that is held responsible for 'going', and is under the obligation to leave. This is made explicit through the markings on the modal verb *devoir*. The main modal verbs of French are *devoir*, *vouloir*, and *pouvoir*. They may take on different modal meanings depending on context.

(49) [PERMISSION]
      Vous   *pouvez*   *partir.*
      you   can-2-sing-formal   to leave
      Subj   Pred   Pred
      You may leave!

(50) [PROBABILITY]
      Elle   *peut*   *avoir*   *trente ans.*
      she   may-3-sing   to have   thirty years
      Subj   Pred   Pred   Comp
      She may be thirty.

(51) [ABILITY]
      Tu   *peux*   *le*   *faire.*
      you   can-2-sing-inf   it   to do
      Subj   Pred   C-clitic   Pred
      You can do it.

Thus, although French Subject and English Subject cannot be identified following the same grammatical criteria, they are clearly similar on semantic grounds and perform the same function in discourse. This reflects again the assumption that we are more likely to find congruence across different languages by approaching their linguistic system from discourse semantics, rather than in terms of syntagmatic structure.

7. Conclusion

In this paper, I have attempted to examine how the French language constructs dialogue – i.e. how it enables the exchange of meanings. At the outset, we drew attention to certain theoretical assumptions. These initial assumptions have been confirmed by the subsequent analysis. Thus, ignoring the details of actual structures, and focussing on its more abstract aspect, we find that the semantics of exchange is realised by MOOD systems which have a prosodic mode of expression both in English and in French. The primary options of the French MOOD potential reflect the primary speech functions of statement, question and command assumed to be common to all languages (see Figure 3a). From a language specific perspective on structure, the modal structure of the French clause is considerably different from that of English. These structural differences result both from the different means of enacting an exchange and the different means of realising MOOD selection. We saw that French makes use of a wider range of prosodic means of realisation i.e. tone, MOOD marker and the order of Subject to Finite or Finite/Predicator. Other interpersonal functions such as negation, modality, and Subject were also found to be realised by prosodic means within the Negotiator of the clause. Nonetheless the French Negotiator + Remainder structure is functionally analogous to the Mood + Residue structure of English. Just as for the purposes of negotiating an exchange in English, it is Mood that is crucial, so also for negotiating French exchanges it is the Negotiator that is the most crucial clausal component.

The French clause as a move was found to have a particular textual organisation making use of tonic pronominals for staging and resolving an exchange, thus creating two textual layers: one unmarked within the interpersonal structure, the other marked, outside this structure. This type of textual organisation seems to support the suggestion that French is becoming more and more polysynthetic (see comments in section 3.1.3). Whilst the tonic pronominals foreground what move the clause is about, the clitic pronominals indicate the relationships between the various entities mentioned.

This overview of the interpersonal organisation of the French clause raises issues as to what should be considered a universal category and what should be considered language specific. It seems clear that Negotiator and Remainder are specific to French and Mood and Residue are specific to English. However, we can assume that all languages will have an interpersonal structure, and all will have some means of realising the clause as exchange. The systemic notions of metafunctions, stratification, realisation as well as system, structure and type of structure give a general theoretical framework for exploring how a particular language construes meaning. It seems that the more general the category the more likely it is to be functional across languages. But what about notions such as Subject and Theme? It appears that Theme is a more general concept than Subject. It is defined by Matthiessen (1992) as the local context of the clause as message and it can be assumed that a clause in any language will have some kind of local context. What would differ would be the realisation of local context across languages and sometimes across registers. So, for example, Theme in French spoken discourse can be positioned clause finally. The Subject, although a category both in French and in English, cannot be assumed to be universal in its manifestation. The French Subject, which together with Finite and Predicator serves to realise MOOD selections in that language, is in some sense the same category as the English Subject. However, across languages there seems to be no question of exact identity of structural elements; and while the functions are similar, they are not identical. A dual perspective on both language specific features and on features that are in common to (many) languages is needed, so that we can identify both the particularities of *a* language and the general characteristics of *all* languages.

Abbreviations

1	1st person	pl	plural
2	2nd person	P-mrkr	Polarity marker
3	3rd person	Pred	Predicator
A-clitic	clitic Adjunct	Pred-mod	modal Predicator
Adj	Adjunct	Q-Adj	que-Adjunct
A-mod	modal Adjunct	Q-Comp	qu-Complement
A-neg	negative Adjunct	Q-Subj	qu-Subject
A-neg-clitic	neg. clitic Adjunct	s+	Speaker-plus
C-clitic	clitic Complement	sing	singular
Comp	Complement	S-clitic	clitic Subject
Fin	Finite	Subj	Subject
Fin-mod	modal Finite	Th	Theme
g-prosody	grammatical prosody	Th-abs	absolute Theme
inf	informal	Th-mkd	unmarked Theme
M-int	interrogative mood marker	Th-rep	reprise Theme

Symbols

(i)   Conventions for system networks: Figure 6.

(ii)   Conventions for displaying a systemic path as **selection expression**:
[y; m: b] = option *b* depends on (symbol for dependency :) the co-selection of options *m* and *y* (symbol for co-selection ;)

(iii)   Conventions for structural representation:

        X^Y   X must precede Y

        X•Y   X and Y are un-ordered vis a vis each other

        (x)   x is an optional function

        X/Y   X and Y are conflated

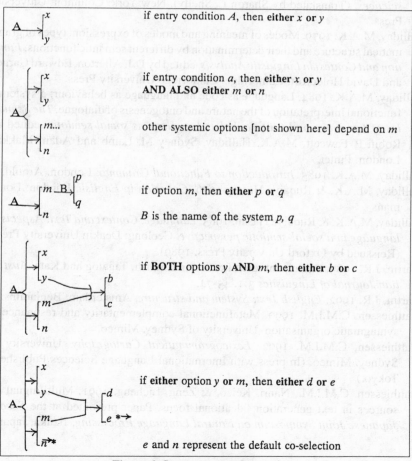

Figure 6: System network notations

References

Battye, A. & M.A. Hintze. 1992. *The French Language Today*. London. Routledge.

Bernstedt, P. 1973. *Viens-tu? Est-ce que tu viens? Formen und Strukturen des direkten Fragesatzes in Französischen*. Tübingen: Narr.

Coveney, Aidan. 1990. Variation in interrogatives in spoken French: a preliminary report. *Variation and Change in French: Essays presented to Rebecca Posner on her sixtieth birthday*, edited by John N. Green and Wendy Ayers-Bennett. New York: Routledge.

De Beauvoir, S. 1945. *Les Bouches Inutile*. Paris: Gallimard.

Hagège, Claude. 1990. *The Dialogic Species: A linguistic contribution to the social sciences*. (Translated by Sharon L. Shelly). New York: Columbia University Press.

Halliday, M.A.K. 1979. Modes of meaning and modes of expression: types of grammatical structure and their determination by different semantic functions. *Function and Context in Linguistic Analysis*, edited by D.J. Allerton, Edward Carney and David Holdcroft. Cambridge: Cambridge University Press.

Halliday, M.A.K. 1984. Language as code and language as behaviour: a systemic functional interpretation of the nature and ontogenesis of dialogue. *The Semiotics of Language and Culture, Vol 1: Language as social semiotic*, edited by Robin P. Fawcett, M.A.K. Halliday, Sydney M. Lamb and Adam Makkai. London: Pinter.

Halliday, M.A.K. 1985. *Introduction to Functional Grammar*. London: Arnold.

Halliday, M.A.K. & Ruqaiya Hasan. 1976. *Cohesion in English*. London: Longmans.

Halliday, M.A.K. & Ruqaiya Hasan. 1985. *Language, Context and Text: Aspects of language in a social-semiotic perspective*. Geelong: Deakin University Press. (Reissued by Oxford University Press, 1989).

Martin, J.R. 1983. Participant identification in English, Tagalog and Kate. *Australian Journal of Linguistics* 3:1, 45-74.

Martin, J.R. 1992. *English Text: System and structure*. Amsterdam: Benjamins.

Matthiessen, C.M.I.M. 1990. Metafunctional complementarity and resonance in syntagmatic organisation. University of Sydney. Mimeo.

Matthiessen, C.M.I.M. 1992. *Lexicogrammatical Cartography*. University of Sydney. Mimeo. (In press with International Language Sciences Publishers: Tokyo.)

Matthiessen, C.M.I.M., Nanri, Keizo, & Zeng, Licheng. 1991. Multilingual resources in text generation: ideational focus. Paper presented at the *Second Japanese Joint Symposium on Natural Language Processing*, Jizuka, Japan.

Rothemberg, M. 1989. Quelques moyens syntaxiques de rhématisation et de thématisation en Français. *Bulletin de la Société de Linguistique de Paris* 84.

Spence, N.C.W. 1976. Pronoms et substituts: la cohésion de l'énoncé. *Le Français Contemporain*. München: Wilhelm Fink Verlag.

Sinclair, J. McH. & Coulthard, R.M. 1975. *Towards and Analysis of Discourse: The English used by teachers and pupils*. London: Oxford University Press.

2

Mood and the Ecosocial Dynamics
of Semiotic Exchange*

Paul J. Thibault
Dipartimento di Linguistica
Università degli Studi di Padova

I. Rethinking Mood

> The concept of substance is a consequence of the concept of the subject: not the
> reverse! If we relinquish the soul, "the subject," the precondition for "sub-
> stance" in general disappears. One acquires degrees of being, one loses that which
> has being.
>
> (Friedrich Nietzsche 1968: 268)

> This social orientation [of the utterance PJT] will always be present in any human
> utterance, not only in a verbal utterance, but also a gesticulatory one (by means
> of gesture or facial expression), no matter what form it may take, whether some-
> one is speaking to himself (a monologue) or two or more people are participating
> in a conversation (a dialogue). The social orientation is indeed one of the active
> organising forces which, together with the environment (the situation) gives shape
> to its purely grammatical structure.
>
> (V.N. Vološinov 1983: 122)

1.1 Mood: The orthodox view

The orthodox view defines mood as a class of basic sentence-types: indicative, interrogative, and imperative. According to Levinson (1983: 242), these
three basic sentence types are likely to have a universal basis. Martin (1992a:

---

* I should like to acknowledge critically important discussion with Ruqaiya Hasan, Kieran
MgGillicuddy, and Bill McGregor at various stages in the preparation of this paper. Their
valuable comments and criticisms have helped me in many ways to improve this paper.
Whatever defects and omissions remain are, of course, entirely my responsibility.

31-91) points out that the systems and structures which derive from these types "have come to be viewed as formal ones – the basic syntax of the English clause". As such, they are a formal and autonomous syntax which encodes the 'literal' meanings of these three types, unless some non-literal meaning takes precedence. Thus, for Levinson the three basic illocutions of questioning, ordering, and stating are not related in a systematic way to the grammatical forms of interrogative, imperative, and declarative. Levinson classifies such illocutions as utterances, not sentences (Levinson 1983: 242-43; Thibault and Van Leeuwen *mimeo*). Here is one orthodox view:

> Mood...is best defined in relation to an 'unmarked' class of sentences which express simple statements of fact, unqualified with respect to the attitude of the speaker toward what he is saying. Simple declarative sentences of this kind are, strictly speaking, non-modal ('unmarked' for mood). If, however, a particular language has a set of one or more grammatical devices for 'marking' sentences according to the speaker's commitment with respect to the factual status of what he is saying (his emphatic certainty, his certainty of doubt, etc.), it is customary to refer to the 'unmarked' sentences also (by courtesy as it were) as being 'in a certain mood'; and the traditional term for his 'unmarked' mood is indicative (or declarative). (Lyons 1968: 307)

Lyons further distinguishes imperative sentences, which "do not make statements at all, but express commands or instructions", and interrogative ones too, which "also stand in contrast to declarative sentences by virtue of their modality" (1968: 307). A later study (Lyons 1981: 189-90) points out:

> ...many languages, including English, do in fact grammaticalise distinctions of sentence-type and mood: and furthermore [that] there is an essential connection between sentence-type and mood, on the one hand, and what we are now calling illocutionary force, on the other".

Thus, the uttering of a statement entails that the speaker simultaneously expresses a proposition and an attitude towards it. Following the standard terminology in modal logic, Lyons calls this the speaker's epistemic commitment. When one asks a question, one indicates to the interlocutor "that one desires him to resolve one's uncertainty by assigning a truth-value to the proposition in question" (1981:190). Commands and requests, etc. entail a different kind of commitment, called deontic commitment. Here, the speaker "commits himself to the necessity of some course of action ... he expresses ... his will that something be so" (1981: 191).

There are two points to make here. First, the basic sentence-types express the literal meanings of their various moods. In contrast to Lyons' claim (1968) that there is an 'unmarked' class of sentences (indicative) which are "unqualified with respect to the attitude of the speaker towards what he is saying", I shall claim later that no utterance is free from the subjective "presencing" of the speaker. Lyons' use of his formal criteria means that he cannot account for the fact that what speakers "intend" or "feel" is, from a linguistic point of view, only decideable on the basis of the discourse level structures and processes into which MOOD, in Halliday's sense of the term, enters in the dynamic exchange of meanings in texts. Analytically, it is the level of exchange structure which shows the linguist how the addressee responds, in turn, to his interlocutor's choice of mood in any given discourse level move.

The second point is that the distinction between epistemic and deontic commitment is founded on essentially *epistemological* criteria concerning the speaker's state of knowledge, whether in the form of a commitment to a proposition (indicative), or to a state of affairs in the world (deontic). This is made very clear when Lyons proposes that the Austinian illocutionary force of statements, questions, commands, and requests can be factorised "into two components": "a component of commitment ("I say so") or non-commitment, on the one hand, and … a modal component of factuality ("It is so") vs desirability ("so be it")" (1981: 191). This is so, Lyons argues, because the distinction between 'factuality' and 'non-factuality' "falls within the scope of what logicians call modality" (1981: 191-92). Thus, for Lyons, as for this entire tradition of thinking about mood, the issue is one of the speaker's commitment either to a factual state of affairs, or to a desired, and, hence, non-factual state of affairs, in the world. Mood is conceived in epistemological terms as the speaker's commitment to expressions concerning the way the world is, or ought to be, i.e. the speaker's knowledge concerning the ontological status of the world. It is not concerned with criteria of action and interaction in the making, negotiating, or exchanging of meanings in discourse. For an alternative account, along these lines, we shall now refer to the interpretation of MOOD in the systemic functional model of language.

1.2 The interpretation of MOOD in SF: making and negotiating meanings in discourse.

In the systemic functional model, following Halliday (1976; 1984; 1985), the grammatical system of MOOD in English is characterised by its relation to four basic types of semantic interact (cf speech act) used to negotiate meaning in dialogue. That is to say, the grammatical system of MOOD has structures as its outputs, and these lexicogrammatical structures are defined in relation to the discourse semantic stratum. The notion of an interact is a semantic one relating to the semantic system of SPEECH FUNCTION in discourse semantics.

1.2.1 The basic MOOD system in SF

The basic assumption rests on the view that the grammatical system of MOOD can be described in terms of the two basic options of [indicative] and [imperative]. Figure 1 shows these two primary options and the secondary options [declarative] versus [interrogative] choice between which depends on the choice of the option [indicative].

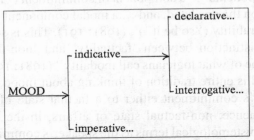

Figure 1: Primary MOOD system: basic options.
(from Martin 1992a: 31)

For each of the three final options of the network in Figure 1, the relevant structural realisation is as shown below:

[declarative]   Subject^Finite^Predicator
[interrogative]   Finite^Subject^Predicator
[imperative]   Predicator

Linguists have generally recognised that there is no one-to-one, or bi-unique link, between the grammatical choices in the MOOD system and the semantics of the SPEECH FUNCTION moves which these help to realise on the discourse stratum. However, both Halliday (1984; 1985) and Martin (1992a) argue that each of these basic Mood choices represents the 'congruent' or non-metaphorical realisation of the basic SPEECH FUNCTION moves, with the exception of offers, which, it is claimed, have no congruent MOOD choice (Halliday 1984:20). The relevant proportionalities are set out as follows:

declarative : statement ::
interrogative : question ::
imperative : command

Martin (1992a) points out that these proportionalities represent a congruent or non-metaphorical level of coding – what Halliday (1984: 14) has called a 'base line' – for relating MOOD choices in the grammar to the 'higher' order semantics of SPEECH FUNCTION which these realise in discourse, implying that the grammar of MOOD is basic to the semantics of SPEECH FUNCTION, while allowing for the fact that a given Mood choice may, nevertheless, and when combined with other systemic choices at a given level of delicacy, realise different choices in SPEECH FUNCTION. Let us now consider a brief illustrative example.

Examples (1i-iii) show how the selections in the three basic MOOD choices have the potential to realise the basic SPEECH FUNCTION of [command]:

(1) i   I'd like a drink.   [declarative]
     ii Could I have a drink? [interrogative]
     iii Give me a drink!   [imperative]

The SPEECH FUNCTION [command] is a semantic construal or interpretation of the meaning potential of some lexicogrammatical form. As such, it selectively attends to and foregrounds some aspects and dimensions of that potential, while backgrounding others. The features which are attended to (whether consciously or not, is irrelevant) for the purposes of a particular semantic construal always occur on the stratum of discourse (Martin 1991: 114-115). Thus, in (1i) the presence of the modulated inclination of desire 'd like means that the clause is, semantically speaking, potentially both a

[*command: request*] and a [*statement*]. The modulation negotiates a difference between 'what the speaker currently does not have' and what the
speaker 'would like to have', i.e. it has a modality of irrealis. The modulation
negotiates the as yet unfinalized difference between these two modal-material states. In (1ii) the presence of the modulation of capacity *could* in the
semantic environment of a demand for goods-&-services means that the
speaker is, semantically speaking, both demanding information – asking a
question – as well as delegating the socially recognised capacity which the
modulation realises to the *you* in this clause.

This suggests that congruent realisations of statement can only negotiate
modality (certainty, probability, usuality), and not modulation (inclination,
capacity, obligation). When features of modulation are selected in the
environment of, say, a declarative clause, semantically speaking, we no
longer have a congruent realisation of a statement, but a semantically much
more complex and indeterminate phenomenon. It would seem that interpersonal grammatical metaphor arises when selections in [indicative] combine
with selections in modulation (not modality).

On this basis, I should like to suggest that it is premature to link specific
choices from the system of MOOD to those in the system of SPEECH FUNC-
TION without first attending to a logically prior stage of the argument. To
create this link, we require a partial redefinition of the semantics of MOOD.
We shall shortly look at this prior stage. But first we shall examine Halliday's conception of the structure of the Mood element.

1.2.2 Halliday's conception of Mood: Subject, Finite and modal responsibility

For Halliday the structural element Subject is located in the interpersonal
grammar. The element Mood is realised by the configuration Subject Finite.
Halliday's conception of Subject is very different from the way this term is
usually talked about in the western grammatical tradition. Generally speaking, Subject is talked about in terms of the referring-and-predicating function
of language. The Subject of the sentence variously 'stands for', 'refers to',
or 'picks out' some real world entity and then predicates some proposition
of it. Thus, the sentence is the abstract propositional coding form of a
referring-and-predicating potential. In a given utterance, speakers understand
this potential to 'pick out' some extra-linguistic entity which the Subject

refers to and to predicate some state of affairs of this as if both Subject and the state of affairs so predicated exist independently of linguistic form and function (Silverstein 1979: 202). Both Friedrich Nietzsche (1968: 267-72) and Benjamin Lee Whorf (1956a) have produced far reaching critiques of the substantivist notions which underpin this conception. Whorf, commenting on this substantivist reductionism, had noted:

> ...the notion became ingrained that one of these classes of entities can exist in its own right but that the verb class cannot exist without an entity of the other class, the "thing" class, as a peg to hang on (1956b: 241).

Whorf, in effect, draws attention to the confusion which arises when this ideology of reference fails to show that the common noun class *per se* does not refer to a given entity 'out there' in the real world. The common noun designates a type; it does not and cannot refer in any direct way to extra-linguistic reality. It is the function of selections in the system of DEIXIS – a system which operates in the nominal group – to 'ground' or anchor a given type-specification as an 'instance' of the type (Hasan 1984).

An exactly parallel situation exists in the case of 'finite' and 'non-finite' in the verbal group. Non-finite verbs designate a type-specification of a verbal process (Davidse 1991:195). Finite verbs, which can only occur in the verbal group, 'ground' the whole proposition in the here-and-now of the speech event as an 'instance' that can be argued about. It is the systems of PRIMARY TENSE, MODALITY, and POLARITY which function to 'instance' some process as an arguable proposition or proposal with respect to the Subject. It is Halliday's claim that the Subject specifies "the entity in respect of which the assertion is claimed to have validity". Subject specifies that which is being held "responsible for the functioning of the clause as an interactive event" (1985: 76). In 'grounding' the verbal process as an 'instance', the Finite element refers the proposition or proposal to a given domain of interpersonal validity (cf. Whorf's 1956c: 113-14 conception of 'assertion'). The Mood element, comprising Subject and Finite, has an orientational function in the modalised space-time of the speech event. It grammaticalises what Vološinov (1983: 122) has called the "social orientation of the utterance" (see also Lemke 1993)

In the traditional account the categories of primary tense, modality, and polarity, which are realised in the Finite element, are seen as predicational categories. Primary tense is interpreted as "predicating states of affairs at

points and in intervals along a seemingly speech-independent time line"
(Silverstein 1979: 202). Similarly, polarity and modality are seen as predicating the existence or otherwise of such states of affairs (polarity) and grading
the speaker's assessment of the truth-value of such predications concerning
state of affairs in extra-linguistic reality (modality).

By contrast, for Halliday, the Mood element coordinates and orients the
Subject as the element in which the speaker invests the modal responsibility
of the utterance in the modalised space-time of dialogic interaction. Whorf's
deconstruction of the folk-ideology of reference aimed to show how language users have rationalised language form and function as having a direct
'standing for' relation with entities located and individuated in physical
space-time. Thus, language more or less transparently reflects or represents
the entities and the relations between them on this space-time grid.

However, the interpersonal grammar, one of whose central components
is the MOOD system, does not simply 'reflect' this space-time grid. Instead,
it dialogically coordinates a modalised orientational framework in relation
to it. In this framework, propositions and proposals are located at socially
recognised locations or person-places – grammaticalised as the Subject –
relative to a modalised orientational framework of deictically grounded
spatial relations, primary tense, and modal responsibility. The MOOD system,
as we shall see, provides the interpersonal grammatical resources for con-
structing this modalised space-time and for orienting the participants in the
dialogic interaction in it. We shall see below how Halliday's fundamental
insights can be further extended and developed. This will involve us in a
renegotiation of the concept of interpersonal meaning. In the process, I shall
also attempt to show how the interpersonal grammar enacts the ecosocial
dynamics of the exchange processes in and through which semiotic-discursive and physical-material domains are cross-coupled, coordinated and
entrained in the social construction of the modalised space-time which is a
feature of every speech event.

I have borrowed the term 'ecosocial' from a recent paper by Jay Lemke
(1993). An "ecosocial" system, such as a human community exemplifies,
is so defined because it exhibits strong, culturally specific "cross-couplings"
of physical-material and semiotic-discursive processes in the making,
maintaining, and changing of social life. In this paper, my concern is with
the central role of the interpersonal grammar of MOOD in coordinating and
entraining precisely such cross-couplings of the physical-material and the

semiotic-discursive domains. Linguistic studies have had very little to say on this question. I argue that this is central to an understanding of both language form and function and the ecosocial dynamics of the cross-couplings of the semiotic and the material that language participates in. The present paper suggests how the grammar of the MOOD system in English is organised in relation to such an ecosocial dynamics - it is concerned with the potential for the MOOD system to engage in such coupling patterns. Further work is required to show the deployment of these couplings in specific ecosocial systems.

I.2.3 The interpersonal grammar of the basic MOOD options: The standard analysis in systemic functional linguistics.

Both Halliday and Martin, I pointed out earlier, describe the MOOD options as realising basic types of interact. This is a good starting point for the argument I should like to develop here. From this point of view, let us reconsider the structural realisations which were used to characterise the interpersonal grammar of the three basic MOOD choices, starting with a declarative clause:

(2)   the man was   pouring   a drink   in the kitchen
       Subject Finite   Predicator Complement Adjunct
      ——**Mood**——   ——————**Residue**——————

In declarative clauses, the Subject is the grammatical entity in which the speaker modally invests in the clause as exchange. The speaker assumes the modal responsibility for the modal investment which is so made. The Finite element is the locus of the speaker's modal investment; it defines a subjective person-place in relation to which the utterance is spoken, and acts as the locus around which the subjective presencing of the speaker is organised. As the following discussion will hopefully show, this may be defined in terms of: (a) time relative to the time of speaking, or primary tense; or (b) the speaker's modal investment in the proposition which is being made with respect to the Subject (Halliday 1985: 75). In declaratives, Subject precedes Finite because the thematic focus is on the grammatical entity – the Subject – in relation to which the speaker subjectively invests the modal responsibility for the proposition. In this way, the speaker may be said to modally bind him/herself to the proposition. Consider now the interrogative structure of (3):

(3)	is	the man	pouring	a drink	in the kitchen
	Finite	**Subject**	**Predicator**	**Complement**	**Adjunct**

In interrogative clauses, it is the Finite element which comes before the Subject. In this way, the subjective presencing of the speaker is put in thematic position. This is motivated by the fact that in an interrogative, the speaker seeks the addressee's modal investment in the Subject. By putting Finite before Subject, interrogatives give thematic prominence to that part of the clause in which the subjective modal presence/investment of the speaker would be located. In effect, the configuration Finite^Subject in interrogatives functions so as to invite the addressee's own subjective investment in this. The initial position of the Finite suggests an exophoric deictic orientation to the addressee, whether explicitly realised or not in its lexicogrammar. The appeal is to whether the addressee will opt to take up a modal stance, i.e. respond, in relation to the proposition and, thereby, be built into the endophoric structure of the text by participating in the construction of the dependency relations whereby interpersonal meanings are exchanged and negotiated on the discourse stratum (Martin 1992a). Let us now consider an imperative clause:

(4)	pour	the drink
	Predicator	**Complement**

Imperatives, as Davidse (1991: 325) points out, do not have an explicit structural realisation of Finite, i.e. the action realised in the Predicator is given no explicit grounding in the here-and-now of the speech situation with reference to a subjective speaking presence. As Davidse also shows, unmarked imperatives exemplified in (4), have a strong exophoric deictic orientation in the sense that the Subject is exophorically recoverable from the speech situation. In an imperative clause like *pour the drink*, the Subject – the implied 'you', or addressee – is exophorically directly retrievable from the situation, and is not in need of further grammatical specification. In other words, there is a semantic disjunction in imperatives between the actually existing state of affairs in the here-and-now of the speech situation, and what the speaker would like the addressee to do about it. The same point can be made in connection with the Finite element. The Finite element, as Halliday (1985: 75) points out, "brings the proposition down to earth, so that it is something that can be argued". It grounds the proposition in the here-and-now of the speech event, as we have already seen. There is thus an absence of the element Mood in unmarked imperatives; and the point that concerns us is the systemic motivation for the choice between the 'presence' or 'absence' of the Mood element. The examples analysed so far have already shown that the presence of the Mood element, consisting of Subject and Finite, realises the feature [indicative]. This contrasts with the absence of this element, which realises the feature [imperative].

The terms 'indicative' and 'imperative' have become so overburdened by linguistic tradition that it is useful to take a fresh look at them. The problem lies in the way in which these two terms already imply a semantic interpretation, and hence a metasemantic consciousness, of the grammatical structures which they gloss. Thus, indicative mood almost invariably becomes associated with the exchange of information, while imperative mood is linked to the exchange of goods-and-services. A better starting point is Halliday's (1985: 74) observation that it is the presence of the Mood element, consisting of Subject and Finite, which realises the feature [indicative]. Similarly, it is the absence of the Mood element which realises the feature [imperative]. The basic systemic contrast is, then, that between 'presence of Mood element' and 'absence of Mood element' in the grammatical structure of the clause. Systemic (and other) linguists have usually glossed this distinction with the terms 'indicative' and 'imperative', respectively, and this in itself is not problematic. The trouble arises, however, when these glosses are univocally linked respectively to propositions i.e. the exchange of information, and proposals i.e. the exchange of goods-&-services. This relationship may well hold, but this is by no means so in any kind of straightforward or bi-unique way.

In my view, a better first step is to inquire into the exchange dynamics of, respectively, the presence and absence of the Mood element, consisting of Subject and Finite. In Halliday's account, Subject is the grammatical entity in which the speaker modally invests the 'success' or 'failure' of the proposition. Finite, which involves the systems of POLARITY, PRIMARY TENSE, and MODALITY, is the locus of the speaker's modal investment in the Subject. The interpersonal grammar of clause as exchange is defined as the configuration consisting of the Mood element and a further structural component, which Halliday has called the Residue. The Residue, which consists of the elements Predicator, Complement, and Adjunct, is, in my view, best defined as the domain or scope for the Mood element in the clause as exchange. For example, in the clause *John is feeling ill,* the Mood element comprises the items *John* (Subject) and *is* (Finite: Tense). *John* is the entity in whom the speaker modally invests a given proposition. The Residue, consisting of *feeling* (Predicator) and *ill* (Complement) defines the scope over which the Modal responsibility of the Subject and the grounding of the Finite extends.

How, then, can we motivate the presence or absence of the Mood element in the clause as exchange? A useful lead is to be found in Gregory Bateson's suggestion that all messages – verbal and nonverbal – are both 'reports' and 'commands', simultaneously:

> When A speaks to B, whatever words he uses will have these two aspects: they will tell B about A, conveying information about some perception or knowledge which A has; and they will be a cause or basis for B's later action. In the case of language, however, the presence of these two meanings may be obscured by syntax. A's words may have the syntax of command, which will partly obscure their report aspects. For example, A may say "Halt!" and B may obey the command ignoring the informational aspects – e.g. the fact that A's words indicate some perception or other mental process of which his command is an indication. Or A's words may have the syntax of report, and B may fail to notice that this report has influenced him in a certain direction. (Bateson 1987: 180)

Thus, indicative clauses such as *I feel ill* are both a 'report' on some state of affairs and, implicitly, a 'command' to the addressee to do something about it. Likewise, an imperative clause such as *Call the doctor!* is both an explicit 'command' to the addressee to respond in a certain way, as well as being an implicit 'report' on a given situation.

Now, the tendency to treat [indicative] and [imperative] in terms of a binary opposition of digital distinctions has often obscured the way in which the presence or absence of the Mood element constitutes, not a binary opposition, but a binary *relation* in which complex semantic homologies link the initial distinction in a still deeper unity. Thus, the presence or the absence of the Mood element in the interpersonal grammar does not mean that the semantics of information and goods-&-services exchange are digitalised as a set of discrete oppositions. My argument is that the grammar of the MOOD system is in need of reinterpretation so as to better account for the ways in which the structural features 'presence of Mood element' and 'absence of Mood element' always have the potential to realise both the 'report' and 'command' dimensions simultaneously. This potential is shared by both [indicative] and [imperative], although the exchange dynamics are different in the two cases. To understand the nature of this dynamics requires us, in the first instance, to inquire into the ecosocial motivation for the presence or absence of the Mood element.

In my view, Finiteness also needs to be extended to include reference to the spatial relations of the interlocutors in the here-and-now of the speech event. We have already noted that in imperative clauses the addressee is not usually realised grammatically as Subject because this is exophorically recoverable from the speech situation. The [imperative] semiotically constructs the addressee as the spatially located being who will enact the process. This does not reduce to a pre-given physical space, but a semiotically constructed one through the orientational function of the MOOD choice itself. Space, then, may be either concrete or abstract. The important point here is that it is semiotically construed and coordinated by the exchange processes under discussion here. Given that imperative clauses are about the exchange of goods-&-services, this orientation necessarily entails a material-spatial dimension in which the semiotic entraining of flows of matter and energy (cf. goods-&-services exchange) can occur in socially constructed space-time. Thus, the congruent realisation of a demand for goods-&-services by imperative MOOD directly grounds the Mood selection in the materiality of matter-energy exchanges and their semiotic entraining in the exchange process. Information exchange, on the other hand, is at one remove from this materiality, which means that its relation to the material-spatial dimension is more abstract, though no less real. I shall return to this point.

2. Reinterpreting the grammar of MOOD

In this section I shall first introduce certain additional concepts and considerations. These are important for understanding how the MOOD system is cross-coupled with physical-material processes in the making and negotiating of interpersonal meaning. (see section 2.1). This will be followed in section 2.2 and its subsections by a discussion of several examples presenting a revised analysis of the interpersonal grammar of MOOD. In section 3 of the paper, the implications of the revised analysis for a reconceptualisation of the MOOD system will be discussed.

2.1 Preliminary observations

The exophoric deictic orientation of imperatives seeks: (a) modally to bind
the Subject – the 'you' – to the proposal; and (b) to ground the proposal in
the material here-and-now of the exchange – i.e. to make it 'finite' – so that
the material individual who is designated as the 'you' is selected as the
Subject who will materially carry out the proposal. Typically in SF descriptions, the element Mood is thought of as comprising the structural functions
Subject and Finite. However, there is another element which is **always**
deictically recoverable from the speech situation, but which is not included
in the SF accounts of the interpersonal grammar of the clause. This is the
semantic function which I shall refer to with the term *SPEAKER* – the I – who
utters the clause. It should be noted here that I have now adopted the termi-
nological convention of upper case letters in italics for designating this term
(i.e. *SPEAKER*) as a functional semantic label. The reasons for doing so will
be developed in due course. It is the *SPEAKER* who both invests in the
Subject as the modally responsible element in the clause and in relation to
whom the Finiteness of the proposition is organised. For this reason, I shall
propose a more complex and, I believe, more complete definition of the
element Mood. I shall do this by making a functional semantic distinction
between (a) the Subject of the modality – typically the *SPEAKER* – the one
who modally invests in the grammatical Subject – and (b) the Subject of the
proposition or proposal – the grammatical Subject in the clause – which is
the entity in whom the former modally invests as the reference point for the
success or failure of the proposition or proposal. It is important to point out
that the *SPEAKER*, in this definition, is not an empirical entity, but a semantic
function which may or may not be realised in the lexicogrammar of the
clause. When it is, then the Subject of the modality, i.e. *SPEAKER*, and the
Subject of the clause may be conflated into a single grammatical element.
SPEAKER is, then, not an element of structure in the lexicogrammar of the
clause. It is a functional semantic value which can be ascribed to the Mood
element in the interpersonal grammar of the clause. For this reason in the
examples to be introduced later (see sections 2.2.1-2.2.8), the semantic
function *SPEAKER* is separated from the clause itself and does not appear on
the line representing the lexicogrammatical analysis.

   The element Mood, as pointed out earlier, is the basic grammatical
resource for organising the orientational function of the clause in social

space-time. This orientational process always occurs in relation to a linguistically constructed speaking presence, whether an empirical flesh-and-blood speaker is present, or not. This always occurs along the dimensions of deictically constructed spatial relations, primary tense, and modal responsibility relative to this speaking presence, as well as in relation to an addressee. Again, the addressee and his/her dialogic response may be spatially and temporally near or far from the initiating speech act in the ensuing exchange. For these reasons, I suggest that our definition of Mood be extended and revised to take account of the functional semantic role *SPEAKER* in the interpersonal grammar and semantics of the clause.

In this revised definition, Mood comprises the following three functional semantic elements: (a) the Finite element which grounds the clause as an interact in the here-and-now of the speech event, relative to the *SPEAKER*. And by virtue of this, the speech event is rendered negotiable along the dimensions of deictic space-time and modal responsibility; (b) the *SPEAKER*, or the Subject of the modality, which is the orientational 'centre' in relation to which a subjective speaking presence, or a person-place, is organised; and (c) the Subject of the clause, realising the proposition/proposal, which is the grammatical entity in which the *SPEAKER* invests the success or failure of his/her utterance. The Subject of the proposition/proposal corresponds to Halliday's definition of Subject, seen as an element of structure in the interpersonal grammar of the clause.

The arguments concerning the exophoric deictic orientation of imperatives can be extended to the entire MOOD system. It will be seen that in (5-12), the exophoric deictic item *here* occurs in each case, as does the second person pronoun *you* with the single exception of (6). Thus, these examples locate the exchange process and the 'you' in a primary structure of spatial location in relation to the Speaker. This does not reduce to physical location *per se*, but to its semiotic construal in relation to the person-place from which the speaker speaks. Exophora, in locating these utterances in the here-and-now of the speech situation, is a useful way into demonstrating the relation between MOOD and the material-physical exchange processes which are entrained and coordinated in semiosis. MOOD, along with the other systems of interpersonal meaning, functions to orient the interactants in a speech event to a secondary structure of social relations – subject positions, speech roles – and the social points of view these enable. It is MOOD that tells us who is speaking, from which point of view, who or what is being talked about, who is being spoken to, what the speaker is doing to the addressee, what is the relationship between these two points of view, how do these relate to the observer – the non-interactant – how a viewing position is constructed for the observer, how does it anticipate or orient itself to possible responses in the ongoing interaction, how does it organise its relationship to the material-physical processes it entrains.

From this point of view, we shall be concerned with the way in which the interpersonal grammar, which is centrally concerned with action and interaction, is cross-coupled with the physical-material processes of energy, matter, and information exchange. It is the interpersonal grammar, whose core component is the MOOD system, which works to coordinate and entrain the material-physical processes with which the semiotic-discursive is always cross-coupled in social semiosis. This cross-coupling is essential for the enactment of social processes, which are simultaneously both semiotic-discursive and material-physical processes (Lemke 1993: 249 ff). One of the arguments to be developed is that the internal functional organisation of the linguistic system is not autonomous; it can only be adequately understood in relation to both the semiotic-discursive and physical-material processes it enters into.

2.2 The revised interpretation of the interpersonal grammar of MOOD.

In the following sub-sections, I shall propose an analysis of the various Mood options according to the revised framework discussed in this section.

2.2.1 Constructing space

Consider example (5):

(5)   *SPEAKER*   you are   here
       Subj Fin:pr/Pred Adj:loc

In this example, the *SPEAKER* is the one who takes up, or invests in, a particular modal position. The Subject of the clause is the entity with reference to which the *SPEAKER* modally invests in the proposition. At the same time, we are told something about the social positioning of the *SPEAKER* in relation to the addressee. In the Finite element, the *SPEAKER*'s subjective (modal) presence is organised in terms of a temporal locus for the act of speaking. The present example is about as close to the material interface as the grammar of a clause with the systemic features [indicative: affirmative: declarative] normally gets. (For the systemic disposition of these features, see Figure 2). One likely context for clauses such as (5) is town maps located in public places. Normally, the clause *you are here* is complemented by an arrow which extends from the clause to the point of the map corresponding to the present location of the 'you', so designated. Thus, the personal pronoun *you* is strongly deictic: it places the addressee in the material situation in relation to the *SPEAKER*. The exophoric deictic element of spatial location, *here*, tells us about the socially organised spatial location of the addressee from the point of view of the *SPEAKER*. Both *you* and *here* would be phonologically salient in this example. However, either of these may receive tonic prominence. The unmarked, and non-contrastive, reading would put tonic prominence on *here*, as the New element, i.e. this is where *you* are now, as distinct from some other location. However, *you* may receive tonic prominence when the pronoun is used contrastively, which would be a marked usage in the given context, i.e. some specific 'you' in particular, as distinct from someone else.

What is interesting about the present example is its strategic dependence on the visual semiotic of the map, town guide, and so on. The grammar of the declarative clause does not interface directly with the material environment in the same way as that of the imperatives. Instead, it construes it as information through the lexicogrammatical resources of signification. In this particular instance, the strongly exophoric spatial deictic orientation of the clause depends on its further contextualisation with the visual semiotic of the map before it can be meaningful for the reader. Thus, in relation to the here-and-now of the material event and the participants taking part in it – the person who is reading the map, in our hypothetical example – Mood constructs a secondary structure of relations between social positions and points of view in social space-time. This does not mean that physical reality has been interpreted through an a priori grid of pre-existing cognitive/perceptual categories. Instead, the primary structure of physical-spatial relations between bodies and the physical events, these occur in, has been construed in terms of a system of social points of view and orientations. MOOD and the other interpersonal systems are the linguistic resources which allow this to happen.

2.2.2 *The presentative function*

Another example of [indicative: affirmative: declarative] is taken from the
Ladybird book for young children *Exploring Maths*. In an exercise on
addition, the clause *Here are four hedgehogs* occurs. It is accompanied by
a coloured illustration showing four hedgehogs.

(6)	SPEAKER	here	are	four hedgehogs
		Adj:loc	**Fin:pr/Pred**	**Subject**

This example illustrates the presentative function of the exophoric
spatial deictic *here*, which is used when the referent of the Subject is present
in the material context. Thus, the deictic element 'presents' or makes relevant to the *SPEAKER* and addressee something which is already present in
the physical scene. The systemic contrast in such cases is with the unmarked
thematic position of *here*, as in *four hedgehogs are here*. Although there are
cases, where the deictic *here* is both phonologically salient and tonic, in the
clause type exemplified by (6), *here* is likely to be phonologically salient,
but probably not tonic. Assuming that (6) displays the unmarked (non-
contrastive) use, tonic prominence will fall on the constituent with the
function of Subject, *four hedgehogs*. By comparison, if tonic prominence had
fallen on *here*, the use would have been contrastive, with a meaning of the
kind 'this physical context, rather than some other'. The systemic selection
expression[1] underlying clause (6) is [indicative: affirmative: declarative;
theme textual/deictic; marked].

2.2.3 *Exclamatives*

In English, exclamations which are realised by major clauses thematise the
Complement as in *what a fool he is!*. The Complement is the focus for the
speaker's attitudinal or emotional commitment. But there also exists another
type of exclamative where a deictic *here* with exophoric reference realises
a thematized Adjunct, as in (7):

(7)	SPEAKER	here	you	are!
		Adj:loc	**Subj**	**Fin:pr/Pred**

---

1. For selection expression conventions, see p 47.

In (7), *here* exophorically presents the physical context in which the *SPEA-KER* and the addressee are located; the deictic expression locates the addressee in a physical space relative to the *SPEAKER*. In (7), *here* exophorically presents the physical context, in which the *SPEAKER* and addressee are located. In this respect, it is no different from (6). Like (6), the thematisation of *here* has a strongly presentative function in the present example as well. The *SPEAKER* emphasises the fact that the person referred to by *you* has, perhaps, just arrived on the scene, or otherwise become relevant in it, relative to the *SPEAKER*'s point of view. In other words, the *SPEAKER* emphasises that the addressee has been brought into the former's spatial purview. But unlike (6) which we have described as [indicative: affirmative: declarative; theme textual/deictic; marked], in (7), *here* has the function of New information around which the *SPEAKER*'s interpersonal (attitudinal, emotional) response is organised. The addressee's arrival on the scene is the focus of the speaker's interpersonal reaction. The presentative function in clause type (7) combines with a strongly attitudinal or emotive orientation, since the marked thematic ordering conflating with the function Adjunct not only draws attention to the physical presence of the addressee on the scene, but may also construe, semiotically speaking, an emotional reaction – surprise, joy, delight – to that event. In [affirmative: exclamative] clauses of this kind, *here* is always phonologically salient. Further, there is a strong probability that it will receive tonic prominence. It is suggested that the systemic description of this clause would be [indicative: affirmative: exclamative; theme textual/deictic; marked].

2.2.4 *Polar interrogative*

Clause (8) is an example of a polar interrogative clause, with the deictic *here* functioning exophorically to construe spatial orientation:

(8) *SPEAKER*   are   you   here?
     Fin:pr/Pred Subj   Adj:loc

In [interrogative: polar] clauses, the *SPEAKER* seeks to know whether something is so, or not. As distinct from declaratives, the *SPEAKER* is not taking up a modal stance or investment with respect to some proposition, and then inviting the addressee to negotiate this stance with him/her. This orientation to modality and its negotiation is made explicit by the tagging which may accompany declaratives. For example, in *Roma's in Queensland, isn't it?*, the SPEAKER takes up a particular modal stance in the declarative, and then invites the addressee's further negotiation of this in the tag clause. In interrogatives, on the other hand, the SPEAKER seeks the addressee's modal stance on the proposition, or some part of it. In the case of [interrogative: polar] clauses, a yes/no response is the minimal requirement for the exchange to be finalized. Thus, a response such as *Yes, I am* comprises two moves in the exchange structure. The *yes* responds to the requirement that the addressee (now turned SPEAKER) takes up and invests in a modal stance with respect to the yes/no polar opposition. This opposition – as a type of modality – is located in the Finite element of the [interrogative: polar] form; *yes* explicitly negotiates this element and thus grounds the new SPEAKER in relation to the here-and-now of the speech event.

The additional move *I am* is an explicit take-up and modal investment in the proposition, as distinct from the Finite, of the prior interrogative form. Either of these responses on its own would be an appropriate response. The difference between the two is that one is oriented to the Finite element, the other to the proposition, in the up-take and negotiation of the [interrogative: polar] form. Interrogatives are oriented to the addressee as the one who is required to take up and invest in a particular modal stance. The SPEAKER seeks to transfer or delegate this modal responsibility to the addressee. It is not directly relevant as to whether the SPEAKER, independently of the interrogative form selected, really does know the answer, or have a point of view on the proposition. The point is that the orientational function of interrogatives is to position the addressee as the one who is required to take up and negotiate the modal responsibility which the SPEAKER delegates to him or her. With the selection of [interrogative: polar] options, it is the element comprising Finite^Subject which is in the unmarked thematic position. That is, the segment realising Mood also has the functions of Theme, with Finite conflating with interpersonal Theme and Subject, with topical Theme. From the SPEAKER's point of view, this complex is in thematic position because it is, in the first instance, the polar opposition between 'yes' and 'no' in the Finite element which is of most interest – the SPEAKER is requiring the addressee to negotiate this, and in the process is signalling that this is the 'point of departure' of the clause.

2.2.5 Exchange of goods-&-services

(9)   *SPEAKER*   here   are   six eggs
                             Adj:loc   **Fin:pr/Pred**   **Subject**

In example (9), it is assumed that the act of uttering the clause is accompanied either by the physical handing over of the goods referred to by the addresser, or, perhaps also, by the performing of some service for the addresser. These non-linguistic physical acts are not, however, independent of the meaning potential of the lexicogrammatical form. They are a necessary and fully semiotic part of the total social act which is performed when clauses of this type are used. For this reason, such non-linguistic acts are a constitutive part of the exchange which is being negotiated on the discourse stratum. On first glance, (9) appears to be no different from (6) *here are four hedgehogs*. This would be so if we appealed only to lexicogrammar in isolation from a number of other factors. The clause *here are four hedgehogs* was systemically described as [indicative: affirmative: declarative; theme textual/deictic; marked] on account of its presentative deictic function in relation to the picture which accompanied it. It was suggested that in (6), the *SPEAKER* asserted or affirmed the physical presence of the entity designated by the Subject in the given physical context. By contrast, in our present example (9), which is accompanied by the *SPEAKER*'s handing over of the goods to the addressee, the exophoric deictic *here* does not so much present an already given physical context, but brings into (semiotic) being the transfer of the goods to the addressee. It brings into being the state of affairs desired by the *SPEAKER*. In this sense, it does not "present" a given physical context, but it creates a particular kind of social relationship by materially enacting the transfer of goods in the given situation. It is the *SPEAKER* who is modally invested with the socially recognised agentive power, or competence, to bring about the state of affairs designated by the clause. We may claim then that *SPEAKER* is here 'empowered'.

Note that the deictic element *here* is again in thematic position: it exophorically indicates the person-place – the SPEAKER – from whom this power flows, relative to the addressee. Apart from the semantics of the clause, there is a further reason – a grammatical one – as to why this clause is not classified as declarative. Declarative clauses can be tagged. Imperative clauses of the type which have 'empower *SPEAKER*' do not appear to be taggable. Tags seek negotiation on the discourse stratum. This may be negotiation oriented to information exchange, or to goods-&-services exchange. In clauses of the type exemplified by (9), which we will describe as having the features [imperative: empower *SPEAKER*], it is the *SPEAKER* who brings about a material and semiotic state of affairs about which no further negotiation is considered desirable.[2] It is not being denied here that the addressee has the discretion to accept or refuse the offer of goods-&-services, but from the *SPEAKER*'s point of view, the meaning is 'this is how things should be; I'm bringing it about'. Thus, the orientational function of this type of imperative does not require the addressee to take up, negotiate, and carry out the *SPEAKER*'s desire. It is the *SPEAKER* who puts this into effect, and who is semanticised as the social being who has the modal authority to do so. This modal authority is invested in the Subject of the proposal – *six eggs*, in our example (9) – which grammatical entity specifies the desirable state of affairs (goods-&-services) which the *SPEAKER* both modally invests in, as well as brings into being in the uttering of the proposal.

The above discussion highlights the fact that a clause such as *here are six eggs* is ambiguous for it may be used either in the unmarked sense of a [declarative] or of an [imperative], as defined above. This ambiguity is itself systemic in origin. The point to be made here is that the meaning potential of such forms may be systematically ambiguous as to the 'report' and 'command' dimensions, discussed earlier (cf Bateson; see section 2.1). Both dimensions are potentially simultaneously present, though one may override the other in any given context. However, I should like to emphasise that a systemic grammar needs to be able to account for this ambiguity in terms of the value-producing distinctions relevant to the MOOD system. For these reasons it is suggested that the systemic description of (9) is [imperative: empower SPEAKER: material focus: goods]. (For these features, see Figure 2).

2.2.6 *Another mode of goods-&-services exchange*

A closely related subtype of clause with features [imperative: empower *SPEAKER*] is illustrated in (10):

2. In "Offers in the Making: A functional perspective", Hasan (1986) semantically characterises offers of this type as [**conclusive**], implying that the business of offer itself is concluded when such a clause is uttered in the course of giving goods-&-services.

(10)   *SPEAKER*   here   you   are
       Adj:loc **Subj** **Fin:pr/Pred**

Unlike the clause in (9), the Subject of the clause in (10) in whom the *SPEA-KER* modally invests the responsibility for the proposal, is the grammaticalised addressee, *you,* rather than the goods or services which are being exchanged. In the previous subtype, the modal responsibility is invested in the successful exchange of the specified goods or services. By contrast, in the present subtype, the speaker invests the modal responsibility in **the addressee**, as the recipient of the goods or services involved in the exchange. Aside from this point, most of the observations made in relation to the previous subtype also apply here. We may also note that the lexicogrammar of this type is parallel to the type exemplified in (6), i.e.[indicative: affirmative: declarative; theme textual/deictic; marked]. Once again, these two types cannot simply be conflated.

In the case of clauses of the type under consideration here – i.e. (10), whose systemic description is [imperative: empower *SPEAKER*: addressee oriented] (compare this with (9) which differs from this by a single feature) – the exophoric deictic does not locate the addressee in the given physical scene as it was said to do in (7). Instead, here the addressee, as recipient of the goods and service, is, metaphorically speaking, spatially located at a person-place such that, when the exchange has taken place, the addressee will be in possession of some object[3] whose spatial location is grammaticalised as the locative Adjunct. This permits the addressee to occupy the social place – the person-place – which was occupied by the *SPEAKER* before the exchange took place. Thus, the exophoric deictic element *here*, in designating a spatial location relative to the *SPEAKER* and in offering some goods-&-services which are exophorically indicated to the addressee, *you*, places the latter in a position semiotically equivalent to the *SPEAKER* prior to the exchange. This metaphorical transference of spatial location – what I have called person-place – from *SPEAKER* to addressee also construes the goods or services in question as passing from the possession of the former to the latter. Thus, it is

---

3. It is to be noted that Hasan (1986), considers clauses of this type as having the same semantic function as that described in (9): both are offers with the semantic feature [**conclusive**], and are expected to occur as a mode of concluding the exchange of goods and services, albeit with certain delicate distinctions.

the *you* who is semantically both someone who participates in the interpersonal exchange act and who is the recipient of the goods-&-services in the experiential semantics: it is the 'you' who by virtue of the utterance, becomes the possessor of those goods. If, in the first type, the SPEAKER brings into being the desired state of affairs, in the second type, the SPEAKER transforms the addressee into the Carrier/Recipient of the desired goods.

These two subtypes of clauses – i.e. (9-10) – do have significant lexicogrammatical features in common with their respective parallel types of declarative clause – features which are both lexicogrammatical and semantic. However, note that the declarative types are oriented to a modality of 'how things are' in the material here-and-now of the speech event; they have the modal feature realis. Their corresponding imperatives in (9-10) are, by contrast, oriented to a modulation of 'how things ought to be', thereby having the modal feature irrealis (Martin 1992b). This is a significant difference.

These two subtypes of clauses considered here may be said to be the congruent realisation of [offer]. This contrasts with the generally received view in systemic functional linguistics that offers have no congruent realisation at primary delicacy in the grammar (Fawcett 1980:105; Halliday 1984: 20; Martin 1992a; however, see Hasan 1986). Fawcett (1980: 105; emphasis mine. PJT) goes so far as to observe that "giving goods and services is not typically a linguistic act ... but it is often *accompanied* by one". My point is that the grammar of the two subtypes of clauses discussed here directly participates in the semiotic entraining and coordinating of matter-energy flows – cf goods and services exchange – from SPEAKER to addressee. The strongly exophoric spatial deictic orientation of these clause types directly participates in the orienting and directing of this flow in relation to the semiotically constructed space-time of the social relations between SPEAKER and addressee. The grammar of these forms is non-arbitrarily related to their participation in these exchange processes, which are simultaneously both physical-material ones of matter-energy flows between spatially located biological individuals, as well as being semiotic-discursive ones of semiotically constructed exchange relations in a space-time of social relations.

2.2.7 Exchange of goods-&-services: further forms

A further subtype includes clauses such as *here I go, here we go, here you go, there you go,* and so on[4]. These clauses are more likely to participate in the social act of performing a service, rather than the handing over of goods. The *SPEAKER* – the Subject of the Modality – who is also the provider of the service, invests the modal responsibility for the proposal in the pronominalised Subject of the proposal – *I, we, you,* in our examples. The *SPEAKER*, in releasing the relevant agentive tendency in the performing of the service, transfers the relevant modal-material competence to the Subject of the proposal, which coincides with the *SPEAKER* when *I* occurs. It is significant that, from the point of view of experiential grammar, the item *go,* in which the structural elements Finite and Predicator are fused, would have to be described as a one-participant material process of the non-goal-directed, or [transitive: middle] type. Experientially, the Subject of the proposal is Actor. In transferring the relevant modal-material competence to the Subject of the proposal, the *SPEAKER*, as Subject of the Modality, is, in effect, endowing the pronominalised Subject of the proposal with the agentive power to carry out the goal-directed task which the receipt of the service entails. The analysis of (11) must include both the interpersonal and experiential dimensions of the grammar so as to highlight this particular movement. Being an intentional, goal-directed movement, it is necessarily one-way in its effects. For this reason, it is solidary with the Deed and Extension model of transitivity proposed by Halliday (1985: 145). The systemic description of clauses of the type (11) only in terms of Mood is offered here as [imperative: empower SPEAKER: service oriented]; the last feature of this description distinguishes it both from (9) and (10), while also showing the similarities. A structural analysis is presented below:

(11) *SPEAKER*   here   you   go
      Adj:loc   Subject   Fin/Pred

In the general subclass of [imperative: empower *SPEAKER*] clauses so far discussed, the Mood element, comprising the functional semantic configuration Subject^Finite in Halliday's definition, is fully grammaticalised in these most congruent realisations of offer. This is so because it is the *SPEAKER* who enacts the exchange, both materially and semiotically, in the here-and-now of the speech event. In saying it, the *SPEAKER* does it, and the only kind of response which the addressee need give so as to finalise the exchange

---

4. For an alternative description, see Hasan 1986.

is to accept or refuse the offer, whether this be done by linguistic or other means. My point is that this subclass of imperative clauses does not seek a nonverbal action on the part of the addressee – it is not a demand for goods-&-services – which means that its finalisation is grounded in the here-and-now of the speech event. This differs from the other main subclass of imperative, whose finalisation is not grounded in the here-and-now of the speech event, but in a negotiable future state of affairs. It is to this type that we shall now turn.

2.2.8 *Imperatives with 'empower addressee' option*

In Halliday's (1984:14) terms, (12) presents the most 'congruent' realisation of the speech function known in SF as command:

(12)   SPEAKER   ADDRESSEE   be   here   at six
                                          Fin:irr/Pred   Adj:loc   Adj

Halliday defines 'congruence' as referring to the most 'typical' realisation of a given semantic function by the grammar. Thus, a lexicogrammatical 'baseline' is postulated in relation to which any given realisation may be perceived as more or less congruent. Halliday (1985: 329-32) has interpreted this baseline as referring to spoken, as opposed to, written language (see also Martin 1991), and is careful to point out (Halliday 1985: 321) that 'congruent' in no way implies 'normative'. I believe Halliday is right to suggest that imperatives of the type illustrated by (12) do represent a kind of baseline for defining the general category of Speech Functions we gloss as command. Halliday's analysis can, I believe, be further extended along the lines I shall discuss in the next paragraph.

'Baseline' imperatives such as exemplified in (12), are said to be clauses without the element Mood, in so far as there is no explicit realisation of the canonical Mood component, comprising Subject and Finite (see for example, Fawcett 1980, Halliday 1984; 1985; Davidse 1991; and Martin 1992a). As I noted earlier, the Subject of the proposal is not realised in the clause because it is clearly exophorically recoverable from the here-and-now of the speech situation. The same observation applies also to the Finite element. So, we can say that this type of imperative has no explicit realisation of the Mood element. This does not mean, in my view, that it is without Mood. Clauses of the type exemplified by (12), which realise the options [imperative: empower addressee], typically function to delegate the modal responsibility for the exchange to the addressee – the exophorically recoverable 'you'. In delegating or transferring this modal responsibility to the addressee, who is the Subject of the proposal, the *SPEAKER* – the Subject of the Modality – is, in effect, saying 'this is how things should be; you bring it about'. There is an orientation to a modulation of 'how things ought to be'. Again, this type of imperative is concerned with the entraining of matter-energy flows in the material-physical processes with which semiotic-discursive processes are cross-coupled. As distinct from the speaker oriented type of imperative we considered earlier, the type now under consideration makes the addressee – not the *SPEAKER* – the modally responsible Subject through which these processes are channelled. Thus, the orientational vector which this type constructs makes the addressee the focal point for the cross-coupling of the semiotic and the material.

My rationale for this suggestion goes something like this: from the *SPEAKER*'s point of view, there is a difference between the ways things are, materially speaking, and the way the *SPEAKER* would like them to be. The *SPEAKER* seeks to renegotiate this difference, **not** by directly acting upon the material, as in the first type, but by delegating the responsibility for doing so to a second party, i.e. the addressee. This also means acting semiotically, not materially, upon the addressee. The *SPEAKER* semiotically channels his/her desire to change the way things are in the here-and-now through the addressee so as to renegotiate the lack of fit, or the difference, between some material state of affairs in the here-and-now and the *SPEAKER*'s semiotic-modal stance on this. It is an attempt, in some local way, to bring the two into alignment – to eliminate the difference. To do so – to produce the necessary finalisation of the exchange – requires the addressee's compliance, both semiotically and materially. This type of imperative is always potentially negotiable, as evidenced by the fact that it may be tagged by clauses such as *won't you?, will you?*, and so on. The addressee's response can be both material and linguistic – s/he may do (or not do) what the speaker wants, as well as respond linguistically by agreeing, refusing, attempting to renegotiate, and so on. Both material and linguistic responses are, however, always semiotic in the context of the exchange process. In so far as they comply – materially and semiotically – to what the *SPEAKER* wants, they are responsive acts finalising the exchange: once the exchange act has been resolved or finalised, they eliminate the semiotically created difference between the *SPEAKER*'s modal-material orientation and his/her final one. The 'elimination' of this difference is always a local and contingent achievement rather than a permanent and totalising one. This is so because the lack – material or semiotic – which constitutes the fundamental principle of human goal-seeking "cannot be exorcised from the code" (Wilden 1980: 431), even though we may try hard to "exorcise" it from the situationally specific interaction.

This closes the revised analysis of clause types to be presented in this paper. The analysis and discussion presented here must be seen as indicative of a certain approach which attempts to link the grammar of a language unequivocally to the discourse-semantic stratum: in other words, it attaches critical importance to meanings, and is not constrained by the wordings as they appear in a string. In the following section we shall attempt to spell out the implications of this approach for the reconceptualisation of MOOD.

3. Revising the conception of MOOD

We have presented only a simplified fragment of the MOOD system network (see Figure 1): there appears no need to present the fuller standard version as this is familiar to most SF linguists. In this section I will first present a revised MOOD system network before turning to its discussion.

3.1 The revised mood network for major clauses

The MOOD network which underlies the above reinterpretation of the basic MOOD options is represented in Figure 2. The considerations underlying this revised MOOD system have been already foreshadowed in the discussion of the example analysed; they are discussed further in sub-section 3.2.

3.2 Orienting participants in modalised space-time

Many SF linguists have pointed out the exophorically retrievable nature of the Subject in the [imperative; unmarked] clause type (Halliday 1978; 1984; 1985; Halliday and Hasan 1976; Fawcett 1980; Martin 1991; 1992a; Davidse 1991, to mention but a few). It has already been noted here that both types of imperative are concerned with the cross-coupling of semiotic-discursive and physical-material processes in the entraining of matter, energy, and

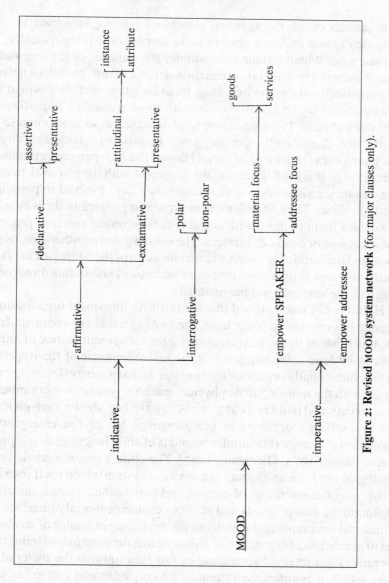

Figure 2: Revised MOOD system network (for major clauses only).

information flows. The grammar of [imperative; unmarked] clauses is organised the way it is because it is maximally congruent with the physical-material processes it seeks to coordinate and entrain. In the here-and-now of the speech event, the material individual who is addressed is given exophorically and does not need to be further specified linguistically. The linguistic work which is done to coordinate the semiotic-discursive and the physical-material into a single orientational frame of reference does not need to grammaticalise the addressee. In so far as language is cross-coupled with the material, it may be said to complete it[5], so as to enable it to perform the social work at hand. Language completes the material so as to organise it in socially and discursively specific ways. In this way, language directly participates in the processes of social labour. The interpersonal grammar of imperatives of this kind is maximally congruent with the physical-material processes they cross-couple with because they have evolved to participate directly in these. Thus, their lexicogrammar is organised in the way which best enables them to mesh with non-linguistic physical-material processes in the exchange of goods-&-services. The use of spatial exophoric items such as *here* and the implicitly exophoric specification of the addressee in clauses with the features [imperative: empower addressee] shows this direct cross-linkage of the semiotic and the material.

Halliday has often argued that the intrinsic functional organisation of language has evolved to relate language to its external environment. In my view, this is where the best explanation for the 'congruent' nature of impera-tives can be found. We suggest that the lexicogrammar of the imperative clause is functionally organised the way it is so that it most effectively cross-couples with the non-linguistic physical-material processes it organises. In this connection, Halliday (1973; 1975; 1991) has shown that goods-&-services exchange develops in protolanguage before the emergence of information exchange (For similar accounts of child language development, see also Painter 1985; Oldenburg 1987). The child's protolinguistic acts of meaning do not have an abstract grammatical system which itself interfaces the two material interfaces of content and expression. Instead, the child's protolinguistic acts of goods and services exchange directly interface with the material environment, i.e. without the mediating influence of an abstract level of grammatical organisation. It may be that the grammar of 'congruent' imperatives has retained something of this bias towards the material pro-cesses which it is functionally required to organise and entrain as social processes through the mediating influence of its grammatical organisation.

5. I am indebted to Kieran McGillicuddy for drawing my attention to this point.

This does not mean that imperatives have a more impoverished grammatical structure than do the other MOOD choices. Instead, it means that the implicit structure of their Mood element – their strongly exophoric nature – has evolved in accordance with the general principle that the internal functional design of the language has developed so as to enable language to respond to its speakers' external environment (Halliday 1978: 52; Martin 1991:121). Vološinov has formulated this most acutely:

> The finalised question, the exclamation, the command and the request, are the most typical examples of whole utterances in daily use. All of them (especially, for instance, the command and the request) require a non-verbal complement, and, in fact, also a non-verbal beginning. The very type of finalisation of these minia- ture real-life genres is determined by the friction between the word and the non- verbal environment, and between the word and an alien word (another person's word).

> Hence the form taken by a command is determined by the obstacles it may meet, the degree of compliance, and so on. The finalisation typical for a given genre is a response to the accidental and the non-repeatable features of the real-life situation.

> It makes sense to speak of special types of genre finalisation in the language of everyday life, only where there are at least some stable forms of everyday commu- nication which have been fixed by life and circumstances. (Vološinov 1983: 116- 117)

The "stable forms" of everyday (spoken) communication are the lexicogrammatical resources of the basic types of MOOD choice in the interpersonal grammar of the clause. The "friction between the word and the non-verbal environment", on the one hand, and "between the word and an alien word", on the other, corresponds to the basic difference in the social work which [imperative], as opposed to [indicative], clauses are required to do. This work always takes place through the processes of negotiation which occur on the discourse stratum. Further, it always requires some determinate discourse genre, or semantic interact (Vološinov 1983; Halliday 1984; 1985; Martin 1992a), so that the meaning exchange may take determinate shape in social space-time. Imperative mood is the primary interpersonal grammati- cal resource for negotiating the difference – Vološinov calls it the "friction" – between the position of the SPEAKER and the state of affairs in the material world which the speaker desires to change. The difference to be negotiated in the exchange is both modal and material. Indicative mood is the primary interpersonal grammatical resource for negotiating the difference between the semiotic-modal position of the *SPEAKER* and that of the addressee. The difference, in the first instance, is a modal one. However, the imperative mood is also used to construe and interpret the physical-material world.

The two main types of imperative which I have proposed, realise most congruently the speech functions (cf. speech acts) of offer and command respectively because, from the orientational point of reference of the *SPEAKER,* there is less "friction" or difference to be negotiated between the *SPEAKER*'s modal-material starting position and the desired modal-material result in the material world in order to bring about a finalised exchange. This would amount to a compliant modal-material response on the part of the addressee. The "accidental and non-repeatable" contingencies of the speech situation may give rise to material and semiotic obstacles; when this happens, the *SPEAKER* may select non-congruent forms – e.g. modulated declaratives – to do the required social semiotic work which the exchange demands for its finalisation. When a 'congruent' form is selected, the *SPEAKER* is making the MOOD selection which requires the least verbal negotiation with either the "alien word" of the other [indicative], or with the "non-verbal environment" [imperative], in order to finalise the semiotic exchange. This is, perhaps, most transparently obvious in the case of [imperative]. Here, congruency involves the 'least' linguistic work to do the social job required. But the basic point is also no less valid for [indicative]. This, I argue, is the missing link in Martin's claim that the baseline for congruent forms is the spoken language. The important point appears to be that it is in spoken language that the cross-coupling of the semiotic-discursive with the physical-material is most obvious and most directly grounded in the exophorically retrievable here-and-now.

The interpersonal grammatical resources of the MOOD system provide the means for orienting the participants in the space-time of social interaction. This occurs along three parameters in relation to the here-and-now of the speech event. These are: (a) the exophoric-deictic spatial relations; (b) tense relative to the time of speaking; and (c) the *SPEAKER*'s modal investment in the Subject of the proposition/proposal. In the examples we have considered above, it is clear that the most congruent grammar for realising the respective speech functions of such choices is tied into the here-and-now of the speech event along these three dimensions with maximum transparency, with respect to the relevant non-verbal material environment. Such most 'congruent' options of the MOOD system would amount to the most transparent or 'automatized' relation between lexicogrammatical form that the element Mood takes and the social work to be done (Havránek 1983; Silverstein 1987).

On the other hand, the social semiotic work to be done by technical and bureaucratic forms of the written language in the entraining of physical-material processes is much more abstracted away from the here-and-now of the relevant nonverbal environment. This is evidenced by the frequent use of metaphorical codings of speech functions such as 'advice', 'recommendation', and 'command' as nominal groups in these types of discourse (see Martin 1993; and Thibault 1991 for further discussion and textual analysis). This does not mean, of course, that the use of such forms – i.e. the tendency to abstraction in technical and bureaucratic discourse – is unrelated to the physical-material domain. On the contrary, these discourses presuppose a high degree of "friction", or modal-material difference, to be negotiated, as evidenced by the increased social work which is required so as to cross-couple such highly metaphorical forms with the physical-material domain. The basic pattern that emerges from these considerations may be set out as in Figure 3.

The distinction I have made here between 'semiotic' and 'material' domains of negotiation is an extreme idealisation of the actual uses to which these systems are put. On the basis of this idealisation, the following proportionalities can be proposed:

Exchange orientation / Domain under negotiation	SPEAKER [=I]	ADDRESSEE [=YOU]
Modality: (Semiotic difference)	declarative	interrogative
Modulation: (Material difference)	imperative: empower speaker	imperative: empower addressee

Figure 3: Congruent MOOD selections, with domains of semiotic or material negotiation (primary options only)

semiotic difference : modality ::
material difference   : modulation.

These proportionalities can, in turn, be related to the following ones:

indicative   : semiotic-discursive negotiation ::
imperative : physical-material negotiation

In actual fact, options from the systems of MOOD, MODALITY, and MODULA-
TION frequently recombine in often subtly indeterminate ways to realise a
very large range of more delicate choices in the system of speech function
(see Hasan 1983 for the English message semantic network, but note that she
has not supported her network by explanations of the type offered here). The
exchange process always involves both semiotic and material negotiation
and exchange, and the two domains are not, in practice, so easily separable.
Figure 3 serves to illustrate the basic systems pertaining to the interpersonal
grammar and semantics which come together in the speech interact and
which coordinate both the cross-coupling of the semiotic and the material
in the exchange process, as well as orient the material individuals who take
part in this as semioticised subjects and agents – as social beings, precisely.

3.3 Declarative vs. interrogative perspectives: An alternative view of MOOD

From another point of view, the basic opposition [indicative] vs. [impera-
tive], from which the interpersonal grammar of the various semantic interacts
is derived, can be reconstrued as the opposition [declarative] vs. [interroga-
tive]. In fact Halliday (1985: 91) has pointed to this possibility, though there
has been no systematic development of this alternative way of viewing the
MOOD system. In fact, this opposition constitutes the second opposition in
the proportionalities for the basic MOOD system which we examined in
section 2.2.1. The first point to make is that the two points of view are
complementary, rather than mutually exclusive. Each sheds light on different
dimensions of the subtly indeterminate semantic relations which can exist
between the four basic types of MOOD options, and their related speech
function semantics. The relevant proportionalities are as follows:

declarative   : empower speaker imperative::
interrogative   : empower addressee imperative

The point may be illustrated with the aid of the following examples. A clause such as *here are six eggs* may be described either as [affirmative; Theme textual/deictic; marked], or as [imperative: empower *SPEAKER*]. If the former, the *SPEAKER* affirms the physical presence of the Subject of the proposition, i.e. *six eggs,* in the here-and-now of the interaction. The thematised spatial exophoric Adjunct *here* presents their being on the scene, and in the process this constitutes a creative enacting of the situation. If the latter, the *SPEAKER* brings into being the material state of affairs he/she desires - i.e. the transferring of the goods, *six eggs,* to the addressee - at the same time that the SPEAKER utters this locution. The *SPEAKER* brings the *six eggs* into being, not literally, but as goods in the semiotics of the exchange process. Clearly, and from another point of view, the *SPEAKER* did not cause the physical-material existence of the *six eggs*. These already existed, prior to their participation in the exchange process, as entities in the pre-semiotic physical-material domain. In this case, the Adjunct *here* brings the relevant entities into the spatial purview of *SPEAKER* and addressee as semioticised material goods in the exchange process. They are brought into being as goods to be transferred from *SPEAKER* to addressee in the here-and-now of the interaction.

From both points of view – [affirmative: declarative] and [imperative: empower SPEAKER] – the interpersonal grammar of these forms is oriented to the speaker, as well as having a modality of realis. The being of something is either affirmed, or else something is brought into being, i.e. as goods to be exchanged, in the here-and-now of the speech event. In both cases, it is the *SPEAKER* – the Subject of the Modality – who either affirms the being of something, or brings something into being. The exophoric locative Adjunct grammaticalises this 'being' or 'bringing into being' at the same time that it grounds it spatially in the here-and-now of the speech event. This is why both these forms have a modality of realis.

Let us now consider the other pair of terms in the relevant proportionalities. This may be illustrated by means of the two clauses *will you be here at six?* and *be here at six!*. Halliday (1985) points out that with ellipsis of the Mood element the [interrogative] clause *will you be here at six?* could be interpreted as an [imperative: empower addressee] clause *be here at six!*. This would obviate the need for the recognition of the grammatical category of imperative mood. However, Halliday goes on to reflect that the "special categories of person and polarity" make it worthwhile to retain imperative mood as a distinct grammatical category. I agree with the argument for retaining these as distinct grammatical categories. Nevertheless, the putative possibility of collapsing [imperative: empower addressee] clauses with [interrogative] one strengthens the arguments for the deeper semantic relationship between them, which is shown in the above proportionalities. Let us now see why.

The clause *will you be here at six?* is [interrogative]; the second *be here at six!* has the systemic options[imperative: empower addressee]. In the first, the *SPEAKER* seeks the addressee's modal investment in the proposition/ proposal in this clause. The exophoric spatial Adjunct *here* grammaticalises the yet-to-be known state of affairs, relative to the here-and-now of the speech event. In the second, as we have already seen, the *SPEAKER* delegates to the addressee the modal responsibility for bringing about the desired state of affairs. The Adjunct grammaticalises the state of affairs desired by the *SPEAKER*, again relative to the here-and-now of the speech event. In both cases, there is a yet-to-be-realised (spatial) state of affairs; the modal responsibility of the addressee is further brought out by the future oriented tags which both forms may take, e.g.*will you?* and *won't you?* Modally speaking, the interpersonal grammar of both forms under discussion here is irrealis.

From both points of view – [interrogative] and [imperative: empower addressee] moods – the interpersonal grammar of these forms is oriented to the addressee, as well as having a modality of irrealis. The *SPEAKER* either requires the addressee to affirm the (future) coming about of the given state of affairs, or else the addressee is required to bring about the state of affairs – the service which is demanded – in some future point relative to the here-and-now of the speech event. In both cases, it is the addressee – the Subject of the proposition/proposal – to whom the *SPEAKER* delegates the modal responsibility for affirming the future coming about of something, or for bringing it about. The exophoric locative Adjunct *here* does not, unlike the first pair, designate the relevant spatial purview of *SPEAKER* and addressee as a conjunctive totality of places in the here-and-now of the speech event. Instead, the future-oriented modality (irrealis) constructs these as a disjunctive totality of moments – a 'now' and a 'later' – whose spatial conjunction is temporally deferred. This is why these forms have a modality of irrealis.

4. Conclusion

This paper began by disputing the idea that what is known traditionally as mood is concerned with the speaker's epistemological commitment to states of affair – actual or desired – in the world. In the course of my arguments, I have given priority to the idea of the interpersonal grammar of MOOD as realising various types of orientational interact. These do not have an 'autonomous' grammar; instead, I have attempted to argue that the internal functional organization of the interpersonal grammar of mood has a complex dialectical (realisational) interdependence with both the semiotic-discursive and the physical-material processes which it entrains and organises in the making, maintaining, and changing of the ecosocial dynamics of the exchange processes in which social beings – subjects and agents – emerge.

NOTE: For abbreviations, and systemic and structural notations, see pp 46-47.

References:

Bateson, Gregory. 1987. Information and codification. In *Communication: The social matrix of psychiatry*, Jurgen Ruesch and Gregory Bateson, 168-211. New York: W.W. Norton.

Davidse, Kristin. 1991. *Categories of Experiential Grammar.* Unpublished Ph.D. thesis, Departement Linguistiek: Katholieke Universiteit Leuven.

Fawcett, Robin P. 1980. *Cognitive Linguistics and Social Interaction: Towards an integrated model of a systemic-functional grammar and the other components of a communicating mind.* Heidelberg: Julius Groos Verlag.

Halliday, M.A.K. 1973. *Explorations in the functions of language.* London: Edward Arnold.

Halliday, M.A.K. 1975. *Learning How to Mean: Explorations in the development of language.* London: Edward Arnold.

Halliday, M.A.K. 1976. *System and Function in Language: Selected papers edited by Gunther Kress.* Oxford: Oxford University Press.

Halliday, M.A.K. 1978. *Language as Social Semiotic. The social interpretation of language and meaning.* London: Edward Arnold.

Halliday, M.A.K. 1984. 'Language as code and language as behaviour: a systemic-functional interpretation of the nature and ontogenesis of dialogue.' *The Semiotics of Culture and Language. Vol. 1. Language as social semiotic,* edited by Robin P. Fawcett, M.A.K. Halliday, Sydney M. Lamb, and Adam Makkai, 3-35. London: Frances Pinter.

Halliday, M.A.K. 1985. *An Introduction to Functional Grammar.* London: Edward Arnold.

Halliday, M.A.K. 1991. 'The place of dialogue in children's construction of meaning.' *Dialoganalyse III: Referate der 3. Abeitstagung, Bologna 1990,* edited by Sorin Stati, Edda Weigand, and Franz Hundsnurscher. 417-430. Tübingen: Niemeyer.

Halliday M.A.K. and Hasan, Ruqaiya. 1976. *Cohesion in English.* London: Longmans.

Hasan, Ruqaiya. 1983. 'A Semantic Network for the Analysis of Messages in Everyday Talk between Mothers and their Children.' mimeo. School of English & Linguistics : Macquarie University.

Hasan, Ruqaiya. 1984. 'Ways of saying: ways of meaning.' *The Semiotics of Culture and Language. Vol. I. Language as social semiotic,* edited by Robin P. Fawcett, M.A.K. Halliday, Sydney M. Lamb, and Adam Makkai, 103-162. London: Frances Pinter.

Hasan, Ruqaiya. 1986. *Offers in the Making: A functional perspective.* mimeo. School of English & Linguistics: Macquarie University.

Havránek, Bohuslav. 1983. 'The functional differentiation of the standard language.' *Praguiana. Some basic and less known aspects of the Prague Linguistic School,* translated and edited by Josef Vachek and Libuše Duskova, 143-64. Amsterdam: John Benjamins.

Lemke, Jay L. 1993. 'Discourse, dynamics, and social change.' *Language as Cultural Dynamic* VI, 1-2 Special issue, edited by M.A.K. Halliday, 243-275.

Levinson, Stephen C. 1983. *Pragmatics.* Cambridge: Cambridge University Press.

Lyons, John. 1968. *Introduction to Theoretical Linguistics.* Cambridge: Cambridge University Press.

Lyons, John. 1981. *Language, Meaning and Context.* Bungay, Suffolk: Fontana.

Martin, James R. 1991. 'Intrinsic functionality: implications for contextual theory.' *Social Semiotics* 1.1, 99-162.

Martin, James R. 1992a. *English Text: System and structure.* (see especially Chapter 2: Conversational structure: negotiating meaning in dialogue). Amsterdam: John Benjamins.

Martin, James R. 1992b. 'Macro-proposals: meaning by degree.' *Discourse Description: Diverse analyses of a fund raising text,* edited by William C. Mann and Sandra A. Thompson, 359-395. Amsterdam: John Benjamins.

Martin, James R. 1993. 'Technology, bureaucracy and schooling: discursive resources and control.' *Language as Cultural Dynamic* VI, 1-2. Special issue, edited by M.A.K.Halliday, 84-130

Nietzsche, Friedrich. 1968. *The Will to Power,* edited by Walter Kaufmann and R.J. Hollingdale (trs). New York: Vintage Books.

Oldenburg, Jane. 1987. Learning the language and learning through language in early childhood. *Learning, Keeping and Using Lamguage, Vol I: Selected papers from the 8th World Congress of Applied Linguistics*, Sydney, 16-21 August 1987, edited by M.A.K. Halliday, John Gibbons and Howard Nicholas, 27-38. Amsterdam: John Benjamins.

Painter, Clare. 1985. *Learning the Mother Tongue*. Geelong (Victoria): Deakin University Press.

Silverstein, Michael. 1979. 'Language structure and linguistic ideology.' *The Elements: A Parasession on linguistic units and levels,* edited by Paul R. Clyne, William F. Hanks and Carol L. Hofbauer, 193-241. Chicago: Chicago Linguistic Society.

Silverstein, Michael. 1987. 'The three faces of "function": preliminaries to a psychology of language.' *Social and Functional Approaches to Language and Thought* edited by Maya Hickmann, 17-38. New York: Academic Press.

Thibault, Paul J. 1991. 'Grammar, technocracy, and the noun: technocratic values and cognitive linguistics.' *Functional and Systemic Linguistics: Approaches and uses,* edited by Eija Ventola, 281-305. Berlin: Mouton de Gruyter.

Thibault, Paul J. and Van Leeuwen, Theo. *Grammar, society, and the speech act: Renewing the connections.* Dipartimento di Linguistica, Università di Padova, Italy. Mimeo.

Vološinov, V.N. 1983. 'The construction of the utterance.' (Translated by Noel Owen) *Bakhtin School Papers. Russian Poetics in Translation Vol. 10,* edited by Ann Shukman, 114-37. Oxford: Holdan Books.

Whorf, Benjamin Lee. 1956a. 'Language, Thought & Reality.' *Selected writings of Benjamin Lee Whorf,* edited by John B. Carroll. Cambridge, Mass.: The MIT Press.

Whorf, Benjamin Lee. 1956b. 'Languages and logic.' (see Whorf 1956a), 233-245.

Whorf, Benjamin Lee. 1956c. 'Some verbal categories of Hopi.' (see Whorf 1956a), 112-124.

Wilden, Anthony. 1980 [1972]. *System and Structure. Essays in Communication and Exchange.* Second edition. London: Tavistock.

3

The English 'Tag Question': A New Analysis, is(n't) it?*

William McGregor

University of Melbourne

I. Introduction

Tag questions have a significant place in linguistic theorising. Their properties were seen by early transformational generative grammarians as evidence for the need of transformations (e.g. Akmajian and Heny 1975: 1-9). More recently, generativists have considered that tags provide evidence for the necessity of formal grammar (e.g. Newmeyer 1983: 30). In systemic functional theory they have been suggested to be a means of identifying the subject of a declarative clause in English (Halliday 1985: 73). Nevertheless, they have not been subjected to really detailed grammatical description either in the generative literature (Newmeyer 1983: 30) – as Matthews (1981: 48) less charitably puts it, "[t]he transformational literature was at one time full of trivial discussion of tags" – or in the systemic literature. The majority of grammatical studies, whatever their theoretical pursuasion, have attached primary importance to formal properties, specifically the formal relations between the subject and auxiliary of the tag question and the subject and object of the stem clause to which it is attached.

Furthermore, most studies of tags by grammarians have been limited by their methodology. Introspection has been the major tool used in the collection of data: rather than observing instances of usage, grammarians have overwhelmingly proceeded by thinking up examples of tags and deciding on their grammaticality or ungrammaticality by introspection. As a result, quite acceptable tag constructions have been wrongly rejected as unacceptable because of the investigator's failure to appropriately contextualise them.

* I am grateful to Ray Cattell, Ruqaiya Hasan, Alan Rumsey and an anonymous referee for useful comments on an earlier version of this paper.

Moreover, failing to observe spoken (and written) English in use, grammarians have unwittingly sanitised their initial data, and missed whole ranges of tag types. In McGregor (1992) I discuss a number of such tag types which have been scarcely mentioned in the linguistic literature, including the interrogative tag (as in *Are you going now are you?*) and the non-finite tag (as in *You going now are you?*). Another consequence of this reliance on introspection has been a failure to appreciate the range of contextual meanings of tags. The value of many studies is limited by the fact that the investigator has singled out a very narrow range of senses, thus, ultimately significantly skewing the perceived 'meaning' of the tag –which usually goes unstated, but appears (by implication) to be identified with a small range of contextual senses. The suggestion that same polarity tags have ironical, threatening and/or challenging senses is an example: these tags can be used in other ways as well.

Sociolinguists, too, have been interested in tags. However, for their part, they appear to take the word of the grammarians, and thus they have tended firstly to focus on those tag types that have been identified by grammarians, and secondly to assume impoverished notions of the meanings and contextual senses of tags. With a few notable exceptions, most sociolinguistic investigators concentrate on statistical patterns in the use of tags by members of different social groups, particularly different genders (e.g. Lakoff 1975). As suggested in McGregor (1992), more interesting and significant sociolinguistic questions than these relate to the different strategic uses members of different social groups put tags to, and the different ways they habitually use tags to achieve their goals, given the different social domains and power relations in which they operate. This point has also been made by Holmes (1986, 1990 and 1992) and Cameron, McAlinden and O'Leary (1990); see also Fishman (1990: 237).

The major purpose of this paper is to begin filling in some of these gaps, by addressing first the fundamental question: what is the syntagmatic relationship involved in tags? It will be argued that it is a whole-whole relationship; an attempt will be made to characterise this relationship more precisely. However, the two entities which enter into this syntagmatic relationship are not the stem and the tag, as in a number of other analyses – e.g. Huddleston (1970) (who proposes a paratactic relation between stem and tag) and Matthews (1981: 234) (who proposes they are juxtaposed) –but rather the stem and the sentential construction of stem plus tag (see analyses below). I attempt to clarify the differences between these competing analyses, as well as the more standard analyses, and present evidence in favour of my own by examining a range of types of tag, including tags to indicative, imperative, exclamative, and interrogative clauses.

According to McGregor's (1990a: 13-20) suggestions about the connections between syntagmatic relations and the metafunctions, the interclausal relationship should be interpersonal, rather than, say "logico-semantic" as proposed by Halliday (1985: 193ff). Some consequences of this are explored here, and it is argued that it is possible to account in this way – to some extent at least – for the 'pragmatic' functions of tags, thus linking grammatical and sociolinguistic descriptions. Finally, certain grammatical facts about the English tag are consistent with this analysis, including the formal relationships amongst the clauses, possibilities of interpolating tags, and possibilities of attaching tags to NPs and framed (quoted) clauses.

I first became interested in tags in 1990 when I became aware of the existence of a number of tag types in Australian English which rate few mentions in the literature, and are sometimes claimed to be ungrammatical (see above). During the following years I recorded over 500 examples of such 'unusual' tag types from the speech of those around me, as well as a few from television. The examples were commited to memory, and written down in a notebook as soon as possible afterwards; only the lexico-grammatical form of the utterance was recorded. McGregor (1992) investigates the syntax and semantics of these 'unusual' tags. This paper represents an attempt to explore the wider significance and validity of my (1992) proposals to tags generally. In addition to the corpus of 'unusual' tags, I recorded a few instances of the better known tag types. This was augmented by a small textual corpus from Halliday and Poole (1978).

The argument is organised as follows. In the next section I begin by outlining the range of tag questions in English, identifying their forms and semantics. Then in the third section I raise and resolve some difficulties for a rank-based grammar and discuss the syntagmatic relationship involved, arguing that it is a whole-whole relationship. Following this, in section 4, I will attempt to show how these suggestions help account for a range of other tagging phenomena which otherwise appear exceptional. Section 5 begins a preliminary exploration of the nature of the whole-whole relation involved in the tag construction. The paper ends with a conclusion which briefly remarks on some further implications of the investigation.

2. Form and meaning of tag questions in English

English has a large number of possibilities for tags, such as do not exist in
many other languages. Polish, for example, is a more typical language,
having, according to Wierzbicka (1991: 37-38), only five or six words that
can be used as 'invariant' tags, much in the manner of the English tags *right*,
OK, *eh*, etc. (See also Caffarel, this volume, on French tags. *Editors*.) Our
best starting point is to make a preliminary list of the major tag types in English, with an example of each. This is done in Table 1.

Table 1: Major types of tag in English

Mood of stem	Polarity	Example
Indicative	Reverse, + −	You're going aren't you
	Reverse, − +	You aren't going are you
	Same, + +	You're going are you
	Same, − −	You aren't going aren't you
Interrogative	Same, + +	Are you going are you
Imperative	Reverse, + −	Come here won't you
	Reverse, − +	Don't come here will you
	Same, + +	Come here will you
	Same, − −	Don't come here won't you
Exclamative	Reverse, + −	What a bank balance, isn't it

Some of the types included in this table have been claimed by some linguists
to be ungrammatical, sometimes explicitly, sometimes implicitly. However,
all are possible, certainly in Australian English, and probably in other
dialects also. In my discussion of the types, I will comment on these differences of opinion later in this section.

There are, of course many finer distinctions not shown in this table. To
begin with, no indication at all is given of tone, and the more delicate
distinctions that are possible on the basis of differences in the number of tone
units the utterance is divided into, and the tone of each unit. In fact, I will be
ignoring tone almost completely in this paper, primarily because it seems to
me that the different tonic possibilities do not affect the core meanings of the
various tag constructions, but modify the degree to which the speaker attests
to the proposition uttered. That is, whether e.g. the tag of *You're going aren't
you* is uttered on a rising tone or on a falling one, the core meaning remains

the same, and all that differs is the 'complexion' the speaker puts on the proposition. A rising tone on the tag indicates an inclination to believe the proposition (Huddleston 1984: 375; cf. Young 1980: 64), and a request for the hearer to indicate whether or not it is true. A falling tone on the tag indicates a commitment to the truth of the proposition plus a request for the hearer's confirmation (Huddleston 1984: 375; cf. Young 1980: 64). In other words, tone constitutes a more delicate system of options, which may be safely ignored in an account of the present degree of generality.

The effect of tagging a clause, I suggest, is to modalise it in some way. The stem clause retains its mood, but with some qualification. Thus tagged declaratives remain declaratives; tagged interrogatives remain interrogatives; tagged imperatives remain imperatives; and tagged exclamatives remain exclamatives. This suggestion is not new, and is implicit in e.g. the system network for the declarative clause in Kress (1976: 105); see also Young (1980: 63) and Hasan (1989: 246-247). It is not, however, shared by all linguists. Hudson (1975: 26), for instance, appears to be suggesting that a reverse polarity tagged declarative is a negatively conducive interrogative (although elsewhere in that same paper he seems to be saying something rather different). And generative analyses based on the *Aspects*-type of framework took the view that declarative tags derived from 'phrase markers' in which there was an element Q(uestion) – in other words, the declarative tag was likened to an interrogative clause in that they have the same meaning, but different derivation (e.g. Burt 1971: 9), or that they derive from the interrogative (e.g. Klima 1964). A somewhat different view is expressed by Dik (1989: 257), who suggests that grammatical illocutionary 'conversion' from declarative to interrogative is involved in the tag. In Dik's opinion the resulting sentence cannot be identified as an interrogative, due to this process of 'conversion'. However, Dik appears not to see it as a type of declarative either. Unfortunately, exactly what Dik (1989) intends illocutionary conversion to involve remains unclear; it is clear, however, that like Hudson (1975), Burt (1971), Klima (1964), etc., he considers tagging to result in a clause of a different mood to the stem.

The type of modalisation tags convey appears to relate to presuppositions, expectations and/or evaluations of the truth or falsity of the proposition expressed by the clause. But this is not all. They also invoke a response from the hearer, at least by implication: if not a verbal response, then either a goods-&-services response, or – to put it rather crassly – a change in the hearer's mental state in relation to the proposition. Further, because of the presuppositions, expectations and/or evaluations involved, tags are conducive – that is, they always invoke an expected response from the addressee, either in the affirmative or negative, depending on the context of utterance and the interactive goals of the speaker.

But we must be more specific than this, and attempt to characterise the meaning of the various types of tag more precisely. Before doing this, however, I reiterate Hudson's (1975: 6) observation that the meaning – that is, the core meaning – of moods has nothing to do with illocutionary force, and therefore that illocutionary force is not needed in discussing the meaning of tags. He suggests instead that what should be included in their core meanings is their sincerity conditions. I will be assuming a version of this suggestion, that something like sincerity conditions – but under a rather different guise – are a part of the meaning of tags. However, other things must also be specified, which relate to presuppositions, expectations and evaluations.

2.1 Declarative tags

Declarative tags are the best studied of all types of tag, and even though there is not full agreement among analysts as to their meaning, there is a reasonable consensus of opinion. I briefly outline – with little or no justification – a possible characterisation of the meaning of the main types of declarative tag, based largely on previously published work on the construction.

Declarative tags are either same or reverse polarity, and the stem is either positive or negative. Reverse polarity tags are normally considered to be the more common or natural, and have been best studied. They represent propositions which the speaker holds, and advances, not necessarily strongly. Examination of the transcripts in Halliday and Poole (1978) shows that for the majority of instances of these tags the speaker elaborates on, or enhances on, what has been previously said, reinterpreting it, advancing the discourse, if you like. This is illustrated by the two bolded clauses in the following extract from Halliday and Poole (1978: 9), where each turn (though not each clause in each turn) is consecutively numbered:

Dialogue I:

Boy   (1)   You learn it if you keep doing it.
Anne   (2)   Aw – crap!

Boy	(3)	You do!
Anne	(4)	You don't need to do exactly the same thing three years in a row, Bill!
Bill	(5)	I do.
Girl	(6)	You do! **It sinks in that way, doesn't it?**
Others	(7)	It sinks in.
Girl	(8)	Would you learn any other way?
Anne	(9)	You don't need to do it – yea, you don't need to do it three times. I can't understand that.
Bill	(10)	**You won't forget it then, will you?**

The bolded clause in (1.6), illustrating a reverse polarity tag to a positive stem, elaborates on the previous discourse by restating it in other words, thus providing an explanation of why the proposition uttered by the boy in the first turn is in fact true, in the face of disagreement by Anne in turns (1.2) and (1.4). Similarly, in the last turn, the reverse polarity tag to the negative stem clause again restates the proposition of turn (1.1) – which, it will be observed, is restated twice, on each occasion more precisely and forcefully.

Reverse polarity tags are thus in a sense speaker oriented: they advance the discourse by adding information which the speaker believes (at least to some extent). But in addition to this, the speaker is soliciting the hearer's agreement with the proposition expressed by the stem clause or its negation (depending on the polarity of the clause), suggesting that not only does the speaker know or believe it, but so also does (or should) the hearer – thus the tag is like a conducive yes/no question. Two distinct types of claim are normally made in relation to same polarity tags. One concerns the status of the proposition in its context of occurrence. It is frequently suggested that the stem clause echoes a previous utterance of the hearer, or expresses a proposition which is derivable from the previous utterance (Wierzbicka 1991: 224ff, Young 1980: 66, Taglicht 1984: 108, Sinclair 1972: 79). However, these conditions are far too strong, as illustrated by the second clause of turn (3) in Dialogue II (from Halliday and Poole 1978: 13):

Dialogue II:

Salesman	(1)	G'day, Steve.
Stephen	(2)	Good day.
Salesman	(3)	Welcome down here. **You're going to be relief staff down here are you?**

Clearly there is nothing in the previous discourse that the tagged declarative in (11.3) echoes. Rather, the proposition that the addressee is on the
relief staff for that department is one which would have been known or
believed by both the speaker and hearer from previous interactions in the
store. In other words, the proposition expressed represents an expectation of
the speaker's based on his interpretation or construal of the situation. Here,
the expectations are based on previous discourses, while the interpretations
concern the present situation as an instantia tion of something relevant to
those previous discourses. It seems to me that it is the interpretative aspect
that is most significant, the distinctive semantic feature of this construction
type, and what distinguishes it from the reverse polarity tag.

The tag also requests the hearer's opinion of the proposition. Hudson
(1975: 26) proposes that the interrogative part, the tag, has a sincerity
condition that the speaker believes that the hearer knows as well as the
speaker whether or not the proposition is true or false. Unlike Hudson, however, I do not regard this as a sincerity condition on the use of the interrogative, but rather a part of its core meaning – part of what is conveyed by the
interrogative mood, rather than a condition on its use.

The other frequently made suggestion about same polarity tags is that
they have hostile, ironic, aggressive, challenging, disapproving, sarcastic,
suspicious, scornful, sceptical overtones (e.g. Huddleston 1970: 221, Quirk
et al 1985: 812, Hudson 1975: 25). My intuitions in relation to decontextual-
ised examples tend to agree. Strangely, however, my corpus (admitedly
small) shows no examples with such overtones (see also Cattell 1973: 614).
This strongly suggests that these overtones are contextual senses, rather than
parts of the core meaning of the same polarity declarative tag.

I have suggested elsewhere (McGregor 1992) that the generalisation in
(a) provides an appropriate characterisation of the semantics of same polarity
positive declarative tags, capturing the properties just discussed.

(a): Same polarity positive declarative tag
I presume that P (the proposition expressed by the clause) may be true on the
basis of an interpretation of the relevant evidence, although without this evidence I would not necessarily have thought so. You are likely to have (or
should have) knowledge at least as reliable as I do; I request your confirmation.

The various attitudinal senses mentioned above emerge as contextualisations of this core meaning: if what leads the speaker to presume P is something done or said by the addressee, the contrast between this and the speaker's erstwhile belief to the contrary may imply disbelief – which naturally leads to the ironic, hostile and other attitudinal overtones.

Same polarity negative tags are quite rare by comparison with the corresponding positive ones. Indeed, some linguists have claimed they are impossible or at best marginally possible to some speakers – for example, Huddleston (1984: 375) claims that they are accepted by only a 'minority of speakers', while Quirk et al (1985: 813) suggest that they are not clearly attested in usage. I myself have not recorded any, but am relying simply on my intuitions, which suggest that the main context is strong disagreement with a proposition previously uttered by the addressee, or predictable from what they have said or done; at the same time, disapproval may be implied. Thus, consider example (1):

(1)   You didn't see him didn't you?

This might be uttered by someone questioning the validity of a previous claim by the addressee that he hadn't seen the person concerned, suggesting strongly that they did not believe this claim.

2.2 Interrogative tags

These are very poorly studied, and barely mentioned in the literature; many linguists claim that they do not exist, and that interrogative clauses (sometimes "questions") cannot take a tag. Cattell (1973) and Bolinger (1957) are exceptions, and contain brief mention of this type of tag. Interrogative tags are, however, the ones I have investigated most carefully myself (McGregor 1992). In brief, my findings are that the interrogative tag is a type of modalised interrogative which differs from the corresponding ordinary interrogative in that it invokes an interpretation of the surrounding circumstances (including what has already been said) as indicating that the proposition is true, even though there is something unexpected about it. Thus, (2) was uttered to someone who was apparently making a move to leave a Little Athletics meeting somewhat before the end of the meeting – the speaker was, that is, interpreting the hearer's actions as suggesting that she was going, but counterposing this to his expectation that she would not (or should not) be going (as it was so early).

(2)   Are you going now are you?

McGregor (1992) proposes the following characterisation of the core meaning of this type of tag:

(b): Interrogative tag

There is evidence that P (the proposition expressed by the clause) may be true, even though I might have thought otherwise. I presume you know at least as well as I do whether P is true; please confirm my interpretation.

In fact, this is not the only type of interrogative tag in English. There are at least four others: (i) non-finite tags, (ii) WH polar tags, (iii) WH non-finite tags, and (iv) WH information tags. We exemplify and briefly discuss each of these types below; a thorough investigation, including justification of the proposals, is beyond the scope of the present paper – see however McGregor (1992).

2.2.1 Non-finite tags

The term 'non-finite tag' refers to a tag to a stem clause which has no Finite (on Finite as clause element, see Halliday 1985: 75) – no first auxiliary (operator) or primary tense marker on the verb.[1] (3) is an example:

(3)   They want to look at other things did they?

McGregor (1992) argues that the Finite element in the stem clause of examples such as (3) has been ellipsed, and that furthermore the elliptical stem clause is interrogative (rather than declarative) in mood. However, ellipsis of the Finite is not motivated solely by its predictability or status as given information. The plain interrogative tag discussed above and the non-finite tag do not just differ in terms of whether the speaker presents the Finite as not predictable or predictable; there is a meaning contrast between the two possibilities. Unlike the former, the latter invoke no contrast between the

1. The term non-finite is not ideal, as it is used elsewhere in linguistics to designate very different types of clause, including to (e.g. to go to Darwin) and -ing (e.g. going to Darwin) clauses. I have retained it for want of a better label; the fact that there is no Finite element in the stem clause, however, means that it is not completely inappropriate.

proposition expressed by the stem clause (i.e. the proposition interrogated) and the speaker's expectations. This, I submit, is why the Finite is ellipsed in the non-finite tag type; that is, the Finite is ellipsed in order not to throw any doubt on the truth value of the proposition: it is not something that the speaker would have previously thought false. Unlike *to* and *-ing* non-finite clauses, however, a proposition which may be true or false, and which may be argued about, is expressed by the clause.[2]

The following characterisation of the core meaning of the non-finite tag construction has been suggested by McGregor (1992):

(c): Non-finite tag

There is evidence that P (the proposition expressed by the clause) may be true. I presume you know at least as well as I do whether P is true; please confirm my interpretation.

2.2.2 WH polar tags

WH polar tags are tags to polar interrogatives which are introduced by the WH interrogative *what*. (4) is an example:

(4)   What did you see him just then did you?

In Australian English *what* need not be set off intonationally from the rest of the stem clause, and indeed it regularly fuses phonetically with the following Finite element. It seems reasonable to regard it as belonging to the interrogative clause. But even if it is not, they are certainly not independent of one another. It is clear that there is a syntagmatic relation between *what* and the following interrogative – the relationship being, I would argue, a scopal one in which *what* holds the interrogative in its scope, and modalises it (see further McGregor 1992). Whether or not a clausal analysis is justified does not affect our analysis of the tag: as we will see later, stems need not coincide with clauses.

The following characterisation is suggested (after McGregor 1992):

---

2. In casual conversation the Finite is also often ellipsed in an independent interrogative clause, as in *You coming?* I believe that this is explicable in a similar way to the ellipsis of the Finite in interrogative tags, rather than by any difference in the information status of the Finite element itself. (I am grateful to an anonymous referee for drawing my attention to this.)

(d): WH *polar interrogative tag*

There is evidence that P may be true, even though I might have thought otherwise. I presume you know at least as well as I do whether P is true; am I right in supposing P to be true – or is there some better explanation?

2.2.3 WH *polar non-finite tags*

In the third type of interrogative tag, the WH non-finite tag, the stem clause is again introduced by *what*, but the finite element is absent.

(5)   What he just born was he?

The following characterisation may be suggested for this type of tag:

(e): WH *non-finite tag*

There is evidence that P may be true. I presume you know at least as well as I do whether P is true; am I right in supposing P to be true – or is there some better explanation?

2.2.4 WH *information tags*

The final type of interrogative tag is attached to a construction which consists of an initial WH information interrogative initiated by *what*, and followed by an NP providing a possible answer. This is illustrated by example (6).

(6)   So what's this a Croydon shopping trolley is it?

I would argue that the WH word, the interrogative and the elliptical possible answer together form a construction, a single unit to which the tag is attached, and which the tag modalises. Again, as pointed out above, whether or not this unit is a single clause is irrelevant to our present considerations. (f) below characterises the meaning of this type of tag:

(f): WH *information tag*

The proposition must hold for some unknown value of one of the arguments, predicates, circumstances or whatever. It is possible that the unknown information is *x*, although this is only a guess, and I have no real evidence for it. I presume you know at least as well as I do whether *x* is the unknown value; please confirm my suggestion.

2.3 Imperative tags

These are also much less well studied than declarative tags, although they are significantly better studied than interrogative tags. I have not made a corpus based study of these tags myself, and the following remarks are gleaned from the literature and my reactions to the claims made therein in relation to the few examples I have recorded. In the imperative tag there is a wider variety of possibilities for auxiliary choice and for the tag subject than for the declarative tag. First, as distinct from the case for declarative and interrogative tags, the auxiliary is not a repetition of the auxiliary of the stem clause; nor need it be a repetition of the auxiliary of the corresponding negative clause (Bouton 1990: 39). Second, the subject of the tag need not necessarily be a pronominal cross referencing the subject of the stem clause – which need not necessarily have a subject (cf. Halliday 1985: 85). Thus, for instance, we have the following examples of reverse polarity imperative tags from Quirk *et al* (1985: 813), which show that the subject of the tag need not even be a pronominal:

(7)   Open the door, won't you?
(8)   Open the door, can't you?
(9)   Open the door, won't somebody/anybody?
(10)   Open the door, can't somebody/anybody?

It is widely agreed that a tag has some effect on the interpersonal meaning or illocutionary force of an imperative clause. On the one hand it has been suggested that it invites the hearer's consent to the performance of the act, and thus is a persuasive softener (Quirk *et al* 1985: 813); that it encodes the option of refusal (e.g. Lyons 1977: 749); that it softens the command by pleading compliance (Bolinger and Sears 1980: 84) or leaving it up to the hearer to decide what to do; that it defers the decision to perform the requested act to the hearer (Young 1980: 71). On the other hand, it has also been observed that an imperative tag can be used to increase the force of directives (e.g. Quirk *et al* 1985: 813) or of offers and good wishes (Bouton 1990: 41).

Table 1 shows the same four types of tag for imperative clauses as for declarative clauses. Some writers – e.g. Huddleston (1984: 376), Quirk *et al* (1985: 813), Bouton (1990: 37), Hudson (1975: 28) – have claimed that only three of them occur, and that same polarity negative imperative tags are not possible. This is quite false. (11), for example, could be uttered by a parent on finding that their child has ignored a demand that they make their bed, in which case it may be an expression of anger or frustration; alternatively it may be a threat or warning of punishment to come if the command is not complied with.

(11)   Don't make your bed won't you?

Quirk *et al* (1985: 813) further suggests that positive tags to negative imperatives are uncommon, and that where they do occur, they usually function as pursuasive softeners. As to the semantic contrast between same and reverse polarity tags to positive imperative stems, Quirk *et al* (1985: 813) suggests that the former is more insistent than the latter. Some support for the insistence of the same polarity positive imperative tag comes from the fact that they are often used to reinforce a previous demand by a parent which has not been complied with by their child. This is illustrated in (12), from Hasan (1992: 97), uttered by a mother to her child, who she has been attempting to coerce into pulling the plug out of the bath:

(12)   Oh well, do it with your toes then would you?

My intuition is that with the negative tag *won't you* (12) would lose much of its force of insistence (and *wouldn't you* seems highly unlikely in this context). Somewhat comparable views appear to be held by the few other writers who discuss the contrast. For example, Wierzbicka (1991: 228) suggests that the former functions as a request while the latter functions as an offer, and Huddleston (1970: 220) suggests that the contrast matches that between the corresponding positive and negative interrogatives used as commands.

Interestingly, there is a rather different use of the same polarity positive imperative tag, as in (13), which I mention because I have not come across discussion of it in the literature. (13) might be uttered by a parent when a child has done – or appears to be intent on doing – something they have been explicitly instructed not to do, again either as an expression of anger or frustration, or as a warning or threat.

(13)   Eat all the chocolates would you?

It is beyond the scope of this paper to propose characterisations for the four types of imperative tag. The discussion above does, however, clearly support the contentions that imperative tags remain imperatives, and that modalisation of the imperative is involved.

2.4 Exclamative tags

These represent a third group of rather poorly studied tags. It seems to be the case though that these are necessarily reverse polarity tags to positive clauses (as an anonymous referee has pointed out to me, negative polarity *how* exclamatives probably do not occur):

(14)   How odd it is, isn't it?
(15)   How odd, isn't it?

According to Quirk *et al* (1985: 813), exclamative tags invite the hearer's agreement; a similar view is expressed by Huddleston (1984: 376), who suggests it is used to seek confirmation with the exclaimed statement. All that needs to be added is that what agreement is being invited to is the proposition which is exclaimed, and not the precise wording of the exclamation itself. So (14) and (15) invite the hearer's agreement with the proposition *It is (very) odd* – not with the wording *It is how odd*. (Note that I am not suggesting that *It is (very) odd* represents an underlying or basic form for the exclaimed clauses in (14) or (15), only that this wording directly represents the proposition expressed by the exclamative clause.) This, incidentally, is the way out of the dilemma noted by Huddleston (1970: 220), that *isn't it* in (14) and (15) cannot be seen as the reduced versions of interrogatives corresponding to *It is how odd*. It is the proposition expressed by the stem clause that is modalised by the tag, and that the tag is accordingly structurally related to as a reduced version of, and not the lexicogrammatical form of the stem clause itself.

3.   Analysing tags: syntagmatic and paradigmatic relations

Now that we have listed and briefly discussed the main distinct types of tags in English, we attempt an analysis. As I have already suggested, there are two 'strands' running through all types of tags:

(i)   that the proposition expressed (as a declarative, interrogative or imperative) is modalised in some way; and

(ii) that they are response soliciting.

Neither or these of its own is adequate to account for the meaning of tags; both are necessary. The assumption made by a number of linguists that the most basic or general meaning of the tag (common to all its contexts of use) is to encourage involvement of the hearer (e.g. Halliday 1985: 69, Holmes 1986) is unfounded; this forms only a part of the core meaning. This is because the tag is distinguishable from a sequence of utterances in which an elliptical interrogative clause follows a declarative, interrogative, or imperative clause by the same speaker. Such sequences are purely response-soliciting, and involve no modalisation of the expressed proposition. The interrogative tag, for instance, contrasts with a sequence of interrogatives such as in (16), spoken by a child aged 7 to another aged 5 whilst they are both sitting together drawing at the kitchen table. The second interrogative occurred on a separate intonation contour following the first after a short interval of silence, which was, however, long enough for the hearer to have begun their reply. The hearer not having replied, the speaker repeated the question in order to more strongly solicit a response. One was in fact then obtained.

(16) Are you doing that the same as mine / are you /

We must now raise the important, though often ignored question: are there one or two (or more) clauses in the various types of tag? That is, does the tagged construction constitute a single clause of its own, or does it constitute a bi- (or multi-) clausal construction? There seems to be a certain amount of evidence in favour of both possibilities. On the one hand, as we have argued, the tag modalises the clause, producing a new construction which has the same mood as the stem clause. This is reflected in various systemic networks such as those in Kress (1976: 105), in which the interpersonal systems of declarative and imperative have mood tag as one of their subsystems. In addition, as argued in McGregor (1992), the fact that the interrogative tag is agnate to – that is, forms a minimal grammatical pair with – the negative interrogative also suggests a single clause analysis.

On the other hand, the single clause analysis is not entirely satisfactory. To begin with, it ignores the obvious formal resemblance between the tag and an elliptical interrogative. Furthermore, granted that I will be arguing later that the meaning of the tag is also consistent with such a characterisation of the tag, it is clear that it is most appropriate to view the tag as an elliptical clause of itself. Secondly, Huddleston's (1970) formal arguments for the tag construction as a type of compound sentence, seem to retain their force. As he argues, it would be difficult, if not impossible to write formal rules which account for all acceptable tag-stem collocations (Huddleston 1970: 218). In particular, problems emerge in regard to tags to certain 'complement' sentence types – which, according to Halliday (1985: 230), involve projection of ideas – such as in *I suppose John's gone, hasn't he* (Huddleston 1970: 216), and in relation to tags to imperative clauses (Huddleston 1970: 217). Problems also emerge in regard to tags to NPs in declarative clauses (see section 4 below).[3] Huddleston's observations argue not only against early transformational analyses of tags such as Klima (1964), but also against any proposal that the tag is no more than a repetition of the subject and finite (first auxiliary) of the stem clause (as suggested for example by Young 1980: 58ff, and Hasan (personal communication)).

But to accept the tag as a separate clause, and the tag construction as a MOOD option at the rank of clause – both of which seem to be strongly justified by the arguments above – gives rise to a contradiction with the rank hypothesis, at least in its standard form (Halliday 1961, 1966; cf. also McGregor 1991a). One way of resolving this contradiction, consistent with Halliday (1985), would be to suggest that grammatical metaphor is involved: that the tag construction is a metaphoric way of expressing a clausal mood. But this is not an appealing position to adopt, since its only motivation is to save the rank hypothesis. A better way around the contradiction is to restrict the rank hypothesis to the experiential metafunction, and permit that else-where – namely when a grammatical construction is viewed from the perspective of one of the other metafunctions – the rank scale does not apply (McGregor 1990a, 1991a). We may presume that there are indeed two separate clauses, the stem and the tag, and that the latter modalises the former. We do not need to classify the construction they form as itself a clause if the relationship is not an experiential one – as it clearly is not. To put it another way, we do not need to presume that the 'entry point' for the system of tagging is the rank of clause; we will be returning to this point in section 4.

What then is the relationship between the clauses of the tag constructions? Huddleston (1970: 215) suggests that the stem and the tag are para-

---

3. Huddleston also remarks on a difficulty with the suggestion that tags constitute a separate clause of their own. We will be suggesting an answer to this objection below.

tactically related; Matthews (1981: 234) makes the similar suggestion that they are juxtaposed. Unfortunately, these suggestions do not help explain the semantics of the construction; modalisation is a semantic relationship not normally (in systemic theory) associated with taxis (except in grammatical metaphor – e.g. Halliday 1985: 332ff), which in my view (McGregor 1990a) should be restricted to logical relations like expansion, elaboration and enhancement (as characterised by Halliday 1985: 202ff). If the semantic relationship between stem and the tag is one of modalisation, an interpersonal function, then the relevant syntagmatic relation should be whole-whole, according to the theory developed in McGregor (1990a). What I want to suggest then is that there are two critical wholes, the stem clause, and the stem plus tag construction; the tag itself is of course also a whole clause, but this is irrelevant to the construction itself (as we will see in section 4). More specifically, what I will be suggesting is that the tag embraces the stem clause in a type of scopal relationship, much in the way that modal operators such as *probably*, *maybe*, *certainly* and so on hold the proposition expressed by the clause in their scope (McGregor 1990a: 28-30), and clauses of speech frame quotations (McGregor 1991c). The remainder of this paper will be devoted to illustrating how this proposal provides useful insights into tags, and explains various facts about tags which would otherwise appear exceptional.

4. Some 'exceptional' uses and characteristics of tags

'Normal' tags in English are attached to the end of single full clauses. Other types of tag do occur, however. We have already seen (section 2.2) that some types of interrogative tags apply to a stem which is arguably larger than a full clause. Alternatively, a tag may be restricted in application to a part of a clause, or to a clause which is not independent. (17) shows a tag which clearly relates to just the NP *an SE*, and not to the entire elliptical non-finite (in the sense above) clause *You using an SE*.[4] (18) (from Matthews 1981: 36)

4. Ruqaiya Hasan suggests (pers. comm) that *is it* in (17) is not a tag, because it does not modalise the clause *you using an SE*, and represents a structure transition, common in speech, in which by the time the speaker gets to the tag he is treating the first clause as *It's an SE (that you're using)*. The first argument is inapplicable because it is not the case that tags must be attached to clauses. And although it is possible to argue that this particular example involves structure transition, not all examples can be accounted for in this way.

is another example of this type. Such tags are not uncommon (see also Matthews 1981: 233).

(17) You using an SE is it?

(18) I spoke to your brother – wasn't it – on Saturday.

Examples (19) and (20) illustrate that tags in English may apply to a non-independent clause. Here the tag relates not to the erstwhile main clause, or to the syntagm constituted by the two clauses, but to the 'complement' clause alone – to the projected (Halliday 1985) or framed clause (McGregor 1991c) – *John's gone* and *It's worth it.*:

(19) I suppose John's gone, hasn't he?

(20) I think it's worth it, isn't it?

Significantly, this type of tag is virtually restricted to 'complements' of clauses of cognition (compare *I saw John taking it, didn't I* vs. *I saw John taking it, didn't he*).

According to McGregor (1990a and 1991c), the so-called 'complement' clause is modalised by the clause of cognition, which frames it, indicating the extent to which the speaker is prepared to attest to the proposition it expresses. So in effect (19) and (20) are subject to dual modalisation: the propositions *John's gone* and *It's worth it* are modalised on the one hand by the clause of cognition, and on the other by the tag, both of which hold it (independently) in their scope. Of course, there is also another proposition involved, namely the one expressed by the clause of cognition. This proposition can also in some cases be modalised by a tag, particularly if the process is one which may be construed as a real cognitive one, as is illustrated by (21) and (22) – which frequently have aggressive overtones, suggesting that the addressee disputes the speaker's beliefs or knowledge.

(21) I believe John's gone, don't I?

(22) I think it's worth it, don't I?

For some clauses of verbal communication both tag types are also possible, although there seems to be a fairly strong tendency for the tag to relate to the clause of speech rather than the framed clause (McGregor

1991c). The viability of both types is illustrated by (23) and (24):[5]

(23)   You told me I could take it, didn't you?

(24)   You told me I could take it, can't I?

Two propositions are expressed by the quotation construction, one framing the other. The tag picks out which of the two the speaker wishes to represent as the most important or significant one. In (23), what is most significant is the issue of whether or not the addressee gave permission to the speaker; in (24), by contrast, it is the issue of whether the speaker is permitted to take the thing.

Tags may also, on occasion, be non-final, as in (25) and (26) (the latter from Hasan and Cloran 1990: 88).[6] Although it is not certain what restrictions there are on the interpolation of tags, it does seem that the constituent which they follow is the focus (in the sense of Taglicht 1984: 9-10); indeed, I would argue that they mark the preceding constituent as the focus of the modalisation they effect. The full clause remains the scope or domain of the tag.

(25)   It was John, wasn't it, who you were talking to just then?

(26)   I'm so quick, aren't I, with the cooking?

Tags themselves, of course, need not be clausal in size, and this adds further support to my proposals. What I am suggesting is that the syntagmatic relation between the tag and the stem is the same for (27) as well as for (28). It is a whole-whole relationship, the relevant wholes being the full clause *You saw her yesterday*, and the whole constituted by this clause together with the tag. The difference between the two types is, I suggest, a function of what

5. Many grammarians would probably regard (24) as ungrammatical or unacceptable. However, I have observed a number of such tags in ordinary conversation, where it is not particularly rare, and goes unnoticed by the speech interactants. Ruqaiya Hasan suggests that this is not a tag, because *can't I* must occur on a separate tone unit. I am not convinced of this: particularly if the polarity of the tag is the same as that of the quoted clause, utterance on a single intonation contour seems to me to be perfectly acceptable.

6. The potential for interpolation of the tag may be seen by some systemicists as evidence that the relationship is indeed an interpersonal one, with the tag being 'scattered' prosodically through the clause. By contrast, however, I regard this as a secondary, non-defining attribute of interpersonal functions, which is by and large a consequence of the fact that scopal relations normally have a focus, which there is a tendency for them to be near to.

realises the tag – whether or not it represents a full proposition.

(27)   You saw her yesterday didn't you?
(28)   You saw her yesterday eh?

As mentioned above (see page 94), many languages show just a few invariant tags. One advantage of the framework I have outlined here is that it permits the same structural analysis for both types of tag, capturing their semantic relatedness. By contrast, analyses such as those proposed by Huddleston (1970: 215) and Matthews (1981: 234) (see section 1) are clearly inapplicable to invariant tags.

At least two other properties of tag constructions underline their relatedness with modalised single clauses. First, interrogative tags form minimal grammatical pairs with negative interrogatives (McGregor 1992); in these the negative element clearly holds the proposition in a type of scoping relationship. Second, tone, as mentioned earlier, has not been included in the investigation. However, it will be noted that modal qualifications very similar to those which I have proposed for the tags in this paper are also conveyed by particular intonation contours in English. Again the 'syntagmatic' relations involved are whole-whole: the lexical clause itself to the clause with overlain intonation contour.

The various apparently exceptional properties of the English tag which have been mentioned in this section together illustrate how rank is irrelevant to the analysis of the construction. Interestingly, there are some striking parallels with properties of framing constructions, including: the potential for a clause of speech or thought to frame a constituent of another clause (as in *He is a believer in transformations as they called them*); the potential for a framing clause to be interpolated within the framed clause; agnation with a single clause expressing the quote (no framing clause), uttered on a distinct intonation contour, usually with a marked voice quality; and agnates with clauses containing morphemes apparently holding the clause in the same sort of relationship (e.g. many languages have evidential particles that could be translated as 'it is said that').

These similarities strengthen the case for regarding the stem as falling within the scope of the tag. The nature of the scoping relationship has so far been spelt out in very general terms only, and it is clearly necessary to state more precisely what is involved in the various scopal relationships I have been talking about. This is what we now turn to.

5. Form and functions of tags

The arguments I have adduced so far are largely metaphorical: they invoke parallels between tags and other grammatical phenomena which they resemble. In order to give more concrete exemplification of the advantages of my proposals, I now consider the relation between the forms and functions or meanings of English tags. Hudson (1975: 23) has suggested a particularly strong relationship, proposing that the meaning of the declarative tag is the

> automatic consequence of the interaction between the meanings of the declarative and the interrogative. In other words, there is really no need to say anything special about the meaning of tagged declaratives, since it is already covered by whatever we say about the meaning of interrogatives and declaratives. ... [O]nce we have said in syntax that reduced interrogative clauses can be added toward the end of the clause on which they are modeled, there is no need to say anything more about them in the semantics.

By contrast, he considers that the syntax of the tag is unpredictable: it would be imposssible to predict the shape of possible tags in English.

The essential details of Hudson's case appear to be as follows. The conduciveness of declarative tags follows from the sincerity condition of the declarative stem and the sincerity condition of the interrogative tag (Hudson 1975: 24). Together they give the sincerity condition that the speaker believes the proposition expressed, and also that the speaker believes the hearer knows as well as the speaker whether the proposition is true or false. More particularly, for reverse polarity tags, the speaker is asking the hearer to consider whether the proposition is true – with the implication that it is true, and the hearer knows this (Hudson 1975: 26). This is represented by the declarative stem, which expresses the speaker's belief in the proposition, and by the reverse polarity interrogative, which has the effect of inquiring whether the hearer thinks that the negation of the proposition is really true – which has the effect of implying that the speaker believes the proposition.[7]

---

7. Hudson further suggests that his analysis shows that, and why, 'reversed-polarity tags are simply instances of negatively conducive interrogatives'. This would seem to be quite false. Whether or not any tag is negatively or positively conducive depends entirely on the context of its utterance, and has nothing to do with its inherent semantics (see also McGregor 1992). Although Hudson is right in relation to the reverse polarity tags of Dialogue 1, had they been uttered in a joking manner by Anne, they could equally have been positively conducive — expecting, that is, disagreement with the proposition expressed by the stem clause.

For same polarity tags, Hudson suggests that the declarative stem indicates the speaker's belief in the proposition, while the interrogative tag indicates the speaker's belief that the hearer knows as well as the speaker whether the proposition is true or false. This, suggests Hudson (1975: 27), accounts for the fact that same polarity tags express shared beliefs, rather than represent something which the speaker wishes to tell the hearer. Hudson suggests that the meanings of imperative and exclamative tags are likewise predictable (1975: 28-29). For the tagged exclamative he suggests that *n't* marks an exclamation, rather than negation, and thus that (appearances to the contrary) exclamative tags are same polarity. For imperative tags he proposes that the interrogative mood of the tag expresses the speaker's belief that the hearer knows as well as the speaker whether the proposition is true – and thus the truth of the proposition depends on the hearer's enactment of it – this contextualises as a polite request, softening the force of the command.

It seems to me that there are difficulties with Hudson's proposals, and that they do not convincingly argue his thesis that the meanings of tag constructions are derivable from the meaning of their parts, and need not be specifically discussed in a grammar of English. For one thing, as we will shortly see, the meanings he suggests for the various types of tag are not without problems: the meanings he suggests for the parts lead to wrong predictions about the meaning of the whole. However, some aspects of Hudson's proposals do appear reasonable, and consistent with the discussion of section 2. First is the notion that part of the meaning of a tag construction relates to the 'sincerity condition' on the interrogative mood whereby the speaker believes that the hearer knows at least as well as the speaker does whether the proposition is true or false. In contrast to Hudson, I regard this not as a sincerity condition on the use of the interrogative mood, but rather as a part of its invariant core meanings – in context, the sincerity condition may not actually obtain, thus giving a specific contextual meaning to the interrogative mood when asserted counterfactually. Those tags for which I have given a semantic description in section 2 all show a clear reflex of the sincerity condition, as does the imperative tag, as Hudson points out – although this does not imply that the tag softens the force of the imperative, as claimed by Hudson (1975: 29). Second, all tags show some element of a request for a response which is also a part of the core meaning of the interrogative mood – even if, again, it is not necessarily an aspect of all contextual uses (e.g. rhetorical questions, rhetorical interrogative tags – on which see McGregor 1992).

It follows from the discussion of the preceding paragraph that it is indeed true that the formal similarity between the tag and the interrogative mood is matched by a commonality of meaning. Not to regard tags as clauses in the interrogative mood would result in missing significant generalisations.

The finer details of Hudson's proposals are less convincing. Firstly, he seems to be suggesting (1975: 26) that the contrast between same and reverse polarity declarative tags is related to the contrast between same and reverse polarity elliptical interrogatives uttered in response to a previous speaker's declarative. In this context, when polarity is reversed, the speaker is representing the negative of the proposition expressed by the previous declarative, and inquiring whether this is held to be true or false by the hearer: the difference of polarity suggests that the speaker in fact believes the proposition to be true. When the polarity is constant, the speaker is simply asking whether the hearer would agree to the proposition or not.

In regard to the reverse polarity declarative tag, what seems unconvincing is the suggestion that an interrogative showing reverse polarity to the declarative stem actually represents the negation of the stem proposition. Let us begin with the case of a negative tag to a positive stem clause. As is well known, negative interrogatives are not simply interrogatives of negated propositions. Rather, they are interrogatives which invoke some interpretation of the circumstances as suggesting that the proposition may in fact be false, even though the speaker would not have thought so (e.g. Quirk *et al* 1985: 808-809). This, I suggest, is crucial to the semantics of the reverse polarity tag to a positive declarative stem, and permits us to formulate something like the following description:

(g): Reverse polarity tag to a positive declarative stem
The speaker asserts the proposition with the qualification that something suggests that it may be false, even though the speaker would not have thought so. The hearer is presumed to know as reliably as the speaker whether the proposition is in fact true or false; and the speaker requests the hearer's confirmation.

The characterisation (g) would seem to provide a more adequate description than Hudson's for the use of this type of tag in turn (6) of Dialogue I *it sinks in that way, doesn't it?*. For the qualification to the speaker's assertion represents, in this instance, the addressee's contrary belief; and the presumption that the hearer knows the polarity of the proposition is a firm attestation that she knows it to be true. This proposal strongly ties in with some recent feminist investigations of tag usage by men and women, such as Cameron *et al* (1990), and Fishman (1990), suggesting as it does that – contra Lakoff (1975) – as interactive devices tags are highly assertive strategies for coercing agreement, express the exercise of power, and are not indicators of tentativeness or politeness.

Can this explanation be usefully extended to reverse polarity tags to negative stem clauses? The semantics of an ordinary interrogative clause contains no interpretative component; perhaps this component in the tag comes from the fact that the tag is an elliptical interrogative. If we presume that the positive tag to a negative clause involves ellipsis of the remainder of the negated clause – the Residue as Halliday calls it (1985: 74) – this is presumably because the proposition itself is given, or presupposed. To interrogate it then would be tantamount to indicating that there is some reason to suppose that it is in fact not the case – and thus there is some reason to suppose the proposition may be true. Thus we would have the following semantic characterisation:

(h): Reverse polarity tag to a negative declarative stem:

The speaker denies the proposition with the qualification that something suggests that it may be true, even though it is presupposed that it is false. The hearer is presumed to know as reliably as the speaker whether the proposition is in fact true or false; and the speaker requests the hearer's confirmation.

This would seem to account for the uses of this type of tag commented on in section 2 above, including turn (10) in Dialogue I *you won't forget it will you?*

In relation to the same polarity declarative tags Hudson's suggestions (1975: 27) are less convincing. First, in regard to positive stems, the interpretative component of same polarity tags (see (a)) is not included in Hudson's characterisation (1975: 27) – and it is difficult to see how it could be. In terms of the theory I am developing here, it is present by virtue of the elliptical nature of the interrogative tag, which represents the proposition as a presupposition. The fact that the proposition is interrogated immediately after it is declared indicates that there is some room for doubt – giving the final clause of the first sentence of (a). Second, in regard to negative stems, Hudson's characterisation appears to give an inappropriate semantic description: according to my observations, these are never used in expressing shared beliefs – but rather are used in strongly disagreeing with a negative proposition previously stated or apparently presumed by the hearer. This, however, seems entirely consistent with the meaning of the negative interrogative, which includes the component that something suggests the possibility that the proposition (i.e. the one negated one) is false even though the present speaker would not have thought so: and will continue not to think so. Given that the former speaker suggests this, the disagreeing use of this tag type follows.

Another contentious aspect of Hudson's proposals is the suggestion that the syntagmatic relation between the stem and tag is irrelevant and requires no explication (1975: 23). But assuming this, there would be no difference between interrogative tags and sequences of interrogatives followed by elliptical interrogatives (as illustrated by (16)). This is false, and so by *reductio ad absurdum* Hudson's proposal must be rejected. Furthermore, the explanations I have just developed to account for the meanings of the four different types of declarative tags invoke different relationships between the meaning of the declarative stem and the meaning of the interrogative tag, depending on whether polarity is reversed or constant.

The above discussion argues that there are at least three essential ingredients to the meaning of tags:
(i)   the meaning of the stem mood;
(ii) the meaning of the elliptical interrogative mood tag (cf. Huddleston 1984: 375); and
(iii) the meaning of the syntagmatic relation involved in the tag construction.

To presume, as does Hudson (1975), that (iii) can be dispensed with is as questionable as presuming that the meaning of relative clause constructions in English are entirely derivable from the meanings of the separate clause types involved, and that the syntactic relationship involved is irrelevant. This is clearly not the case. A grammar of English does need to describe relative clauses – their properties cannot be derived simply from the properties of WH interrogatives. The same holds for tag constructions. The best we can hope for is some reasonable, principled association between the form of the clauses involved in the constructions and the uses to which the construction is put – and thus ultimately their meanings. This would seem to be manifestly the case for tags.

Clearly much further work is required on each of (i)-(iii) above, but most particularly on (ii) and (iii). As to (ii), it is commonly believed that ellipsis relates to the information status of that which is ellipsed; if, as per McGregor (1991b), information packaging falls into the interpersonal metafunction, then the use of ellipsis in tags is explicable. The 'structural' ellipsis of the Residue represents the status of the proposition (which is put forward in different ways according to the mood of the clause) as presupposed – and this is a central ingredient in the meaning of all types of clausal tags in English. Ellipsis thus emerges as critically important at the level of sentence, and not just beyond it, in the text, as has been suggested by e.g. Halliday and Hasan (1976: 8-9) and Halliday (1985: 288).

In regard to (iii), as proposed both here and in McGregor (1992), the interrogative tag contrasts minimally with the negative interrogative. This means that (29) and (30) are agnates:

(29) Are you going now are you?

(30) Aren't you going now?

What I have been proposing in this paper is that the same whole-whole relation is involved in these two constructions – that is, between the interrogative clause *are you going* and the entire sentence. This is manifested in the relation between the negative enclitic *n't* in (30) and the interrogative clause, and between the reduced interrogative mood (tag) and the interrogative in (29). In other words, *are you* and *n't* relate in essentially the same way to *are you going*.

6. Conclusions

In this paper I have proposed a new analysis of English tags according to which the syntagmatic relation between stem and tag is accorded primary importance, and the tag is seen as a type of 'operator', modalising the stem clause. This wording is not accidental. It invokes a rather different perspective on mood to that adopted in Halliday (1985): mood, according to the analysis suggested here, is a type of 'operator', modifying the proposition expressed by the clause. All clauses, irrespective of mood, thus express a proposition. Instead of the contrast between propositions and proposals (Halliday 1985: 71), I prefer to speak of differences between asserting and proposing propositions (see also McGregor 1990b: 383). The stem relates to the whole construction as whole to whole, as per my (1990a) proposals about the nature of the interpersonal metafunction. This suggestion is more concrete and usable than Halliday's suggestion that the interpersonal meta-function is 'typically' associated with prosodic relations – seen as embracing scattering – and thus is more amenable to analysis. It also permits us to link together various apparently disparate phenomena, including tagging, framing (quotation), negation, repetition, etc. This paper, admitedly, has not succeded in providing a fully rigorous characterisation of the type(s) of whole-whole relation involved in tags: I have been restricted to as yet not fully developed parallels to scopal relations such as are involved in negation. To develop an adequate characterisation of these whole-whole relations is an important goal for future research.

Given that the tag serves the interpersonal function of modalising the proposition expressed by a clause it is significant that the two elements of the tag constitute what Halliday (1985: 73) calls the Mood, the pivot on which the validity of the proposition (in my sense – see above) expressed by the clause rests and may be argued or challenged. Thus the argument may be seen as lending further support to Halliday's proposal that the Subject in English is an interpersonal category, and represents that "something by reference to which the proposition can be affirmed or denied", that entity on which the validity of the proposition rests. Indeed, my argument would seem to suggest that this characterisation of Subject applies not just to declarative, but also to imperative clauses.

But what of the case in which the tag has scope over a clausal constitu-ent? For examples such as (17) and (18), it does not make sense to say that the tag modalises the whole clause, modifying the proposition it expresses. However, it does not seem unreasonable to suggest that the tag serves an interpersonal function, focussing on the involvement of the clausal constitu-ent in the proposition. This clausal constituent is in fact the thing picked up by the Subject of the tag. In other words, the validity of the proposition expressed by the tag itself hinges on this entity as that which is "modally responsible". It is at best a tendency for what is modally responsible for the proposition expressed by the tag to be also modally responsible for the proposition expressed by the clause to which the tag is attached – and this is a consequence of the tendency for the proposition expressed by the tag and the clause to be the same.

On the one hand, this argument is part of a more general argument that syntagmatic relations must be reinstated to a central position in systemic functional grammar. Syntagmatic and paradigmatic relations are mutually defining, but orthogonal: neither one may be derived from the other. Where then does the paradigm fit in this account, in which it is (to the systemicist at any rate) conspicuous by its absence? The answer is not at all clear to me at present. I have employed the method of paradigmatic contrast in the process of attempting to determine the meaning of the various types of tag, both here and in McGregor (1992). But I have not attempted to draw any networks for the oppositions involved. One difficulty in drawing a network would be to determine its location, its point of entry. For, as we have seen, it is not possible to associate tags with any particular grammatical rank, which may then be seen as the point of entry for the system. It would, of course, be possible to draw separate networks of options for each rank where tagging is found, and then, for each subtype within the ranks where distinctive tagging behaviour is found. Irrespective of the descriptive and pedagogic advantages of doing this, theoretically it does not seem to be a particularly insightful solution. For the evidence we have discussed does seem to indicate that there is a certain degree of commonality across all tag types, and that furthermore there are gaps in the paradigms which are predictable once we take into account the core meaning of the stem, the tag and the relationship between them: this explains, for example, why reverse polarity interrogative tags do not exist.

References:

Akmajian, A. and F. Heny. 1975. *An Introduction to the Principles of Transformational Syntax*. Cambridge Mass: MIT Press.

Bolinger, D. 1957. *Interrogative Structures of American English*. Alabama: University of Alabama Press.

Bolinger, D. and M. Sears. 1980. *Aspects of Language*. New York: Harcourt, Brace, Jovanovich.

Bouton, L. 1990. The imperative tag – a thing apart. *World Englishes* 9, 37-51.

Burt, M. 1971. *From Deep to Surface Structure*. New York: Harper and Row.

Cameron, D., F. McAlinden, and K. O'Leary. 1990. Lakoff in context: the social and linguistic functions of tag questions. *Women in Their Speech Communities*, edited by J. Coates and D. Cameron, 74-93. New York: Longman.

Cattell, R. 1973. Negative transportation and tag questions. *Language* 49, 612-639.

Dik, S. 1989. *The Theory of Functional Grammar. Part 1: The structure of the clause*. Dordrecht: Foris.

Fishman, P. 1990. Conversational insecurity. *The Feminist Critique of Language: A reader*, edited by D. Cameron, 234-241. London and New York: Routledge.

Halliday, M.A.K. 1961. Categories of the theory of grammar. *Word* 17, 241-292.

Halliday, M.A.K. 1966. The concept of rank: a reply. *Journal of Linguistics* 2, 110-118.

Halliday, M.A.K. 1985. *An Introduction to Functional Grammar*. London: Arnold.

Halliday, M.A.K. and Ruqaiya Hasan. 1976. *Cohesion in English*. London: Longman.

Halliday, M.A.K. and M. Poole. 1978. *Talking Shop: Demands on language*. Sydney: Film Australia.

Hasan, Ruqaiya. 1989. Semantic variation and sociolinguistics. *Australian Journal of Linguistics* 9, 221-275.

Hasan, Ruqiaya. 1992. Meaning in sociolinguistic theory. *Sociolinguistics Today: International perspectives*, edited by Kingsley Bolton and Helen Kwok, 80-119. London and New York: Routledge.

Hasan, Ruqaiya. and C. Cloran. 1990. A sociolinguistic study of everyday talk between mothers and children. *Learning, Keeping and Using Language, Volume 1: Selected papers from the 8th World Congress of Applied Linguistics*, Sydney, August 1987, edited by M.A.K. Halliday, John Gibbons and Howard Nicholas, 67-99. Amsterdam and Philadelphia: John Benjamins.

Holmes, Janet. 1986. Functions of *you know* in women's and men's speech. *Language in Society* 15, 1-22.

Holmes, Janet. 1990. Hedges and boosters in women's and men's speech. *Language and communication* 10/3, 185-205.

Holmes, Janet. 1992. Women's talk in public contexts. *Discourse & Society* 3/2, 131-150.

Huddleston, R. 1970. Two approaches to the analysis of tags. Journal of Linguistics 6, 215-222.

Huddleston, R. 1984. *Introduction to the Grammar of English*. Cambridge: Cambridge University Press.

Hudson, R. 1975. The meaning of questions. *Language* 51, 1-31.

Klima, E.S. 1964. Negation in English. *The structure of Language: Readings in the philosophy of language* edited by J. Fodor, and J. Katz, 246-323. Englewood Cliffs: Prentice Hall.

Kress, Gunther. 1976. ed. *Halliday: System and function in language*. London: Oxford University Press.

Lakoff, R. 1975. *Language and Woman's Place*. New York: Harper and Row.

Lyons, J. 1977. *Semantics*. Cambridge: Cambridge University Press.

Matthews, R.H. 1981. *Syntax*. Cambridge: Cambridge University Press.

McGregor, W. 1990a. The metafunctional hypothesis and syntagmatic relations. *Occasional Papers in Systemic Linguistics* 4, 5-50.

McGregor, W. 1990b. *A Functional Grammar of Gooniyandi*. Amsterdam: John Benjamins.

McGregor, W. 1991a. The concept of rank in systemic linguistics. *Functional and Systemic Linguistics: Approaches and uses*, edited by E. Ventola, 121-138. Berlin: Mouton de Gruyter.

McGregor, W. 1991b. Information as an interpersonal function. Paper presented at the Nineteenth International Systemic Congress, Tokyo, Japan.

McGregor, W. 1991c. Quoted speech and thought in Gooniyandi – perspectives from semiological grammar. Paper presented at workshop on Theoretical Linguistics and Australian Aboriginal languages, Australian Linguistics Society Conference, Brisbane, Australia.

McGregor, W. 1992. Ja hear that didja? Paper presented at the Australian Linguistics Society Conference, Sydney, Australia.

Newmeyer, F. 1983. *Grammatical Theory: Its limits and its possibilities*. Chicago and London: University of Chicago Press.

Quirk, R. *et al.* 1985. *A Comprehensive Grammar of the English Language*. New York: Longman.

Sinclair, J. McH. 1972. *A Course in Spoken English: Grammar*. London: Oxford University Press.

Taglicht, J. 1984. *Message and Emphasis: On focus and scope in English*. London and New York: Longman.

Wierzbicka, A. 1991. *Cross-cultural Pragmatics: The semantics of human interaction*. Berlin and New York: Mouton de Gruyter.

Young, D. 1980. *The Structure of English Clauses*. London: Hutchinson.

4

"Nothing" Makes Sense in Weri:
A Case of Extensive Ellipsis of Nominals
in a Papuan Language

Maurice Boxwell
Summer Institute of Linguistics
Papua New Guinea

1. Introduction

It is generally accepted that co-referentiality is an important means of establishing textual continuity. At first glance the concept of co-reference appears fairly straightforward. There are two conditions that need to be met in creating co-referentiality:

(a)   that there are at least "two instances of reference" (Huddleston 1978: 345), and

(b)   that reference must be to the same thing (Grimes 1975: 182; Halliday & Hasan 1976: 3; Lyons 1977: 191; de Beaugrande 1980: 56; de Beaugrande & Dressler 1981: 133; Huddleston 1984: 278-9; Hasan 1984a: 196, 205).

Co-referentiality requires the "relationship of situational identity of reference" (Hasan 1985: 73). However, there is disagreement in the details of the interpretation of the conditions, particularly regarding the first one, as to what constitutes an instance of reference. The difference relates directly to which of two basic views of reference one holds. The first of these two views is held within the philosophical tradition and represented in linguistics by such linguists as Lyons (1977) and Huddleston (1984) among others. According to this view reference can only be made to particular entities. Thus, in discussing

(1)   Wash and core **six cooking apples**. Put **them** into a fireproof dish.

(Halliday & Hasan 1976: 2)

Huddleston rejects *them* and *six cooking apples* as being co-referential, because *six cooking apples* is a nonidentifying expression and, for him, it "is not being used referringly" (Huddleston 1978: 345). Note in passing that in this and most other examples throughout this paper, the elements under discussion are highlighted. The only exceptions to this convention are found in four examples, noted at the appropriate point in the text, where the practice would confuse rather than assist the reader.

According to the second view of reference, it is maintained that all signs refer. Thus the term reference is viewed as synonymous with the Saussurean term signification. This view allows reference to nonspecific and abstract entities, as well as to particular entities. Thus, in this view, not only are such non-controversial linguistic items as *my son* and *he* co-referential in a straightforward example like

(2)   While **my son** was on holidays **he** broke his arm.

but so also are *six cooking apples* and *them* in (1), regardless of whether they are specific or nonspecific.

The grammatical categories which are generally recognised as establishing the relation of co-referentiality are the implicit devices known as pronoun and demonstrative (Hasan 1985). A third, and less widely recognised, device is that of ellipsis. This is not to suggest that ellipsis has not been identified as an implicit cohesive device. On the contrary, scholars describing the cohesive resources of English (eg., Halliday and Hasan 1976; de Beaugrande 1980) have pointed to the contribution ellipsis can make to the texture of text. However, in most of these cases ellipsis has not been associated with co-referentiality, and rightly so in the majority of cases for English, where its overwhelming function is that of co-classification (Hasan 1984a; 1985).

Co-classification is the meaning relation in which "the things, processes, or circumstances to which [the cohesively related elements MB] refer belong to an identical class, but each [element MB] refers to a distinct member of this class." (Hasan 1985: 74). For example, in

(3)   There are **ants** in the sugar and even **ants** in the biscuits.

the relation between the two occurrences of *ants* is one of co-classification, not co-referentiality, because they do not refer to the same ants but to two different groups within the total class of ants. Grimes (1975: 184) also recognises that this relation is different from that of co-referentiality, referring to the former as "sameness of recognition" and the latter as "sameness of reference".

The aim of this paper is to examine the extensive use of ellipsis of nominal elements in establishing the semantic relation of co-referentiality in the Weri language of Papua New Guinea. But before turning to the discussion of ellipsis in Weri, I will touch briefly, in section 2, on the Weri people and their language, providing a cultural and linguistic background for what follows. I will go on to present a condensed account of certain formal features of Weri. These features are important to the present discussion, since they become instrumental in the identification and/or interpretation of co-referential ellipsis. In section 3, I shall go on to say a few words on the concept of ellipsis, since it has been described in different terms by different scholars. This will pave the way for section 4, which is concerned with the discussion of the different types of ellipsis of nominals which enter into extensive co-referential chains in Weri. In particular, this discussion will revolve around the role of Subject ellipsis and Complement ellipsis in establishing co-referentiality to an extent which is so much greater than in English.

2. Some features of Weri

The Weri are a group of approximately 4,500 people living in the headwater region of the Waria River and in the Ono and Biaru valleys in a rugged and remote corner of the Wau Sub-district of the Morobe Province of Papua New Guinea. Their language is a member of the Goilalan stock level family of the Trans New Guinea Phylum of Papuan languages (Wurm, Voorhoeve & McElhanon 1975: 12; Dutton 1975: 631; Foley 1986: 234). It belongs to an area which has been described as the most linguistically complex in the world (Wurm 1982: 1), having "a language density unparalleled elsewhere" (Foley 1986: 8). Crammed into the land area of 900,000 km² of the New Guinea mainland and surrounding islands are some 1,000 languages, almost one quarter of the world's total number. Of these, approximately 250 languages belong to the Austronesian language family, with the remaining number, some 750, belonging to upwards of 60 language families which are collectively called Papuan (or Non-Austronesian) languages. Weri is just one of those 750 Papuan languages.

Two features of the Weri grammar interrelate with co-referential ellipsis which forms the main focus of this paper. It will be helpful to briefly describe these. The first is what is commonly called medial verbs, the second a sentence and paragraph linking device called tail-head linkage. It will also be helpful to briefly distinguish the ranks of group, clause, sentence and paragraph which will be mentioned at one point or another in this paper.

2.1 Medial verbs

Weri shares with most other Papuan languages a distinction between sentence medial verbs and sentence final verbs, based on a different morphology for each (Wurm, Laycock and Voorhoeve 1975: 171; Wurm 1982: 81, 83–5; Foley 1986: 11–21). They are generally called medial or dependent verbs and final or independent verbs respectively. The latter have the full range of inflectional possibilities, including person, number, tense and mood, while the former are much reduced, taking their specification for the missing inflections from those of the final verb (Foley 1986: 11). The relationship of the medial verb to the following verb is normally one of temporal sequence but can also be that of temporal overlap. For the purposes of this paper I will focus on examples of sequential relationship only. A simple example may be seen in (4). A key to all abbreviations and symbols, including orthography, is given at the end of the paper.

(4) *Pi yokot-up   pës   **mö-ak** //   nga   **më-ë-a.***
     he boy-**sg.cl** rod hit-**comp** angry 3-say-**3.pst**
     After he₁ caned the boy₂ (he₁) spoke angrily (to him₂).

In (4) the medial verb *möak* in the first clause carries no inflection for person, number or tense, but receives its specification from the final or independent verb *mëëa* 'spoke to him' in the second clause.

In Weri, as with other Papuan languages with medial verbs, medial verb constructions are not limited to two clauses. Rather, any number of clauses, each with a medial verb, may be strung together in a chain before the main clause containing a final verb. Robert Longacre likens the structure to a series of train carriages hooked together with the engine at the end (1972: 2). Such strings of clauses will be seen in several examples below.

In addition to the temporal relationship between a medial verb (or strings of medial verbs) and the final or independent verb, each medial verb also indicates whether the subject of the following verb is same or different from the current subject. Some languages go further and specify the person and number of the subject of the following verb. Examples of such languages include Hua (Haiman 1976: 259-60), Fore (Scott 1978: 124) and Kanite (McCarthy 1965: 60). In Weri, for temporal sequences the medial verb is marked by −Vn, normally -ën, indicating that the following verb has a different subject (ds); by contrast, the absence of -Vn indicates that the following verb has the same subject. For example, in

(5) *Pi yokot-up* **mö-ön** // *nga   më-ë-a.*
     he boy-**sg.cl** hit-**ds**   angry 3-say-3.**pst**
     He₁ caned the boy₂ and (he₂) spoke angrily (to him₁).

the different subject suffix -*ön* on the medial verb *möön* 'hit' in the first clause signals that the verb of the following clause will have a different subject from that of the first clause. Thus, while the subject of *möön* in the first clause is *pi* 'he', the subject of *mëëa* 'spoke to him' is *yokotup* 'the boy', the complement of the first clause. The possibility exists that the subject of the second clause could have been some other element which is presupposed exophorically from the immediate situation (see Halliday & Hasan 1976) or from earlier in the text. This issue will be taken up in 3.2 below. However, here, because of the proximity of 'the boy', as the complement of the first clause, it is the preferred candidate for the subject of the second clause. Compare (4) where the absence of the different subject marker on the verb *möak* of the first clause indicates that there is no change of subject for the following clause.

2.2 Tail–head linkage

Another common feature of Weri, which has also been reported in a number of Papuan languages, is the joining of the sentences or paragraphs (see 2.3 below for the distinction between the two in Weri) by what has been called "tail–head" linkage (Scott 1983: 162-3; Reesink 1987: 163, 275). In it the verb at the end of a sentence or paragraph (the tail) is repeated in medial form (see 2.1) at the beginning of the next sentence or paragraph (the head). That is, the verb at the end of a sentence or paragraph occurs with its full inflectional possibilities. However, when it is repeated in the first clause of the following sentence or paragraph, the verb is greatly reduced inflectional-

ly. In many cases the only inflection required is the presence or absence of
the different subject suffix -*Vn*, although the completed action suffix -*ak* is
regularly present, particularly where -*Vn* is absent (see (5) and (4) above
respectively). This type of linkage is the normal way of progressing from one
sentence to another in Weri narrative and other discourse types like proce-
dural discourse which require the expression of temporal sequence or
overlap.

The most common form of tail–head linkage is repetition by means of
the pro–verb construction, *pël ëën* or *pël ëak*, rather than repetition of the
lexical verb. The pro-verb is comprised of the demonstrative *pël* 'that way'
and the verb *ë* 'do', plus either the different subject suffix -*ën* or the completed action suffix -*ak*. The pro-verb construction is used to join sentences
in sequential relation and to indicate different subject or same subject
respectively in the following clause. Because the pro-verb is semantically
a linking device, it is often shown as a conjunction rather than a clause in
free translations into English. The matter of its equivalence in English is
dealt with further in the final paragraph of this section. Examples of the two
pro-verb forms are given in (6) and (7).

Before proceeding with these examples, a word of explanation would
be helpful. These and similar Weri examples provided throughout the paper
form part of texts which may have very long sentences. To avoid distraction
by material outside our immediate concern, it has proved convenient to take
for some of our examples small sections of particular texts. This requires
commencing and closing the examples mid sentence. Wherever such extracts
are taken as examples, three dots (...) are used to indicate the existence of
preceding and/or following cotext. In addition, sentence juncture is indicated
by three slashes (///) to distinguish it from clause juncture, indicated by two
slashes (//). Sentence juncture is marked only when it occurs within one
speaker turn and *not* when it occurs at turn transition between one speaker
and the next, as for example in (28), (30) and (31). (See 2.3 below for the
difference between a clause and sentence in Weri). Further, wherever
examples contain more than three clauses, each clause is numbered with
lower case Roman numeral (i, ii,... etc.) for both the vernacular examples and
their free translations.

Turning back to the pro-verbs *pël ëën*, indicating change of subject in
the following clause and *pël ëak*, indicating same subject, an example of the
two forms may be seen in (6) and (7) respectively.

(6) ...// (i) *lup-t-ak*   *is* //   (ii) *won ye-s.*///
       middle-**sg.cl-loc** rise   no   **act**-go
       (iii) *P-ël*   *ë-ën* //   (iv) *wë-ën-ak* //...
            that-way   do-**ds**   be-**ds-comp**
     ...(i) (the sun) rose to the middle (of the sky) (ii) and disappeared [in eclipse].
     (iii) Then (iv) (we) remained and...

(7) ...// (i) *kër-öt*   *ë-ëpën-ëak*   *pö-t*//
       middle-**sg.cl-loc**   do-**3.fut-des** that-**sg.cl**
       (ii)   wi-it   wetë rë-ak//   (iii) wet   ya-wi.///
            string-**cl**   first break-**comp**   twist   **act**-put
       (iv) *P-ël*   *ë-ak*//   (v)   *wi-it-ön*   *itaangk-ën*//
            that-way   do-**comp**   string-**cl-Rec** see-**ds**
       (vi) *kësang ë-ën-ak*//...
            big   do-**ds-comp**
     ...(i) if (some women) want to make string bags, (ii) (they) first [lit. act first]
     (iii) twist the string. (iv) When (they) do that (v) (they) see the string (vi) that
     it is long and...

In (6) *pël ëën* in clause (iii) recapitulates the final clause of the preceding sentence *won yes* '(the sun) disappeared' and also indicates by means of the different subject marker *-ën* on the verb that there is a change of subject in the following clause (iv). In (7) *pël ëak* in clause (iv) recapitulates the final clause of the preceding sentence *wet yawi* '(they) twist (the string)' and also indicates by means of the absence of the different subject marker that the following clause has the same subject.

While the pro-verb is grammatically a standard clause, it does not represent a new event. It adds no experiential content, but functions textually as a linking device. As a clause it can be translated as 'Having done that,' '(x) did that and' or 'When (x) did that', but it is often freely translated as 'Then' or 'And' or sometimes not translated at all.

2.3 Ranks in Weri

A number of units of different sizes are referred to in this paper. They range in a scale which Halliday (1985) calls rank (though some others have also referred to it as *level*). The ranks which Halliday recognises are, from smallest unit to largest: morpheme, word, group, clause and clause complex (Halliday 1977: 177; 1978: 129). Berry (1975) follows this, but has also used sentence as an alternative to clause complex. In addition, she admits the possibility of the rank of paragraph (1975: 94). The ranks adopted in Weri are: morpheme, word, group, clause, sentence and paragraph.

The first four need little comment. Of these the morpheme and word are recognised only implicitly, through references to suffixes and to lexical items such as verbs. Reference to the rank of group occurs in the discussion of the nominal group (called noun phrase in other frameworks). A clause is the unit which, simplifying somewhat for this paper, has the obligatory elements of Subject^Predicator or Subject^Complement^Predicator. However, the reader should be aware that, like other languages in many parts of the world, Weri also has verbless clauses of an equative or stative nature (see Boxwell 1978).

A little more needs to be said about the ranks of sentence and paragraph. A sentence is a structure whose elements are realised by clauses. These clauses are in particular relationships to each other, the specifics of which are irrelevant here, but include temporal and logical relations of various types. A sentence is distinguished from a clause in that it is closed by an independent verb with person, number and tense specification (see 2.1 and 2.2 above), and has final intonation contour. A paragraph is a structure whose elements are realised by sentences. Like clauses in a sentence, the sentences in a paragraph stand in particular relationships. A paragraph is distinguished from a sentence by its closure, in which the pitch drops further and following which there is a longer pause than for a sentence. It is also distinguished from a sentence by its opening. For example, the form of tail-head linkage used to open a sentence is repetition of the final verb of the preceding sentence by means of a pro-verb construction, such as *pël ëak* or *pël ëën*, described in 2.2 (see (6) and (7)). In contrast, the form of tail-head linkage used to open a paragraph is repetition of the lexical verb of the final clause of the preceding paragraph, as exemplified in (8) below, where the new paragraph commences at clause (v).

(8) (i)   *Maip   ka-k   së //*   (ii)   *kaömp   ar   ë-ak //*
           Maip   village-**loc** go   food   cook do-**comp**
     (iii) *n-ak //*   (iv)   *ka   ur-a. ///*
            eat-**comp**   sleep   sleep-**3.pst**
     (v)   *Ka   ur-ak //*
           sleep   sleep-**comp**

(vi) *röökëër wal ë-ak // ...*
     early   rise do-**comp**
(i) Maip went to the village, (ii) cooked food, (iii) ate (it) (iv) and slept.
(v) When (he) had slept (vi) (he) rose early and ...

The item, *ka urak* in clause (v) of this example recapitulates, by lexical repetition of the verb *ka ura* '(Maip) slept', the final clause of the preceding sentence, and thus signals the opening of a new paragraph.

3. Ellipsis

Discussion of ellipsis in the literature reveals a wide range of views on the subject and, as de Beaugrande (1980: 155) notes, has "been marked by controversy". It is important, therefore, to define what is meant by ellipsis in this paper, and to determine what ellipsis is and what it is not. This will be done in 3.1, following which the subsequent section will discuss ways in which ellipsis enters into co-referential relations.

3.1 What is ellipsis?

The Macquarie Dictionary defines ellipsis as "the omission from a sentence of a word or words which would complete ... the construction". Halliday and Hasan (1976: 142) reflect this definition with the non-technical terms "something left unsaid" and "something understood". They are more specific in their definition when they state that "an elliptical item is one which, as it were, leaves specific structural slots to be filled from elsewhere" (1976: 143). Ellipsis, then, is characterised by the noticeable omission of element(s), and the resultant incompleteness of structure and the recoverability of the omitted element(s) from the context. Consider the following examples:

(9)   Look at those two Ø.
(10) I **had** chicken, Jenny Ø fish, and Robin Ø beef. (had)
(11) **Jack** fell down and Ø broke his crown. (Jack)
(12) Who'll **go to the shop for me**?
      – John Ø. (will go to the shop for you)

All are examples of ellipsis because in each case there is omission, structural incompleteness and recoverability from the context. In (9), *those two* is an elliptical nominal group. Its structure is incomplete because of the absence of Thing, which in this case is recoverable from the immediate situation and not the cotext. In (10), the verb *had* has been omitted from the second and third clauses. In (11), the Subject *Jack* has been omitted from the second clause. In (12), the response *John* is elliptical because the missing elements are recoverable from the preceding question.

It goes without saying that it is not possible to determine whether an expression is elliptical or not without a knowledge of the type of construction to which it belongs; different construction types may have different obligatory structural elements. Taken in isolation, a given expression may belong to one of a number of construction types. Thus (13) below is a question-answer sequence in which the response is a statement which is typically realised as declarative, having the structure here of Subject^Predicator^Complement.

(13) Who **killed Lincoln**?
      –Booth Ø (killed Lincoln)   (Dik 1968: 200)

In this example, the clause represented by *Booth* is elliptical because the obligatory elements Predicator and Complement have been omitted. Similarly in (14), in another question-answer sequence, *Booth* is elliptical because the structurally obligatory elements Subject and Finite have been omitted, leaving only Complement.

(14) What **is his name**?
      – Ø Booth. (His name is)

However, consider (15) below, where again *Booth* is the sole element overtly expressed in the clause.

(15) **Booth!**

Here *Booth* is a call of address to someone of that name. In terms of systemic functional grammar, it represents a minor vocative clause. As such there is no structural incompleteness. Since *Booth* already realises the only obligatory element in this clause type, the clause is not elliptical.

Structural incompleteness, then, is a necessary condition for ellipsis. However, for an expression to be elliptical it must not only be structurally incomplete, in addition the omitted element(s) must be recoverable from the environment, whether that be the context or cotext. Thus in (9) above, there would be a strong expectation that the omitted element would be recoverable from the immediate situation. Likewise, in (10) to (14) the omitted element(s) would be recoverable from the cotext. In (10) and (11) the elements are recovered from an earlier point in the same sentence, while in (12) to (14) the preceding cotext functions as a source for the recovery of the omitted elements.

In establishing what the necessary conditions for ellipsis are, the question arises as to what does not constitute ellipsis. We need to go back to the essential features of ellipsis just discussed. Is the expression structurally incomplete? Can omitted element(s) be retrieved from the context? Unless the answer to both of these questions is affirmative, then the expression is not elliptical. Thus *Booth!* in (15) above is not elliptical, because the expression is not structurally incomplete. Likewise in

(16) John: No one is to say another word.
      Jim: **But John–**
      John: No buts! That's enough!

But John is not elliptical, even though there is clear omission and it is structurally incomplete, because the missing elements are not recoverable here. They have been cut off by the interruption of the first speaker.

In concluding this section, several other observations can be made regarding what does not constitute ellipsis. Firstly, not everything that can be said in a given situation is ever said. The speaker chooses to include certain information and to exclude other information. Such omission does not constitute ellipsis (Halliday & Hasan 1976:143; Brown & Yule 1983: 193). So we cannot say of a statement like

(17) It rained.

that it is elliptical even though information about where, when, and the intensity with which it rained has not been included. Such information is not structurally required. So its absence does not make the expression elliptical. The same may be true, even when the missing information can be retrieved from context. For example in

(18) It rained **yesterday** and I got drenched.

it is clear that the time element *yesterday* in the first clause could also be inserted in the second clause. But that clause is not elliptical because there is no structural incompleteness.

Secondly, what Quirk et al. (1985) call "semantic omission" is not ellipsis. For example in

(19)   **Frankly**, he is very stupid. (Quirk et al. 1985: 884)

the modal Adjunct (see Halliday 1985) *frankly* expresses the speaker's comment on what he is saying. But although we can expand it to something like *I am speaking frankly when I say* ... or *If I may put it frankly I would tell you* ... there is no grammatical omission which can be supplied from the context.

Thirdly, the simple definition of ellipsis as something understood breaks down if it is taken to refer to implied information. As Hasan (1984b: 123) says:

> The recognition of ellipsis is not based on the perception of implied meanings for
> if this were the case every linguistic string produced would be elliptical, since
> implication is a constant condition of encoding.

She draws attention to the example:

(20)   Someone's at **the door**.

and notes that although the nominal group *the door* in such a clause would normally be understood as 'the front door', this does not allow us to treat *the door* as an elliptical expression because there is no structural requirement that every English nominal group must have the element Classifier in it.

3.2 Ellipsis and co-referentiality

Before discussing the use of ellipsis to establish co-referentiality, it is important to state quite clearly that it does not always do so. In fact, as we have already noted in section 1, the typical tie relation of ellipsis in English is not co-referentiality but co-classification. As we saw there, co-classification is the relation between nonidentical members of an identical class. Examples may be seen in (21) and (22).

(21)   Roslyn **bought** a bottle of coke and Linda Ø a milkshake.
(22)   I must have left my **pen** at home. Can I borrow yours Ø.

In (21), the relation between the ellipsis and its presupposed item represents a relation between different acts of buying. In (22), it represents a relation between different entities belonging to the same class, namely pens. Thus in both cases the relation is one of co-classification and not of co-referentiality.

Another use of ellipsis which is not co-referential occurs where ellipsis is interpreted exophorically from the situation (see Halliday & Hasan 1976). For example, when a customer in a fast food shop points to a tray of pies and says

(23)   I'll have one of those Ø please.

the ellipsis does not enter into any co-referential relation, since it receives its interpretation not from another linguistic item but from entities in the situation, namely certain pies.

While ellipsis has been described as typically entering into relations other than co-referentiality, there are certain types of uses where ellipsis is regularly co-referential in English. The most notable of these is Subject ellipsis. Indeed Hasan has recognised this in her description of co-referential or identity chains, which include ties created through Subject ellipsis (Hasan 1984a; 1985). A second, and lesser, contributor to co-referential ellipsis is Complement ellipsis, and very occasionally ellipsis of Thing in the nominal group will also be found to be co-referential. Examples of each may be seen in (24), (25) and (26).

(24)   **The lad** weeded the lawn, Ø watered the garden and then Ø collected his pay.
(25)   The fisherman pulled in Ø, and his companion untangled, **the fishing line.**
(26)   When we arrived home we saw **a car** sitting in the driveway. It was, in fact, Laurie's Ø.

In each of these examples the ellipsed item and its presupposed item have the same situational referent, and so are co-referential. In (24) the Subject ellipsis in the second and third clauses is co-referential with *the lad* in the first clause, in (25) the Complement ellipsis in the first clause is co-referential with *the fishing line* in the second clause, and in (26) the ellipsis of Thing in the second sentence is co-referential with *a car* in the first. Note too that ellipsis may be anaphoric, as in (24) and (26), or cataphoric, as in (25).

4.   Ellipsis through nominal elements in Weri

I now turn to ellipsis in Weri. Here ellipsis can be described in broadly similar terms to Halliday and Hasan's (1976) description for English. In

Weri ellipsis can occur in the sentence - where one or more whole clauses (its structural elements) are omitted; in the clause - where one or more (but not all) of its structurally obligatory elements are omitted; and in the nominal group – where the structurally obligatory element Thing is omitted and one of the other elements in the experiential structure (for example Qualifier or Epithet, etc.), conflates with Head.

However, it is in looking at ellipsis in Weri from another perspective that its important function in text can be seen – that of ellipsis of nominals, and in particular ellipsis of the MOOD elements Subject and Complement. I have already noted in 3.2 above that Subject ellipsis in particular and Complement ellipsis regularly enter into co-referential relations in English. In Weri they are typically co-referential and, in fact, together account for the large majority of all co-referential relations.

Three types of ellipsis of nominals may be identified: Subject ellipsis (SE), Complement ellipsis (CE) and ellipsis of Thing (TE) in the nominal group. All three satisfy the requirements for ellipsis defined earlier: that there is noticeable omission of elements, resultant structural incompleteness, and recoverability of the omitted elements from the context. The first two types, ie., the ellipsis of Subject and of Complement, are overwhelmingly more common and involve ellipsis of the whole nominal group. By contrast, the last type, ie., the ellipsis of Thing, is what Halliday and Hasan (1976) call nominal ellipsis. The first two, being ellipsis at the clause rank, differ from the last, which is ellipsis at the group rank. Nevertheless, they all have one thing in common. The ellipsis has to do with the nominal group. Either there is ellipsis of the whole nominal group or of part of it, so that we can say that they all represent ellipsis of nominals.

In my discussion of ellipsis in Weri, I will first describe ellipsis of Thing in the nominal group, which only occasionally establishes co-referentiality. This will be followed by the discussion of Subject ellipsis and Complement ellipsis, the two major contributors to co-referentiality in Weri.

4.1 Coreferentiality involving ellipsis in the nominal group

Halliday (1985: 302) points out that ellipsis of Thing in the nominal group is the type of ellipsis in which co-classification is most clearly seen. It signals another member of the same class rather than the same member as would be the case for co-referentiality. An example in English was given in (22) above. In Weri too, ellipsis of Thing in the nominal group typically establishes the relation of co-classification. An example may be seen in (27).

(27) *Pi itaangk-ën* // **muri** *narö* *utpet* *ë-ën* //
    he see–**ds** orange some.**cl** bad do-**ds**
    Ø *ompyau-rö* *pëën* *kër-ëëp-ök* *waul-a.*
    TE good-**pl.cl** only string.bag-**sg.cl-loc** put-**3.pst**
    He saw that some oranges were bad and put only the good (oranges) in the string bag.

Here the ellipsed element 'oranges' in the third clause does not refer to the same oranges as *muri* in the second clause.

However, occasionally ellipsis of Thing in the nominal group signals the same member and thus establishes the relation of co-referentiality, as for example in (28).

(28) *I* *pip-ët* *es* *nga ya-ë* *ma?*
    water that-**sg.cl** hot hard **act**-do **q**
    – *Won Ø* *ep-ët* *ëp* *ya-ë.*
    no, TE this-**sg.cl** cold **act**-do
    Is that water hot?
    – No, this (water) is cold.

In this example the ellipsis of Thing in the response is co-referential with *i* 'water' in the question.

4.2 Coreferentiality involving Subject ellipsis

One of the most productive environments for ellipsis in general lies in the informal interaction of dialogue, in question-answer and other rejoinder sequences (see Halliday and Hasan 1976: 207). However, in such sequences in English, Subject cannot normally be omitted alone, but must be omitted with some other element(s). Thus, in (29) the response is not acceptable.

(29) Where has **Laurie** gone?
    –* *Ø* Has gone to the beach.

But the responses to the same question in (29 i and ii), where more than the Subject element is omitted, are acceptable.

(29) i   Ø Ø Gone to the beach.
      ii   Ø Ø Ø To the beach.

In (29i), not only the Subject, but the whole Mood element Subject^Finite (*Laurie has*) has been omitted. Similarly in (29ii), not only has the Subject been omitted, but, as is more usually the case in the response to such a question, so too have the elements Subject^Finite^Predicator (*Laurie has gone*) been omitted.

In Weri, however, the Subject alone can be omitted in rejoinders. Consider (30) and (31).

(30) **Karong** *pol–öp*   *wisang ë-a*   *ma?*
      Karong pig-**sg.cl**   shoot   do–**3.pst**   **q**
      – *Won,*   *Ø*   *pol-öp*   *wisang na–ë–n*   *ë-a.*
         no   **SE**   pig-**sg.cl**   shoot   **neg-do–neg**   do–**3.pst**
      Did Karong shoot the pig?
      – No, (he) didn't shoot the pig.

(31) **Ni–m**   *koont–up*   *Mosupi*   *wë*   *koröp.*
      you.**sg–pos**   girl–**sg.cl**   Port.Moresby   be   probably
      – *Won,*   *Ø*   *Lae–t–ak*   *wë.*
         no   **SE**   Lae–**sg.cl–loc**   be
      Your daughter is probably in Port Moresby.
      – No, (she) is in Lae.

The Subject ellipsis in the rejoinder is co-referential in (30) with *Karong* and in (31) with *nim koontup* 'your daughter'.

While dialogue provides many examples of Subject ellipsis in Weri, it is in monologic discourse that the proliferation of Subject ellipsis can be seen. This is particularly true of such discourse which comprises sequences of one or more dependent clauses, each with a medial verb, plus an independent clause with a final verb. This type of construction, commonly known as a medial verb construction, was briefly described in 2.1. In it the specification of person, number and tense is marked only on the final, independent verb. A simple example may be seen in (32) below, in which the medial verb *ar ëak* 'cook' in the first clause is followed by the final verb *na* 'ate' in the second clause.

(32) **Öng-öp**   *kaömp*   *ar*   *ë-ak //*   *Ø*   *n-a.*
      woman-**sg.cl**   sweet potato   cook   do–**Comp**   **SE**   eat–**3.pst**
      The woman cooked sweet potato and (she) ate (it).

In this example, Subject ellipsis in the second clause presupposes and is co-referential with *öngöp* 'the woman' in the first.

A further feature of such constructions, which is of particular interest in this paper, is the highly attenuated constituent structure of the clause. It is not uncommon to find a string of clauses in Weri, each realised by a verb and at the most just one other element. Very often there is no overt Subject or Complement element at all. A typical example of this may be seen in (41) in section 5 below. In the examples in this section, however, I will be marking Subject ellipsis only, even though Complement ellipsis may also be present, since it is the question of Subject which we are addressing here. Thus in (32) above, Complement ellipsis is not marked in the second clause even though it occurs there. Similarly in (33) and (34) below, although Complement ellipsis occurs in a number of clauses it is not marked, except in the free translation where it is needed in order to maintain the naturalness of English. Complement ellipsis will be discussed separately in 4.3.

Example (32) is an extremely simple one. More frequently, this type of construction extends over a number of clauses, generating multiple Subject ellipses. Consider example (33) below, which is taken from an oral narrative text describing an encounter with a snake. The example consists of the final part of one sentence plus the first part of the following sentence. The first sentence has eight clauses, with medial verbs in the first seven and a final verb in the eighth. The second sentence has four clauses, each with a medial verb.

(33) ...// (i) **Moris**   *kakaati*   *ilë* //
                Maurice   inside   enter

     (ii) Ø   *öp–pel*   *të–ak* //
           SE   knife-**sg.cl** take.out-**comp**

     (iii) Ø   *w–ak* //
           SE   get-**comp**

     (iv) Ø   *orö* //
           SE   emerge

     (v)   Ø   *öp–pel*   *om*   *w–eë*//
           SE   knife-**sg.cl** just   hold-**dur**

     (vi) Ø   *wet*   *kaal*   *ë–ak* //
           SE   first   first   do-**comp**

     (vii) Ø   *pës–empel–ring*   *kepön–ö–ök*   *mö* //
           SE   stick-**sg.cl**-with   head-**sg.cl**-**loc**   hit

     (viii) Ø   *öngk*   *yanga–ak*   *olë–a.* ///
            SE down   ground-**loc** throw-**3.pst**

(ix)	Ø	Tomök	së //
	SE	outside	go
(x)	Ø	rangk	ngep	ë–ak //
	SE	top	press	do–**comp**
(xi)	Ø	öp	mö //
	SE	knife	hit
(xii)	Ø	wi	ulmë–ak //...
	SE	put	do.**3**–**comp**

...(i) Maurice went into the house, (ii) (he) took out the machete (iii) (he) got (it) (iv) and (he) came out (v) and (he) holding the machete, (vi)(he) first [lit. acted first] (vii) (he) hit (it) on the head with the stick (viii) and (he) threw (it) down on the ground. (ix) (He) went outside, (x) (he) trod on (it), (xi) (he) cut (it) with the machete (xii) and (he) left (it) and...

In this example, Subject ellipsis occurs in eleven successive clauses. The ellipsis thus creates an identity chain, the members of which are co-referential (see Hasan 1984a; 1985) so that each instance of Subject ellipsis successively links back through its predecessor to, and is co-referential with, the overt Subject *Moris* in the first clause. Co-referential chains are not necessarily restricted to one sentence, but may span sentence boundaries, as can be seen between clauses (viii) and (ix) in (33).

Moving forward in a text, each instance of Subject ellipsis is co-referential with its immediate predecessor, unless there is some indication otherwise. Change of Subject in a given clause is signalled by the presence of the different Subject marker -*Vn* on the verb of the preceding clause (see 2.1). No such signal is given in (33), so all twelve clauses have the same Subject and all eleven instances of Subject ellipsis are co-referential.

Where change of Subject is signalled there is no requirement that it be followed by overt Subject; the realisation of Subject is often covert, resulting in ellipsis. An example of continuing Subject ellipsis, even where there is a change of Subject, can be seen in (34) below. In all examples to this point, the ellipsis and the overt item which the ellipsed item presupposes have been highlighted in order to assist the reader. However in (34), where we are discussing multiple ellipsis belonging to more than one chain, highlighting the overt item clearly serves no useful purpose. Rather than assisting the reader, it is more likely to confuse. The practice will, therefore, be discontinued here, and in other similar examples, *viz.*, (39), (40) and (41).

(34) ...// (i) ne   o   tang–it–ak   is //
                I   up   steep–**sg.cl–loc** go.up
         (ii)   Ø   kora–kaim //
                SE   wait–**cont**
         (iii) Ø   o   kaalak së //
                SE   up   again   go
         (iv)   Ø   o–ol   koliil   pö–r–ek   së //
                SE   up–way direction   that–**sg.cl–loc** go
         (v)   Ø   kora–kaim //
                SE   wait–**cont**
         (vi)   Ø   wë–ën //
                SE   be–**ds**
         (vii) Ø   apr–a. ///
                SE   come.up–**3.pst**
         (viii) Ø   P–ël   ë–ën //
                SE   that–way   do–**ds**
         (ix)   Ø   koir–ak//
                SE   find–**comp**
         (x)   Ø   im //
                SE   go
         (xi)   Ø   o   kan   kou–r–ak   is // ...
                SE   up   path dark–**sg.cl–loc** go.up

...(i) I went up the steep slope (ii) (I) waited, (iii) and (I) went on again, (iv)
and (I) went up the other side (v) (I) waited (vi) and (I) remained (vii) and
(they) came up. (viii)Then [lit. (they) did that and] (ix) (I) met (them) (x) and
(we) went on (xi) and (we) went up the track and...

In this example there is Subject ellipsis in ten successive clauses even though
change of Subject in the following clause is signalled twice, by means of the
different Subject verb suffix -ën in clauses (vi) and (viii). There are two main
co-referential chains, each maintained solely by Subject ellipsis. The first
one commences with ne 'I' in clause (i) and extends through to and including
the Subject ellipsis in clause (vi). It is broken after clause (vi) by the different Subject marker -ën on the verb of that clause, indicating change of
Subject for clause (vii). The ne chain is reestablished without overt Subject
selection in clause (ix), following the second use of the different Subject
suffix -ën on the verb of the preceding clause.

The second co-referential chain takes up in this example with the Subject ellipsis of clause (vii) Ø *apra* '(they) came up'. However, this Subject ellipsis presupposes *pit* 'they' outside the example eight clauses earlier, and finds its ultimate interpretative source (see Hasan 1984a) in the explicit identification of a particular man and his wife a further four clauses earlier in the cotext and outside this example. As already stated the chain resumes in this example without any overt Subject in clause (vii), following the signal of different Subject suffix *-ën* in the preceding clause, and extends to clause (viii).

In clause (x) chain conjunction (see Hasan 1984a) takes place with the conjunction of the two chains to form a chain which is a composite of the two. No different Subject marker is required, because this is seen as an expansion of the existing Subject. The composite chain reaches from clause

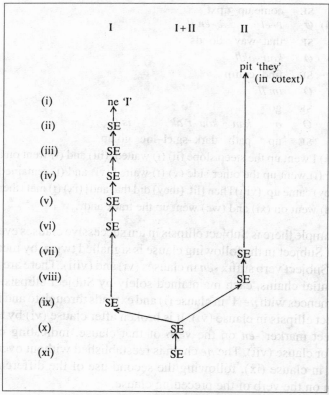

Figure 1: Co-referential chains in (34)

(x) to (xi). Figure 1, adapted from Hasan (1984a:196), displays the co-referential chains established by Subject ellipsis in (34). The figure takes no account of Complement ellipsis in clause (ix). Clause numbers are indicated by the lower case Roman numerals (i)-(xi) down the left side and the chains are identified by the upper case numerals across the top: I for the narrator, II for the man and his wife, and (I+II) for a combination of the two.

4.3 Co-referentiality involving Complement ellipsis

Complement ellipsis in Weri follows the same pattern as Subject ellipsis, occurring in two main contexts, rejoinder sequences and sequences of medial verb(s) and final verb. In rejoinder sequences, Complement ellipsis, like Subject ellipsis, can occur in question–answer sequences of both the yes/no and WH- type, and also in rejoinders to statements. An example of each can be seen below in (35) (36) and (37) respectively.

(35)   *Ni*   ***ne–m yokot-up–ön***   *iten-aup*   *ma?*
     you-**sg**   I-**pos**   boy-**sg.cl–rec**   see-**sg.pst q**
     –Won,   *ne*   *Ø*   *it–na–angk–ën.*
     no   I   CE   see-**neg**–see–**neg**
     Did you see my son?
     –No, I didn't see (him).

(36)   *Tal–ëp*   ***pep***   *ep–wer*   *retëng*   *ë–a?*
     who-**sg.cl**   paper   this-**sg.cl**   write   do-**3.pst**
     –Ne   *Ø*   *retëng*   *ë–aut.*
     I   CE   write   do-**pst**
     Who wrote this letter?
     –I wrote (it.)

(37)   *Ni-m*   *pol-öp*   ***ne–m***   ***ëm–ö***   *utpet wes-a.*
     you.**sg-pos**   pig-**sg.cl**   I-**pos**   fence-**sc.cl**   bad   make-**3.pst**
     –Won,   *pi*   *Ø*   *utpet ne–was–ën*   *ë–a..*
     no   it   CE   bad   **neg**–make–**neg**   do-**3.pst**
     Your pig damaged my fence.
     –No, it didn't damage (it).

Thus, in (35) the Complement ellipsis is co-referential with *nem yokotupön* 'my son', in (36) it is co-referential with *pep epwer* 'this letter', and in (37) it is co-referential with *nem ëmö* 'my fence'.

However, as in the case of Subject ellipsis, co-referentiality established by Complement ellipsis most frequently occurs in sequences of medial verb(s) and final verb. A simple example occurs in (38).

(38) *Tisa-ap*   *pi-m*   *runga-ap*   **pep-ewer**   *ma-ngk-ën//*
      teacher-**sg.cl** he-**pos** child-**sg.cl** paper-**sg.cl**   **3**-give-**ds**
      pi Ø   *sangk*   *kel-a.*
      he **CE**   read   read-**3.pst**
      The teacher gave his student the book and he read (it).

Here Complement ellipsis in the second clause is co-referential with *pepewer* 'the book' in the first.

Again, as with Subject ellipsis, Complement ellipsis is not limited to simple two clause examples such as (38). More often a number of instances of Complement ellipsis occurs across a series of clauses, establishing a co-referential chain. An example of this can be seen in (39), from a text about a flat battery. This example, like most natural text material, contains instances not only of Complement ellipsis but also of Subject ellipsis. However, for ease of description Complement ellipsis alone will be marked here and in (40), in both the Weri text and the literal translation . However, in the free translation of (39) and (40) some, but not all, instances of Subject ellipsis are expanded in order to maintain the naturalness of English.

(39) (i)   *Pateri–it*   *utpet*   *ë–ën //*   (ii) *Ø*   *yokot–aar ma–ngk–ën//*
             battery–**sg.cl** bad   do–**ds**   **CE** boy–**dl.cl** **3**–give–**ds**
      (iii) *Ø*   *w–ak //*   (iv) *Karain*   *ka–k*   *së //*
             CE get–**comp**   Garaina   village–**loc** go
      (v)   *Ø*   *ompyaö*   *wes–ak //*   (vi) *Ø*   *w–ak //*
             CE good   make–**comp**   **CE** get–**comp**
      (vii) *wais //*   (viii) *Ø*   *Ø*   *ma–ngk–ën //*
             come   **CE** **CE** **3**–give–**ds**
      (ix)   *Ø*   *ök*   *ë–ak //*
             CE try   do–**comp**
      (x)   *Ø itaangk–ën //*   (xi) *pangk*   *na–ë–n.*
             CE see–**ds**   correct   **neg**–do–**neg**

      (i) The battery was flat (ii) and (he) [=Maurice] gave (it) to the two boys (iii) and (they) got (it) (iv) and went to Garaina, (v) (they) charged (it) (vi) and got (it) (vii) and (they) came (viii) and gave (it) (to him) (ix) and (he) tested (it) (x) and (he) saw (it) (xi) but (it) was no good.

In (39) Complement ellipses in clauses (ii), (iii), (v), (vi), (viii), (ix) and (x) are co-referential with *pateriit* 'the battery' in clause (i). In addition, there is also co-referentiality between a second instance of Complement ellipsis in clause (viii) and Subject ellipsis in clause (ii).

Co-referential chains involving Complement ellipsis, as is also true for Subject ellipsis, are not confined to within a sentence, but can reach across sentence boundaries, as for example in (33), reproduced below in part as (40) with Complement ellipsis marked here.

(40) ...// (i) Ø   *pës–empel–ring*   *kepön–ö–ök*   *mö* //
              CE   stick–**sg.cl**–with   head–**sg.cl**–**loc**   hit
    (ii) Ø   *öngk*   *yanga–ak*   *olë-a.* ///   (iii) *Tomök së* //
         CE   down   ground–**loc**   throw–**3.pst**   outside go
    (iv) Ø   *rangk*   *ngep*   *ë–ak* //   (v) Ø   *öp*   *mö* //...
         CE   top   press   do–**comp**   CE   knife   hit

...(i) (he) hit (the snake) on the head with the stick (ii) and threw (it) down onto the ground. (iii) (He) went outside, (iv) (he) trod on (it) (v) and (he) cut (it) with the machete and ...

Thus the Complement ellipses in clauses (i) and (ii) in the first sentence are co-referential with the Complement ellipses in clauses (iv) and (v) in the second sentence and are ultimately interpreted by reference to 'a snake', an item explicitly mentioned in the cotext outside this example and nine clauses earlier than the clause numbered here as (i).

5. Conclusion

In presenting the account of co-referential use of Subject and Complement ellipsis in Weri, I have focused mainly on the density of these devices. If the examples above are taken as typical, it is obvious that these two types of ellipsis are used very extensively in the language. However, Weri is not alone in this. Similar patterns have been reported in languages as widely scattered as Mangga Buang, an Austronesian language of Papua New Guinea (Healey 1988), Urdu (Hasan 1984b) and Italian (Piccioli 1988). And based on a general knowledge of Papuan languages, it would be safe to say that this pattern of extensive Subject and Complement ellipsis would be found amongst many more of them.

In many Weri texts, examples of co-referential Subject and Complement ellipsis are found in almost every clause. For example in (33), Subject ellipsis occurs in eleven successive clauses and in (34), in ten successive clauses. Similarly in (39), Complement ellipsis occurs eight times in eleven clauses, including twice in clause (viii), and in (40), four times in five clauses.

In addition, it is worth noting that such chains of Subject and/or Complement ellipsis extend across sentence boundaries, as can be seen in (33), (34) and (40). Admittedly all the above examples were chosen to highlight the frequency and extent of Subject ellipsis and Complement ellipsis in Weri, but they were taken from natural texts, and many similar examples could have been used.

To avoid any appearance of exaggeration let me briefly mention the quantitative results obtained from the analysis of three naturally occurring complete texts. Each of these texts represents a distinct genre, and the three were analysed in detail in a separate study to examine patterns of cohesion in Weri (Boxwell 1990). When the occurrence of co-referential ellipsis in these three texts was compared with the occurrences of other implicit devices such as pronouns and demonstratives, which too have the potential of being used co-referentially, the former – ie., ellipsis – was highly favoured. The figures are displayed in Table 1, which shows 90.4% of all clauses had co-referential ellipsis. In addition, co-referential ellipsis accounted for 63.7%

Table 1: Co-referential items in texts 1-3

Genre	Text 1 Letter: mixed	Text 2 Narrative	Text 3 Hortatory
Pronouns	15	18	20
Demonstrative (total)	10	20	14
simple items	2	7	2
extended items	8	13	12
Ellipsis (total)	24	110	36
SE	16	96	25
CE	8	14	10
Thing			1
Total coreferential items	49	148	70
No. of clauses	30	120	38

of the entire co-referential implicit devices for the three texts put together. In other words, over the three texts, co-referential ellipsis occurs almost twice as often as all the other implicit devices, such as pronouns and demonstratives, put together.

Obviously in a presentation of this scope, it is impossible to reproduce all three texts and their analyses. However, let me conclude this discussion with one example already used to demonstrate Complement ellipsis. I refer to (39), which was used earlier to demonstrate the density of Complement ellipsis in Weri. This same example will be reproduced below as (41) in order to highlight the extensive use of both Subject and Complement ellipsis.

(41) (i) *Pateri–it utpet ë–ën //*
   battery–**sg.cl** bad do–**ds**

 (ii) Ø Ø *yokot–aar ma–ngk–ën //* (iii) Ø Ø *w–ak //*
   SE CE boy–**dl.cl** **3**–give–**ds**   SE CE get–**comp**

 (iv) Ø *Karain ka–k së //*
   SE Garaina village–**loc** go

 (v) Ø Ø *ompyaö wes–ak //* (vi) Ø Ø *w–ak //*
   SE CE good make-**comp** SE CE get–**comp**

 (vii) Ø *wais //* (viii) Ø Ø Ø *ma–ngk–ën //*
   SE come   SE CE CE **3**–give–**ds**

 (ix) Ø Ø *ök ë–ak //* (x) Ø Ø *itaangk–ën //*
   SE CE try do–**comp** SE CE see–**ds**

 (xi) Ø *pangk na–ë–n.*
   SE correct **neg**–do–**neg**

(i) The battery was flat (ii) and (he) gave (it) to the two boys (iii) and (they) got (it) (iv) and (they) went to Garaina, (v) (they) charged (it) (vi) and (they) got (it) (vii) and (they) came (viii) and (they) gave (it) (to him) (ix) and (he) tested (it) (x) and (he) saw (it) (xi) but (it) was no good.

Within these 11 clauses, there is a total of eighteen instances of ellipsis in all; ten of these are instances of Subject ellipsis and eight of Complement ellipsis; moreover, three such ellipses occur in just one clause *(viz.,* viii). Yet this is a natural text , not one that was specifically designed to make the linguist's point, and it is notable that there is no loss of meaning. Far from blocking the exchange of meaning as we might expect from a simplistic literal coding point of view, ellipsis actually facilitates the exchange of meaning. In other words *"nothing" makes sense in Weri.*

Abbreviations

act	actual aspect	pl	plural
CE	Complement ellipsis	pos	possessive
cl	noun classificatory suffix	pst	past tense
comp	completed action	q	question
cont	continuous action	Rec	Recipient
des	desiderative	SE	Subject ellipsis
ds	different subject marker	sg	singular
dur	durative	TE	Thing ellipsis
fut	future tense	v	vowel
loc	locative	3	third person
neg	negative		

Symbols

.	links units of multiword or multifunction gloss
Ø	ellipsis
-	morpheme break
//	clause boundary in sentence
///	sentence boundary in paragraph
[ ]	phonetic script; author's comment
^	concatenation
*	ungrammatical
Subscript₁ ... subscript₁	identity of referents
Subscript₁ ... subscript₂	nonidentity of referents

Orthography

The phonetics symbols for the Weri orthography used throughout this paper are as follows (for more details see Boxwell & Boxwell 1966): p [p], t [t], k [k], s [s], m [m], n [n], ng [ŋ], l [l], r [l̃], w [w], y [y], i [i], ë [ɪ], e [ɛ], a [a], o [o], ö [ʋ], u [u].

References

de Beaugrande, Robert. 1980. *Text, Discourse and Process*. London: Longman

de Beaugrande, Robert and Wolfgang Dressler. 1981. *Introduction to Text Linguistics*. London: Longman

Berry, Margaret. 1975. *An Introduction to Systemic Linguistics*. Vol. 1. London and Sydney: Batsford

Boxwell, Helen and Maurice Boxwell. 1966. Weri phonemes. *Pacific Linguistics* A7, 77-93.

Boxwell, Maurice. 1978. *Weri Clauses*. Unpublished manuscript. Summer Institute of Linguistics, Ukarumpa, Papua New Guinea.

Boxwell, Maurice. 1990. *Co-referentiality through Nominal Elements in Weri*. Dissertation submitted in requirement of Ph.D. Macquarie University.

Brown, Gillian and George Yule. 1983. *Discourse Analysis*. Cambridge: Cambridge University Press.

Dik, Simon C. 1968. *Coordination: Its implications for the theory of general linguistics*. Amsterdam: North–Holland.

Dutton, T. E. 1975. South-Eastern Trans-New Guinea Phylum languages. Wurm (ed.) 1975, 613-664.

Foley, William A. 1986. *The Papuan Languages of New Guinea*. Cambridge: Cambridge University Press.

Grimes, Joseph E. 1975. *The Thread of Discourse*. The Hague: Mouton.

Haiman, John. 1976. Presuppositions in Hua. *Chicago Linguistic Society* 12, 258-270.

Halliday, M.A.K. 1977. Text as semantic choice in social contexts. *Grammars and Descriptions*, edited by Teun A. van Dijk and Janos S. Petöfi. Berlin: de Gruyter.

Halliday, M.A.K. 1978. *Language as Social Semiotic*. Baltimore: University Park Press.

Halliday, M.A.K. 1985. *An Introduction to Functional Grammar*. London: Edward Arnold.

Halliday, M.A.K. and Ruqaiya Hasan. 1976. *Cohesion in English*. London: Longman.

Halliday, M.A.K. and Ruqaiya Hasan. 1985. *Language, Context and Text: Aspects of language in a social–semiotic perceptive*. Geelong, Vic: Deakin University Press. (Re-issued Oxford: Oxford University Press 1989).

Hasan, Ruqaiya. 1984a. Coherence and cohesive harmony. *Understanding Reading Comprehension*, edited by James Flood, 181-219. Newark, Delaware: International Reading Association Press.

Hasan, Ruqaiya. 1984b. Ways of saying: ways of meaning. *The Semiotics of Culture and Language. Volume 1: Language as social semiotic*, edited by Robin P. Fawcett, M.A.K. Halliday, Sydney M. Lamb and Adam Makkai, 105-162. Dover: Francis Pinter.

Hasan, Ruqaiya. 1985. The texture of a text. Halliday and Hasan 1985, 70-96.

Healey, Joan. 1988. *Coreference in Mangga Buang*. Dissertation submitted in requirement of M.A. Honours. Macquarie University.

Huddleston, Rodney. 1978. On classifying anaphoric relations. *Lingua* 45, 333-345.

Huddleston, Rodney. 1984. *Introduction to the Grammar of English*. Cambridge: Cambridge University Press.

Longacre, R. 1972. *Hierarchy and Universality of Discourse Constituents in New Guinea Languages: Discussion*. Washington D.C.: Georgetown University Press.

Lyons, John. 1977. *Semantics*. Vol. 1. Cambridge: Cambridge University Press.

McCarthy, Joy. 1965. Clause chaining in Kanite. *Anthropological Linguistics* 7, 59-70.

The Macquarie Dictionary, 2nd revised edn. 1987. Arthur Delbridge (ed.). Sydney: The Macquarie Library.

Piccioli, Maria Theresa. 1988. S-ellipsis in Italian: a systemic interpretation. *Rassegna Italiana di Linguistica Applicata* 2, 43-54.

Quirk, R., S. Greenbaum, G. Leech and J. Svartvik. 1985. *A Comprehensive Grammar of the English Language*. London: Longman.

Reesink, G. 1977. *Structures and their Functions in Usan*. Amsterdam: John Benjamins.

Scott, Graham. 1978. *The Fore Language of Papua New Guinea*. Pacific Linguistics B47.

Scott, Graham. 1983. Discourse cohesion in a highland language of P.N.G. *Language and Linguistics in Melanesia* 14, 150-174.

Wurm, S.A. (ed) 1975. *Papuan Languages and the New Guinea Linguistic Scene*. Pacific Linguistics c38.

Wurm, S.A. 1982. *Papuan Languages of Oceania*. Tübingen: Gunter Narr Verlag.

Wurm, S.A., D.C. Laycock, and C.L. Voorhoeve. 1975. General Papuan characteristics. Wurm (ed.) 1975, 171-189.

Wurm, S.A., C.L. Voorhoeve and K. McElhanon. 1975. The Trans-New Guinea Phylum in general. Wurm (ed.) 1975, 299-322.

5

Subjectlessness and Honorifics in Japanese:
A Case of Textual Construal*

Motoko Hori
Tokai Women's College

I. Introduction

1.1 General approaches to honorifics in Japanese linguistics

There has been a long continuing controversy among Japanese scholars over
the description of honorifics. The two most influential theories may be those
of Yamada (1924) and Tokieda (1941), each representing a different view.
While Tokieda thinks of honorifics as a kind of lexical phenomenon, Yamada finds syntactic features significant for their description. Still others place
honorifics outside the discussion of grammar altogether (Watanabe 1971).
A more recent trend is to expand the coverage of honorifics from the original
'keigo' – literally meaning 'language of respect' – to *'taigu hyogen'*, that is
to say, 'expressions of how to change one's language and attitude according
to the interactant and situation'. This latter includes not only deferential
expressions but also derogatory and/or ordinary ones, and sometimes even
nonverbal behaviour (Komatsu 1963; Miyaji 1971; Minami 1974, 1977;
Oishi 1983). This approach seems to have been influenced to a certain extent
by politeness theory in sociolinguistics.

So far as the grammatical description of honorifics is concerned, it is
notable that the ancient European concept of 'person' was not recognised in
Japanese studies, much less was it employed in the description of honorifics,
until the late 19th century when Japan first experienced the influence of the

* This paper was originally presented at the 19th International Systemic Functional Congress,
Macquarie University, Sydney, July 13-18, 1992. I am thankful for the valuable comments
on its revised version by the anonymous referees and the editors.

Western world. To Yamada (1924) is attributed the suggestion that there exists a relation between the category of 'person' in the subject and honorifics in the verb which is somewhat similar to the subject-verb agreement in Western languages. His perspective was developed by several grammarians such as Ishisaka, Kindaichi, and Tsujimura with some changes (Kitahara 1978; Tsujimura 1992: 9-30). With a view to combining 'person' and honorifics, Ishisaka (1951) proposed the new terms 'self-referent, other-referent, and general-referent honorifics,' to replace the traditional terms 'humbling, respectful, and polite honorifics.'

Tsujimura (1977) reviewed the grammatical expression of honorifics in a number of languages such as Korean, Tibetan, and Javanese. According to him, Javanese simply changes vowels and/or consonants of ordinary terms to make them function as honorific terms, while in spite of its syntactic similarity to Japanese, Korean does not have prefixes similar to the Japanese ones, like *gyo, go, on, o* and *mi*. (See Notes 1 and 9.) He speculates that Tibetan may be most similar to Japanese, since like the latter, it has honorific prefixes which attach to nouns and honorific auxiliaries which attach to verbs.

Apart from traditional grammarians, some scholars, following Western linguistic theories recognise the grammatical relation between the subject and its honorific verb but, in doing so, they take it for granted that, like Western languages, every Japanese sentence must have a subject and that the honorific verbs are 'triggered' by the choice of that subject. Typically the examples they cite to support this view turn out to be artificially constructed ones, which, in the words of Lyons (1981: 165), might be described as "the de-contextualized, abstract, units of language system ... [which MH] have no psychological validity at all". Such scholars seldom examine natural conversations (Kuno 1973a, 1973b; Harada 1975; Inoue 1989; Miyagawa 1989; Tonoike 1991, etc.).

There are also sociolinguistic approaches, where the honorifics are described mainly from the point of view of male/female differences and/or politeness theory. Scholars following these approaches are usually not concerned with analysing the grammatical aspects of honorifics (Ide 1982, 1988, Ide and McGloin 1991; Loveday 1986a, 1986b; Matsumoto, 1988; Coulmas 1992; Shibamoto 1990; Smith 1992, etc.). In fact, I myself took this position up to quite recently (Ide et al. 1984, 1985, and 1986), though my interests did tend to turn to the morphological analysis of honorifics as well (Hori 1986,

1988a, 1988b, 1988c, and 1989). Continued engagement with these issues has convinced me that Japanese honorifics represent a qualitatively different phenomenon[1] as compared to politeness in English. Thus I am in agreement with Levinson (1983: 92) that honorific concord should be treated with some reference to "the socially deictic values of particular morphemes" because pervasive patterns of "honorific concord can... become an intricate aspect of morphology". This I believe is the position in Japanese.

The treatment of honorifics as social deixis is exemplified in Wetzel (1985) and Tokunaga (1992), both of whom analyse honorifics from a sociological viewpoint. Wetzel regards verbs of giving and receiving when used in the expression of honorifics as a manifestation of Levinson's 'social deixis'. She treats the concept of social grouping, that is, ingroup vs. outgroup, as the critical factor underlying such usage. Accepting the concept of ingroup and outgroup (*uchi* and *soto*, respectively) as basic in interpreting utterances in the Japanese language, Tokunaga in his work also introduces the notion of 'control' as underlying some of the typical honorific auxiliaries, *naru* (as realized in the form of *o-* ... *ni-naru*) and *rare*. (See examples and discussions in Dialogues 3 and 5 below). My own position is close to these scholars. Thus Hori (1989) presents a diagram of honorific verb formation incorporating the concept of *uchi/soto* as the crucial regulator of the overt appearance of honorifics on the surface level of discourse.

Studies such as these have provided rich insights into the nature of honorifics in the Japanese language. In this paper, I hope to make a small contribution to this growing literature, by attempting to relate Japanese honorific expressions to the problem of subject in Japanese. The crucial question is whether subject should be treated as a necessary element in the structure of all Japanese clauses. In my view the answer to this question is

---

1. Concerning Korean politeness and honorifics, Jung (1991) recommends that politeness and deference (honorifics) should be treated as separate concepts. In support, he quotes Hwang (1990: 53-54) as claiming that "politeness may be identified with 'sentiments', a matter of psychology, and honorifics with 'conventional norms', a matter of social code". Jung also refers to Sohn's argument (1986: 412) that honorifics are based on a closed, language-specific system consisting of a limited set of structural and lexical elements, while politeness is based largely on universal pragmatics and can be traced to an open-ended pattern of language that is applicable in principle, to any speech participants regardless of their age, sex, kinship or social status. These definitions of honorifics and politeness in Korean can be applied to Japanese to a large extent.

closely related to the function of the honorifics. Further, it is futile to attempt an answer without clarifying the concept of subject. Accordingly, in subsection 1.2, I will present a brief overview of approaches to this concept. I will argue specifically against the position, which seems to have become a rigid preoccupation of modern linguistics that human language has a universal grammar which is entirely independent of its cultural context. I believe, with Halliday, that language as code bears a systematic relation to the culture in which it is embedded.

> Just as each text has its environment, the 'context of situation' in Malinowski's terms, so the language system has its environment, Malinowski's 'context of culture'. The context of culture determines the nature of the code. As a language is manifested through its texts, a culture is manifested through its situations; so by attending to text-in-situation a child construes the code, and by using the code to interpret text he construes the culture. Thus for the individual, the code engenders the culture; and this gives a powerful inertia to the transmission process. (1985: xxxii)

However, placing the code of language in its context of culture inevitably introduces a functional perspective. A good deal of recent work on Japanese subject derives from recent views in formal linguistics on subject in English. In my opinion, these approaches fail to reveal the essence of the category subject. I shall, therefore, adopt a functional approach to the conceptualisation of both subject and honorifics. Accordingly, in subsection 2.1, I shall briefly draw attention to Halliday's functional treatment of the same concept in the context of English. Using in essence the sorts of argument that Halliday uses for postulating the element subject as essential to the description of mood choices in English, I will argue, in section 3, that the concept of subject in Japanese is fundamentally different from that of subject in English, that subjectlessness in clauses is the default condition, rather than an exception, and that the absence of overt subject in Japanese bears a logical relation to the prevalent use of honorifics. I will attempt to demonstrate these points, in the various subsections of section 4, through a close examination of several examples of clauses with and without subject; these examples are taken from naturally occurring dialogues which form part of the data collected by Ide and other researchers, including myself (Ide et al. 1984) to investigate the use of honorifics by women in contemporary Japanese. By interpreting 'text-in-context', I will attempt to construe the nature of Japanese subject and its relation to Japanese honorifics.

1.2 The subject in Japanese

In traditional literature on Japanese studies, it is very rare to find a chapter, even a small section, devoted to subject alone. The term, *shugo*, meaning 'subject', almost never appears in tables of contents. Linguists discussing the problem of subject, always use the term *shukaku*, meaning 'subjective or nominative case' in connection with the case marking particles *wa* and *ga*. That is to say, because the nouns and pronouns bear no case markers, the employment of a case marking particle elsewhere is indispensable no matter what function a particular NP is going to have.

It is actually impossible to assign an NP the function of 'subject' or 'object' if it is not followed by a particle. Therefore, the discussion of subject should inevitably rest on the discussion of *ga* and *wa*, markers of subject and theme respectively. The tendency to pay very little attention to subject is also obvious in the discussion of honorifics. Thus most chapters are devoted to the description and categorisation of honorifics in the verbs and auxiliaries; however, nouns and pronouns are rarely touched upon and their nominative functions are seldom discussed. The fact of the matter is that overt subject is a rarity in the Japanese clause, while the verbs and the auxiliaries are quite unavoidable: the fact that subject is seldom discussed in traditional literature is witness to its peripheral nature.

According to Morino (1971) the absence of subject in the Japanese clause can be traced back to a distant history of the language. As early as 9th to 12th century, in the Heian Period, speakers avoided referring to a person by his/her real name, when describing their action. To refer directly by name to a person could be interpreted as expressing a derogatory attitude to them. This practice could conceivably be related to similar conventions in other Asian countries which too avoid calling and referring to people by their real names. For example, Errington (1988: 192-193), reporting on honorific speech in Javanese, points out that when the Javanese want to speak deferentially they avoid "overtly direct reference" thus marking that person "as object of felt deference." Hattori (1959: 261-262) draws attention to some Altaic languages, like Turkish, Mongolic, and Tungus, where an independent clause might be without subject, consisting of the predicate alone, though he does not comment on honorifics in relation to such subjectless phenomena.

If referring to persons by their name was problematic, pronouns were

no solution to the problem either: pronouns could not be used freely as
subject in ancient Japanese. This was because every pronoun conveyed some
specific interpersonal attitude. (See Note 4). Indeed, Morino (1971) main-
tains that there were almost no neutral pronouns such that they could be used
as free of contextual constraints. As for the particles, *no* and *ga*, these were
used as subject markers, but there was strict restriction on their use. It would
appear from Morino's account that *no* usually followed common nouns and
personal pronouns which were derived from locatives (such as *koko, soko*,
literally meaning, 'here', 'there', but also functioning as pronominals, 'I',
'you', respectively), while *ga* followed more intensified personal pronouns
(such as *wa, maro*, both meaning 'I'). They often had some derogatory
meaning, and this is how *ga* itself came to bear a similar derogatory connotation. Morino relates an anecdote about a man named Sata, who was furious
on hearing a woman say *"Sata ga ... "* (Sata did...), first, because his real
name was pronounced by a woman, perhaps of lower status, and then this
insult was further compounded by the derogatory *ga* following his real
name!

Among modern Japanese linguists, Mikami (1960) is perhaps the one
best known as an advocate for limiting or even abolishing the use of the term
'subject' in the grammar of Japanese. He observes that theme, overtly
signalled on the surface by the particle *wa* has control of the whole clause,
extending its influence to the end of the clause, while subject, followed by
ga does not exert its control over its direct verb. It is Mikami's position that
from this point of view, subject expressed by NP-*ga*, is no more essential to
the structure of the clause than the object, NP-*o*, or the locative noun phrase,
NP-*ni*. Mikami goes on to suggest that the natural word order in a Japanese
clause is that where the locative, NP-*ni*, precedes the subject, NP-*ga*, and
cites in support of his view the results of a survey made by the National
Institute of the Japanese Language according to which the locative followed
by subject construction (NP-*ni* ... NP-*ga* ...) appeared 344 times while the
subject followed by locative construction (NP-*ga* ... NP-*ni* ...) appeared only
in 95 instances (Mikami 1960: 260).

Mikami's proposal has found favour with some linguists. For example,
Kiyose (1989: 23-24, 38-40) raises strong doubts about the subject as an
indispensable entity in a clause; he points out that *ga* marks the subject in
written texts only, being usually omitted in spoken contexts. He identifies
this 'zero morph' as the original nominative case in the history of Japanese,

and taking the theme-rheme structure as basic to Japanese, he rejects the relatively recent label 'double/multiple nominative structure,' which is the standardised term for 'NP-*ga* ... NP-*ga* ...' construction in the formal generative approaches (Kuno 1973a: 71-78; Inoue 1989; Shibatani 1990: 293-96). However, it would be wrong to suggest that the proposal to abolish the use of the term *shugo* (subject) has met with unanimous support; this much Mikami himself admits. Thus several objections have been raised by Shibatani (1978b: 178-220)[2]. (See also his more recent discussion of subject (1990: 257-306), which, however, does not directly refer to Mikami's position).

Nitta (1991: 13-15), considering the subject from a functional viewpoint, brings a somewhat different perspective to the discussion. He regards language as an activity, a means of communication, and its structures as reflecting its functions, taking text and context into consideration. Thus for Nitta, declarative clauses are divided into two classes, descriptive and judgmental: the former describes the ongoing event or the phenomenon the speaker is experiencing at the time of speaking; the latter denotes the speaker's judgment about something. According to Nitta, a descriptive clause has no theme and the whole clause consists of new information with NP-*ga* as the subject. This construction with nominative *ga* covers all objective cases such as the description of natural phenomena, story telling, news reporting, speaker's own physical conditions, and academic writings (Nitta 1991: 123-34). Once the particle *wa* is attached to a noun phrase, the whole clause becomes judgmental; the speakers/writers of such clauses will be heard as expressing judgment concerning the NP which precedes *wa*. By contrast, a descriptive clause with NP-*ga* does not require such a judgmental interpretation (Nitta 1991: 116-17).

These studies suggest that, subject in Japanese is not quite as indispensable, not quite as central to the structure of the clause as the element with the same name is in English. However, most publications on the subject, particularly those in English using the framework of formal generative grammars, insist on describing Japanese as if subject is an indispensable entity in a Japanese clause as well. Let me refer here specifically to just two well-known scholars – Kuno and Shibatani. In the introduction to his voluminous

---

2. According to Shibatani some parts of his argument in (1978b) are based on Shibatani (1977 and 1978a), written in English.

book, Kuno (1973a) devotes one section to ellipsis, where he mainly discusses pronoun deletion in isolated clauses, concluding with a plea for
"further studies" because "It is not clear at present when subjects, objects,
and other elements of sentences can be deleted and when they must not be
deleted" (Kuno 1973a: 18).

Shibatani takes a broader approach than Kuno. He has more recently
(Shibatani 1990: 360-65) focused on the description of pronoun ellipsis, as
an aspect of 'pro-drop' phenomena[3], where he uses terms such as [e], PRO,
PROarb, and pro, each denoting a different kind of pronoun ellipsis. Although
Shibatani seems to be examining pro-drop phenomena from a functional
point of view, discussing meteorological expressions, cookery recipes,
speaker hearer relations, and honorifics, the main focus of his analysis are
single clauses, discussed in isolation from texts. Quoting other linguists'
observations that "the role of the honorific system [is] a compensatory
mechanism for the recovery of elliptical elements," Shibatani (1990: 364)
seems inclined to see a systematic grammatical relationship between subject
and honorifics in Japanese. He points out that "the honorific endings
indicate to a large extent whether the action is ascribed to the speaker or the
hearer or a third person." So Shibatani may be taken as treating the honorifics as a mechanism for avoiding direct reference to a person, suggesting that
this might be an "extreme of defocusing mechanisms" similar to the plural-
isation of pronouns in referring with deference to a singular person, which
is observed in some of the Western languages.

The above will serve as a brief summary of the various observations on
the grammatical status and analysis of subject in Japanese. Once again I
would dissociate myself from the view that subjectless constructions in
Japanese are the result of subject deletion or a manifestation of the pro-drop
phenomena. I believe that a clause without subject is a self-supporting

3. In his critical comment on universal features in language, Comrie (1989: 54) gives an
example in Italian to explain the phenomenon of 'pro-drop': "... the pro-drop parameter
covers not only the possibility of freely omitting unstressed subject pronouns (whence the
name pro-drop), but also the presence of widespread encoding of the person-number of the
subject of the verb". The seeming ellipsis of the subject in Japanese might share a lot with
the pro-drop phenomenon in languages such as Italian, and "the person-number of the subject
of the verb" might share some of the honorific 'agreement' with the hidden subject in
Japanese. I have, unfortunately, not seen any direct comparison of the two languages on these
points.

construction in Japanese. When no subject appears on the surface, this simply means that the element subject is not needed in that clause. If the subject is needed, it appears on the surface taking the particle *ga,* though it does not necessarily appear at the beginning of the clause as the subject in English typically does. Restating the same fact in terms of markedness, we might claim that subject appears on the surface in a Japanese clause only when it is marked; when it is unmarked, it does not do so. If the subject is the theme of the clause and the theme is also marked, it appears on the surface but in that case, the following particle must be *wa.* It is perfectly possible for both *wa* and *ga* to appear on the surface in the same clause with each particle following different noun phrases. In such cases, the subject, NP-*ga,* completes its function with its own verb, while the theme, NP-*wa,* extends its force to the end of the clause, sandwiching the subordinate clause governed by NP-*ga* between the theme, NP-*wa,* and its verb, the predicate of the main clause (Mikami 1960: 99-154).

In this paper, I will demonstrate these characteristics of Japanese subjectless constructions, using in the majority of cases naturally occurring clauses to show what functions are expressed by the Japanese honorifics and where and why subject surfaces in everyday Japanese discourse. However, first we need to be clear about the nature and function of the element subject.

2. Functional approaches to the Subject

2.1 Definition of the Subject

In *An Introduction to Functional Grammar,* (IFG), Halliday (1985: 35) claims that the traditional definitions of subject simply represent a conjunction of three distinct concepts. These are:

(i)   Psychological Subject that is the concern of the message;
(ii)   Grammatical Subject of which something is predicated;
(iii)   Logical Subject that is the doer of the action.

Since these functions are not logically dependent on each other, they are separated in his functional grammar, each receiving a distinct label. Thus, (i) psychological Subject is re-named Theme; (ii) grammatical Subject is re-named Subject; (iii) logical Subject is re-named Actor. To demonstrate the logical non-dependence of these three functions, Halliday shows how

Theme, Subject, and Actor can be separated. Let me repeat his examples.

(1)   The duke gave my aunt this teapot.
       Theme
       Subject
       Actor

(2)   This teapot my aunt was given by the duke.
       Theme   Subject   Actor

(3)   My aunt was given this teapot by the duke.
       Theme   Actor
       Subject

(4)   This teapot the duke gave to my aunt.
       Theme   Subject
                      Actor

(5)   By the duke   my aunt was given this teapot.
       Theme   Subject
       Actor

Here in the first example, one constituent, *the duke*, serves to realise all
three functions. According to Halliday this is the default form typical of the
declarative clause in English when "… there is no context leading up to it,
and no positive reason for choosing anything else" (Halliday 1985: 36). The
contrast to this pattern is seen in the other clauses. In (2), each of the three
functions is separated from the others and a distinct function is assigned to
each of the three noun phrases. In (3)-(5), some of the functions are conflated, being expressed by one constituent. All clauses (1)-(5) are semantically related but at the same time they differ subtly and significantly. In order
to clarify the differences among them, Halliday (1985: 36-37) provides a
functional definition for each of these three notions.

(i)   The Theme is a function in the CLAUSE AS A MESSAGE. It is what the
       message is concerned with: the point of departure for what the speaker is
       going to say.
(ii)   The Subject is a function in the CLAUSE AS AN EXCHANGE. It is the element
       that is held responsible: in which is vested the success of the clause in
       whatever is its particular speech function.
(iii) The Actor is a function in the CLAUSE AS A REPRESENTATION (of a pro-
       cess). It is the active participant in the process: the one that does the deed.

By these steps the traditional term subject has been analysed as a composite of the three different functions shown above. This separation enables us to be clear which concept we are dealing with at any point. So it becomes possible to focus on the grammatical Subject.

How is Subject in English recognised? According to Halliday (1985: 73), Subject in a declarative clause can be identified as an "element which is picked up by the pronoun in the tag". Subject typically appears on the surface of the English clause no matter how simple or short a clause may be. Even in a short dialogue, where the main body of the clause is understood from the cotext or context, the Subject must be repeated every time with a part of the verb, the Finite element. These two elements, the Subject and the Finite, combine to form the Mood element; the incidence of subject deletion ie., ellipsis is very rare. The element Finite is realised by a class of word, known as 'finite auxiliary', consisting of a small number of verbal operators. A Finite either expresses the primary tense of the clause, as *was* does in *An old man was crossing the road* or it expresses modality, which is the speaker's judgment of what s/he is saying, as *may* does in *It may happen sometime.* Polarity is treated as a feature of the Finite element: every Finite indicates either positive or negative polarity, as in *did/didn't, can/ can't*, etc.

The Mood element, consisting of Subject and Finite, is the core of the interpersonal structure of the clause in English. It is the presence of the Mood element that realizes the feature 'indicative.' Further, the more delicate grammatical distinctions require reference to the elements Subject and Finite. If a clause has the order Subject^Finite, it is declarative; if it has the opposite order, Finite^Subject, it is a yes-no interrogative. In a WH-interrogative, the order of Subject and Finite depends on whether the WH-element is Subject or not: if it is, then the order is Subject^Finite; if not, Finite^Subject. To say that the element Subject is indispensable in English is to say that the element plays a crucial role in the grammar of mood.

2.2 Unmarked Subjects

It is not as if even in English Subject is always present overtly. Halliday (1985: 90-91) mentions "one condition in which clauses in English systematically occur without Subjects, one that depends on the notions of giving and demanding." The clue to the interpretation of the absent Subject is said to be facilitated by two features: (i) intonation often signals the mood choice of the subjectless clause; and (ii) the giving or demanding function of the clause indicates the specific nature of the missing Subject. In a giving clause, the unmarked Subject is *I* while in a demanding clause the unmarked Subject is *you*. So, if the clause is an offer or a statement, the hearer knows, without it being overtly indicated, that the Subject is the speaker, *I*, whereas if the clause is a question or a command, the Subject would be *you*. In such ellipses, usually the whole of the Mood element is omitted: *(Shall I) Carry your bag? (Will you) Play us a tune!*. However, the Finite element is not always ellipsed in the environment of Subject ellipsis; it may be overtly present, if tense or modality needs to be expressed, as in *(I) Might see you this evening,* or when primary tense is fused with the Predicator, as in *(I) Met Fred on the way here.*

Japanese, as I suggested above, is a language where typically Subject is absent to begin with; it is, therefore, not surprising that under the conditions identified above by Halliday for English, the unmarked Japanese Subject will be absent. In a dialogue between two people, personal pronouns marked as the Subject by the nominative particle *ga* are quite rare; further, it is almost obligatory to omit the first person pronoun like *watashi* in a statement or offer, and the second person pronoun in a question or demand.[4] Quite frequently, therefore, a dialogue between two Japanese participants may continue for a considerable extent of time without a single occurrence of the Subject so long as Subject can be deduced on the basis of the cotext and/or the context. We shall see, later, how a dialogue with subjectless clauses is possible. First, I will look at a typical dialogic exchange in English to show what role the element Subject plays in this exchange. This will allow me to ask whether Subject has a similar function in Japanese, and if not what elements, if any, characterise a Japanese dialogic exchange.

4. The use of a second person pronoun requires a lot of deliberation in Japanese because there is none that can be used to one's seniors with an appropriate degree of respect. In teaching English in the classroom context, *you* is easily translated into *anata*. However, its use is not free of problems because it has come to imply two completely different meanings, one derogatory and the other intimate, which is why the use of the second person pronoun is usually avoided. When this use is necessitated, the speaker selects the best alternative from among several common nouns such as *o-taku* (your house), *oku-san* (someone's wife, used to a woman only), *danna-san/go-shujin* (someone's husband, used to a middle-aged male only), *sensei* (teacher, used to anyone higher or seemingly higher in status), or role names such as *kacho, bucho, shacho*, etc. (each denoting a role position in a company).

2.3 The Mood elements in English and in Japanese

In a normal series of dialogic exchanges in English, only the Mood elements are tossed back and forth as a means of information exchange, as exemplified in (6)-(13), taken from Halliday (1985: 71).

Dialogue 1: The duke and the teapot (English Original)

(6)   The duke's given away that teapot, hasn't he?
(7)   Oh, has he?
(8)   Yes, he has.
(9)   No, he hasn't!
(10) I wish he had.
(11) He hasn't; but he will.
(12) Will he?
(13) He might.

In (6)-(13), the Mood elements are: (6) *the duke's, hasn't he* ; (7) *has he*; (8) *he has*; (9) *he hasn't*; (10) *he had*; (11) *He hasn't, he will*; (12) *Will he*; and (13) *He might*; it is the use of these that carries the dialogue back and forth between the speakers. Subject is thus crucial to the 'clause as exchange'. But what about Japanese? Does Subject have the same role in Japanese? Let me translate Dialogue 1 into Japanese so as to answer this question. But here we encounter a problem: it is possible to translate the original English dialogue into at least twelve different versions, each varying in correlation with variation in the participants' sex, social status, and their relationships with the persons being talked about. Even where the participants are the same, if the roles of the speaker and the hearer are exchanged, the expressions change accordingly.

To economise on space, I will present only two of the twelve possible translations. In both of these, the participants are assumed to be adult speakers of Standard Japanese. Other contextual features relevant to the dialogues will be stated at the head of these translations. Note that in the idiomatic English translation of Japanese clauses, the ellipsed/deleted Subject is indicated not by omission or zero but by enclosing the intended item in parantheses. The key to the symbols in the inter-linear translation is given at the end of this paper.

Dialogue 2: The duke and the teapot (Japanese version 1: A casual conversation)
Note, this is a variety of gossip between close friends. They are not related directly
to the duke; therefore show no respect to him. Both are male.

(14) *Koshaku wa ano kyusu o yacchimatta ne?*
duke **th** that teapot **obj** give-finish-**pst** **fp**
The duke's given away that teapot, hasn't he?

(15) *E? yacchatta no?*
oh give-finish-**pst** **fp**
Oh, has (he) given (it) away?

(16) *Un, so da yo.*
yes so be **fp**
Yes, (that)'s right.

(17) *Iya, yatte nai yo!*
no give-finish not **fp**
No, (he) hasn't given (it) yet!

(18) *Yatte-itara ii noni na.*
give-**cond** good-**cond** **fp**
It would be good if (he) had given (it) away.

(19) *Mada yatte nai yo. Demo yaru daro ne.*
not-yet give-finish not **fp** but give be-**fut** **fp**
(He) hasn't given (it) yet; but (he) will give (it).

(20) *So daro ka?*
so be-**fut** **q**
Will (it) be so ?

(21) *Kamo ne.*
possible **fp**
(That) is possible.

Since this is offered as translation, it must be semantically the same as
Dialogue 1. Are there, then, elements which are tossed back and forth like
the Mood elements in English? There are, but with an important difference:
there is no pronoun, comparable to *he* in English, which could be identified
as Subject. This can be shown through a clause by clause commentary. Thus
in the opening clause (14), the verb equivalent to the English *'s given away*
is *yacchimatta*, a conjugated form of the main verb *yaru*, meaning 'has
finished giving away.' In this clause, *the duke* features in the form of
NP...*wa* and may be treated as the Theme and Subject of the clause. The

English tag question *hasn't he* is expressed in a sentence final particle *ne* which is often used in translating the English tag; however, it has no pronominal element in it, and is also used as the translation equivalent of French *n'est-ce pa*. In (15), the Japanese equivalent to the English *has he?* is *yacchatta no?*, a combination of the verb *yaru* and a sentence final particle *no*, which can express a question if pronounced on a rising tone. In (17, 18 and 19) only the conjugated forms of *yaru* are repeated; there is no Subject in these clauses, though there are sentence final particles. Clauses (16), (20) and (21) have no main verb; they consist of an adjective or an adverb followed by other items such as an auxiliary, a copula, or a sentence final particle. In (16) and (20) an adverb *so* acts as a substitute for the action of the duke *giving away the teapot*. In (18), an adjective *ii* and *noni*, a conjunction introducing a conditional clause, stand for the clause *I wish..* There are two items in (21), *kamo* and *ne*. *Kamo* is a conjunction combining a clause of future possibility with the main clause; its use sometimes expresses the possibility of an event occurring. Thus, (21) can be interpreted as indicating the possibility of the duke giving that teapot away in the future. In all of this, notably, there is no nominal or pronominal trace of *the duke* as Subject.

We need to make two points about this dialogue: (i) that there is certainly something repeated in its clauses, and this something is what carries forward the information exchange in the dialogue; and (ii) that this something cannot be treated as Subject. In fact the repeated items belong to two classes: (a) the conjugated forms of the main verb, *yaru*, as in *yacchatta* (15), *yatteitara* (18), *yattenai* (17, 19) and *yarudaro* (19), and (b) the sentence final particle such as *ne, yo, no, na, ka*. It seems obvious that in Japanese the element comparable in function to the English Mood includes not only primary tense and modality but also the main verb, sentence final particles, and other items like adjectives and adverbs depending on the content; the one thing that is not present in such an element is the Subject.

Let me now translate Dialogue 1 into a more polite conversation to see how this contextual change affects the language of the dialogue.

Dialogue 3: The duke and the teapot (Japanese version 2: A polite conversation) Note, this is a variety of polite conversation between acquaintances of similar status and age, who are not close but know each other fairly well. They also know the duke fairly well; so show him respect. Gender is immaterial; the speakers could be male or female.[5]

(22) *Koshakusama wa   ano kyusu   o   o-age-ninatta-n   desu   ne?*
      duku-**hon**   **th** that teapot **obj** **hon**-give-**hon-pst** be-**hon** fp
      The august duke has given away that teapot honorably, hasn't (he), sir?

(23) *E? so   desu   ka?*
      oh so   be-**hon** q
      Oh, has (he) done so, sir?

(24) *Ee   so   nan desu   yo.*
      yes so   that be-**hon** fp
      Yes, (that)'s right, sir.

(25) *Iie, sonna hazu   wa ari-masen   yo.*
      no   such possibility **th** exist-**hon**-not   **fp**
      No, there could not be such possibility.

(26) *O-age-ninatte   itara   ii-n desu   ga.*
      hon-give-**hon** be-**pst-cond** good be-**hon** though
      It would be good if (he) had given (it) away, though.

(27) *Mada desu   yo. Demo o-age-ninaru   desho   ne.*
      not-yet be-**hon** fp   but **hon**-give-**hon** be-**hon-fut** fp
      (He) hasn't yet, sir; but I think (he) will honorably give (it).

5. That Japanese is a language with male/female difference has received a good deal of emphasis; yet features specific to sex are not as prevalent as honorific features. They are limited to personal pronouns, especially the first and second person, conjugated forms of the copula *da*, and sentence final particles. (See Note 6.) Other features also frequently mark the speaker's sex, but they are more or less common to other languages (like women's frequent use of hedges, indirect speeches, rising intonation, etc). The sex-specific features appear only when the speaker is relaxing, talking with family members, intimate friends, or acquaintances known for a long time. They are a kind of sign that the speaker is feeling free to reveal his/her real person, as a man or a woman, so they do not appear when the speaker is cautious, deliberate, and/or paying lots of attention to his/her words. In a formal setting, there should not be any features particular to either of the sexes because using gender-specific terms in such formal situations will be regarded as a sign of intentional disrespect to the people of dignity. Therefore, there is little difference in speech between male and female speakers at formal settings like the Diet, the court, the city council meeting, the faculty meeting, etc. Even when talking privately, if both participants are not well acquainted, the conversation will show few sex-specific features. It is really difficult, to translate such Japanese dialogues as exemplified here, saturated with hon(orific) markers, into English.

(28) *So desho   ka?*
      so be-**hon-fut**   q
      Will (it) be so, sir?

(29) *Tabun   so   nasaru desho   ne.*
      perhaps so   do-**hon** be-**hon-fut**   fp
      Perhaps (he) will honourably do so, sir.

The most outstanding difference between Dialogue 2, a casual conversation between close friends, and Dialogue 3, a social one between acquaintances, is that in the latter the main verb is enveloped in an honorific auxiliary when it denotes the action of the duke: the main verb *ageru* is itself an euphemistic suppletive of *yaru* (to give); nonetheless, it is further enveloped in an honorific auxiliary *o-* ... *ninaru* to be finally realized in the verb *oageninaru*, literally meaning, 'the Subject honourably gives.' This honorific envelopment implies that the Subject (the Actor of the main verb) is known fairly well to the speakers and holds a higher status than either of them. By contrast, in Dialogue 2, the speakers do not use such honorifics because they are simply two close friends, gossiping about the duke whom they do not know personally. No matter how high the status a person holds within the society, if s/he is not directly acquainted with the speaker and/or the hearer, then in a Japanese dialogue s/he will not be referred to with honorifics.

Another respect in which Dialogue 3 is quite different from Dialogue 2 is that in the former, each clause has either *des-* or *mas-* as a part of the main verb. Of these two, *des-* is an honorific copula; and *mas-* an honorific auxiliary. The use of these particles indicates the speaker's polite attitude toward the hearer; the interactants are showing respect to each other by using these sentence final honorifics. By contrast when the honorific *o-...ninaru* is used, this indicates who the Subject/Actor is through the speaker's respectful attitude toward the Actor. The choice between *mas-* or *des-* is also fully determined. *Mas-* can only follow verbs, while *des-* and its ordinary form *da* can follow a noun phrase, an adverb, or a locative.

In addition to the elements that have already been discussed above, both Dialogue 2 and 3 have other small items eg., *ne, yo, no, na,* and *ka* which occur at the end of a clause. These are known as sentence final particles, which do not appear in formal writing, but are indispensable in dialogic exchange. It is these particles that build up solidarity between the speaker and the hearer and help conversation go back and forth by acting as turn taking cues[6]. Speaking more specifically, *ka* is an interrogative particle. Its presence in a clause marks the clause as interrogative regardless of the intonation of the clause. *Ne* and *no* can also indicate that the clause is interrogative, but only if it is said with a rising intonation. *Yo* almost always affirms the declarative statement to which it is added, and *ne* and *no* can also have the same function if pronounced with a falling intonation. *Na* shows the speaker's wish or desire. Among all of these particles, *ne* is most frequently used perhaps because its other connotation is to ask for the listener's agreement, so that it creates a softening effect. The particle *ne* can follow not only verbs and auxiliaries but also other content words and particles. Although these particles are very small, they are quite important in Japanese discourse, not least because one of them, *ka*, does change the grammatical function of the clause without any involvement of the Subject. So these particles indicate important interpersonal meanings, and their function is comparable to English Mood, as shown by Dialogue 2 and 3. Also, they modify the clause attitudinally with the speaker's feelings which might not be expressed explicitly in content words.

If this interpretation is accepted, it would appear that the Japanese Mood element consists of the auxiliaries denoting tense, modality, and honorification, together with various sentence final particles; the Subject is typically not expressed. Instead, the auxiliaries explicitly reveal the speaker's relations to the hearer, to the person being talked about, and to certain other features

6. Sentence final particles may be among the few elements in Japanese that help build solidarity among the participants. The use of these particles at the end or in the middle of the speech allows the speaker to show his/her warm feeling toward the hearer. The continuation of the conversations depends on their use. Sentence final particles appear very often in a casual, relaxed situation, as when talking with family members or close friends, though they are used in conversations with others, too, if the speaker wants to approach them to gain their favour. These particles, placed mainly at the end of a clause, sometimes after other grammatical elements, can be classified into three groups, man-favoured, woman-favoured, and neutral or both sex-favoured. Some of the man-favoured particles are *yo, na, zo, ze, yona* and their combinations with the copula *da*, like *dayo, dana, dayona, daze, dazo*, etc. Some of the woman-favoured particles are *wa, yo, nano, nanoyo, nanoyone, noyo, noyone*, and their combinations with the copula *da*, like *dawa, dawayo, dawayone*, etc. Others like *ne, no, sa, kana*, etc. are used by both sexes. The particle *ne* is rather special because it is inserted almost in any place in an utterance to make the speech sound soft. Its connotation is close to French *n'est-ce pa*.

of the context of situation. These relations are expressed directly through the use or non-use of honorifics attached to the verb, which in turn indirectly but unmistakably signals information about Subject. The speaker must decide whether or not to use honorifics, and if so, which ones so as to make his/her speech convey the intentions correctly and to maintain relevance.

Moreover, when talking about the third person or persons, the speaker has to classify the third party according to that party's relation to both the hearer and the speaker him/herself. If the third party belongs to the hearer's group, the speaker has to use the same level of honorifics as s/he uses to the hearer, not only in referring to the third party, but also in describing their actions. On the other hand, if the third party belongs to his/her own group, no honorifics should be used either in referring to them or to their actions. Such demeaning reference to one's own group is another method, traditionally established in Japanese grammar, to exalt the other group, ie., the hearer and his/her group[7].

It is not surprising, then, that even though the Japanese Mood element does not include the Subject, its identity is seldom in question. The conclusion seems justified that in Japanese, Subject is not needed for effecting the dialogic exchange; this function is carried out by the honorifics. Nor is it needed for indicating mood choices. I pointed out in subsection 2.2 that the systemic contrast between declarative and interrogative in English is typically expressed by the order of the elements Subject and Finite in the clause. By contrast in Japanese, this systemic contrast is expressed by the presence/absence of certain particles and/or the intonation of the clause. The element Subject is superfluous in Japanese so far as the grammar of mood is concerned. In the next section, I will analyse the clauses in some examples of naturally occurring conversation in order to show how Subject may be interpreted in subjectless constructions purely on the basis of the honorifics[8].

---

7. This is a typical case of what Levinson calls "relational variety" of honorifics (1983: 90). All the four relations he lists (referent honorifics, addressee honorifics, bystander or audience honorifics, and formality levels) can be applied to Japanese honorifics. His observation that "in some [languages] the distinction formal/informal is firmly grammaticalized, for example in Japanese by so-called *mas-* style" (1983:91) is true but it identifies only a minute part of the pattern. There are many more "firmly grammaticalized" elements which function to distinguish several relations, not only among participants but also to bystanders and to the setting (see Note 10).

8. More complete explanation and examples of Japanese verb formation with honorific auxiliaries are given in Harada (1975: 506-507) and Hori (1986: 375-377, 1988a, 1989).

3.   Dialogues without the Subject

3.1 A casual conversation

In 1982-84, I worked in a research project to investigate the use of honorifics
by women in contemporary Japanese. This project collected a large body of
conversational data (Ide et al. 1984), where the main speaker, a housewife,
was audio-recorded while interacting with 47 different persons, over the
course of 41 interactive scenes. I will use two such scenes from the transcription of these dialogues to see if the subjectless structures found in the
translated dialogues in section 2.3 also occur in natural conversations. In
Dialogue 4 the husband (H) and wife (W) are talking about when it was that
the wife watered the flowers.

Dialogue 4. Watering flowers (Ide et al. 1984: 223)

(30)   H: *Hana   ni mizu   yatta   no? Kyo?*
           flower   to water   give-**pst** **fp** today
           Did (you) water the flowers? Today?

(31)   W: *Yarimashita   yo.*
           give-**hon-pst** fp
           Yes, (I) did.

(32)   H: *Un.*
           hum
           Hum.

(33)   W: *Asa.*
           morning
           In the morning.

(34)   H: *Un?*
           huh
           Huh?

(35)   W: *Asa   yarimashita.*
           morning   give-**hon-pst**
           (I) watered in the morning.

(36)   H: *Un. Yugata nanka   genkan   noho   yatta   mitai ne?*
           yeah evening somehow entrance direction give-**pst** seem **fp**
           Yeah. Seems (you) watered around the entrance in the evening,

(37)   w: *Asa   yaru no wasureta kara yugata yatta-n   desu.*
             morning give that forget-**pst** as   evening give-**pst** be **hon**
             As (I) forgot to water in the morning, (I) watered in the evening.

I shall ignore the inconsistency in the wife's responses about the time of watering as irrelevant to the present discussion. What is relevant is that there is no Subject in any of the utterances of Dialogue 4. The main verb is *yaru* (to give) and its conjugated forms, *yatta* in (30), (36), and (37) and *yarimashita* in (31) and (35). Here, together with the noun, *mizu* (water), this verb means 'to water,' and irrespective of whether *yaru* appears in questions eg., (30) and (36) or in answers eg., (31), (35), and (37), it has no Subject. The verb is followed by the tense marking auxiliary *ta* as in (30), (31), (35), (36), and (37) and in the wife's responses it is followed by an honorific auxiliary *mashi* as in (31) and (35) or an honorific copula *desu* in (37), but there is no constituent in any of the clauses which may be said to act as Subject. In (37), there is another verb *wasureta* (forgot), but this too has no Subject. In fact, not only is Subject absent, but also there is no overt Theme in any of the clauses, nor is the Actor of the actions of 'watering' or 'forgetting' indicated.

Halliday points out that in English conversations the Subject of a giving clause is often the first person *I* and that of a demanding one is often the second person *you*. Does the same generalisation hold true for Japanese dialogues? If so, then it should be possible to insert *I* and *you* appropriately in the Subject position of each declarative (which gives information) and interrogative (which demands information) respectively in Dialogue 4, without causing any other change of meaning than that associated with making Subject explicit. This is certainly the case: we can indeed appropriately insert *you* or *I* in the various clauses of this dialogue as the material in the parentheses shows. If such a doctored version of Dialogue 4 were translated back into English, all that would be needed to provide an idiomatic translation, would be the removal of the parantheses in the present one since the items in these parentheses simply indicate the absent but understood Subject, and the resultant would be true to the Japanese meaning.

What can be argued from this fact? It could be taken to suggest that in Japanese, everyday conversation has no Subject so long as the Subject of a giving clause is the first person and the Subject of a demanding clause is the second person. In effect then the situation is like that in English: when the

Subject is unmarked, it does not appear overtly, but the interpretation is unproblematic since the mood function of the clauses acts as a guide. The question is, then, what happens in those cases where a clause is complex with different Subjects for each embedded clause, without overt presence of Subject in the form of 'NP-*ga*' ? Is it possible to interpret Subject in these cases? To answer this question, let me examine another conversation from the same body of data.

3.2 A polite conversation

Dialogue 5 is taken from a conversation between the same woman (W) as in Dialogue 4 and a well-known writer, Mr. K, whose daughter went to school with W's daughter. Mr K had contributed to the PTA and W, being in charge of the PTA, visited him with three other women as a sign of gratitude.

Dialogue 5: A visit (Ide et al. 1984: 3)

(38) W: *Hontoni   arigato   gozai   mashita.*
          really   thank-you be-**hon hon-pst**
          Thank you very much, Mr. K.

(39) K: *Aa. Itsumo agatte itadaka-nakute moshiwake   nai*
          oh   always step-up receive-**hon**-not excuse-**hon**   not
          Not at all. (I)'m sorry (I) never asked (you) to come into the house …

(40) W: *Ie,   ie,   mo. Ano nanka   shichigatsu ni o-hairi-nina-rare*
          no   no   no   well somehow July   in **hon**-enter-**hon-hon**
          mashitara sugu go-ryoko de   rassharu -tte koto   o   ne
          hon-cond soon **hon**-trip on   be-**hon**   that thing **obj   fp**
          No, no, that's nothing, Mr. K. (I) thought (I)'d heard that (you)'d soon
          be taking a trip when July came …

(41) K: *Ie, ie.*
          no   no
          Well …

(42) W: *Uketamawatte ori   mashita   mono desu   kara …*
          hon-hear   be-**hon hon-pst** thing be-**hon** as
          As (I) heard from somebody that (you)'d be (taking a trip) …

(43) K: *Ano …*
          well
          Well, (I) …

(44) w: *Motto   hayakuni* ...
      more   early
      (I) thought (I) should have come much earlier ...

(45) K: *Ise   Zingu   e ne.*
      Ise   Shrine   to **fp**
      (I)'m going to Ise Shrine.

(46) w: *Hah?*
      oh
      Oh?

(47) K: *Ano, Ise Zingu e chotto   itte   konaito* ...
      well Ise Shrine to a little   go   must
      Well, (I) must go to Ise Shrine.

(48) w: *Aa,   sayode irasshai   masu   ka.*
      oh   **hon**-so be-**hon**   **hon**   q
      Oh, is that so, Mr K?

Here again, no overt Subject is to be found in any clauses of the Japanese Dialogue. But it is clear from the free English translation, that both *I* and *you* are understood in each utterance. Besides, there are a number of honorifics scattered around in nearly all of the woman's utterances. It is these honorifics which identify the Subject of each clause.

For example, in (40) the woman's *shichigatsu ni ohairini narare mashitara* literally means 'if it honourably happened that July honourably came.' This 'honorability' is expressed by such auxiliaries as *o-* ... *nina-,* -*rare-*, and *-mas-*. The first two are auxiliaries exalting to the highest degree the Subject/Actor of the main verb, 'to enter'. This honorific envelopment of the verb clearly indicates that the person who would do something in July could not be the speaker, even though this is a giving clause.

This exclusion of the speaker from the Subject status implies that the Subject must be somebody other than the speaker. Who then could the Subject be? Note that in this particular situation there are only five persons involved: the speaker, the hearer, and the speaker's three friends, and the purpose of the visit is to thank the hearer. Taking these features of context into account, the most likely interpretation is that the focus of such exaltation would be the hearer, Mr. K. Thus the only logical interpretation of this clause is that the person who does something in July is not the speaker or her companions but the hearer, even though no pronoun designating the second person is used.

The auxiliary *mas-* often appears in Dialogue 4 showing the wife's polite attitude toward the husband. A similar interpretation fits in Dialogue 5 as well; both *mas-* (the root of *mashita, masu,* and *masho*) and *des-* (the root of *desu, deshita,* and *desho*) show that the speaker is addressing the hearer politely, that is, treating that person as somebody either higher than the speaker herself or not close to her. This justifies the assumption that the woman is talking to Mr. K., and not to her friends who have come with her. Thus, this clause *shichigatsu ni ohairini narare mashitara* clearly designates the hearer as the Subject of the verb.

The second clause of (40) ie., *sugu goryoko de rassharutte koto o ne,* literally means 'the fact that soon (someone) honourably is on an honorable trip.' Here again, there are two honorifics, *go* and *(i)rassharu*. *Go* is a prefix which exalts the noun followed, showing that whatever is referred to by the noun is related to someone higher than the speaker[9]. And *(i)rassharu* can be used as an honorific suppletive of any of *iku, kuru,* or *iru*, meaning 'to go', 'to come', and 'to be', respectively, for the purpose of exalting the doer of the action. So, once again, the Subject/Actor of *being on a trip* cannot be the speaker or her friends, but the hearer, Mr K.

As the last example from this dialogue, let me examine (42), where the woman says *uketamawatte orimashita mono desu kara,* literally meaning, 'as the thing is such that (someone) was in the humble state of humbly having heard.' The main verb *uketamawatte* is a suppletive deferential alternative of the verb *kiite,* a conjugated form of *kiku* (to hear), and *ori-mashita* is an agglutination of a verb *ori-* and *mashita*, an honorific auxiliary in the past tense. *Oru* (the root of *ori-*) is a suppletive deferential alternative of the verb *iru* (to be), implying a highly deferential attitude on the part of the Actor/ Subject of this verb. By these devices, the Subject/Actor of this clause seems to be lowering him/herself, metaphorically speaking, right

9. Although these honorific prefixes were originally used only to exalt the person who possessed the item to which the prefix was agglutinated, their use has been extended even to such items as have nothing to do with respect. At present, they are quite easily attached to any entity according to the speaker's mood; if s/he wants to make speech sound more elegant, s/he adds one of these prefixes to a noun in the speech. Which of them to employ is basically decided by the following noun: if the noun is a native Japanese word, the prefix should be *o, on,* or *mi*; if it is a word of Chinese origin, the prefix should be *go* (Harada 1975: 504-5). The reason for their prevalence may be the ease with which they can be used. Their overuse and misuse has often been deplored by purists and some linguists.

down to the ground. Who else could be the Actor of such humbling behavior but the speaker herself? If it is not the speaker, it must be someone belonging to her ingroup. In the present situation, the Subject/Actor might include both the speaker and her friends. This interpretation is highly probable since the speaker and her friends are considered to belong to the same group, though temporarily; at least, they belong to a group different from that of Mr κ's[10].

The phenomena to which I have drawn attention appear quite regularly in naturally occurring conversations; and they might be thought of as a basis for the conclusion that in a Japanese conversation, whenever possible, the speaker will try not to refer to the participants of the dialogue by either using a name or by employing the first or second person pronouns; instead, s/he would be inclined to use rather indirect means such as the use of respectful honorifics added to the verb if the hearer is the Subject, and/or the use of humbling honorifics added to the verb if the speaker him/herself is the Subject[11].

10. The concept of ingroup and outgroup is one of the fundamental keys to interpret Japanese society (Lebra 1976), and language use clearly reflects it. The basic principle is well exemplified in the main text: 'when the participants can be divided into two groups, ingroup and outgroup, use respectful honorific verbs if the outgroup is the Subject, and use demeaning honorific verbs if the ingroup is the Subject'. However, in practice, there is a problem since the division of ingroup and outgroup is not absolute. Apart from the certainty that one's family is always one's foremost ingroup, the group membership is dependent on the participants and the immediate situation relevant to the conversation. The group defining lines are volatile and can shift if there is some change in the participants and/or the situational setting.

11. Harada (1975: 516-31) uses the terms 'subject honorification' and 'object honorification' to explain the phenomena of subject raising predication and object raising predication. His purpose is to write rules for the Japanese honorific system within generative theory, that is, he tries to generate an honorific expression like o-yomi-ninaru (someone honourably reads) o-hanashi-suru (someone humbly talks). The former is called 'subject honorification' because the doer of the action 'reading' is exalted and the latter is called 'object honorification' because the hearer (receiver) of the action 'talking' is exalted. These terms have been used in most writings in generative theory, but they are rather confusing for obvious reasons. Since my purpose is to see how Subject and honorifics are related, I have preferred to use simpler terms like 'respectful honorifics' and 'humbling honorifics' placing the Subject of the verb as the Actor of the action referred to by the verb, whether the Subject is stated overtly or not. My usage is, in fact, much closer to Japanese traditional terms sonkeigo (words of respect) and kenjogo (words of humbleness), for which Bloch (1946) uses the terms "esteem" and "humility", respectively.

This systematic relation between the Subject and honorifics might be one of the reasons why the first person and second person pronouns themselves do not appear for the most part as Subject in Japanese conversation. However, it would be wrong to give the impression that Japanese never permits the appearance of overt Subject in daily conversation; this is patently not true. Japanese does employ overt Subject when necessary. The problem is figuring out when it is necessary. In order to suggest an answer to this problem, I will analyse a dialogue with overt Subjects in section 4.1.

4. The function of the Subject in Japanese

4.1 A dialogue with the Subject

It is a widely held view in the grammar of modern Japanese that the Subject is followed by the particle *ga* and that the Theme is followed by the particle *wa*. But as pointed out at the beginning of this paper (See section 1), these two particles do not appear very often. What are the conditions for the use of *ga* and *wa* in Japanese?

To answer this question, I will analyse a dialogue between the same woman (w) and one of her students (s). For several years, the woman had been teaching cookery at her house. Dialogue 6 is triggered by the presence of the tape-recorder the woman is carrying to record her speech. The cookery students are worried that their words are also going to be recorded and would be subjected to analysis. They want to be reassured that this will not happen.

Dialogue 6. Tape recording (Ide et al. 1984: 138)

(49) w: *Dakara   omoni watakushi ga, ano are nan   desu*
        therefore mainly I   **nom** well that thing be-**hon**
     yo ne. Dakara   do-nenpaino hito,   sorekara
     fp   therefore same aged   person   and
     meueno   hito,   sorekara shitano   hito   ni ne,
     senior/higher person and   junior/lower person to **fp**
     doyufuni sono onaji kotoba o   tsukai-wakeru ka
     how   that same   word   **obj** use-separate   **q**
     to   yu-koto rashii desu.
     that to say   seem   be-**hon**

So, it's something like this, you know, how I talk to people of my age, to people above me, and to people below me, I mean, how I talk, that is, how I use words differentiatingly. That's what they want me to record, I suppose.

(50) s: *A   so   desu ka.*
oh   so   be-**hon** q
Oh, I see.

(51) w: *Dozo   o-kininasara   naide   kusasai   mase.*
please   **hon**-be-worried   not   please-**hon**   **hon**
So, please don't be worried (about this tape-recorder).

(52) s: *Aiteno   hito   wa   haira-nain desu   ne?*
interacting person   **th**   enter-not   be-**hon** fp
So you mean, our words aren't going to be recorded, are they?

(53) w: *Un.*
yeah
No.

(54) s: *Sensei-no kotoba   ga   omo ne?*
teacher's   word   **nom** main fp
It's your words mainly, isn't it?

This conversation contains one of the very few occurrences of the first person pronoun with the nominative particle *ga* (see 49). In a total of 13,286 utterances which represent all the conversations audio recorded during a whole week, only 45 instances of nominative *ga* follow the first person pronoun: (*wataskushi ga* 9; *watashi ga* 14; *atakushi ga* 8; *atashi ga* 12; and *boku ga* 2). Even if the two intensified first person nominative cases, *watashi-jishin ga*, 'I myself' are included, the total number is only 47. Nonetheless it is obvious that the nominative *ga* can occur in daily conversation. Let me now examine clauses (49), (52) and (54) to probe the motivation for the occurrence of the particles *ga* and *wa* in Dialogue 6.

In (49), w uses *watakushi ga* to clarify what the Subject/Actor of the verb *tsukai-wakeru* ('use differentiatingly') is, presumably because she considers it necessary to make an excuse for recording her interaction with these women. So in fact what she is implying is some such message as, "It's me whose words are being recorded." By using *ga*, she separates herself from her students who may not wish their words to be recorded. The overt Subject indicates the identity of the referent, and sets it clearly aside from any other likely candidates.

In (52), the student uses the particle *wa* in the clause *aiteno hito wa hairanain desu ne*. The noun phrase *aiteno hito* literally means 'the inter-actants' but its intended meaning is 'the interactants' words.' Why does the student use the particle? Because she wants to know what will happen to the words of the students themselves. As they are talking with the teacher, it is inevitable that their words will be recorded. But if the teacher's words are the only target, then the students need not feel threatened, because so far as their own words are concerned, they would not be subjected to analysis. Again, the overt use of Subject identifies the referent, setting it apart from other likely entities.

But if the function is the same, then, why is this noun phrase followed by *wa*, not by *ga*? If it is the Subject of the verb *hairanai*, it could clearly take the nominative *ga*, rather than *wa*. Essentially, the Subject NP-*ga* refers to new information alone, a simple description of something (Nitta 1991). In the case of this student's question, the problem of their words being recorded is not at all new; indeed, that is precisely what is under discussion. The student, therefore, thematises this NP, indicating thereby that this is her point of departure. It is well known that in Japanese, Theme can appear at any place in a clause, since unlike English, it is not realised by the order of the constituents; instead, Theme in Japanese is realised by the attachment of the post-position *wa*. Further, it has been observed by several scholars that when Theme and Subject happen to be realised by the same NP, *ga* is absorbed in *wa* (Mikami 1960). By making *aiteno hito* her Subject and her Theme, the student is able to dissociate herself from the earlier Theme, *viz.*, 'the teacher's words' and to introduce her own Theme 'the students' words', thus indicating what she is 'on about'. As Halliday (1985) has pointed out, Theme is in fact "the point of departure for what the speaker is going to say."

The fact that this phrase comes at the beginning of a clause has nothing to do with its thematic function. The order of the constituent may be a decisive fact in the recognition of Theme in English; it does not follow from this that the same is true of Japanese. In Japanese Theme is realised by the post-position *wa*; the constituent expressing Theme can, therefore, be placed anywhere in the clause, as illustrated by (55i-iii).

(55)   (i)   *Aiteno   hito   wa   tepu ni haira-nai-n   desu   ne?*
             interacting person   **th**   tape in enter-not   be-**hon fp**
             Other people's words aren't going to be recorded, are they?

(ii) *Tepu ni aiteno   hito   wa   haira-nai-n   desu   ne?*
tape in interacting person **th** enter-not **be-hon fp**
Other people's words aren't going to be recorded, are they?

(iii) *Tepu ni haira-nai-n   desu   ne,   aiteno   hito   wa?*
tape in enter-not **be-hon fp** interacting person **th**
They aren't going to be recorded, are they, other people's words?

All three examples in (55) have the same experiential meaning, *viz.*, 'Other people's words aren't going to be recorded, are they?' In all three clauses, *aiteno-hito* is the Theme. Also, this Theme is the Subject of the verb and the Actor of the action of 'entering.' These functions which are conflated in one noun phrase, are not affected by the position of that constituent.

In (54), the student's *sensei no kotoba ga omone* where *ga* follows the noun phrase *sensei no kotoba* (the teacher's words), indicates that this noun phrase is the Subject of the clause. Why was it necessary for the student to use an overt Subject? If this clause had been subjectless, it would have consisted only of the Finite element, *omo ne* (mainly, 'isn't it?'). The assumption under this condition would be that the Subject of this clause is the same as that of the preceding one, *aiteno hito* ('the interactants' words'). So clause (54) would come to mean that it is mainly the interactants' words that are to be recorded and analysed. This is clearly the opposite of what the speaker intends, for the student wants to make sure that it is the teacher's words that are going to be recorded and analysed but not hers or other students'. So, she must state her Subject overtly and put the nominative *ga* after it, in order to prevent any confusion in identifying the Subject. By using this particle, she can clearly separate 'the teacher's words' from 'the students' words' and dissociate herself and other students from the recording[12].

4.2 The function of the Subject, realized by NP-ga

As a native speaker of Japanese, I find the above analysis intuitively satisfying. This might imply that the definition and function of the Subject in Japanese, realized in a clause as NP-*ga,* needs to be reexamined. The first and

---

12. Some results concerning the differentiated use of words, including honorifics, in the conversations recorded in our data are reported both in Ide *et al.* (1985, 1986) and in Hori (1986, 1988a, and 1988c).

second person pronouns appear very infrequently as Subject in everyday conversation[13], as illustrated by Dialogue 4 and 5 and as further emphasised by the low occurrences of such NPs in our data. When these NPs do appear overtly, there is a very clear reason for it, whose motivation lies in the dialogic process, as the above discussion of (49) and (54) has attempted to demonstrate.

The speaker employs particle *ga* under conditions where the purpose of identifying the Subject overtly, and/or marking the Subject off as distinct from other entities, can be attributed to him/her; in other words, NP-*ga* appears only when marking is needed. When the Subject is unmarked, it does not appear on the surface. The rare occurrence of *ga* can be attributed at least partly to the fact that when the Subject, the Actor, and the Theme are conflated as in (52) and (55), the nominative *ga* is obligatorily absorbed in the thematic *wa*. In these cases the function that is made explicit is that of Theme; the function Subject still remains covert, and must be deduced from context, since the conflation of Theme and Subject is only a default condition, not a necessity.

It could be argued, then, that Subject is not an indispensable item in a Japanese clause. It appears as an item only when the speaker wants to express it overtly for the purpose of identifying the referent of the Subject NP, thus clearly separating it from other possible noun phrases. In such cases, if it is not stated overtly, it could lead to misunderstanding, but so long as this clear separation is not required the clause will remain subjectless.

5. Conclusion

In his discussion of several of the phenomena of reference and honorifics in Asian languages, Levinson deplores the neglect of the notion of social deixis. He suggests that this neglect "is no doubt simply due to the disproportionate amount of recent linguistic work that has been done on English or to closely related languages" (Levinson 1983: 94). It is certainly true that most Japanese data referred to or analysed in major linguistic journals or books, particularly when written in English, have been analysed using the "recent

---

13. The number of occurrences of the second person pronouns in the nominative case is only 16 in the whole data: *anata ga* 12; *anata-tachi ga*(pl.) 3; *kimi ga* 1. The other forms, such as *omae* and *anta,* appear in the data but do not precede *ga.*

linguistic [frame]work" whose focus is fundamentally confined to single clauses; they almost always ignore any information except that which is directly and overtly coded within linguistic items. Further, the blue-print for the description of all languages by an unspoken assumption happens to be English. This leads to considerable distortion of the facts of other languages.

The phenomenon of subjectless clauses is so prevalent in Japanese that to call it 'subject deletion' appears counter-intuitive at least to this native speaker of that language. The fact that decontextualized 'double/multiple nominative construction' is taken to be 'natural' is especially questionable. Dissatisfaction with these descriptions was the primary reason for my interest in the problem of Japanese Subject. Mikami (1960) is perhaps the first one to point out the inappropriateness of using the term 'subject' for the Japanese NP-*ga* in the same sense as that in which the term Subject is used in the description of Western languages in general and English in particular. My analyses of honorifics have led me to believe that the information permeating every part of the honorific system is a powerful mechanism for identifying the Subject of the clause, without its overt presence in the form of NP-*ga* in the clause. To this should be added the observation that there is a long-standing tradition in Japanese against referring to a person directly by his/her own name. Even today, this social convention is well observed. Mentioning the hearer's name in the midst of a conversation is often taken as not a sign of friendliness, much less that of respect; a better way to show respect is to refer to that person indirectly. That is the cultural background that underlies the system of honorifics, established in the language now for many centuries. The appreciation of the "socially deictic value of particular morphemes" that Levinson (1983: 92) recommends, requires placing the system of language into the context of its culture, and so to recognise the specificity of the grammar of each language. From this point of view, my paper is a contribution to the discussions of subjectlessness in the various languages of the world, which are being forced to require the element Subject under the influence of English as the prototype manifestation of universal grammar.

Abbreviations

cond   - conditional mood
fp   - sentence final particle
fut   - future tense
hon   - honorific
nom   - nominative particle
obj   - objective particle
pst   - past tense
q   - interrogative particle
th   - thematic particle

(The present tense is not marked specifically.)

References

Bloch, Bernard. 1946. Studies in colloquial Japanese II: Syntax. *Language* 22, 154-184.

Comrie, Bernard. 1989. *Language Universals and Linguistic Typology: Syntax and morphology.* Second Edition. Oxford: Basil Blackwell.

Coulmas, Florian. 1992. Linguistic etiquette in Japanese society. *Politeness in Language: Studies in its history, theory and practice*, edited by Richard J. Watts, Sachiko Ide, and Konrad Ehlich, 300-323. Berlin: Mouton de Gruyter.

Errington, Joseph J. 1988. *Structure and Style in Javanese: A semiotic view of linguistic etiquette.* Philadelphia: University of Pennsylvania Press.

Halliday, M. A. K. 1985. *An Introduction to Functional Grammar.* London: Edward Arnold.

Halliday, M. A. K. and Ruqaiya Hasan. 1989. *Language, Context, and Text: Aspects of language in a social-semiotic perspective.* Oxford: Oxford University Press.

Harada, S. I. 1975. Honorifics. *Syntax and Semantics 5: Japanese generative grammar* edited by Masayoshi Shibatani, 499-561. New York: Academic Press.

Hattori, Shiro. 1959. *Nihongo no Keito* [The Genealogy of Japanese]. Tokyo: Iwanami Shoten.

Hori, Motoko. 1986. A sociolinguistic analysis of the Japanese honorifics. *Journal of Pragmatics* 10, 373-386.

Hori, Motoko. 1988a. *Nihongo no Keii Hyogen: Eigo tono hikaku* [Honorific Expressions in Japanese: A comparison with English]. Sakado, Saitama: Josai University, Women's Junior College.

Hori, Motoko. 1988b. Politeness strategy on the morphological level: a case study of Japanese. *The Tsuda Review* 33, 187-206.

Hori, Motoko. 1988c. Language forms reflecting social hierarchy and psychological attitude. Microfiche. ERIC. USA.

Hori, Motoko. 1989. Keigo no hasso-ten wa doko ka? [What is the starting point of the concept of honorifics?]. Paper presented at the Ninety-ninth Linguistic Society of Japan, Osaka, Japan.

Hwang, Juck-Ryoon. 1990. Deference versus politeness. *International Journal of the Sociology of Language* 82, 41-55.

Ide, Sachiko. 1982. Japanese sociolinguistics: politeness and women's language. *Lingua* 57, 357-385.

Ide, Sachiko. 1988. Introduction. *Multilingual 7-4, Special Issue: Linguistic politeness* I, 371-374.

Ide, Sachiko, Shoko Ikuta, Akiko Kawasaki, Motoko Hori, and Hitomi Haga. 1984. *Shufu no Isshukan no Danwa Shiryo* [Data of A Week's Conversations between a Housewife and Others]. Publication of a special research project subsidised by the Ministry of Education.

Ide, Sachiko, Motoko Hori, Akiko Kawasaki, Shoko Ikuta, and Hitomi Haga. 1985. *Josei no Keigo no Gengo-keishiki to Kino* [Forms and Functions of Honorifics Used by Women]. Publication of a special research project subsidised by the Ministry of Education.

Ide, Sachiko, Motoko Hori, Akiko Kawasaki, Shoko Ikuta, and Hitomi Haga. 1986. Sex differences and politeness in Japanese. *International Journal of the Sociology of Language* 58, 25-36.

Ide, Sachiko and Naomi Hanaoka McGloin, eds. 1991. *Aspects of Japanese Women's Language*. Tokyo: Kurosio Publishers.

Inoue, Kazuko. 1989. Shugo no imi-yakuwari to kaku-shihai [The thematic role of the subject and case marking]. In Kuno and Shibatani (eds.).1989, 79-101.

Ishisaka, Shozo. 1951. Keigo-teki ninsho no gainen [Concept of honorific person]. *Hobun Ronso* [Papers in Humanities] 2. University of Kumamoto. Reprinted in Kitahara 1978, 65-80.

Jung, Jae-Hoon. 1991. A systemic-functional approach to politeness and honorifics phenomena in Korean. Paper presented at the Eighteenth International Systemic Congress, Tokyo, Japan.

Kitahara, Yasuo, ed. 1978. *Ronshu Nihongo Kenkyu 9: Keigo* [An Anthology of the Studies of Japanese 9: Honorifics]. Tokyo: Yuseido.

Kiyose, Gisaburo Norikura.. 1989. *Nihongo-bunpo Shinron: Hasei-bunpo josetsu* [A New Approach to Japanese Grammar: An introduction to derivational analysis]. Tokyo: Ofusha.

Komatsu, Hisao. 1963. Taigu-hyogen no bunrui [A classification of expressions for treating people]. *Kokubungaku: Gengo to bungei* [Japanese Literature: Language and literature] Vol. 5, No. 2. Reprinted in Kitahara 1978, 122-128.

Kuno, Susumu. 1973a. *The Structure of the Japanese Language*. Cambridge, Mass.: The MIT Press.

Kuno, Susumu. 1973b. *Nihonbunpo Kenkyu* [A Study of Japanese Grammar]. Tokyo: Taishukan.

Kuno, Susumu and Masayoshi Shibatani, eds. 1989. *Nihongogaku no Shin-tenkai* [A New Development in the Study of Japanese]. Tokyo: Kuroshio Shuppan.

Lebra, Takie S. 1976. *Japanese Patterns of Behavior*. Honolulu: The University Press of Hawaii.

Levinson, Stephen C. 1983. *Pragmatics*. Cambridge: Cambridge University Press.

Loveday, Leo J. 1986a. *Explorations in Japanese Sociolinguistics*. Amsterdam and Philadelphia: John Benjamins.

Loveday, Leo J. 1986b. Japanese sociolinguistics. *Journal of Pragmatics* 10, 287-326.

Lyons, John. 1981. *Language and Linguistics: An introduction*. Cambridge: Cambridge University Press.

Matsumoto, Yoshiko. 1988. Re-examination of the universality of face: politeness phenomena in Japanese. *Journal of Pragmatics* 12, 403-426.

Mikami, Akira. 1953. *Gendai Goho Josetsu* [An Introduction to the Modern Usage]. Tokyo: Toho Shoin. Chapter 2: Keigo-ho no A-sen [The addressee-line in honorifics]. Reprinted in Kitahara 1978, 143-146.

Mikami, Akira. 1960. *Zo wa hana ga nagai* [An Elephant has a Long Nose]. Tokyo: Kuroshio Shuppan.

Miller, Roy Andrew. 1967. *The Japanese Language*. Chicago: University of Chigago Press.

Minami, Fujio. 1974. *Gendai Nihongo no Kozo* [The Structure of Modern Japanese]. Tokyo: Taishukan Shoten.

Minami, Fujio. 1977. Keigo no kino to keigo kodo [The function of honorifics and respectful behaviour]. Ono and Shibata (eds.) 1977, 1-44.

Miyagawa, Shigeru. 1989. *Syntax and Semantics 22: Structure and case marking in Japanese*. San Diego: Academic Press.

Miyaji, Yutaka. 1971. Gendai no keigo [Modern honorifics]. Tsujishima, Kasuga, Morino, Sakurai, Komatsu, and Miyaji (eds.). 1971, 368-425.

Mizutani, Nobuko. 1985. *Nichi-ei Hikaku: Hanashi-kotoba no Bunpo* [Japanese-English Contrast: A grammar of spoken texts]. Tokyo: Hobunkan.

Morino, Muneaki. 1971. Kodai no keigo II [Ancient honorifics II]. Tsujimura, Kasuga, Morino, Sakurai, Komatsu, and Miyaji (eds.) 1971, 97-182.

Nitta, Yoshio. 1991. *Nihongo no Modarity to Ninsho* [Modality and Persons in Japanese]. Kasukabe, Saitama: Hitsuji Shobo.

Oishi, Hatsutaro. 1983. *Gendai Keigo Kenkyu* [A Study on Modern Honorifics]. Tokyo: Chikuma Shobo.

Ono, Susumu and Takeshi Shibata. 1977. *Nihango 4: Keigo* [Japanese 4: Honorifics]. Tokyo: Iwanami: Shoten.

Shibamoto, Janet S. 1990. Sex related variation in the ellipsis of *wa* and *ga*. Ide and McGloin (eds.) 1990, 81-104.

Shibatani, Masayoshi. 1977. Grammatical relations and surface cases, *Language* 53, 789-809.

Shibatani, Masayoshi. 1978a. Mikami Akira and the notion of subject in Japanese grammar. *Problems in Japanese Syntax and Semantics*, edited by J. Hinds & I. Howard. Tokyo: Kaitakusha,

Shibatani, Masayoshi. 1978b. *Nihongo no Bunseki: Seisei-bunpo no Hoho* [An Analysis of Japanese: The Generative Approach]. Tokyo: Taishukan.

Shibatani, Masayoshi. 1990. *The Language of Japan*. Cambridge: Cambridge University Press.

Smith, Janet S. 1992. Women in charge: Politeness and directives in the speech of Japanese women. *Language in Society* 21, 59-82.

Sohn, Ho-Min. 1986. Cross-cultural patterns of honorifics and sociolinguistic sensitivity to honorific variables: evidence from English, Japanese, and Korean. *Linguistic Expeditions,* edited by Ho-Min Sohn, 411-437. Seoul: Hanshin.

Tokieda, Motoki. 1941. *Kokugogaku Genron* [A Fundamental Theory of the Study of Japanese]. Tokyo: Iwanami Shoten.

Tokunaga, Misato. 1992. Dichotomy in the structure of honorifics of Japanese. *Pragmatics* 2, 127-140.

Tonoike, Shigeo. 1991. The comparative syntax of English and Japanese: Relating unrelated languages. *Current English Linguistics in Japan*, edited by Heizo Nakajima, 1991, 455-506. Berlin: Mouton de Gruyter.

Tsujimura, Toshiki. 1976. Nihongo no keigo no kozo to tokushoku [The structural characteristics of Japanese honorifics]. Ono and Shibata (eds.). 1977, 45-94.

Tsujimura, Toshiki. 1992. *Keigo Ronko* [Studies on Honorifics]. Tokyo: Meiji Shoin.

Tsujimura, Toshiki, Kazuo Kasuga, Muneaki Morino, Mitsuaki Sakurai, Hisao Komatsu, and Yutaka Miyaji. 1971. *Koza Kokugo-shi 5: Keigo-shi* [Lectures on the History of Japanese 5: History of Honorifics]. Tokyo: Taishukan.

Watanabe, Minoru. 1971. *Kokugo Kobunron* [The Structure of Japanese]. Tokyo: Hanawa Shobo. Appendix: Keigo taikei [The honorific system] reprinted in Kitahara 1978, 109-21.

Wetzel, Patricia J. 1985. In-group/out-group deixis: situational variation in the verbs of giving and receiving in Japanese. *Language and Social Situations*, edited by Joseph P. Forgas, 141-157. New York: Springer-Verlag.

Yamada, Yoshio. 1924. *Keigo-ho no Kenkyu* [Studies of Honorifics]. Tokyo: Hobunkan. Chapter 2: Keigo-ho no taikei [Principles of honorifics] is reprinted in Kitahara 1978, 37-40.

6

A Dynamic Perspective:
Implications for Metafunctional Interaction
and an Understanding of Theme[*]

L. J. Ravelli
University of Wollongong

I. Introduction

In recent years, linguists have recognised the need to account more explicitly for the dynamic nature of language, and to provide dynamically oriented models which allow for this aspect of language to be explained. Within systemic linguistics, Halliday (1991) has discussed the different ways in which the term 'dynamic' can be seen to be relevant to language. With respect to one of these dimensions, that of an instance of language – a text – being seen to be dynamic, Martin (1985) has defined the relevance of this perspective, and established the fundamental opposition between 'dynamic' and 'synoptic'. Innovative attempts to establish a linguistic model which is dynamically oriented have been made by Ventola (1987) and Fawcett *et al* (1988). The semantic implications of a dynamic approach have been explored by Lemke (1991), computational applications by Bateman (1989), and its relevance to conversational analysis by Fine (1991), O'Donnell (1990) and others. The independence of a dynamic perspective from the nature of the data being examined, and the fundamental components of a dynamic perspective, have been established by Ravelli (1989; 1991). While attention to this domain is by no means confined to systemic linguistics, it is interesting to note some specific problems in language description posed by the synoptic conceptualisation of language in the systemic functional model, which we address in this paper.

* I am indebted to Michael Hoey for numerous and stimulating discussions regarding the content of this paper; my thanks are due also to Margaret Berry, as well as the editors and anonymous referees for their comments and suggestions.

The paper falls into two main sections. The first part examines the nature of a dynamic perspective, its central characteristics, and the basic contrasts with standard modelling in systemic linguistics. The discussion is confined to general principles and parameters, and so does not fully elaborate all the modelling issues which need to be considered when adopting a dynamic perspective. The second part of the paper applies the principles of a dynamic perspective to an understanding of the metafunctions of language (Halliday 1973; 1976), and in particular, to the problem of defining the extent of the *Theme* of a clause.

2. A brief overview of the dynamic perspective

A dynamic perspective arises from an interest in the dynamic nature of language: language as process, rather than product. This interest provides a particular challenge for contemporary linguistic theory, as our available linguistic models are much more suited to accounting for the finished, static nature of language, where texts are presented and received as complete wholes, than for the unfinished, fluid nature of language, in which a text may be presented and received as something unfolding and ongoing.

Generally, available linguistic models encourage a global or totalising view of text, one which is eminently suited to an account of language as a finished product. This perspective has been termed 'synoptic' by Martin (1985), drawing on Bourdieu (1977) (note, however, that Hasan *in press* disputes Martin's interpretation of Bourdieu). The synoptic perspective is clearly closely associated with the study of written language, which – because texts in this mode are presented as complete wholes – encourages a global and static overview of the text. In contrast, spoken language, which presents text as active and ongoing, encourages a view which is less totalising, and more process-like. To account for this aspect of language, a dynamic perspective is needed. Yet it is too easy to make a false equation between written language and a synoptic perspective on the one hand, and spoken language and a dynamic perspective on the other. Their equation with the synoptic and dynamic perspectives arises largely because of the *presentation* of the respective modes. Spoken language is both produced and presented as an ongoing process: it preserves all the hesitations, false starts and changes of direction which characterise text production. Written language, on the other hand, is produced as an ongoing process, but edits out all features which typify this, and presents itself as a finished product (Halliday 1985b). It is therefore inappropriate to equate one mode with only one perspective: all language is both product and process. Given that linguistic models have largely arisen in conjunction with the study of written language, the relatively recent focus on spoken language has revealed the inability of available models to account for the process nature of language. However, both modes can – and should – be accounted for from both perspectives. This suggests that a perspective on language should be independent from any 'intrinsic' qualities of the data. A dynamic perspective, then, is a way of modelling or explaining language as, or as if it were, unfolding.

Within the systemic functional approach the dynamic perspective has tended to be most vigorously pursued in relation to certain linguistic phenomena. These phenomena include the study of generic structure (the stages which are typically negotiated in a particular text type), the analysis of clause complexes (how individual clauses are built up to form larger units) and the analysis of turn taking in conversation. As these phenomena can be seen to unfold in time, and to be dependent on the nature of the current environment, they could be said to be 'inherently' dynamic. Certainly, a full account of them demands that they be considered as processes, and doing so reveals inadequacies and weaknesses in synoptically oriented models. However, the suggestion that some types of linguistic phenomena are 'dynamic', and that by inference, others are not, is an equation as false as the equation of the dynamic perspective with a specific mode of discourse. A dynamic perspective should not be reserved just for certain types of data, but should be applied broadly to language as a whole.

The primary work instigating interest in this domain within the systemic school is Martin (1985). Drawing on Hjelmslev (1969), Martin elaborates the concepts which are critical to an understanding of a dynamic perspective, namely the comparison of *dynamic* with *synoptic*, the distinction of *process* and *product*, and the cross-classifying dichotomies of *actual/potential* and *active/static*. He illustrates that a dynamic approach deals with an active view of potential, resulting in a view of text as process, whereas a synoptic approach deals with a static view of potential, resulting in a view of text as product. Given that text is both product and process, both approaches are necessary to give a full account of text, and both approaches must interact. He exemplifies this interaction with a game of bridge, where the various possible moves in the game relate to its synoptic potential, while the sequence of actual moves relate to its dynamic potential. Our global understanding of the game gives a sense of the types of possible moves – a sense of the synoptic potential of the game as a static product. But in playing an actual game, only particular moves are appropriate at particular moments – and for this we need a sense of the game's dynamic potential, as an active process.

However, Martin's appraisal of the synoptic/dynamic distinction entails one problem. He has made a valid and useful observation that every instance of language (the 'actual') is both product and process. In relation to the actual, the difference between product and process is clearly a matter of perspective: while a given instance may foreground either the product or process nature, any instance can be viewed in either way. Thus, a spoken text is clearly process-like in nature, but may be *treated* as either a product or a process, and the reverse is true for a written text. This aspect of Martin's case is clear and convincing. The problem arises in Martin's evaluation of potential. His argument is that the static and active perspectives give rise to two different kinds of potential: a 'synoptic system' and a 'dynamic system'. While he acknowledges that both must be seen to 'symbiotically interact' in order to produce the actual, it is in fact the case that the 'dynamic system' is seen to generate 'dynamic' features (such as the variable sequencing of generic structures, or turn-taking in conversation), and the 'synoptic system' is seen to generate 'synoptic' features (namely those which have typically been the focus of linguistic descriptions in the past: for example, the components of a linguistic unit and how they relate to each other). But as Martin himself argues, the product/process distinction in relation to actual is one of perspective; it would therefore seem logical to extend this to potential as well, such that there is only one system of potential, with the nature of that potential (active, static) differing according to how it is being viewed (dynamically, synoptically). As is the case for the description of the actual, potential should be seen to vary *according to perspective*.

Unfortunately this insight is buried in Martin's work. The consequence is that the nature of the perspective (synoptic or dynamic) is seen to be dependent on the nature of the data being examined (product or process). So a dynamic perspective becomes reserved for data where process aspects are foregrounded, such as conversations, while a synoptic perspective is reserved for the areas with which it has always been associated, where the product aspects dominate, as in the grammar of written texts. The nature of the perspective is equated with the nature of the data, rather than being seen as independent. As a result, the dynamic perspective takes on a secondary role, filling in 'gaps' where the synoptic system fails to explain the data. And in an ironic contrast, it is also equated with everything that is new and interesting in language, whereas the synoptic is equated with everything that is staid and unrevealing. These are problems which can be easily overcome if Martin's insight regarding the dual nature of the actual (as both product and process) is applied to potential as well. The ideal is not to develop two separate systems accounting for two types of data, but to recognise that the perspective is independent of the data, and hence, that two *complementary* approaches to the data are required. Synoptic and dynamic perspectives need to be interwoven, and both should be applied simultaneously to data, to achieve a full understanding of text.

2.1 The synoptic bias in systemic modelling

However, Martin is certainly right that a model which can provide a synoptic perspective only, is necessarily limited in what it can say about language as both product and process. Available linguistic models are largely confined to a synoptic presentation or understanding of language. In the SF model, this takes the form of *system networks* which are the primary theoretical tool for language description. A system network models the paradigmatic potential of language, as a network of inter-related, inter-dependent options (see Halliday and Martin 1981). While a network may be read or used in either a dynamic or a synoptic way (*cf* Halliday 1985a: xxvii), and while it may be used to model 'dynamic' data, the network provides a synoptic representation of language: it is the product of a product point of view.

In a network, choices from a system have structural consequences: the options in the system are *features*, and each feature has an associated realisation, that is, the linguistic reflex of choosing that feature from that system. An output is generated from the network by tracing a path through the network from left to right (this movement being an increase in *delicacy*), making a selection from each system and collecting all the associated realisation statements for that path; this enables a structure to be produced. While it may take time for someone to actually read through a network, the intention is that the selections have no real-time implications for generation. Importantly, all the selections relevant to one structure are made simultaneously, collected together, and then realised to produce one structural output. As Ventola explains (1987: 66), the process of generation is thus 'explosive'. While the network represents the meaningful choices which contribute to the structure of a unit, the choices are made with respect to a unit *as a whole*. This is why current systemic modelling is largely confined to a synoptic perspective. The model represents structure, which is manifested on the syntagmatic axis, as a *consequence* of paradigmatic choice. However, the dynamic perspective highlights the syntagmatic dimension, such that the unfolding of a text is seen to have a certain structural 'life' of its own in terms of an unfolding process. Clearly, if a dynamic perspective is to account for units as they unfold, progressively, then it will not be possible, in generation, to pass through a whole network, collect the relevant features and then explode them into a structure. Nor, in analysis, can a whole unit be examined for all its paradigmatic features. Other, less synoptic, ways of modelling are required.

At issue is the relationship of the two perspectives to language (in the sense of the system of language) and to text (in the sense of an individual instance of language). A system network is appropriate for a synoptic perspective because it presents language as a system of potential – what it is possible to say in the language as a whole. From this, instances of actual texts can be generated from and explained in relation to the overall system. But the potential itself is necessarily static, because what is true for the system, which is understood to be operative for all occasions, is not necessarily true for an instance, that is, the options which would be selected on a given occasion in a given set of circumstances. Opposed to the view of language presented by the system network is the possibility of accounting for language as something actual, an instance of language in use, where language must be seen as something active, with choices being made in response to the exigencies of the moment. The representation of a dynamic perspective therefore requires something other than a system network. It is not simply the case that a dynamic perspective is needed to represent text, in the sense of the actual unfolding of a text, but that language itself must be viewed dynamically, so that the active potential which is available as the text unfolds can be considered.

Clearly, such an account needs to be related to the synoptic description in some way, so that it has some general validity – we would not suggest that what is already known about meaning should be rejected. At the same time, the synoptic description should be related to the dynamic, so that actual instances can be accounted for. Thus, both perspectives are intertwined, but nevertheless bring their own understanding to language and to text.

2.2 Inter-relation of the dynamic and synoptic perspectives

How, then, do the two views of potential relate? Consider the way in which structure, an output or selection from potential, is typically explained. In a systemic model, it is the paradigmatic axis which is primary: choices among elements *in absentia* provide the resource for making meaning, and structure is on the whole a consequential feature following from paradigmatic choices. For example, the choice in English between an interrogative or declarative clause will determine the word order of the clause: whether the Finite precedes or follows the Subject (Halliday 1985a: 68-100). The choice pertains to the unit as a whole, the clause, and the consequence of the systemic choice is a particular structure for the clause. The paradigmatic choice therefore acts as a type of umbrella for the unit in question, opening out to give a particular structure for that unit. This is represented in Figure 1.

In Figure 1, the features are paradigmatic options pertaining to the clause; their selection (between, say, *active* or *passive*, *declarative* or *interrogative*, and so on) determines the nature of the structure, or syntagm, for that clause. The principles of this explanation apply to other *ranks* in grammar, and to other linguistic levels.

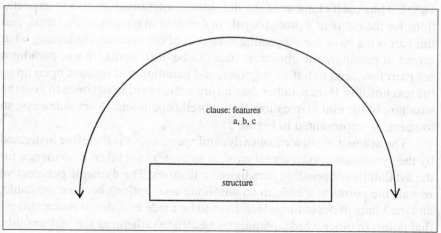

clause: features
a, b, c

structure

Figure 1. Structure from a synoptic perspective

But a dynamic perspective challenges this explanation of the relationship between paradigm and syntagm. Because of the progressive nature of the dynamic perspective, the structure – whether of a clause element or a particular genre – is only revealed as the text unfolds. The paradigmatic choices pertaining to the whole structure cannot be described, because the whole structure cannot be seen.

Yet it would be most unsatisfactory if the synoptic interpretation of paradigm and syntagm had to be entirely abandoned to facilitate what is, after all, supposed to be a change of *perspective*. The systemic model, while synoptically formulated, provides a theory of language which enables us to explain how it is that people mean. If the contribution of the paradigmatic axis to this theory was rejected, this explanation of meaning would be lost, as meaning is seen to derive from paradigmatic contrast: something is meaningful as much for what it isn't, as for what it is.

Importantly, the dynamic perspective does not reject the synoptic formulation of paradigm/syntagm, but interprets it in a different way. Rather than exploring paradigmatic relations as realised by syntagmatic structures, the structures are examined *as a reflection of* paradigmatic options. That is, the structural result of one choice is observed, and on the basis of some knowledge of the language system, this is used to try and explain what choices, to be realised in what structures, might come next. For example, if the element *goods handover* has just been realised in a service encounter, there would be a strong expectation for a *pay* element to follow (Ventola 1987). Thus each element of the unfolding structure gives rise to expectations for the element's probable role or function in paradigmatic terms, and this forms the basis for suggesting what part of the structure, reflecting what aspect of paradigmatic choice, is likely to be next. Syntagm and paradigm are therefore seen to unfold together, and paradigms of options open up as the text unfolds. Hence, rather than an umbrella opening out once to give the structure of the unit in question, the umbrella opens and closes sideways, so to speak, as represented in Figure 2.

The account of choice from a dynamic perspective is therefore instigated by the syntagmatic axis: actual choices in the text are taken as evidence for the availability of possible paradigmatic features. The dynamic perspective reveals the points at which, in an unfolding text, options become available, and the kinds of decisions which have to be made in order to proceed from that point. In other words, paradigms become available as the text unfolds.

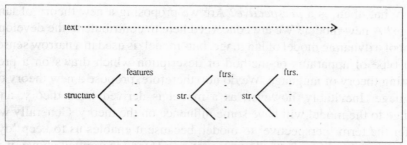

Figure 2. Structure from a dynamic perspective

The synoptic account of paradigmatic choice is essential to inform the dynamic perspective: the system behind the text must be understood in order to be able to hypothesize the role of a given current element. But it is also the case that the dynamic perspective *itself* adds to the understanding of *function*. Because the dynamic perspective shows that paradigms become available as the text unfolds, it becomes meaningful to *move forward in one way rather than another*. From the expectations which arise at places in the unfolding structure, an actual choice is made, from which the text moves forward again. The choice of the actual becomes significant when it is a selection from a paradigm. When a dynamic perspective is adopted, the syntagmatic axis is no longer entirely secondary to the paradigmatic axis, but has its own role to play in the organisation of linguistic choice.

As a way of explaining the significance of choice from a dynamic point of view, consider a conversation between friends in which one participant wishes to make a criticism. If the actual criticism is made without any prior modification or 'softening', it is likely to be interpreted as being very direct and harsh. If, on the other hand, the criticism is preceded by a whole series of qualifications, the blow of the criticism will be much softer. The criticism will still be delivered and received as a criticism, but part of its meaning will have been altered by the circuitous route chosen to deliver it. This can also be explained synoptically, because from a retrospective position, we can observe the nature of the other choices made prior to the criticism, and explain them systemically, observing the contribution of the structure as a whole to the meaning being made. But being able to explain the same situation dynamically, as a process, enables us to see that the very process of delaying the actual criticism changes part of the meaning of that criticism.

What, then, is a *perspective*? Are we proposing a new theory of language? A new model? We are concerned here to contribute to the development of a dynamic model of language, but 'model' is used in a narrow sense, as a type of apparatus or method of description which draws on a preexisting theory of language. We do not, therefore, propose a new theory of language. Inevitably, however, as a model is derived from theory, any change to the model will have some influence on the theory. Generally we prefer the term 'perspective' to model, because it enables us to keep 'dynamic' as a Modifier, instead of using it as a Head (as implied above, it is not appropriate to refer to 'the dynamics' of language). But 'dynamic model' suggests that the model itself must have certain active characteristics, whereas it is the modelling *of* the phenomenon in question which needs to be dynamically oriented. We therefore adopt the term 'perspective', to suggest a way of looking, a way of treating or approaching what is being looked at.

At this point, it is useful to address the question of what exactly is being modelled, and from whose point of view. The question arises as to whether the aim of a dynamic perspective is to model a speaker's intentions or a hearer's process of understanding. Given that the presentation of the arguments is typically from the point of view of the analyst, the emphasis naturally falls on the position of the receiver, and to strategies of decoding, parsing, or interpreting. However, both the speaker's and the receiver's positions are equally relevant, and nothing in the model should preclude the explanation of speaker-related strategies, of generating, producing, or encoding. The aim is to account for the linguistic choices which are possible as a text unfolds, including both the way in which a speaker *can* choose to develop a text, and how a receiver *might* interpret what is being said.

This position is relatively easy to accept as long as the discussion is confined to, say, the unfolding generic structure of a text, or the ongoing flow of speaker-turns in conversation. In such cases, it is easy to see the relevance of trying to account for what *might* happen. Yet as argued above, a perspective should be independent of the nature of the data. It should, therefore, be as relevant to the description of, say, grammar within a clause, as to any other aspect of language. Here, however, objections are likely to be raised (and indeed, have been, for example by Martin 1985 and O'Donnell 1990), as grammar is, after all, one of the least 'inherently' dynamic areas of language. Yet we would argue that it is relevant to consider the flow from one element in, say, a nominal group, to the next element within the same group.

Firstly, while speakers very probably do 'know what they are going to say', and therefore probably do frequently generate units as a whole (that is, select all the relevant features of a nominal group before expressing it), it is certainly not the case that generation can *always* be explained in this way. Explosive generation may be a convenient way of modelling for an analyst, but there is little evidence to suggest that speakers do produce entirely 'explosively'. To do so would mean that all the features of a particular unit are chosen before the unit is actually expressed: this situation therefore entails the assumption that the speaker has a clear idea of the extent of the main unit in a text.

Let us consider the case for explosive generation in relation to grammar. The highest rank in grammar is that of the clause, and clauses can be joined into complexes, which may be both long and deep (that is, many clauses are joined together in a multi-layered construction; *cf* Halliday 1985a: 192-251). While it is assumed that speakers have certain intentions at the start of a clause complex, there is no suggestion that the speaker has planned all the clauses and all their interrelations before beginning to express them. The case for explosive generation here is therefore weak, and we are not aware of any linguist who would argue for it. For the choices relating to an individual clause, the case for explosive generation is stronger, but still not convincing. It would certainly be counter-intuitive to suggest that a speaker proceeds without prior intention, that is, without having any idea what it is that he or she wishes to say. But there is ample evidence that in an unfolding text, speakers may diverge from the planned path, taking up a path which is later judged to be unsatisfactory, or perhaps finding themselves in a branch of a path which has led them into semantic or structural difficulties, from which they need to extricate themselves, (see, for example, de Smedt and Kempen, 1987.)

Even at the rank of group, the case for explosive generation is weak. Consider, for instance, a nominal group, where it is possible to extend an unfolding nominal group by adding Epithets, by making the Head a complex Head, or by tacking post-Modifying elements onto other post-Modifying elements (as in *This is the cat that chased the rat that...*), and so on. The possibility of a speaker extending these structures, on the spur of the moment, as it were, works against the potential for entirely explosive generation. If generation could be explained explosively, then the dynamic perspective would indeed have no relevance, but generation is certainly not wholly, and possibly not even partially, explosive.

Thus a dynamic perspective is relevant to description at any level, even when it may not appear to be an obvious perspective to take. To provide a linguistic analogy, a nominal group which has an extensive list of, say, Epithets as Pre-Modifiers (Halliday 1985a: 159-175), can be explained synoptically as incorporating a great deal of description. From a dynamic perspective, we would want to say that the process of adding Epithet after Epithet has another effect; not merely building up the description, but creating a 'delay' of some sort. This could be motivated by a variety of factors – such as giving the speaker time to think of an actual Head, or adding to suspense in a narrative. It is relevant, therefore, to consider the effect of the process of including multiple Epithets, rather than just observing that multiple Epithets exist.

3. The fundamental characteristics of a dynamic perspective

We will now outline the fundamental characteristics of a dynamic perspective, explaining how it is that such a perspective draws on, but is different from, a synoptic perspective.

A dynamic perspective applies both to the actual, that is the data itself, and to the potential, that is the system behind that data. Its central characteristics are that it is (i) progressive, (ii) active and (iii) probabilistic. The progressive characteristic arises from the fact that, in contrast with the synoptic perspective, the dynamic perspective cannot stand outside of, and *totalise*, the object in question (Bourdieu 1977:4-5). A text, therefore, cannot be viewed as a static object: it is not possible to 'see' all the choices that have been made in the text. Rather, the choices must be observed moment by moment, in a progressive fashion, as they unfold. The aim is to explain what might come next, considering the available options in light of what has already been chosen.

This would appear to have implications for the consideration of time in relation to a dynamically oriented model. A global, synoptic perspective operates *hors du temps,* or 'outside' of time; the flow of time does not impinge upon a point of view which stands outside or above text. On the other hand, a progressive, dynamic perspective necessarily looks forward from its starting position, and so seems to demand the incorporation of a time dimension. However, this does not necessarily mean that *real* time should be accounted for; rather, what needs to be described are the points at which options become available, as a text unfolds.

However, it is the case that there is a strong association between the nature of the perspective and certain positions in relation to time. A global perspective tends to encourage a *retrospective* position, one which looks back on the components of the object in question, and a progressive perspective tends to encourage a *prospective* position, one which looks forward from a given point to what might be coming next. Both prospection and retrospection are possible within both perspectives, but the noted associations are very strong tendencies. Further, as argued in Ravelli (1991), a strong focus on prospection, in a dynamically oriented model, tends to encourage as much independence as possible from the synoptic perspective. For instance, while it is clearly an option for language users to 'go back' in a text and either retrospectively adjust what they have said or written, or clarify what they have heard or read, it is not *essential* for such processes to be explained in retrospective terms. An alternative, although less immediately obvious, option is to explain such a process in prospective terms, by *bringing forward* any previous actualised text to the current position.[1]

The second central characteristic of a dynamic perspective is that it be active. Because the dynamic perspective applies to actual texts, and because it describes and explains those texts as something growing and changing, continually responsive to their environment, then the active characteristic is essential.

Treating a text as active requires the potential behind the text to also be treated actively: at issue are the options which open up in a given text, in a given context. At a particular point in an unfolding text, it is certainly not the case that the entire (synoptic) potential of the linguistic system is relevant: only a portion of that potential is viable. The actually available options depend on both the nature of the text leading up to the current point – the

---

1. An example of how text can be 'brought forward' is found in Emmot (1989). She argues that pronominal referents in narratives are not interpreted anaphorically, by going back in the text to find the appropriate referent, but by bringing forward a frame of reference with the text, so that at any stage in the narrative, the appropriate characters are *primed*, or in ready focus.

text that has already been seen – and on the context within which the text as a whole occurs.

There are four factors which facilitate an active view of potential. Firstly, while an active view of potential has been opposed to a synoptic, static one, it must still draw on a synoptic understanding of potential in order to have some foundation on which to base expectations. It would not be possible to suggest the available options at a given point unless the language being dealt with is known, that is, unless the system of the language is understood. The system represents the static potential of language, it is from this that we begin to draw our expectations for any given text[2].

The general, synoptic potential is subject to conditioning factors: it is this which makes the view active and which narrows the options available at any given point. One feature which contributes to this is *experience of the system in operation*. Rather than just being aware of the options which occur in the (static) system, it is important to be aware of the patterns of typical choice in the system as a whole, that is, to know which options in the system have a strong likelihood of co-occurrence (cf Firth 1968:181, on collocation, and Nesbitt and Plum 1988 on the co-occurrence of options in the clause systems of *taxis* and *logico-semantic* relations).

Knowledge of and experience of the system must then be embedded within a particular context. As is well established within systemic functional linguistics (see, for instance, Halliday 1978 or Halliday and Hasan 1985), selections from the linguistic system are motivated by the context of situation. This view of context is fundamental to a synoptic perspective, and in relation to the dynamic perspective, context can be seen to *activate* certain parts of the linguistic system, and to therefore affect the expectations which are posited as the text unfolds. However, the dynamic perspective requires a slightly different use of contextual information than is currently formulated from a synoptic point of view. Context itself must be viewed actively, as something which may shift or change in response to selections in the unfolding text. Unfortunately, we do not have space to elaborate on this aspect

---

2. While the general, static potential captured by a synoptic perspective is critical to the operation of a dynamic perspective, it should also be noted that a dynamic perspective provides the basis for an understanding of a synoptic system. This is because it is from experience of actual text that abstractions are made about the system as a whole, and each encounter with a text subtly changes the system as a whole (Halliday 1991). Thus the flow of information between the perspectives is bidirectional.

here, but it is described further in Ravelli (1991), and is explored by Hasan (1981; *in press*); the notion of *activation* in relation to context is also discussed by O'Donnell (1990).

Finally, it is essential to account for the history of the text as it unfolds: the choices available in the middle of a text, for example, are not the same as those available at the beginning. Each choice made in the development of the text has the potential to influence choices later in the text. As Lemke observes (1991: 26), we need to know "how the selections *up to now* condition the probabilities for selections *now*." (original emphasis).

In summary, a dynamic perspective incorporates an active characterisation of potential: it requires an understanding of the *possible* in terms of the potential of the system at a given point, and of the *likely*, in terms of the factors conditioning that potential in a given text. While all these factors themselves require some synoptic understanding of the system, it is using that knowledge instantially, in text, which facilitates an active view. The appropriate question to ask is 'what (systemic) choices are relevant at *this* point, in *this* text?'

The final characteristic of a dynamic perspective is that it is essentially *probabilistic* in nature. As a dynamic perspective takes a progressive view of text, the options which open up from a given point are invariably *options*, that is, multiple in nature. Importantly, these are weighted in terms of relative likelihood; some being more likely to occur than others. A probabilistic evaluation of choice is therefore an integral part of a dynamic perspective, and gives rise to *expectations*, that is, options weighted according to the conditioning factors of the moment. The weighting should be in relative, not exact, terms; what is needed is an understanding of what is more likely to occur or less likely to occur in a particular instance.

Again, for further details about the nature of this probabilistic weighting we refer to Ravelli (1991), but one consequence to note here is that probabilistic weighting facilitates a plausible explanation of features such as surprise or markedness in text. Notions of marked and unmarked choices can be equated with notions of *typical* and *untypical* choices. Berry (1982: 88) notes that "the rules specify what is typical, thereby providing a basis for explanation of our recognition, interpretation and evaluation of the untypical." Tsui (1986) relates this comment to the concerns of a dynamic perspective, equating *expected* with *typical* and *actual* with *untypical*. This equation reflects the situation where expectations relate to what is most likely to occur in a particular context, while an actual choice may in fact take up an unlikely option. However, we should add that it is also possible for the actual choice to be the most expected one, that is, to be the typical choice for that context. This means that the probabilistic weighting does not apply *between* the expected and actual choices, but *to* the expectations themselves. The actual option to be selected will come from this range of potential, and may be one which was highly or only marginally expected in the context. This emphasises the meaning attached to the selection of one option rather than another: when a dynamic perspective is adopted, the actual can be seen to *negotiate with* potential. A dynamic perspective therefore highlights a hitherto unexplained aspect of meaning potential.

Bourdieu provides an analogy here, when discussing the meaning of the exchange of gifts. He argues (1977: 4ff) that "an act receives its meaning ... *from the response it triggers off*" (emphasis added). For instance, when a gift is offered by one person to another, the meaning of the exchange depends on the way in which it is received; if the gift is refused, an exchange cannot be seen to have taken place. In other words, whenever a gift is offered, it may always be refused. The refusal does not necessarily have to reclassify the intended meaning of the gift, but the exchange as a whole has been affected by the chosen response to the gift. A similar situation is observed by Willis (1987) who, in discussing the analysis of linguistic exchanges, argues that each move in an exchange has a range of potential, and that the response to that move will take up one aspect of that potential. Choosing how to respond is therefore more than just the synoptically derived meaning of the response itself; there is also meaning in the relation of that response to what has gone before, and to what might follow.

Other features which typify a dynamic perspective, and which are consequential upon the characteristics discussed above, include the fact that the description must embody a flexible definition of what actually constitutes a choice. From a progressive, unfolding point of view, any part of actualised structure may have a role to play at a variety of ranks and levels, and the expectations posited from such a point can relate to any or all of these. The exact nature of these expectations is of course language-specific, but the principle should be generally valid. For example, in English, in an unfolding text, a current word will be assumed to be part of a group and of a clause, and so expectations will be posited in relation to the structure of these elements. But as the text continues to unfold, the group or clause of which that word is a part will eventually be seen, and different expectations will be posited from that point. From a synoptic point of view, this issue does not arise, as the global overview of the text enables the whole unit to be seen, and so for the analyst, it is only a question of deciding which components to focus on.

As a flexible definition of the unit must be allowed, it is then also the case that simultaneous analyses must be allowed. Given that multiple possibilities have to be held open at the same time, it may frequently be the case that the next option could be interpreted as taking up *more than one* expectation posited by the preceding choice. This may seem to invite the spectre of unconstrained analyses, as each element potentially gives rise to a multitude of expectations. Yet the main point of the dynamic perspective is that it makes this problem tractable: a dynamic analysis does not necessarily consider every option which is structurally or grammatically viable, but only those which are active in the context of the unfolding text.

4. The basis of the model

Clearly, then, the dynamically oriented model outlined here adopts the Hallidayan view of language as a resource for making meaning, in which the notion of choice among paradigmatic alternatives is central to an understanding of meaning (see, for example, Halliday 1975, 1985a). What is known of language from a synoptic perspective is drawn on heavily to inform the dynamic. What, then, does the dynamic perspective add?

The key differentiating feature of the dynamic perspective is that it is able to explain actually unfolding choices. This means not just representing a complex array of possibilities for the unfolding of a text, but also giving a functional interpretation to the progressive unfolding of choice. This aspect is essential if a dynamically oriented model is to be more than a sophisticated representation of synoptically-acquired information. Here, we propose a simple metaphor,[3] that of a *path*, to give functional value to the unfolding of choice.

The path provides a mechanism for keeping track of choices as they unfold in a text. A dynamic perspective means that options become available

---

3. The SF model has employed the metaphor of "path" since the early 60s to refer to the sytemic choices which specify some category. It is the path that is represented in the selection expression underlying the structure of a syntagm. My use of the term "path" differs somewhat. See section 4.2 for discussion.

as a text unfolds: wherever a text is *now* provides the environment for what may follow. But as the text unfolds, the relevant environment will shift. Thus, the environment has to be monitored. Bateman (1989) uses the terms *current* and *next* to keep track of the relevant environment. Wherever the text is *now* is the *current* environment, and this sets up the potential for choices at the *next* point in the text. However, a continuous flow is established so that each next choice becomes a current choice as the text continues to unfold.[4]

Current –>Next/Current –>Next/....

This enables movement from 'here' to 'there', from 'current' to 'next' to be monitored. The *current* environment consists of a choice made in the context of preceding choices (although it should be noted that the first actual choice in a text is a different case, *cf* Lemke 1991). It is assumed that from each current environment, a variety of options opens up. Thus, the *next* environment also consists of multiple options: when a selection is made, it in turn becomes the environment for following choices. In this way, the potential available at the next point depends on which option was selected from the current point.

Given this ongoing movement of choice, a *path* of development, of potential, can be seen to flow through a text, opening up and closing down as the text progresses. Such a path is illustrated in Figure 3. This figure represents different choices (potential paths) opening up from each current point; the thick line represents the path which is actually taken up; the other paths are left behind as the text unfolds.

In the fuller model, which we are not able to elaborate here, the multiple options will be contextually weighted, such that the options in the current environment have the status of *expectations*.

Once the mechanism for keeping track of choices has been established,

4. It should be noted that in Bateman's proposal, *current* and *next* have a technical role to play in the modelling of recursive systems. He introduces them as logical micro-functions, associated with the selection of a feature within a recursive system: when a feature is selected, it has a particular consequence for the current and next selection. In this way, it is possible to keep track of the development of a univariate structure. Bateman himself ultimately rejects this proposal because of its unsuitability for computational modelling, but for this paper, the basic concept is useful. Here, then, the terms are not used in the technical sense in which they were established by Bateman, but are used more broadly and generally. Their precise definition depends on the nature of the description to which the general model is applied.

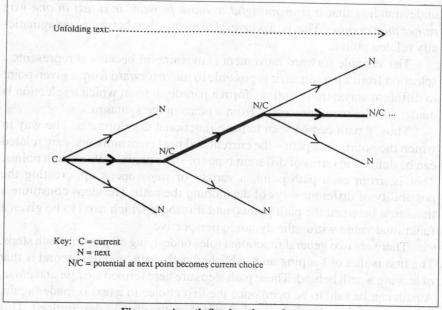

Figure 3. A path flowing through a text

it is then necessary to give a *functional interpretation* to the nature of the
movement in the unfolding path. The current and next environments are the
transition points on the paths, and these are defined according to the description to which the model is applied. For example, an application to the
description of genre will mean the current and next points are defined as
generic stages; in discourse, it could mean that each turn in a conversation
is considered for the potential it opens up for a following turn. In grammar,
a grammatical unit could be taken as the current choice, and other grammatical units as the potential next choice. But for the purposes of developing a
general model, an abstract notion of the way in which these path points may
relate to each other is required. The relevant question is *what sort of path
development is possible? Or, in what ways can the current, actual choice set
up expectations for the next choice?*

The dynamic perspective suggests that any current point will set up
different possible ways of relating to the next point; but, as only one of these
multiple options will be taken up at the next point, this leads us to the

understanding that *it is meaningful to move forward in a text in one way rather than another.* That is, a *potential to mean* arises between syntagmatic-ally related points.

The variable forward movement is meaningful because it represents a selection from a paradigm: it is possible to move forward from a given point in different ways; these options form a paradigm from which a selection is made, and the paradigm arises from a place in the syntagm.

Thus, a path can be seen to have functional development. The way in which the *points* on a path – the current and next environments – are related can be defined in terms of different types of *steps* between those path points. That is, from each path point, a variety of *steps* opens up, creating the possibility of different ways of developing the path. The steps constitute a transition between the path points, and it is these which need to be given a functional value within the dynamic perspective.

There are two general functional roles underlying all possible path steps. The first is that of keeping an established path open, and the second is that of leaving a path behind. These path steps are here termed *sustain* and *close*. A path can be said to be open once the first choice in a text is made (again, the nature of that choice being dependent on the chosen description). This means that the potential for further development of the text is available. The first choice characterises the chosen path, and if another choice is made, this constitutes a step in the path, either sustaining or closing it. If a path is sustained, the option to sustain or close continues to be available. Figure 4 illustrates these most general types of path steps. The term *open* represents the initial choice in the path, and the terms *sustain* and *close* represent possible path steps from that initial point. The lines represent a transition to be made between successive environments in a text, that is, between current and next points. It should be indicated that a close option, if selected, not only closes the current path, but simultaneously opens a new path. While this is not actually captured in the diagram, it is the opening of a new path which signals that the previous path has been left behind.

These path steps may be applied to a variety of linguistic descriptions. Consider an example where a description of the *exchange* is in question (the exchange being a rank of discourse as proposed by Sinclair and Coulthard 1975, although the following terminology derives from Fawcett *et al* 1988). In an exchange, an initiating move which seeks information may be re-sponded to supportively by the next speaker, by, for example, giving an

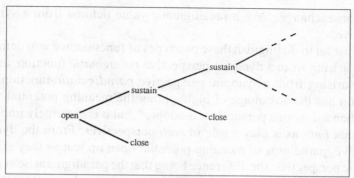

Figure 4. Basic path steps

answer, or non-supportively by, for instance, keeping silent or initiating another exchange. In path terms, the initiating move *opens* a particular path, and sets up a variety of possible options for the next speaker, one of which will be taken up. If the supportive response is taken up, this keeps the path of the exchange *open*, and succeeds in *sustaining* it. If the non-supportive response is taken up, this effectively *closes* the potential for further development of that exchange.

While different path steps are possible, it is also the case that for most descriptions, each path step may be accomplished in more than one way. For example, in the exchange, a closing step can be achieved by either keeping silent or by initiating another exchange. So, a range of options may succeed in effecting a particular type of path step, and a further modelling device is needed to account for the probabilistic weighting of those options, and the way in which one choice is made from the multiplicity of options. Simplifying somewhat, this notion is essentially a means of accounting for the weighting of options using a version of computational *stacks* (for further details, see Ravelli (1991).

Yet it is important to note that two definitions of function arise in this model, as a result of the fact that one path step can be effected in more than one way. From a dynamic perspective, the path step is a functional transition between choice points, so *sustain* and *close* are functional in this, syntagmatic, sense. But the options which effect these path steps have a functional value in a synoptic model of linguistic potential: thus *keep silent* and *reinstate*, while both effecting a close step in a dynamically oriented description of the exchange, have a paradigmatic value defined from a synoptic perspective.

It is useful to distinguish these two types of function; we will define the function arising from a dynamic perspective *syntagmatic* function, and the function arising from a synoptic perspective *paradigmatic* function. This distinction has the advantage of highlighting the meaning potential which arises when a dynamic perspective is adopted, but it is extremely important to note that *both* axes play a role in *both* perspectives. From the dynamic perspective, paradigms of meaning potential open up just as they do from a synoptic perspective, the difference being that the paradigms arise at places in syntagmatic structure. From the synoptic perspective, the syntagmatic axis is also accounted for, but in a way which is consequential upon the choices made on the paradigmatic axis. Therefore, while the terms *syntagmatic function* and *paradigmatic function* are used to distinguish meaning potential from the different perspectives, they should not be taken to indicate that only one axis is relevant to either perspective.

The notion of path steps is a simple way of describing the progressive unfolding of choice in a functionally motivated way. The description can be expanded by differentiating further types of path steps. Both the sustaining and closing steps may be further classified in at least two ways. A path can be sustained by allowing it to *continue* along the lines established by the preceding part of the path. In essence, a continue step means that the next choice repeats the functional potential (in the *paradigmatic* sense) of the preceding choice. So in a continue step, the nature of the relation between the current and next choice is that the units at each path point would play the same role in a synoptic description. In other words, when one point on the path is followed by another which has the same paradigmatic potential as defined in a synoptic description, the step between the two is interpreted as a *sustain: continue.*

The continue step itself may be further classified. A continuation might be achieved by explicitly joining together two choices with a marker of concatenation. Consider a nominal group such as *tanks and guns,* where *tanks* sets up a path about this nominal group, and *guns* continues this path, concatenating an element with the same role as the preceding choice. This type of continue step is called *concatenate.* Alternatively, the continuation may be achieved by juxtaposing two elements with the same (paradigmatic) functional potential, as in *small, pretty flowers*, where *small* sets up a nominal group path, and plays the role of describing the Head in some way, and *pretty* plays the same role, continuing to contribute to the description of this nominal group. This type of continue step is termed *add*. The nature of the continue transition is that the second choice adds something to the unfolding path, but does so in such a way that it repeats the functional potential of the preceding step, either through concatenation or addition. In general terms, the continue step keeps the path unfolding along the lines established by the preceding choice.

Another way in which a path can be sustained is by adding an element which keeps the path open, but which also *changes* the general direction of the path in some way. In this case, the next choice clearly belongs to the unfolding path, but plays a functional role different to that of the preceding one. Consider the nominal group *two army tanks*. In this group, *two* sets up a nominal group path, and tells us something about the nominal group, describing the number of the group; *army* sustains the nominal group, but changes it by classifying the group, and *tanks* also sustains the path, but changes it again by defining the Head of the group. In comparison with a continue step, a *change* step means that each point in the path has a different role to play in relation to that path.

The option to close a path can also be achieved in more than one way. First, closure can be accomplished by *completing* the current path, that is, by adding an element which fulfils the expectations set up by the path up to that point. For instance, the path set up by the nominal group cited above, *the two army tanks*, could be sustained by continuing the group, perhaps concatenating another Head, or by changing it with a post-Modifying element. As it is a nominal group path that is in question, the path is potentially complete once *tanks* is reached, because *tanks* can function as Head. This means that the next element following *tanks* could successfully close the group, by moving out of the nominal group path and into a different type of group, say, a verbal group, as in *two army tanks were* .... The step into *were* constitutes a completion because the expectations for the basic nominal group structure have been satisfied. (Simultaneously, the step into *were* succeeds in *opening* a verbal group path; a post-Modifying element would not succeed in closing the nominal group, because it is part of that same nominal group path, and so does not open any new path.)

On the other hand, a path can be closed without the essential expectations being fulfilled, and a step such as this is termed *abandon*. For instance,

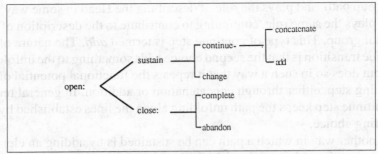

Figure 5. Finer classification of the basic path steps

if the above example had been *two army were...,* the step into *were* still succeeds in closing the nominal group path, but in this case, the expectations set up by *two army* have not been fully satisfied, as the appropriate conditions for a nominal group have not been fulfilled. These path steps are illustrated in Figure 5. The square brackets indicate finer distinctions of the basic path steps.

These choices are based on the premise that it is meaningful to move forward in *one way rather than another,* and they illustrate the *function* of a dynamic perspective. That is, the nature of the step between the current and the next environment in an unfolding path has a function attributed to it. This enables the unfolding of a text to be explained in functional terms: the path presented here is not just a way of showing complex syntagmatic relations, but one which presents a dynamic perspective on choice. The transitions between choice points, as well as the choice points themselves, have a functional value attached. Clearly, the above examples are very much based on the operation and nature of English; application to other languages would, no doubt, result in a different conception of the choices involved, and in different ways of achieving and accounting for the steps between current and next choices. However, it is the *principles* which are important: that choices should be considered as they unfold, and that the syntagmatic relation of one choice to another can be interpreted functionally.

A dynamic perspective therefore encompasses two different types of choice. The first is in the nature of the path step itself: whether from a given current point the options to *continue, change, close,* are taken up. This aspect of choice is a way of functionally interpreting the syntagmatic relations between successive units. The second type of choice concerns the way a particular path step is accomplished: for instance, there may, in the description in question, be more than one way of effecting a *change* step, or more than one way of *completing* a path. This second aspect of choice is informed by our synoptic knowledge of linguistic potential, and is a way of functionally interpreting the paradigmatic possibilities at a given point. In this way, each next path point represents a multiplicity of options, relating both to the type of path step which is in question, and to the way in which any one path step may be achieved.

Given these two interrelated views of function, the question arises whether one is accorded greater priority than the other or not. While the positions of the producer and the receiver are somewhat different in relation to this question, it is not that one view of function is theoretically more important than another: the separate notions of function interact in such a way that it is impossible to give one type priority. Certainly for the analyst, the two views of function are necessarily treated simultaneously: the nature of the transition between choice points and the nature of the options selected at the choice points must operate in conjunction with each other.

For the producer of a text, it would certainly be the case that the path steps are secondary in relation to choices at path points if, and only if, the process of generation was understood to be explosive. But as argued above, explosive generation cannot be taken as an unquestioned given. Yet even so, it is the case that from the producer's point of view, secondary weight is accorded to function arising from a dynamic perspective, that is, to the nature of the path steps. This is because semantic intentions are generally understood to be prior to the actualisation of any choice (Hasan 1981:115), so the intentions precede the unfolding path; in other words, the speaker will have some idea of which features to select in relation to the unit about to be produced. But this does not mean that function arising from the dynamic perspective is less important – it is in fact an essential component in modelling speaker production of a dynamically unfolding text. For example, having commenced a certain path in order to realise a particular meaning, the speaker might find him/herself obligated (structurally) to complete the path; or a selection at one path point might open up path possibilities which the speaker had not previously considered, allowing the text to take an unanticipated direction. Further, in producing a text, a speaker typically self-monitors what is being produced, therefore simultaneously playing the role of receiver, with a receiver's perspective on the unfolding text. For the producer, then, a certain priority is accorded to the choices at path points, over the path steps themselves. But it is not by any means the case that, in an unfolding text, the role of the latter is obviated.

In contrast, for the receiver of a text, primary weight is accorded to the path steps, and secondary weight to the choices at path points. The receiver of a text uses the current choices to set up hypotheses about what is to come next, and interprets the next actual choice in light of these. The actual choices are understood against the background of what the receiver expects the text to be meaning at that point. Hoey (1983) argues a similar case for the reader making sense of a written text. The role of the dynamic perspective is reinforced by the fact that receivers are occasionally 'wrong-footed' and have trouble 'fitting in' the current (path point) choice to their cumulative understanding of the text.

Given the predominance of the synoptic perspective in linguistic modelling, it would be natural to interpret the dynamic perspective as secondary, being at best an interpretation strategy to understand relations between choices which have been predetermined, that is, which already 'exist'. But the dynamic perspective adds to the understanding of the meaning potential of an unfolding text: it is not just the case that certain choices must follow others at sequential points. Rather, there is an option to choose what will come next in an unfolding text; the choice relates to the way to develop that text, and is not necessarily predetermined by a synoptic understanding of meaning potential.

This model of unfolding choice entails several interesting features. Firstly, it differentiates *expected* from *actual* choices. That is, a choice which is the most expected at the next point, given the current state of the description, may not necessarily be the choice which actually occurs in the unfolding of the text. The comparison of the expected with the actual allows effects of markedness to be explained. Secondly, what is not chosen at the next point but which was expected can have a residual effect, termed *latent potential*. Latent potential arises when one linguistic realisation at a path point manifests more than one potential functional role (as, for example, in the case of a verbal item which could be playing the role of either auxiliary or main verb). It may give rise to simultaneous paths. However, not every possible role of every item must always be accounted for – an account of context will generally constrain the analysis of latent potential. Similarly, it might be the case that a later choice in a text will require a reinterpretation of something chosen earlier, in which case the latent potential of an earlier item needs to be *brought forward* to assist that interpretation. In either case, the unactivated potential of a current choice can be taken up at a later stage in the path, and can affect the interpretation of ongoing choices. This latter effect is called a *shadow*, and both latent potential and shadow will be referred to further below.

A further distinctive feature of this model is in the definition of unit boundaries. Given the path model described above, the boundary of a unit cannot be determined *until that boundary has been passed*. That is, a path cannot be understood to be *closed* until another has *opened*. For example, in an unfolding text, a structure might represent a potentially complete nominal group; however, until a step into another group is achieved, the nominal group boundary cannot be confirmed. Again, while our knowledge of what constitutes a particular unit type derives from a synoptic understanding of language, it is nevertheless the case that in the application of a dynamic perspective, the implementation of that knowledge needs to be re-evaluated. The determination of unit boundaries from a dynamic perspective in some ways contrasts with our usual (synoptic) understanding of unit boundaries.

A further point to note is that the path notion must apply to a description which has a structure consisting minimally of two *ranks* (rank being the scale of abstraction accounting for the hierarchical arrangement of linguistic units, such as *clause-group-word* in English; see Halliday 1961). Steps between units are interpreted in terms of their role in the next highest rank. For instance, steps between *words* are interpreted in light of their role in a *group*. Or, in discourse, steps between *moves* are interpreted in light of their role in an *exchange*, and so on. Once the highest rank in any description is reached, it is necessary to move up a level of description in order to be able to interpret the highest rank.

Most importantly, because the path movement allows for different possibilities in the development or forward movement of the text, *this movement is meaningful*. In other words, in this model, it is meaningful to move forward to 'here' rather than 'there'. The path steps give a value or meaning to the transitions between choice points. This feature differentiates the model outlined here from other attempts at dynamic modelling, as explained below.

4.1 Comparison with other dynamically oriented models

Numerous other models have been proposed which try to provide a dynamic representation of various linguistic phenomena. For example, Ventola (1987) explores *flowcharts* as a possible representation for the unfolding of generic structure in texts. Fawcett *et al* (1988) develop *systemic flowcharts* to account for the unfolding of an exchange. The *Augmented Transition Networks* developed by Woods (1970), have also been explored as a possible dynamic representation.

All these models are able to account for different possible forward movements in a text, and all of them overcome some of the synoptic limitations of modelling with a network. Ventola's flowchart, for example, models the way in which speakers can interactively negotiate the generic stages of a text (specifically, a *service encounter*), by making various decisions or taking particular actions which enable the text to move forward. Instead of describing all the systemically potential options for generic stages, the flowchart lays out a variety of paths which might be followed by speakers in interactively producing a text. Thus choice is represented non-explosively, with the ultimate structure of the finished text being achieved incrementally, each actual choice being the environment for the next choice.

Woods' Augmented Transition Network (ATN) is in many respects very similar to the flowchart. It represents movement from one *state* to another (Bates 1978), using *arcs* to accomplish movement between states. While developed for grammar, ATNs have been used by O'Donnell (1990) to represent behavioural options, and by Reichman (1985) to represent aspects of discourse. They have the same advantages as the flowchart, showing that the next possible choice is dependent on the choices that have previously been made. Hence choice is modelled progressively, as something which unfolds, rather than as something which explodes.[5]

The systemic flowchart, developed by Fawcett *et al* (1988), develops Ventola's proposals, providing a more complex representation than the basic flowchart of actually available choices (the choices in Ventola's flowcharts

---

5. While often associated with transformational grammar, there is ample evidence that the principles of the ATNs can be extended to other descriptions. O'Donnell (1990), Reichman (1985) and Leal (1975) explore their application in systemics, discourse analysis and tagmemics respectively.

being essentially limited to binary options). Flowchart and network representations are integrated, using flowchart relations to link up many small system networks. So by following the flowchart, it is possible to generate the syntagmatic relations in the text as the text unfolds, and the systems represent the paradigmatic relations of choice. In this way, paradigms become available as the text unfolds, which is clearly an advantageous feature for a dynamically oriented model.

All these representations are in many ways successful at modelling the progressive unfolding of choice. They all succeed in showing how the selection of one option at one point affects the possible routes which can be taken from that point. In this respect, they overcome the global view of choice necessitated by a synoptic perspective, and represent the linear, non-global, unfolding aspect of choice.

However these models all have one particular limitation. There seems to be no way of describing what it *means* to take one path or route rather than another. The paths may lead in different directions, but this says nothing more than that different steps follow different steps. The path itself has no significance, and is nothing more than an observed transition between different parts of the data.

As a result, the potential routes in these models are necessarily finite in number, and limited to the routes which have been observed in actual data. All the possibilities must be laid out in advance, and only pre-observed structures can be accounted for. Such models therefore present a *static* view of potential: the models must exist *in toto* before the text description begins. The way in which that potential is used as a text unfolds may be dynamically oriented, as potential is seen to unfold progressively, but the overall potential of the linguistic resources described by these models is synoptically conceived. The meaning captured in the model continues to be meaning as understood from a synoptic perspective. No meaning or function is attributed to the dynamic perspective, and so, while texts might be seen to unfold in a particular way, the significance of this cannot be explained. If a model cannot give a functional purpose to the nature of transitions between choices, it will be necessarily limited in its representation of a dynamic perspective. In particular, any new or additional structure in the relevant description has to be added in an ad-hoc fashion, simply extending the model to incorporate the new description.

Of course it is not the case that the patterns which exist for any one aspect of description are infinite in the sense of being random. But new structures and novel use of familiar structures do arise, and a model which attempts to account for an actually unfolding text must be able to allow a moment by moment reformulation of the meaning potential of the text. If the model exists *in toto* before the text description begins, it necessarily presents a static view of potential, even if the way of moving through that model is dynamic.

Thus the path model proposed above differs from the flowchart, ATN and systemic flowchart in that only the path model attributes a functional value to the dynamic perspective. In the other models, different potentials for ongoing development do depend on the current choice, but no value is given to the process of choosing from among these alternatives. That is, no meaning is ascribed to the choice to move forward in one way rather than another, and the 'meaning' of the selection derives only from being able to compare it, synoptically, with other possibilities at the same point. As a result of this restricted view of potential, the relevant models must be described and built in advance of the text, so to speak: all the (synoptically) possible means of developing the text have to be accounted for. However, given the notion that a path may have its own dynamic function, *and* given what is known about synoptic potential, it is possible to build the path *in conjunction with* an unfolding text. The nature of the unfolding path from a dynamic perspective therefore draws on an understanding of the system, but responds to the exigencies of an actual text.

4.2 Comparison with standard systemic modelling

It is important to differentiate the paths proposed here from a system network. It might at first sight be tempting to compare the paths with a path being traced through a system network: Bateman (1989: 272) says that a system network can be interpreted as if it were a flowchart, "walking through" the network, "following connections and making choices". But the comparison is valid in name only: the actual nature of these two types of path is very different. In a system network, the type of path Bateman refers to does indeed take a particular direction, and various options are available along the course of that path. But essentially, such a path must be followed from the initial selection to a final realisation statement, resulting in explosive generation. As the environment of choice is defined paradigmatically, there is no possibility of tracing the flow between the current and next environments for choices in an actually unfolding text.

Additionally, while the basic path steps can be further classified, this finer classification is not equivalent to an increase in delicacy in the system network. Conceptually the two are very similar, but formally, an increase in delicacy adds further features to a given unit, while in a dynamic path model the finer distinctions are different ways of talking about the same thing – that is, they describe the same type of path step, without adding further 'features' to it.

Related to this, a further point of difference is that delicacy is the *only* type of movement possible in the network. Once a 'path' is started in the network, it needs to be followed until a point of realisation is reached which can be included in a selection expression. Thus, certain options and directions are virtually obligatory. A dynamic representation is able to use the knowledge from the synoptic system in a more fluid way than this.

The path model proposed here is therefore different from tracing a path, in general terms, through a system network. Yet interestingly, reference has often been made in the systemic field to a 'dynamic system'. Martin (1985) and Ventola (1987) refer to this, although they do not necessarily use the term 'system' in a technical sense. However, Bateman (1989) O'Donnell (1990) and Fine (1991), among others, do explore the term in its technical sense. As should be clear from the arguments presented in this paper, and as Hasan (*in press*) has argued, a 'dynamic system' is a 'theoretical oxymoron'. Systems may be used to model phenomena which have 'dynamic consequences', as Bateman does for the modelling of dependency structures, but this does not necessarily mean that a dynamic perspective on choice has actually been represented. Even O'Donnell, who is able to modify the network to show how current choices constrain available next choices, is confined to a synoptic view of meaning, where motivation for selection of options from a system arises from their different paradigmatic potential. There is nothing to explain why a text would unfold in one way rather than another.

Yet, as stated in this paper, it is a fundamental characteristic of the dynamic perspective that it draws on an existing synoptic system. This can be achieved if, when applying a dynamic perspective, the synoptic network is 'frozen', so that the dynamically oriented analysis can draw on the network without being obliged to traverse a whole system. In a dynamically oriented analysis we need to consider what path steps might be possible from

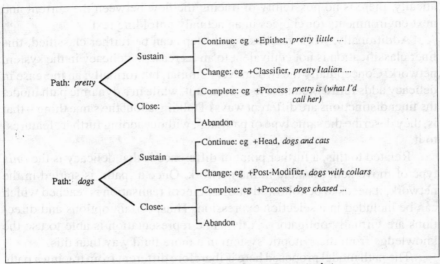

Figure 6. Different nominal group constraints

a particular current point, and the current point has to be identified in terms of its probable paradigmatic potential. This locates it in terms of the system network. Thus from the network, it can be determined what would constitute the different path steps from that point; for instance, a continue step would repeat the network feature selected by the current point; a change would be accomplished by selecting from a simultaneous system; a complete would be achieved by moving into a different, unrelated system, and an abandon would be inexplicable in terms of the activated system. The dynamically oriented model therefore draws on the information contained within available networks, but formulates the information in a different way. It is something other than a simple trace through a network. Figure 6 exemplifies the way in which the status of the current choice may give rise to different path potentials, by reference to unfolding nominal groups, the first being opened by *pretty*, which is located in the network as a Pre-Modifier, specifically an Epithet; the second being opened by *dogs*, located as Head.

As Figure 6 shows, the types of options available vary markedly according to the status of the current choice. Paradigms of choice are activated as the text unfolds, and so vary according to the current status of the text. The synoptic representation is needed to inform a dynamic perspective, but the actual nature of the paradigms within a dynamic perspective are syntagmatically defined.[6]

5. Relevance to the metafunctions

Having spent considerable time establishing some of the fundamental features of a dynamic perspective, we will now apply the dynamic perspective to an understanding of the interactional unfolding of the ideational, interpersonal and textual metafunctions within a clause. However, rather than applying the dynamic perspective to its full extent, we will apply only the 'essence' – as it were – of the model. This is because space is insufficient to elaborate and apply the model at length. Our aim will not be to explore all the implications of a dynamic perspective, but to illustrate the influence that a 'forward-looking' approach can have on our understanding of an aspect of language. We will begin by examining a particular problem in the description of *Theme*.

6. Similarities might also be drawn between the path model proposed here and finite state grammars, also called Markovian or stochastic processes. The latter was rejected by Chomsky (1957) as in inadequate representation of linguistic structure. But again the similarity is at a superficial level only. The path model does move from state to state, but because the nature of the current and next choices are taken from the synoptic understanding of language operative in a systemic model, the whole conception of language is rather different from that represented in the original finite-state grammars (*cf* Shannon and Weaver, 1949).

An additional feature of a Markovian process is that the current environment provides all the necessary information for moving on to the next environment. It is debatable whether the path model is equivalent to this or not. To describe the dynamic unfolding of a text as Markovian in this sense, would seem to place too much emphasis on the movement from current to next, ignoring the fact that any 'current' choice is but one link in an ongoing chain, in which different choices would have led to different 'current' points. Yet, in the fuller model, the previous history of the text is *carried forward* with the unfolding text (rather than preserving the previous history of the text so that it is available to 'go back to'). Thus, all necessary information does seem to be available from the current point only. This is the position implicit in Sinclair's (1991) model of *encapsulation*, where the current sentence embodies all that is relevant to interpret the text, both encapsulating the previous text/sentence and prospecting the next text/sentence. In Sinclair's model, the previous text appears to lose its importance, because it is encapsulated by the current text. But it remains true both in the path model and in Sinclair's, that the current text was arrived at by following a particular unfolding path; a different path would have led to a different point from which to proceed.

5.1 Problems in the description and delimitation of Theme

There currently exists some debate as to the way the boundary of Theme is delimited. Halliday (1985a) describes Theme as extending up to and including the first ideational element of the clause, that is, up to the first topical Theme. Interpersonal and textual elements are therefore thematic if occurring before the topical element, but not after, and only the first topical element can be thematic. This is, of course, the description of Theme *in English*. It is not necessarily true for other languages and is not the functional *definition* of Theme. The definition of Theme can be taken as that which functions as the 'starting-point' of the message (Halliday 1985a: 39). It should be noted that Halliday (1967: 219) does allow a thematic role to multiple Adjuncts in clause initial position: "... the function of theme, restricted elsewhere to single clause elements, can in the case of adjuncts extend over two or more." In other words, the topical theme can extend over more than one ideational element. However, this aspect is not foregrounded in the 1985a description.

The current debate exists with respect to the description in Halliday 1985a. For example, Berry (1992a; 1992b) argues that the boundary of Theme should be extended to include everything which is *pre-verb*. This permits complex Themes which include more than one topical Theme, as in (1) (Note thematic elements are in bold type):

(1) **On Saturday, there** is a market .... (Berry 1992a)

It also permits complex Themes with textual or interpersonal elements occurring *after* the topical Theme, as in (2).

(2) **The alternative to dogmatic realism, fortunately**, is not....
(Berry 1992a, citing VandeKopple 1991)

Berry argues that examples such as these are stylistically, but not functionally, different from the more strictly Hallidayan examples (where neither *there* nor *fortunately* would be analysed as thematic).

Matthiessen (1992) contributes to the debate. He observes the difficulty in drawing the dividing lines of Theme, and agrees with Berry that "... experiential Adjuncts may pile up at the beginning of the clause, and the effect is clearly one of successive thematic contextualisation." (1992: 50). Matthiessen (1992: 51) cites example (3), an extract from Muriel Spark, to illustrate his point:

(3) A: 'Do you mean we're overdressed?' said the charming father of the
        Family.
     B: '[Place:] In England, [Time:] at this moment, [Purpose:] for this occasion,
        [Carrier:] we [Process:] would be [Attribute:] quite overdressed.'

Matthiessen suggests that in (3), all the elements up to the Process have
a thematic role to play, giving a complex Theme consisting of three Circumstantial elements (Place, Time, Purpose) and the element Carrier. He notes
further that the Subject element in clauses with marked Themes can be seen
to be part of the thematic development of a text. This point is illustrated with
the help of example (4) (from Matthiessen 1992: 52; Themes in bold;
marked Theme in bold italics).

(4) **Autumn** passed and **winter** [passed], and ***in the spring*** the **Boy** went out to
     play in the wood. While he was playing, two rabbits crept out from the
     bracken and peeped at him.

Here, in (4), the third clause has a marked Theme (*in the Spring*)
followed by Subject *the boy*, which according to Matthiessen (1992: 52)
"seems to have some thematic value." In Halliday's description, this
element would not count as thematic; and Matthiessen comments on the fact
that the item is picked up as Theme of the following clause. On this basis he
concludes that "In this [third] clause, the Subject [ie… *the boy* LR] still falls
within the diminuendo of the thematic wave."

Thus both Matthiessen and Berry suggest that the boundary of Theme
needs to be broadened, because elements following the first topical element
can be important in the thematic development of a text, contributing to a type
of diminuendo effect in the Theme. Interestingly, there seems no doubt that
the Process element is part of the Rheme; that at least is one clear dividing
line. Why, then, is there doubt about the *extent* of Theme, and why is there
certainty as to its absolute limit? It is in relation to these questions that a
dynamic perspective offers some interesting suggestions.

5.2 The metafunctions from a dynamic perspective

A dynamically oriented description describes each metafunction *as a clause
unfolds;* information about each metafunction thus builds as the clause
proceeds. Here, we present in the most general terms what can be said about

the grammatical components of Theme (pertaining to the textual metafunction), Mood (interpersonal) and Transitivity (ideational). We do not consider other grammatical systems relevant to the respective metafunctions.

At this stage, we are not attempting to apply a dynamic perspective to its full extent, but merely to *transfer* known synoptic analyses to a 'frontloaded' point of view, to see what this simple shift in orientation enables us to say – or to think – about this aspect of language. This is an initial stage in developing a dynamically oriented description, and does not fully reflect the potential of such a description nor the details of integrating synoptic and dynamic models. However, this may serve as an appropriate starting point for the purposes of initiating a debate on the dynamic perspective in language description.

The synoptic description of Theme clearly transfers readily to a dynamic perspective, as – at least in English – Theme comes first in the clause, and is followed by the Rheme. Thus, any initial element of the clause will be taken to *open* the Thematic path; once a candidate for a topical element is reached, steps into further elements will be taken to close the Theme path and open the Rheme. The description is therefore initially very informative, but trails off rapidly.

In the synoptic analysis of MOOD, the Mood element in indicative clauses is realised by the presence of the Finite and Subject elements, and their relative order determines whether the MOOD selection is declarative or interrogative. A dynamic analysis will encounter the elements in Mood as they unfold in the clause, hence if a Finite or wh-element is encountered first, the Mood will most probably be interrogative. If a nominal element is encountered first, then it is highly likely that a declarative is being formed, although in some cases the classification of the clause as declarative has to be held off until more of it has been seen (as in the following example: *These days, can we afford not to be more vigilant?*, where an element of the Residue precedes the Finite^Subject structure of the Mood element). In most cases, it can be quickly determined whether the clause is declarative or interrogative.

However, the identification of the element taking on the role of Subject in the clause is not so straightforward. For interrogative clauses, where the Finite or wh-element comes first, the most probable next option is that the next nominal element will be functioning as Subject (as in *are the soldiers...?*) For declaratives clauses, it is necessary to identify elements which are potential Subjects, and then to wait for a Finite element (or fused Finite and Predicator element) to confirm this. This is because clauses can begin with multiple ideational elements, where elements of the Residue precede the Subject (as in *before dawn, the protesters gathered...*), or where a Residue element intervenes between the Subject and the Finite (as in *the soldiers, without prior warning, began....*). Once a Finite element is reached (and given that a potential Subject element has been identified, that is, that a declarative structure is unfolding), the Mood analysis ceases to be of interest, as further steps must pertain to the Residue. The remainder of the clause is still of interest in *interpersonal* terms, however the path pertaining to Mood itself is closed with the step from the Finite to the Predicator. Where the Finite and Predicator are fused, the two steps from the Subject to the Finite and from the Finite to the Predicator occur simultaneously.

For Transitivity, the synoptic analysis hinges on the nature of the Process in question. While different Participants in different Processes have distinct grammatical characteristics (Halliday 1985a: 108), it is still necessary to determine the nature of the Process itself before being able to assign roles to the Participants. Thus, assuming the structure Participant^Process^Participant, for a declarative clause, it is clear that from a dynamic perspective, very little can be said about ideational meaning as the path begins to unfold. What can be said will increase as the path continues to develop, and will become most informative when the Process element is reached.

5.3 Interaction of the metafunctional analyses

How, then, do these brief sketches of the metafunctional paths relate to the delimitation of the Theme boundary? The answer is in the interaction of the analyses as they unfold, particularly in the interaction of the Theme and Mood paths. The discussion will be illustrated with reference to (5), which is taken from Ravelli (1991); the actual string in (5) occurred in a radio news broadcast.

(5)   ... and there this morning protesters gathered again after dawn ...

This example illustrates the concerns raised by Berry and Matthiessen: a Hallidayan analysis of Theme would have to conclude that the Theme path closes after *there*, yet *this morning* and *protesters* seem to be just as much a 'departure point' of the message as is *there*. In examples such as this, the area of contention concerns groups like *there* and *this morning* which have the potential to function either as Adjunct or as Subject.

In a dynamic analysis, as a clause unfolds, the role of such elements cannot be determined until the element is passed and other elements encountered. In other words, these elements have a *latent potential*. Importantly, this latent potential is operative in terms of the Mood analysis, that is, they could be functioning as either Adjunct or Subject. For every clause-initial element which has these characteristics, these simultaneous expectations apply. Once a step into a verbal group is effected, this shows that the Subject path has been taken up, and so no further expectations are required for the Mood analysis.

However, the simultaneous expectations in the Mood analysis affect the Theme analysis. Because of the unmarked association between Subject and Theme (*cf* Halliday 1985a), even a latent potential for a Subject gives rise to a parallel expectation that the element has a thematic role to play. Thus, each time a simultaneous Adjunct/Subject analysis is posited for a fronted element, this gives that element the effect of a *shadow* Theme, that is, Theme by virtue of the unactivated potential affecting our interpretation of the element. The element is *interpreted* as being Thematic, because in the Mood analysis, the same element has the potential to function as Subject. Hence in these cases, the Theme is not in fact 'trailing off' (Matthiessen 1992), but is being constantly revised as the clause unfolds, until the point at which the clause unequivocally moves into Rheme. This analysis is captured in Figure 7. The elements of the example are presented down the page in a column; similarly, the analyses should be read downwards. The sign '<->' means that that step is not functional in terms of the current analysis; the sign '/' means that the analyses presented either side are simultaneous; the sign 'x' means that the analysis ceases at that point. The vertical lines, sometimes shown as branching, are included to facilitate tracking of the analyses.

In order to explain the details of Figure 7, we will 'talk through' the analyses represented therein. In the Mood analysis, the element *and* is not functional in Mood terms; the next element, *there*, might be functioning as an Adjunct or a Subject, but the following element, *this morning*, picks up the Adjunct potential of the path, and so identifies which of the simultaneous paths is in question. However *this morning* may itself be either an Adjunct or a Subject, so the same simultaneous analysis is represented again. The next element, *protesters*, again shows that the Adjunct path has been picked

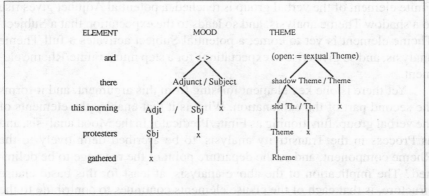

Figure 7. Interplay of Mood and Theme Analyses

up. Thus for both *there* and *this morning*, there has been a latent potential for these elements to be functioning as Subject. *Protesters* can be assigned a Subject role with reasonable certainty, and the next element *gathered* confirms this.

In relation to the analysis of Theme, the first element, *and*, opens a Theme path, and is a textual Theme. This gives rise to the expectation that the Theme path will be sustained by the addition of interpersonal or topical Themes. The next element, *there*, is a topical Theme, and at this point, a Hallidayan analysis would analyse the Theme path as being completed. However other ideational elements may follow, and as the Subject has not yet been definitively analysed, there is still a sense in which the departure point of the message has not yet been fully elaborated. Thus, a simultaneous thematic analysis is posited for *there*, allowing it to be a part of a larger Theme path (hence *shadow Theme*) or to be the whole of the Theme path (hence *Theme*). As the element following *there* is *this morning*, this shows that the shadow potential of *there* has been taken up; again, the same type of expectations are posited from *this morning*, as either shadow Theme or Theme, and the next element, *protesters*, again takes up the shadow Theme potential of the preceding element. However, because of the strong expectation that *protesters* is Subject, this suggests that the departure point of the message has been elaborated, and that Theme will be completed here by a step into Rheme. The next element, *gathered*, confirms this.

Thus the expectations for Mood and Theme are inter-related. Before the

Finite element of the verbal group is reached, a potential Adjunct gives rise
to a shadow Theme analysis, and so leads to the expectation that a Subject/
Theme element is yet to come; a potential Subject activates a full Theme
analysis, and so gives rise to expectations for a step into a Finite/Rheme element.

Yet there is one key element missing from this argument, and it forms
the second part of the explanation. What is it that enables the elements of
the verbal group, functioning as Finite/Predicator in the Mood analysis, and
as Process in the Transitivity analysis, to be ascribed definitively to the
Rheme component, and so the departure point of the message to be delimited? The implication of the above analysis, at least for this basic clause
structure, is that each of the clause elements continues to contribute to the
'departure point' of the message, but that once the Process is reached, the
clause is unequivocally 'under way'. This analysis therefore broadens
Halliday's explanation of the departure point of the message, and needs to
be justified.

When a dynamically oriented analysis is applied, and given that the
metafunctional paths unfold in conjunction with each other, it could be said
that each of the metafunctional paths has to 'get under way'. Every path
needs to be opened and developed in its own terms. Again, we will restrict
our discussion to a basic declarative structure. In the analysis of ideational
meaning (at least as captured by the system of Transitivity), it is the presence
of the Process element which marks a critical dividing line in the ideational
path between 'little' and 'significant' information: the sense of what the
clause is 'about' in ideational terms grows as the clause grows, with the
Process providing the essential pivot. At the same time, the path analysis for
interpersonal meaning gives 'advance warning' of the Process in ideational
terms. This is because an element which is likely to be functioning as Subject
will be in intimate relation with the Finite element of the verbal group; that
is, a Finite or fused Finite/Predicator will be expected to be next, and these
will form part or all of the Process from an ideational point of view.

Ideationally, then, there is a sense that the departure point of the clause
is not fully elaborated until the Process is reached, and it is the interpersonal
structure which gives rise to the expectation that the message is off the
ground and ready to be elaborated. Textually, everything up to that critical
dividing line can be seen to be thematic; once there is an element which is
not only thematic but also likely to be functioning as Subject, the ideational

information is expected to be increased imminently, and the departure point of the message is therefore fully elaborated.

A dynamically oriented analysis thereby seems to re-evaluate the boundaries of Theme, by revealing an additional role of the Subject element in a Mood analysis. The Subject, from a dynamic perspective, indicates a core element of the clause around which a great deal of information hinges. Of course, this is exactly what the synoptic analysis says: that the Mood component consists of two elements, Subject and Finite, on which the validity of the proposition rests. But the dynamic analysis reveals that Mood is not only important for identifying the 'resting point' of the proposition, but also for acting as a focussing element in relation to the other metafunctions. The Mood component acts as a hinge between the simultaneously unfolding analyses of Theme and Transitivity; until a potential Subject element is confirmed, the Theme analysis is still relevant, as the message is not yet fully 'off the ground'. But once the Subject element is confirmed, by a step into a Finite/Predicator element, attention shifts to an analysis of Transitivity, as this will reveal what is of interest in the proposition. The comparative growth and decline of the metafunctions, revealed from a dynamic perspective, enables us to reconsider the roles of these analyses in an unfolding text.

The interaction of the metafunctions as described above is represented graphically in Figure 8. The diagram shows that the analysis of textual meaning, in terms of Theme, is highly informative at the beginning of the clause, but that it trails off as the clause unfolds. On the other hand, the analysis of ideational meaning, in terms of Transitivity, is uninformative at the beginning of the clause, but expands as the clause progresses. Like Theme, Mood has its weight at the beginning of the clause, but in the early stages, is never as informative as Theme, and cuts off abruptly once the Finite is reached. It is therefore presented as a box, the right-hand edge of it providing a pivotal, cross-cutting point between the other two metafunctions.

In Figure 8, the names of the specific grammatical systems are retained, viz, Theme, Mood and Transitivity, and are taken to refer to their respective metafunctional domains. Again it should be emphasised that these grammatical systems do not represent the full potential of the metafunctions; for example, alongside Theme, information systems should be considered for the textual metafunction; Modality alongside Mood in the interpersonal

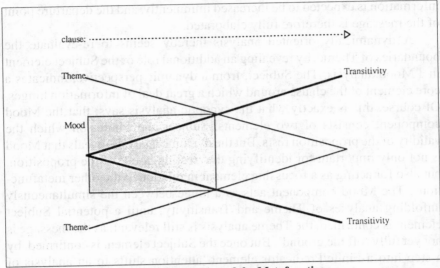

Figure 8. Interaction of the Metafunctions

metafunction, and Ergativity alongside Transitivity in the ideational metafunction.

The figure is clearly restricted to declaratives only and does not in any
way account for all clause types. For example, a clause beginning with a
Process would present a different weighting of the metafunctions. However
Figure 8 is presented as an illustration of the way in which metafunctional
interaction can be considered from an unfolding point of view.

Additionally, this explanation of the unfolding interaction of the metafunctions is pertinent to our earlier discussion of what a dynamic perspective
adds to an understanding of meaning. If it is accepted that thematic boundaries can be redefined in the way suggested, then we can contrast examples
where there is a 'delayed' topical Theme (as in the example discussed
above), and examples where there is an ordinary, single topical Theme.
Where Theme is re-defined as being 'delayed', the final topical Theme still
functions as Theme, but somewhat differently from the case where it is not
preceded by or delayed by other topical elements: the final topical Theme
has a different 'weight' because of the delay. Of course a synoptic model can
account for the difference by explaining what the additional elements
contribute in structural terms, but the dynamic orientation shows that the

process of delaying that topical Theme is also functional in itself.

It is interesting to compare our figure of metafunctional interaction with Bolinger's (1952) conception of the sentence as a 'complex semanteme': a pointed structure with hyperbolic flaring sides, as illustrated in Figure 9.

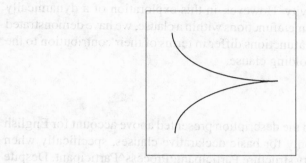

**Figure 9. Bolinger's notion of the sentence
as complex semanteme**

The structure in Figure 9 represents the fact that in a progressively developed sentence, "beginning elements have a wider semantic range than elements towards the end." (Bolinger 1952: 1117). He goes on to elaborate this position (p. 1118):

> Before the speaker begins, the possibilities of what he will communicate are practically infinite, or, if his utterance is bound within a discourse, they are at least enormously large. When the first word appears, the possibilities are vastly reduced, but that first word has, in communicative value for the hearer, its fullest possible semantic range. The second word follows, narrowing the range, the third comes to narrow it still further, and finally the end is reached at which point the sentence presumably focusses on an event …

While our figure is somewhat different to Bolinger's, the two positions are not so far apart: initially, a broad range of expectations and possibilities exist, but they are narrowed or reweighted by further elements. Bolinger's position is perhaps closest to that presented here with regard to Transitivity: while our diagram represents the ideational path as growing as the clause progresses, complementary metaphors are equally appropriate, including Bolinger's of the initially broad range being narrowed down to a finer point. The main point of difference between our diagram and Bolinger's is the more elaborate conception of meaning in the former. This draws on and reinforces Halliday's description of the metafunctions, showing that each has a separate and important role to play in the clause. Also, in our figure, the conjunction of the different metafunctional analyses coincides with the Process element, and this parallels the centrality of the process in the synoptic analysis of Transitivity. However, in this exploration of a dynamically oriented analysis of the metafunctions within a clause, we have demonstrated where and how the metafunctions differ in terms of their contribution to the development of an unfolding clause.

6. Conclusion

Obviously Figure 8 and the description presented above account for English only – and there too only for basic declarative clauses, specifically when they have the transitivity structure Participant^Process^Participant. Despite such limitations, it is interesting that, firstly, we have provided a potential explanation as to why the boundaries of Theme are problematic to define, and if that explanation is accepted, then we have provided an extension of the definition of Theme as 'departure point of the message'. Secondly, we have suggested an additional explanation of the role of the Mood element, serving as a hinge or a focussing element between aspects of the other two metafunctions. While we have already acknowledged that the above is anglocentric, it is interesting to note that Caffarel (this volume) sees the clause nucleus of French as a hinge between Theme and information systems. Further, Martin (1992) notes that in Tagalog, dependency structures, an aspect of ideational (specifically, logical) meaning, seem to be used to delimit the domain of interpersonal meaning. Such observations may not be directly comparable to what has been described here, but suggest that the interaction of the metafunctions merits further exploration from all points of view. Halliday (1968: 214-5) provides an initial account of this interaction, noting the interplay of thematic prominence with transitivity, "but through the modal structure rather than directly, since initial position in the clause also functions to signal speech function." It would seem that the interplay of the metafunctional components can signal significant points of development or transfer of responsibility between metafunctions. While all three are always present, one or two can be highlighted as being more informative or pertinent at particular points in the development of the clause.

These observations have been achieved by attempting to look at an 'old' domain from a 'new' point of view. Simply considering the clause as something which unfolds has enabled the interaction of the metafunctions and their respective roles to be re-assessed. As we have already acknowledged, the exemplification is highly restricted, and does not exploit the dynamic perspective as outlined in this paper to its full potential. But it does suggest that the dynamic perspective is worth further exploration, and that it is possible that such an analysis can complement and supplement our existing notions of meaning.

References

Bateman, John A. 1989. Dynamic systemic-functional grammar: a new frontier. *Word* 40: 263-286.

Bates, M. 1978. The theory and practice of augmented transition network grammars. *Natural Language Communication with Computers*, edited by L. Bolc. Berlin: Springer-Verlag.

Berry, M. 1982. Review of M.A.K. Halliday, 1978, Language as Social Semiotic: The social interpretation of language and meaning. *Nottingham Linguistic Circular* 11.1: 64-94.

Berry, M. 1992a. Theme and Variation. Plenary address to the 1992 conference of the Applied Linguistics Association of Australia, University of Sydney.

Berry, M. 1992b. Bringing systems back into a discussion of Theme. Plenary address to the 19th International Systemic Functional Congress, Macquarie University.

Bolinger, Dwight. 1952. Linear Modification. *PMLA* 67: 1117-1144.

Bourdieu, Pierre. 1977. *Outline of a Theory of Practice* (Translated by Richard Nice). Cambridge: Cambridge University Press.

Chomsky, Noam. 1957. *Syntactic Structures*. The Hague: Mouton.

Davies, Martin and Louise Ravelli. (eds.). 1992. *Advances in Systemic Linguistics: Recent theory and practice*. London: Frances Pinter.

Emmott, C. 1989. *Reading Between the Lines: Building a comprehensive model of participant reference in real narrative*. PhD dissertation, School of English Language and Literature. Birmingham: University of Birmingham.

Fawcett, R.P. and D.J. Young. (eds.) 1988. *New Developments in Systemic Linguistics, Volume Two: Theory and Application*. London: Frances Pinter.

Fawcett, R.P., A. van der Mije, and A. van Wissen. 1988. Towards a Systemic Flowchart Model for Discourse Structure. R.P. Fawcett and D.J. Young (eds.), 1988: 116-143.

Fine, J. 1991. The static and dynamic choices of responding toward the process of building social reality by the developmentally disordered. Eija Ventola (ed.). 1991: 213-234.

Firth, J.R. 1968. A synopsis of linguistic theory, 1930-1955. *Selected Papers of J.R. Firth 1952-1959* edited by F.R. Palmer.168-205. London: Longman.

Halliday, M.A.K. 1961. Categories of the theory of grammar. *Word* 17.3: 241-292.

Halliday, M.A.K. 1968. Notes on transitivity and theme in English, Parts 2 & 3. *Journal of Linguistics* 4: 153-308.

Halliday, M.A.K. 1973. *Explorations in the Functions of Language.* London: Edward Arnold.

Halliday, M.A.K. 1975. *Learning How to Mean.* London: Edward Arnold.

Halliday, M.A.K. 1976. Functions and universals of language. Gunther Kress (ed.) 1976: 26-31.

Halliday, M.A.K. 1985a. *Introduction to Functional Grammar.* London: Edward Arnold.

Halliday, M.A.K. 1985b. *Spoken and Written Language.* Deakin: Deakin University Press.

Halliday, M.A.K. 1991. Towards probabilistic interpretations. Eija Ventola (ed.) 1991. 39-62

Halliday, M.A.K. and Ruqaiya Hasan. 1985. *Language, Context and Text: Aspects of language in a social-semiotic perspective.* Deakin: Deakin University Press.

Halliday, M.A.K. and J.R. Martin (eds.) 1981. *Readings in Systemic Linguistics.* London: Batsford.

Hasan, Ruqaiya. 1981. What's going on: a dynamic view of context in language. *The 7th Lacus Forum 1980,* edited by J.E. Copeland and P.W. Davis. 106-121. Columbia: Hornbeam Press.

Hasan, Ruqaiya. in press. The conception of context in text. *Discourse and Meaning in Society: Functional perspectives – Meaning and choice in language: Studies presented to Michael Halliday, Vol 3.* edited by Peter H. Fries and Michael Gregory. Norwood NJ: Ablex. (Mimeo from School of English and Linguistics, Macquarie University).

Hjelmslev, Louis. 1969. *Prolegomena to a Theory of Language* (Translated by F.J. Whitfield). Wisconsin: University of Wisconsin Press.

Hoey, Michael. 1983. Three metaphors for examining the semantic organisation of monologue. *Analysis: Quaderni di Anglistica* anno 1. n.1: 27-53.

Kress, Gunther (ed.). 1976. *Halliday: System and function in language: Selected papers.* Oxford: Oxford University Press.

Leal, W. M. 1975. Transition network grammars as a notation scheme for tagmemics. *Network Grammars,* edited by J. Grimes. A publication of the Summer Institute of Linguistics at the University of Oklahoma.

Lemke, Jay L. 1991. Textproduction and dynamic text semantics. Eija Ventola (ed.), 1991: 23-38.

Martin, J.R. 1985. Process and text: two aspects of human semiosis. *Systemic Perspectives on Discourse, Volume One,* edited by James D. Benson and William S. Greaves, 248-274. Norwood, NJ: Ablex.

Martin, J. R. 1992. Logical meaning, interdependency and the linking particle *na/-ng* in Tagalog. Paper presented to the July 1992 Australian Linguistics Society Conference, Sydney.

Matthiessen, C.M.I.M. 1992. Interpreting the textual metafunction. Martin Davies and Louise Ravelli (eds.), 1992: 37-81

Nesbitt, C. and G. Plum. 1988. Probabilities in a systemic functional grammar: the clause complex in English. Fawcett and Young (eds.), 1988: 1-38. London: Frances Pinter.

O'Donnell, M. 1990. A dynamic model of exchange. *Word* 41: 293-328.

Ravelli, L.J. 1989. A dynamic perspective on systemic grammar: getting the perspective right. Paper presented to the 16th International Systemics Congress. Hanasaari: Finland.

Ravelli, L.J. 1991. *Language from a dynamic perspective: models in general and grammar in particular* Unpublished Ph. D. Dissertation. Birmingham: University of Birmingham.

Reichman, R. 1978. Conversational coherency. *Cognitive Science* 2: 283-297.

Reichman, Rachel. 1985. *Getting Computers to Talk Like You and Me: Discourse, context, focus and semantics (An* ATN *model).* Cambridge MA: MIT Press.

Shannon, C.E. and W. Weaver. 1949. *The Mathematical Theory of Communication.* Urbana: The University of Illinois Press.

Sinclair, J. McH. 1991. Trust the text. Martin Davies and Louise Ravelli (eds.), 1992: 5-19.

Sinclair, J. McH. and Coulthard, R.M. 1975. *Towards an Analysis of Discourse: the English used by teachers and pupils.* Oxford: OUP.

de Smedt, Koenraad and Gerard Kempen. 1987. Incremental sentence production, self-correction and co-ordination. *Natural Language generation: New results in artificial intelligence, psychology and linguistics,* edited by G. Kempen, 365-376. Dordrecht: Martinus Nijhoff Publishers.

Tsui, Bik-May Amy. 1986. *A Linguistic Description of Utterances in Conversation.* Dissertation, Birmingham: University of Birmingham.

Vande Kopple, W.J. 1991 Themes, thematic progressions, and some implications for understanding discourse. *Written Communication* 8.3: 311-347.

Ventola, E. 1987. *The Structure of Social Interaction: A systemic approach to the semiotics of service encounters.* London: Frances Pinter.

Ventola, Eija. (ed.) 1991. *Functional and Systemic Linguistics: Approaches and uses.* Berlin: Mouton de Gruyter.

Willis, D. 1987. An analysis of directive exchanges. *Discussing Discourse.* edited by M. Coulthard. *Discourse Analysis Monograph* 14. Department of English: University of Birmingham.

Woods, W.A. 1970. Transition network grammars for natural language analysis. *Communications of the* ACM 13: 591-606.

7

On Theme in Chinese:
From Clause to Discourse

Fang Yan
Tsinghua University

Edward McDonald
University of Sydney

Cheng Musheng
Tsinghua University

1. Introduction: the descriptive problem

The syntactic analysis of Chinese in this century, since the introduction of Western-style linguistics, has been hampered by the perception that Chinese is a language "without grammatical signals" (Li and Thompson 1978); and by the consequent, and seemingly unresolvable debates on problems like the nature of subject in Chinese (Tsao 1980: 7). We believe that approaching Chinese grammar from the point of view of its textual function, in particular the systems of THEME and INFORMATION (Halliday 1985: see especially chapters 3 and 8), can help us understand the types of grammatical patterning present in Chinese. Using this approach enables us not only to delimit the boundaries of the clause and explain the ordering of elements within the clause, but also to see how this sort of patterning operates in the organisation of discourse. In this paper, we will attempt to show how the insights about clause structure embodied in Chinese linguistics and Prague School linguistics can be more comprehensively developed within the framework of systemic functional theory (Halliday 1985). We will go on to show that the principles underlying the internal organisation of the clause in Chinese can be generalised to account for the ordering of two or more clauses joined in a clause complex. Finally we will identify some ways in which these same principles operate in the construction of texts.

2. Background to the study: Theoretical traditions

Before setting up the framework for the current study, we will briefly review the two main relevant theoretical traditions: (a) theories of clause structure in Chinese; and (b) functional theories of clause structure.

2.1 Theories of clause structure in Chinese

In the Chinese descriptive tradition, one of the most controversial issues has been what element in the clause can be identified as subject. Generally speaking, those answering this question fall into two main schools: those who work with the notion of subject only; and, secondly, those who recognise subject and topic as two separate notions.

2.1.1 The subject only view

Zhu (1981: 95-96) gives a structural definition of the subject (*zhuyu*) in contrast to the predicate (*weiyu*): in most cases, the subject precedes the predicate, is marked off from it by an optional pause and/or particles, and may be omitted if understood from the context. Zhu then gives two interpretations of the subject-predicate relation: semantic, and expressive. Semantically, the subject may enter into a number of different relations with the predicate: e.g. agent, patient, recipient, time etc. This view diverges from that of a number of scholars such as, for example, Wang Li (quoted in Tsao 1980: 8) for whom the subject "denotes something (or some person) [to which FY *et al*] the behaviour (active or passive), property or nature indicated by the predicate belongs", i.e. experientially it must be a participant rather than a circumstance (for more detail see 3.2.2 below.) Expressively, the relation of subject and predicate is explained as follows (Zhu 1981: 96): "What the speaker chooses as subject is the topic he is most interested in, the predicate is then a statement about the topic chosen." For example, in the following two clauses, the choice of agent or time as subject is explained by its expressive function:

(1) i *Women*   *zuotian*   *kai* *le* *yi ge*   *hui.*
        we   yesterday   hold **asp**[1] one **meas** meeting
        Subject ——————————**Predicate**——————————
        We held a meeting yesterday.

---

1. The key to abbreviations for grammatical words in these and following examples is given immediately following the main text.

    ii   *Zuotian   women kai le   yi ge   hui.*
       yesterday we   hold **asp** one **meas** meeting
       Subject   ————————**Predicate**————————
       Yesterday we held a meeting.

Further, the predicate of a clause may itself be a "subject-predicate construction": thus, in effect the clause contains two subjects, the first being the subject of the whole clause, the second the subject of only the predicate part of the clause as illustrated in (2):

(2)   *Zhe ge   ren   xinyan'r   hao.*
      this **meas** person heart   good
      ————**Subject**————   ——**Predicate**——
                           Subject   **Predicate**
      This person is kind-hearted.

Chao (1968: 67-69, 78-80) defines subject and predicate structurally in a very similar way to Zhu, also allowing for the possibility of what he refers to as an "s-p predicate", exemplified by *xinyan'r hao* 'heart good – kind-hearted' above. Chao goes on to characterise the "grammatical meaning" of subject and predicate in Chinese as "topic and comment, rather than actor and action" (p. 69), explaining this as follows (p.70): "The subject is literally the subject matter to talk about, and the predicate is what the speaker comments on when a subject is presented to be talked about." Furthermore, since "the subject sets the topic of the talk and the predicate gives the information by adding something new" (p.76), there is a strong correlation between subject and "definite", and between "predicate" and "indefinite", as shown by the following examples :

(3)   i   *Huo   zhao le.*
         fire   start **asp**
        Subject **Predicate**
        The fire is lit.
    ii *Zhao   huo le!*
        start   fire **asp**
        Subject **Predicate**
       (There has) started a fire - there is a fire!

Chao (pp.78-80) makes a further distinction between two types of predicate: the "grammatical" predicate, in other words the comment; and the "logical" predicate, i.e. the point of the message. The logical predicate is "normally located in the [grammatical] predicate" but "may be located in any part of the sentence" if marked by "contrastive stress". Chao notes that there is in fact a much stronger tendency in Chinese than in English for the two types of predicate to coincide, i. e. for the final element of the clause to be both grammatical and logical predicate (see also Gao 1994). In the following examples, the respective (logical) points of the two sentences are the equivalent "too many/*tai duo*". In English it is expressed grammatically as a modifier to part of the grammatical predicate 'are...people here' as in (4i); in Chinese it is the grammatical predicate (see 4ii):

(4)   i   *There*   *are too many people here.*
          Subject ————**Predicate**————
     ii   *Zhe'r de ren*   *tai duo.*
          here **sub** person   too many
          Subject   **Predicate**
          The people here are too many. (= there are too many people here)

2.1.2 The subject and topic view

In contrast to Zhu and Chao, for whom subject and topic are largely equivalent notions, Li and Thompson (1981: 85-92) consider these as entities of quite different kinds. They distinguish between the subject, "the noun phrase that has a 'doing' or 'being' relationship with the verb" (p.87), and the topic, "what the sentence is about" (p.86); for them, "a topic sets a spatial, temporal, or individual framework within which the main predication holds" (p.86). Structurally, they define topic in a very similar way to Zhu's and Chao's subject: it "always occurs in sentence initial position" and "can be separated from the rest of the sentence by a pause or by one of the pause particles" (p.86). Since topic and subject bear a distinct relationship to the rest of the sentence, their co-occurrence is independent of each other. Li and Thompson recognise four possibilities: (a) both topic and subject discretely present; (b) a topic identical to the subject; (c) topic present but not subject; or (d) neither topic nor subject present. We reproduce their original examples (Li and Thompson 1981: 88-90) as illustration, showing relevant items in bold; in (5.i) the topic – *na zhi gou* – precedes subject *wo*; in (5ii) *wo* is both

subject and topic; in (5iii) *nei ben shu* is simply topic, not subject; in (5iv)
the second clause is elliptical, with neither subject nor topic:

(5)   *(a): +Topic, +Subject*

   i   **Na zhi   gou, wo**   yijing   kan-guo le.

      that **meas** dog I   already look **asp asp**

      That dog, I've already seen.

   (b): Topic = Subject

   ii **Wo** xihuan chi   pingguo.

      I   like   eat   apple

      I like eating apples.

   (c): +Topic, -Subject

   iii **Nei ben   shu**   chuban le.

      that **meas** book   publish **asp**

      That book has been published.

   (d): -Topic, -Subject

   iv *(Ni kan-guo Lisi ma?)*

      you look **asp** Lisi **mod**

      (Have you seen Lisi?)

      ____ *mei kan-guo.*

      neg look **asp**

      (I) haven't seen (him).

Tsao (1980: 36-38) agrees in outline with Li and Thompson's analysis,
but argues that topic and subject belong to different levels of grammatical
organisation. While subject is an element of sentence structure which "bears
some selectional relation to the main verb of a sentence" (p.84), topic is a
"discourse element" which "may ... extend its semantic domain to more
than one sentence" (p. 88). In example (6), all three sentences share the topic
ta 'he' which is omitted after the first sentence (for a fuller justification for
viewing *ta* as topic rather than subject in this example, see Tsao 1980: 11-13):

(6)   *Ta   duzi   e*

    s/he stomach   hungry

    ____ *you zhao-bu-dao   dongxi chi*

    also seek **neg** reach thing eat

    ____ *suoyi tang-zai   chuang shang   shui-jiao.*

    so   lie at   bed   on   sleep nap

He was hungry, and couldn't find anything to eat, so (he) lay down on his
bed and slept.

2.1.3 Relevant features of Chinese clause structure

The above descriptions of clause structure in Chinese have drawn attention to the following four characteristics:

(a)   The clause is commonly defined in "message" terms; in other words "the clause...has some form of organisation giving it the status of a communicative event" (Halliday 1985: 38);

(b)   structurally, the clause divides into two parts: the first part, the beginning of the message; the second part, the continuation of the message;

(c)   the different parts of the clause tend to have different information status: the first part known, definite; the second part new, indefinite; and

(d)   the first part of the clause is significant in the creation of discourse.

2.2 Functional theories of clause structure

The concepts relevant to the "message" organisation of the clause found in definitions of clause structure in Chinese were first introduced in the 1930s by Prague school linguists. Since then, they have been extensively applied in other functional schools, such as systemic functional theory (e.g. Halliday 1967: see especially pp. 211-215). The relevant concept here is that of Theme, which was first defined by Mathesius in 1939 as "that which is known or at least obvious in the given situation and from which the speaker proceeds" (see Fries 1981: 1). We briefly review the different ways in which this notion has been developed, and attempt to explain why the version current in systemic functional linguistics is most suitable for our purposes.

2.2.1 Theme in functional theories

Fries analyses Mathesius' definition of Theme as containing two distinct aspects: firstly, that which is "known or obvious in the situation", and secondly, that "from which the speaker proceeds" (1981: 1). He then distinguishes two approaches to the concept of "Theme": the "combining" approach, which uses both of these criteria to define Theme; and the "separating" approach, which takes only the second as definitive of Theme. The difference between the two approaches to Theme is shown in Table 1, adapted from Fries (1981: 1-2):

Table 1: Combining and separating approaches to Theme

(a): combining approach	
Theme:	that which is known or obvious in the situation that from which the speaker proceeds
(b): separating approach	
Theme:	that from which the speaker proceeds (point of departure of the message)
Given:	that which is known or obvious in the situation

Commenting on the analysis of Theme in the English clause, Fries (1981: 3) sums up the differences between the two approaches as follows:

> The difference ... between the combining and the separating approach to the definition of Theme is that while the combiners either ignore the contribution of word order [to the realisation of Theme as point of departure FY *et al.*] ... or treat it as contributing to the same concept as the given-new distinction ... separators tease out and separate the contributions of word-order and of the distinction between given and new information, and they use the term theme to indicate the meaning of initial position in the clause.

2.2.1.1 Thematic progression   The separating approach assigns Theme to a particular position in the clause (in English, this is the initial position) and identifies it as the "point of departure of the message" (Fries 1981: 4; see also Cloran, this volume). If Theme is defined as the point of departure of the message, then its significance can only be understood by seeing how it contributes to the progress of the message in texts. Fries, borrowing a term from Daneš, refers to this as the **thematic progression**. The patterns of thematic progression are identified by reference to the way a text moves forward from Theme to Rheme, within each clause, and between clauses (for some more discussion of this notion, see Fries, and also Cloran in this volume). From this point of view, we can see the Theme Rheme structure of each clause as textually motivated, organising the text as a whole.

2.2.2 A multifunctional view of clause structure

If we refer back to Zhu's definition of subject in Chinese given in 2.1.1, we find that at least part of his definition corresponds very closely to the way Theme is defined for English in the separating functional theories: i.e. Theme takes the initial position in the clause, and is a topic on which the predicate comments. While Zhu's definition works well in analysing single clauses, it is not designed for analysing extended stretches of text, and thus does not particularly help us to determine why particular elements are chosen as subject, apart from the vague formulation "what the speaker ... is most interested in" (Zhu 1981: 96). The notion of Theme does deal with the discourse considerations involved in the choice of clause Theme (Zhu's "expressive subject"); however, it fails to address Zhu's other main feature of subject, its "semantic" relationship with the predicate in terms of agent, patient etc.

Systemic functional theory incorporates both of these types of meaning relation into a framework that explicitly recognises the multifunctional nature of the clause as a "combination of three different structures deriving from distinct functional components" (Halliday 1985: 158). Two of these components, generalised abstract functions of language known as "metafunctions", correspond to Zhu's two interpretations of the meaning of subject in Chinese. The first, corresponding to Zhu's "semantic", derives from the **ideational** metafunction, which analyses the clause from the point of view of its "representational meaning: what the clause is about ... typically some process, with associated participants and circumstances" (Halliday 1985: 158). The second, corresponding to Zhu's "expressive", derives from the **textual** metafunction, which focusses on the "organisation of the message: how the clause relates to the surrounding discourse, and to the context of situation in which it is being produced" (Halliday 1985: 158). The third component, not treated by Zhu, is the **interpersonal** metafunction, which is concerned with "interactional meaning: what the clause is doing, as a verbal exchange between speaker/writer and audience" (Halliday 1985: 158).

In the grammar of the clause in English, each of these three components or metafunctions "contributes a more or less complete structure, so that a clause is made up of three distinct structures combined into one" (Halliday 1985: 158). In Chinese, however, the interpersonal metafunction does not define a distinct clause structure in the same way the ideational and textual metafunctions do[2] For this reason, in the discussion that follows we will

---

2. Arguments for recognising only two functional structures at clause rank in Chinese can be found in McDonald 1992: 437-440. In terms of Halliday's (1979) claim that each metafunction "typically generates different kinds of structural mechanism" (p.61), the system of Mood in Chinese is realised "prosodically" (p.66), by clause final modal particles and certain types of verbal group marking in conjunction with polarity.

focus mainly on the realisation of the ideational and textual metafunctions in Chinese grammar.

In summary, if we adopt the multi-functional approach of a systemic functional grammar, we are able to (a) capture all the relevant types of meaning for the analysis of Chinese clause structure, and (b) take the analysis from the micro – i.e. clause – level to the macro – i.e. discourse – level.

3. Framework for current study

In this study we aim to look at the textual organisation of the clause from the point of view of its role in the formation of discourse. We will trace this organisation from the level of single clauses to that of two or more clauses joined together in what in the systemic functional framework is known as the **clause complex**. We will also examine one example of a complete text in order to see how this same organisation is manifested through a whole text. The analysis will involve two main types of textual organisation: structural, and non-structural or cohesive.

3.1 Units of analysis

In the following discussion we will set up units of analysis on the basis of their textual organisation: i.e. in terms of their Theme-Rheme structure. We will define two units, related to each other by constituency: a "clause complex" is made up of "clauses".[3] The definition of these units also involves two other aspects of functional organisation: for the clause, its experiential function; for the clause complex, its logical function (in systemic functional theory, these are known collectively as the ideational metafunction).

3.1.1 Clause

The clause in Chinese may be defined from two points of view. Firstly, from the point of view of its textual function, the clause is made up of Theme (starting point of message), and Rheme (continuation of message). This is

3. An earlier version of this research may be found in Fang 1989.

characterised as the thematic structure of the clause. The Theme normally comes first in the clause, and may be marked off from the Rheme by a pause and/or a textual particle such as *a, ba, me, ne* (Chao 1968: 67; Zhu 1981: 95). The Rheme normally follows the Theme, and may itself be followed by an experiential (aspectual) particle and/or an interpersonal (modal) particle. The Rheme may precede the Theme only if the Theme is put in as an afterthought (Chao 1968: 69), with the aspectual/modal particles still following the Rheme:

(7) i *Ni   (a)   gan   ma   (ne)?*
        you **text** do   what **asp**
        Theme   ——**Rheme**——

     ii *Gan   ma   ne,   ni?*
         do   what   **asp** you
         ——**Rheme**——   **Theme**
         What are you doing?

Secondly, from the point of view of its experiential function, the clause divides into a Process (what is going on), one or more Participants (who/what are taking part), and associated Circumstances. This is known as the transitivity structure of the clause. From this viewpoint, the centre of the clause is the Process, what is going on; different types of Process define different configurations of Participants and, to a lesser extent, Circumstances. There are a number of accounts of transitivity in Chinese in systemic functional terms (Tam 1979; Long 1981) as well as in comparable frameworks such as case grammar (Li 1971; Tang 1972) and Chafeian grammar (Teng 1975). Since this is not the main focus of the current study, we will not be treating transitivity in any detail here; the framework used will be the simplified one presented in McDonald 1992, which has the advantage that each of the three main Process types recognised, action[4], state and relation, has a distinct kind of textual organisation: that is, action clauses are textually very flexible, while state and relation clauses tend to have a more fixed thematic structure (see 4.1 below). In this framework, the example given above can be analysed as follows (particles omitted from transitivity analysis here):

---

4. In this framework, "action" subdivides into "material", "mental" and "verbal" (McDonald 1992: 440-441).

(7) iii *Ni* *(a)* *gan* *ma* *(ne)?*
          you **text** do what **asp**
     Actor   **Process** **Goal**
     What are you doing?

A clause in Chinese is thus defined as the combination of a single thematic structure and a single transitivity structure. There are a couple of points that need noting here: first, the Process – particularly of the action type – may be realised by more than one verb. In that case the two verbs share the same thematic and transitivity structure; in other words, there is only one Theme-Rheme structure, and the two verbs share the same set of Participants and Circumstances as in (8):

(8) *Ni* *gan* *ma* *qu le?*
     you do what go **asp**
     Theme ———**Rheme**———
     Actor Pro- **<Goal> cess**
     What are you going (somewhere) to do?

Secondly, the elements of the thematic and transitivity structures which define the clause are not necessarily isomorphic; what this means is that it is possible to have a thematic element which has no transitivity function in that clause. In (9), which is adapted from Tsao (1980: 104), *nei kuai tian* 'that piece of land' does not function as an element of the experiential structure of the clause. If it had been part of the experiential structure, then as a Circumstance of location it would have needed to be in the form (*zai*) *nei kuai tian li* 'in that piece of land'. Here, while the reference to location in *nei kuai tian* is clearly related collocationally to the experience the clause is representing, structurally it merely serves as the starting point for the message:

(9) *Nei kuai tian* *daozi* *zhang* *de* *hen da.*
     that piece field rice grow **ext** very big
     ——**Theme**—— ————**Rheme**————
          Actor **Process** **Circumstance**
     (In) that field, the rice grows very large.

3.1.2 Clause complex

A clause complex is made up of two or more clauses, and it may be described from two related points of view: the textual and the logical. From the point of view of the logical component of the ideational metafunction, clauses in a clause complex consist of one **primary** clause and one or more **secondary** ones. These are linked by two kinds of logical relations: **interdependency** relations of **parataxis** (coordination) and **hypotaxis** (subordination), and the **logico-semantic** relations of **expansion** or **projection**. The main categories of logical relation with their appropriate notations are displayed in Table 2 . (For the definition and discussion of these, see Halliday 1985: 196-197):

Table 2: Logical relations in the clause complex

subtypes	status of clauses	
(A): Interdependency relations		
	primary	secondary
parataxis	I (initiating)	2 (continuing)
hypotaxis	α (dominant)	β (dependent)
(B): Logico-semantic relations		
I: EXPANSION		
a: elaboration	= (primary equals secondary)	
b: extension	+ (primary is added to secondary)	
c: enhancement	x (primary is multiplied by secondary)	
II: PROJECTION		
a: locution	" primary projects secondary as wording	
b: idea	' primary projects secondary as meaning	

From the textual point of view, two considerations appear important. First, the clauses in a clause complex may share a common Theme, though as illustrated by (6), the shared Theme may not occur overtly except in the first clause of the clause complex. Secondly, the clause complex as a whole has a point of departure, so that a thematic structure needs to be recognised which is specific to the clause complex as such and independent of the thematic structure of its constituent clauses. In the English clause complex, the initial clause is regarded as the Theme, with the remaining clauses making up its Rheme. The thematic structure of the clause complex is to a certain extent determined by the types of logical relations between its clauses. Specifically, some combinations of interdependency and logico-semantic relations may entail a fixed order for the primary and secondary clause: irrespective of this constraint, it is the initial clause that is automatically treated as the Theme of the clause complex. The justification for recognising thematic structure in the clause complex lies in the fact that there do exist combinations of the two relations – interdependency and logico-semantic – that permit variation in the order of clauses in a clause complex (Halliday 1985: 56-59). In these cases, it is the thematic progression of the text that determines which clause will occur initially, thus acting as Theme.

As Ouyang (1986: xi-xii) points out, the equivalent of clause complex in Chinese linguistics, *fuju* ("complex sentence"), does not make a clear distinction between interdependency and logico-semantic relations, nor does the notion of *fuju* cover the full range of possible relations between clauses in Chinese. In section 3.2.1.2 we will use Ouyang's classification of types of clause complex in Chinese, and give definitions and examples of the different types of interclausal relation. An example of a clause complex showing different kinds of interdependency and logico-semantic relations is given below:

(10)	i	**I**	*Mama*	*mai le*	*yixie taozi,*		
			mum	buy **asp**	some peach		
	ii	$^+2^x\beta$	____	*chi-diao*	*shiba*	*zhi*	*hou,*
				eat up	18	**meas**	after
	iii	2α	____	*hai* *sheng*	*liu zhi,*		
				still remain	6 **meas**		
	iv	$^+3$	*mama*	*mai-lai*	*duoshao*	*zhi*	*taozi?*
			mum	buy come	how-many	**meas**	peach

Mum bought some peaches, after 18 were eaten, 6 still remained: mum bought how many peaches altogether?

In example (10), we have both paratactic and hypotactic relations. The former has three terms, one initiating a paratactic relation, and hence shown as **I** in clause (10i), the remaining two continuing, shown as **2**, **3**, (10ii-iv). These terms are related by paratactic extension, shown as **+**; the relation is interpretable as temporal addition: i.e. **I** and then **2** and then **3**. The hypotatic relation occurs at the second term, which is itself made up of two parts, related by hypotactic enhancement, shown as **x**, with the dependent clause (β *chi-diao shiba zhi hou* 'after eighteen were eaten') providing a precondition for the dominant clause (α *hai sheng liu zhi* 'six still remained').

3.1.3 Textual organisation through a text

Once we go beyond the boundaries of the clause or clause complex, we are dealing not with grammatical units, but rather with semantic units: in other words, with (parts of) complete texts (Halliday and Hasan 1976: 1-2). It is in this context that the concept of thematic progression really comes into its own. However, in order to understand the contribution of thematic progression to what Halliday and Hasan refer to as the **cohesion** of a text (1976: 4-6), in other words how the text hangs together, we need also to take into consideration the different functional varieties of language – or **registers** – and the different text types (or **genres**) that define particular texts. This would take us far beyond the scope of the present study; what we propose to do is to look at the thematic progression of one complete text – called **Dreams** – (see Appendix 1), to see how some of the patterns we have identified at the level of the clause and clause complex contribute to the structure of text. The first three clauses of **Dreams** are analysed below as example (11i-iii), to show how the pattern of thematic progression contributes to the introduction of the main information of the text:

(11)　i　ˣβ *Dishang*　*mei*　*you*　*gui,*
　　　　　 earth-on　**neg**　exist　ghost
　　　　　 Theme　——**Rheme**——

　　　ii　α *gui*　　*zai*　*na'r?*
　　　　　 ghost　　be-at　where
　　　　　 Theme　—**Rheme**—

　　　iii　 *Gui*　　*dou*　*zai*　　*renxin*　　*litou.*
　　　　　 ghost　　all　be-at　people-mind　inside.
　　　　　 Theme　　　————**Rheme**————

　　　(If) there are no ghosts on the earth, (then) where are the ghosts? The ghosts are in people's minds.

This extract from **Dreams** presents two main pieces of information: an entity (*gui* 'ghosts'), and its various locations. The Theme of (11i) – (*dishang* 'on earth') – is a location which sets the scene for the introduction of a new entity in the Rheme (*gui* 'ghosts'). This entity then becomes Theme, functioning as the starting point for the next two clauses, while the main point of the paragraph, the location of the ghosts, is dealt with in the Rhemes of these two clauses.

3.2 Methods of analysis

The analysis[5] of textual organisation in Chinese can be divided into two kinds: structural, and non-structural or cohesive (Halliday 1978: 133). The units of clause and clause complex were defined above according to structural criteria; once we begin to look at how clauses and clause complexes are formed into texts we need to consider cohesive criteria. As a preliminary step to the analysis, we will briefly review the implications of these two kinds of criteria.

3.2.1 Structural relations

Structural relations in the systemic functional framework are seen as multifunctional: that is, for any concrete structure, there will be more than one functional principle relevant to its interpretation. For the clause, different functional components define different abstract structures which interact with each other to determine the concrete ordering of the clause. For the clause complex, component clauses are linked to each other via different combinations of logical relations.

3.2.1.1 Structural relations in the clause There are three grammatical systems which define distinct functional structures for the clause: the textual systems of THEME and INFORMATION, and the experiential system of TRANSITIVITY. Strictly speaking, only the systems of THEME and TRANSITIVITY have the clause as their structural unit. However, alongside the clause, we can recognise another structural unit, in this case not a grammatical one like clause, but rather a phonological one, the **tone group**, "the carrier of one complete tone contour" (Halliday 1978: 133). The tone group serves as the device for the realisation of the **information unit**, which is

5. Unless otherwise noted, all statements about structure etc. refer to Chinese, not English or any other language.

defined as follows by Halliday (1985: 274-275):

> The information unit is what its name implies: a unit of information. Informa-
> tion…is a process of interaction between what is already known or predictable and
> what is new or unpredictable…Hence the information unit is made up of two
> functions, the New and the Given.

While these two units are in principle distinct, we can take it as a general
rule that "one information unit will be co-extensive with one clause"
(Halliday 1978: 133), and we can therefore recognise Information structure
also in written texts. This gives us the following distinct functional structures
in a clause:

Table 3: Functional structures in the clause

system	structural unit	structural elements
THEME	clause	Theme, Rheme
TRANSITIVITY	clause	Pro, Participant(s), (Circ(s))
INFORMATION	information unit	Given, New

In the concrete structure of the clause, which is a realisation of these
three distinct functional structures, the different structures are **conflated**: i.e.
in different contexts, the elements of these structures will map on to each
other in different ways. The textual systems define two points of message
prominence in the clause: Theme, which is the point of departure of the clause
as message, and New, which constitutes the news in the clause as information.
The Theme occurs at the beginning of the clause; the New normally falls at
the end of the clause, i.e. within the Rheme. Fries (1992:464) has coined **N-
Rheme** (for New conflated with Rheme) as the term to refer to this "particular location in the clause"; in the present simplified description, we will
assume that the last element of the Rheme is New unless otherwise stated. In
characterising clause structure in Chinese, we will, for the sake of simplicity,
consider the conflation of different elements of transitivity structure with
these two structural points, Theme and New, in the clause.

3.2.1.2 Structural relations between clauses   As noted in 3.1.2, underlying
the syntagmatic structure of a clause complex are relations of two kinds:
interdependency – parataxis and hypotaxis – and logico-semantic – expansion and projection. The intersection of these two types of relation is signifi-

cant to the thematic structure of the clause complex. Thus, in a paratactic clause complex, the primary clause always comes first – precisely because the relation of parataxis is one based on the order of its constituents, with the initiating member followed by the continuing. So in a paratactic clause complex, whether expanding or projecting, the first clause will automatically be Theme of the clause complex: the structural order is fixed. The relation of hypotaxis, in contrast, is based on subordination between the primary and the secondary clauses. But the dependency may be expressed simply by the order of the constituent clauses. So in an expanding clause complex, the secondary clause normally precedes the primary, while in a projecting one the primary clause precedes the secondary. However, if this relation is marked by a structural device, clearly indicating which is the dominant and which the dependent clause, then variant ordering is possible.

Table 4 (adapted from Ouyang 1986: 18) presents the various possible combinations of interdependency and logico-semantic relations in the Chinese clause complex; where variant order is possible, the unmarked order is shown first. The table shows that variation in the structural order for thematic effect is possible only when the relation of hypotaxis combines with enhancement or projection. Where parataxis combines with projection, the structural order is invariant; what changes is whether the primary clause is projecting or projected.

Table 4: Types of clause complex in Chinese

Logico-semantic relation	Interdependency relation	
	PARATAXIS	HYPOTAXIS
I: EXPANSION		
a: elaboration	$1\ {}^{=}2$	
b: extension	$1\ {}^{+}2$	${}^{+}\beta\ \alpha$
c: enhancement	$1\ {}^{\times}2$	$\{{}^{\times}\beta\ \alpha$
		$\{\alpha^{\times}\beta$
II: PROJECTION		
a: locution	$\{1\ {}^{\text{“}}2$	$\{\alpha\ {}^{\text{“}}\beta$
	$\{{}^{\text{“}}1\ 2$	$\{{}^{\text{“}}\beta\ \alpha$
b: idea	$\{1\ {}^{\text{‘}}2$	$\{\alpha\ {}^{\text{‘}}\beta$
	$\{{}^{\text{‘}}1\ 2$	$\{{}^{\text{‘}}\beta\ \alpha$

3.2.2 Cohesive connections

On the basis of the structural relations already set up, we can identify further relations which act alongside structural relations, but unlike them are not confined to the clause/clause complex. These non-structural or "cohesive" relations extend over a whole text, serving to bind it together into a whole. Two main types of cohesive relations are relevant here: thematic progression, and cohesion proper.

3.2.2.1 Thematic progression We have indicated above some of the different possibilities, in terms of the grammatical structures, for what is chosen as the Theme of a clause or clause complex. However, we have not explained why particular lexical material is chosen as Theme, nor how this fits in with the overall organisation of the text. The notion of thematic progression (Fries 1981) is designed to provide a framework for answering this question. Following Fries (1981: 20), if we ask why a particular piece of information is chosen as the Theme of a clause, the answer is that the Theme of a clause is the point of departure of the message of that clause. As for the nature of the relationship between the information contained in the Themes of successive clauses in a paragraph or some significant segment of a text, it is suggested that this relation is what creates the method of development of that paragraph and/or textual segment.

Apart from these positive features, the choice of Theme also has a negative characteristic: that is, the choice of what information is **not** put in the Theme but rather in the Rheme is also significant. Thus, if we ask why a particular piece of information is chosen as Rheme of a clause, then again, we would suggest, following Fries (1981:20-21) that a particular piece of information is put in the Rheme of a clause because it is the (main) point of the message of that clause. Further, the relationship between the information contained in the Rhemes of successive clauses is that together they form part of the (main) point of the paragraph. (See both Fries and Cloran, this volume, on the textual contribution of Rheme.) In section 4, we will show some of the possible patterns of thematic progression in Chinese.

3.2.2.2 Cohesion A cohesive relation may be defined as the "semantic relation between an element in the text and some other element that is crucial to the interpretation of it" (Halliday and Hasan 1976: 8). This sort of relation, as was pointed out above, exists alongside the structural relations found in clause and clause complex, and may be marked in various ways. The main types of cohesive relation (Halliday and Hasan 1976) are the following:

a: reference
b: substitution/ellipsis
c: conjunction
d: lexical cohesion

As explained above (3.3.1), a full treatment of text-forming relations, of which cohesive relations are only one part, would involve consideration also of the register (Halliday and Hasan 1976: 22-26) of the text, and would moreover require detailed analysis of actual texts. This takes us beyond the scope of the current study. We have included this brief discussion of cohesion for the sake of completeness; furthermore we have taken some account of cohesive relations in the analysis of the appendix text. Basically for this study, the point to be noted is that thematic progression always implies, at least, some lexically expressed semantic relations between the various clauses occurring in the text.

4. Textual organisation in Chinese

In the following sections we will present a systematic overview of textual organisation at and above clause level in Chinese. Our aim is to set out the different possibilities for the conflation of theme, transitivity and information structures in the clause and the clause complex. We are not presenting this as a comprehensive framework, but rather as an introduction to some characteristic textual patterns in Chinese. Large-scale text analysis, drawing from a wide range of different text types, will be needed to fill out and modify the outline given here. Most of the examples are extracts from actual (written) texts; in addition, we have provided one example of a complete (short) text in the appendices.

4.1 Clause

As noted in 2.2.1.1 above, the concrete structure of the clause in Chinese can be seen as the conflation of three distinct structural functions which express the choices from three different systems. The basic, unmarked, structural functions associated with THEME, TRANSITIVITY, and INFORMATION are set out below in Table 5. The information provided in Table 5 is of course far from exhaustive, but it will suffice for our needs in this paper.

Table 5: Clause structures in Chinese

system	functional structure
THEME	Theme^Rheme
TRANSITIVITY:	
action:	Actor^Circumstance(s)^Process^Goal
state:	Carrier^Circumstance(s)^Process
relation:	Participant A^Circ(s)^Pro^Participant B
INFORMATION	Given^New

While every clause contains a Theme-Rheme and a Given-New structure, there are a number of different, mutually exclusive transitivity structures. The three main types of transitivity structure recognised in this framework, action, state and relation (McDonald 1992: 437-442), have different possibilities for ordering, and therefore for textual organisation. As noted in 2.2.1.1 above, we will discuss the textual organisation in terms of the conflation of different elements of transitivity structure with Theme (initial position in the clause), and New (final position in the clause).

4.1.1 Textual organisation in Action clauses

Of the different clause types, action clauses tend to contain the largest number and variety of distinct functional elements. For most of these elements we can recognise a default or unmarked position in the clause, but they also have the possibility of being moved into positions of textual prominence.[6] This gives a two-fold choice for Circumstance, between initial

---

6. Halliday's discussion of Theme in the clause in English distinguishes "unmarked" and "marked" Theme according to its conflation with the various elements of Mood Structure (1985: 44-49). Since we are not recognising a Mood structure at clause level in Chinese we are unable to use similar criteria; and moreover, the fact that almost any transitivity element of the clause can be conflated with Theme simply by moving it to initial position, without the need for any other structural changes, makes it very difficult to identify "basic" or "unmarked" Theme in the clause. For these reasons we have chosen not to characterise the various possibilities as marked or unmarked; further research may be able to establish a discourse basis for such a distinction.

position conflating with Theme, and post-initial position at the beginning of
Rheme. Ignoring the function of Range in this simplified description, for
Participant type roles – i.e. Actor and Goal – there is a three-fold choice: the
element may occur in the clause initial position, thus conflating with Theme;
or in post-initial position; or in a final position, thus conflating with New.
Process occurs in clause initial position either as a result of the ellipsis of a
Participant function as in clause (20) of the Text in Appendix 1, or due to
inversion as exemplified in (17) below. The first case would be analysed
here as one of ellipsed Theme while the second is treated as a case of Process
conflating with Theme. Examples (12-17) illustrate these basic possibilities
under headings *a-f*. The slash "/" shown in the heading titles – as in Ac-
tor/Theme, New/Goal – signifies that the elements on either side of the slash
are conflated. Note that in the analysis of the examples, the function New is
indicated not by entering the name of the element itself but by putting that
transitivity function in bold italics with which the element New is conflated,
eg *Goal* under heading *a*. in (12):

a: Theme/Actor, New/Goal

(12) | *Ta* | *zuotian wanshang* | *zuo-wan le* | *zhe jian* | *shi.* |
|---|---|---|---|---|
| s/he | yesterday evening | do finish **asp** | this **meas** | matter |
| **Th** | ——————————**Rheme**—————————— | | | |
| Ac | Circ | Process | ———***Goal***——— | |

He finished doing this last night.

b: Theme/Circumstance, New/Goal

(13) | *Zuotian wanshang* | *ta* | *zuo-wan le* | *zhe jian* | *shi.* |
|---|---|---|---|---|
| Yesterday | s/he | do finish **asp** | this **meas** | matter |
| **Theme** | ——————————**Rheme**—————————— | | | |
| Circ | Actor | Process | ———***Goal***——— | |

Last night he finished doing this.

c: Theme/Actor, New/Process

(14) | *Ta* | *zhe jian* | *shi* | *zaojiu* | *zuo-wan le.* |
|---|---|---|---|---|
| s/he | this **meas** | matter | long-since | do finish **asp** |
| **Theme** | ———**Rheme**——— | | | |
| Actor | ———Goal——— | | —Circ— | ***Process*** |

He finished doing this long ago.

d: Theme/Goal, New/Process

(15)	*Zhe jian shi*	*ta*	*zaojiu*	*zuo-wan le.*
	this **meas** matter	s/he	long-since	do finish **asp**

Theme ——————————**Rheme**————————————

Goal   Actor   Circ   *Process*

This, he finished doing long ago.

e: Theme/Circumstance , New/Actor

(16)	*Huran*	*pao-lai le*	*yi zhi*	*tuzi.*
	suddenly	run come **asp**	one **meas**	rabbit

Theme ——————————**Rheme**————————————

Circ   Process   ————*Actor*————

Suddenly there ran out a rabbit .

f: Theme/Process, New/Actor

(17)	*Qu le*	*chuan hong de*	*(hai you*	*gua lü*	*de.)*
	go **asp**	wear red **sub**	still exist	hang green	**sub**

Theme —**Rheme**—

Pro   ————*Actor*————

(Though) gone were those in red, there still remained those in green.

4.1.2 Textual organisation in state clauses

In a clause with a state Process, the ordering of the (single) Participant (the Carrier of the state or property) and the Process is fixed, and only circumstantial elements may vary between initial (Theme) and post-initial position.

a: Theme/Carrier, New/Process

(18)	*Ni*	*zuijin*	*mang*	*ma?*
	you	recently	busy	**mod**

Theme ——————————**Rheme**————————

Carrier   Circ   *Process*

Have you been busy recently?

b: Theme/Circumstance, New/Process

(19) Zuijin ni mang ma?
recently you busy **mod**
Theme ――――**Rheme**――――
Circ Carrier *Process*
Have you been busy recently?

  The only exceptions to these two orderings are where an afterthought Theme is found (see 3.1.1. above):

(19') *(Ni)* mang ma, zuijin?
you busy **mod** recently
――――**Rheme**―――― **Theme**
Carrier Process *Circ*
Have you been busy recently?

4.1.3 Textual organisation in relational clauses

A relational clause structure always includes two participants (these were indicated as Participant A and Participant B in Table 5, p. 254); the type and ordering of these participants vary in the four subtypes of relational clause that have been recognised here. In a clause with a relation Process, ordering is part of the realisation of transitivity structure. This implies that the Theme is always conflated with the same functional element, i.e. Participant A. In most cases the New is conflated with Participant B. In one subtype,viz. the existential, the New may be conflated with the Process.

a: existential clause: Theme/Location, New/Existent

(20) Dishang mei you gui,
earth-on **neg** exist ghost
Theme ――**Rheme**――
Loc Process *Existent*
(If) there are no ghosts on earth...

b: locational clause: Theme/Existent, New/Location

(21) gui zai na'r?
ghost be-at where
Theme ――**Rheme**――
Existent Pro *Location*
...(then) where are the ghosts?

These two examples, from the opening clause complex of the appendix text, show how in relational clauses, the use of different lexical verbs determines the textual organisation, with the existential verb *you* 'exist' and the locational verb *zai* 'be located' defining transitivity structures that are mirror images of each other, and therefore placing textual prominence on exactly the opposite participant functions.

In an existential clause, the New may also be conflated with the Process. Furthermore, the Location may be omitted, in which case we have the equivalent of a Theme-less clause, with a distinction between Existent as New, or Process as New exemplified in (22) and (23), respectively:

(22)   *(Zhe'r)*   *you mei you*   *niunai?*
          here   exist **neg** exist   milk
          Theme   ————**Rheme**————
          Loc   —Process—   ***Existent***
          Is there any milk (here)? i.e. do you sell milk here?

(23)   *(Zhe'r)*   *niunai*   *you mei you?*
          here   milk   exist **neg** exist
          Theme   ————**Rheme**————
          Loc   Existent   ***Process***
          Is there any milk (here)? i.e. do you have any left?

c: attributive clause: Theme/Carrier, New/Attribute

(24)   *Zhanggui*   *shi*   *yi fu*   *xiong*   *liankong,*
          boss   be   one **meas** brutal   face
          Theme   ————**Rheme**————
          Carrier   Process   ————***Attribute***————
          The boss had a brutal face...

A characteristic of attributive and equative relational clauses is that either of the participants may be a clause or part of a clause embedded through nominalisation with the subordinating particle *de*: Note that the embedded status of a clause, as *keyi huodong de* in example (25) is shown by enclosing it within double square brackets:

(25)   *Ta*   *de*   *erduo*   *shi*   *[[keyi*   *huodong*   *de]].*
          s/he **sub** ear   be   can   move   **sub**
          Theme   ————**Rheme**————
          Carrier   Process   ————***Attribute***————
          Its ears are moveable.

d: equative clause: Theme/Identified, New/Identifier

(26) Tamen   bu   shi   gui
     they   **neg** be   ghost
     Theme   ——**Rheme**——
     Identified Process   *Identifier*
     They are not ghosts.

(27) Kepa   de   shi   [[hai you   ni mei jian guo... de ren]].
     frightening **sub** be   still exist you **neg** see **exp sub** person
     Theme   ——**Rheme**——
     Identified   Pro   ——————*Identifier*——————
     The frightening thing is there are still people you've never seen.

The lexical material of an equative clause may be reversed: in this case, the function structure of the clause remains the same, i.e. Theme/Identified, New/Identifier as shown in (28):

(26') Tamen   bu   shi   gui.
     they   **neg** be   ghost
     Theme   ——**Rheme**——
     Identified Process   *Identifier*
     They are not ghosts (they are something else).

(28) Gui   bu   shi   tamen.
     ghost   **neg** be   they
     Theme   ——**Rheme**——
     Identified Process   *Identifier*
     The ghosts aren't them (the ghosts are something else).

All types of relational clauses also admit Circumstances, with the same potential for either initial or post-initial position:

(29) Yuanlai   ta   shi   wode   laoshi.
     originally   s/he   be   my   teacher
     Theme   ——**Rheme**——
     Circ   Identified Pro *Identifier*
     Originally she was my teacher.

(30)   *Ta*   *yuanlai*   *shi*   *wode laoshi.*
        s/he   originally   be   my teacher
        Theme   —————**Rheme**—————
        Identified Circ   Pro   *Identifier*
        She used to be my teacher.

4.1.4 Possibilities of textual prominence for transitivity functions

Table 6 is designed to present a summary of the possibilities that are open to the different transitivity functions for conflation with either Theme – when they occur in initial position – or with New when they occur in final position; by comparison, the post-initial position usually means that an element has not been chosen as Theme of that clause, nor is it conflated with New. Note that certain positions are not open to certain functions in certain clause types. Thus, Process in action clauses, cannot occur in post-initial position, while in state clauses its position is the clause final one. In the table, those positions not open to a transitivity function in some clause type are indicated by a dash in the column. Of the transitivity functions, the two with the greatest potential for movement in the clause, are the participant functions Actor and Goal, which can occur in any of the three possible locations.

Table 6: Positions of textual prominence in the clause in Chinese

Clause type	Position of functions in the clause		
	initial /Theme	*post-initial*	*final/New*
action	Actor	Actor	Actor
	Circumstance	Circumstance	–
	Goal	Goal	Goal
	Process	–	Process
state	Carrier	Carrier	–
	Circumstance	Circumstance	–
	–	–	Process
relation	Participant A	Participant A	–
	Circumstance	Circumstance	–
	–	–	ParticipantB
existential	Participant A	Process	Process
	–	Participant B	ParticipantB

4.2 Clause complex

The textual possibilities for ordering of clause complexes in Chinese may be viewed from two perspectives: the combinations of taxis and logico-semantic relations; and, secondly, thematic progression. A brief illustration of both is provided below in that order.

4.2.1 Basic combinations of parataxis/hypotaxis and expansion/projection

a: paratactic expanding clause complex, lexical material reversible:

(31) i **1Theme** *Feng ye zhu le,*
           wind also stop **asp**

   ii **+2Rheme** *yu ye ting le.*
           rain also stop **asp**

The wind has stopped, the rain has stopped too.

(31′) i **1Theme** *Yu ye ting le,*
           rain also stop **asp**

   ii **+2Rheme** *feng ye zhu le.*
           wind also stop ASP

The rain has stopped, the wind has stopped too.

b: paratactic clause complex – (32ii-iii) – nested inside first clause (32i); note that the Rheme of (32i) follows the interrupting paratactic clauses:

(32) i **1Theme** *Zhe ge ren*
           this **meas** person

   ii **=21** *ni bu zhidao*
           you not know

   iii **+22** *wo ke zhidao*
           I really know

      1Rheme *huai-tou le.*
           bad through **asp**

This person - you don't know, (but) I really know - is very bad.

c: paratactic projecting clause complex, with either projecting or projected clause thematic:

(33)   i   **1Theme**   *Xiao   Ming   shuo*
                          young   Ming   say

      ii   **"2Rheme**   *"Wo mingtian bu   qu   shang   xue"*.
                            I   tomorrow   **neg**   go   attend   school

           Ming said: "I'm not going to school tomorrow."

(33')   i   **"1Theme** *"Wo mingtian bu   qu   shang   xue"*,
                         I   tomorrow   **neg**   go   attend   school

      ii   **2Rheme**   *Xiao   Ming   shuo.*
                         young   Ming   say

           "I'm not going to school tomorrow", said Ming.

d: hypotactic expanding clause complex, with initial (subordinate) clause thematic to following (dominant) clause:

(34)   i $^\times\beta$ Theme   *Tangshi   gai   de   bu hao*
                        if   write **ext**   not good

      ii   α *Rheme*   *duzhe   keyi   xie   wenzhang   piping.*
                        reader   can   write   article   criticise

           If (this book) is not well-written, readers can write articles to criticise (it).

e: hypotactic expanding clause complex, with initial (dominant) clause thematic to the following (subordinate) clause in (35) and the reverse in (35'):

(35)   i   α **Theme** *Tian yiding   hen   leng,*
                     sky   definitely   very   cold

      ii $^\times\beta$ Rheme *yinwei   shui   jie   le   bing.*
                      because   water   form   **asp**   ice

           The weather must be very cold, because the water has frozen.

(35')   i $^\times\beta$ **Theme** *Yinwei   tian   hen   leng,*
                     because   sky   very   cold

      ii   α **Rheme** *suoyi   shui   jie   le   bing.*
                     therefore   water   form   **asp**   ice

           Because the weather is very cold, (therefore) the water has frozen.

f: hypotactic projecting clause complex, with either projecting or projected clause as thematic:

(36)   i   α **Theme** *Women dou   renwei*
                          we   all   consider
       ii 'β **Rheme** *zhe ge   banfa   hen   hao.*
                          this **meas** method very good
We all think this is a good way of doing it.

(36') i   'β **Theme** *zhe ge   banfa   hen   hao,*
                          this **meas** method very   good
       ii α **Rheme** *women dou   renwei.*
                          we   all   consider
This is a good way of doing it, we all think.

4.2.2 Thematic progression in the clause complex

In the following examples, for the sake of clarity, we have not shown the logical relations between clauses, and only the thematic structure of each individual clause (not that of the clause complex) has been indicated.

a: All clauses share common Theme/Actor, Theme is ellipsed after first clause; and Rhemes describe actions performed by Theme/Actor:

(37)   **Theme Rheme**
       i   *Ta   qu-chu   kapian,*
           s/he   take out   card
       ii _____ *sai-jin   yidou,*
                     stuff in pocket
       iii _____ *likai   bangongshi,*
                     leave   office
       iv _____ *congcong gan xia   lou,*
                     hastily   rush descend stair
       v   _____ *ti   tade mishu   ban shi   qu le.*
                     for   his secretary do   matter go **asp**
He took out a card, stuffed it into his pocket, left the office, hurried downstairs and went to do some things for his secretary.

b: initial and final clause share common Theme/Actor; *taozi* 'peaches' is New in the Rheme of (38i); it is the ellipsed Theme of (38ii-iii); and the following Rhemes specify amount of 'peaches'.

(38)

		Theme	Rheme	
i	*Mama*	*mai le*	*yixie taozi,*	
	mum	buy **asp**	some peach	
ii	_____	*chi-diao*	*shiba zhi*	*hou,*
		eat up	18 **meas**	after
iii	_____	*hai sheng*	*liu zhi,*	
		still remain	6 **meas**	
iv	mama	*mai-lai duoshao*	*zhi*	*taozi?*
	mum	buy come	how-many **meas**	peach

Mum bought some peaches, after 18 were eaten, 6 still remained: mum bought how many peaches altogether?

c: Theme of initial clause (39i) is elaborated in Rhemes of (39i-iv); the Theme of (39i) is presupposed by ellipsis in (39ii-iv):

(39)

		Theme	Rheme				
i	*Laike*	*ye bu shao,*					
	guest	also not few					
ii	_____	*you*	*songxing*	*de,*			
		exist	see-off	**sub**			
iii	_____	*you*	*na*	*dongxi*	*de,*		
		exist	bring	thing	**sub**		
iv	_____	*you*	*songxing*	*jian*	*na*	*dongxi*	*de.*
		exist	see-off	concurrently	bring	thing	**sub**

There were quite a few guests also, there were those who came to see (them) off, there were those who came to carry things, and there were those who came to see (them) off and carry things as well.

d: Initial clause (40i) has Theme/Circumstance (location); in its Rheme, New and Actor are conflated; the constituent realising New/Actor consists of two nominal groups in coordination, each one extended in the separate following clauses:

(40)

		Theme			Rheme			
i		*Dongwuyuan zhong*			*ji-man*	*le*	*daren*	*xiaohai,*
		zoo	in		crowd	full	**asp**	big-person small-child
ii		*da*	*de*		*jiao,*			
		big	**sub**		shout			
iii		*xiao*	*de*		*tiao.*			
		small	**sub**		jump			

The zoo was full of grown-ups and children, the big ones shouting, the small ones jumping.

e: expanding clause complex: with Actor/Theme in clause (41i); in (41ii-iii) conjunctions are thematic:

(41)

	Theme	Rheme						
i	*Ta*	*hao bu rongyi de-dao*		*le*	*chu-guo*		*huzhao,*	
	he	very **neg** easy gain reach		**asp**	leave country		passport	
ii	*dan yinwei*	*youxie biyao*	*de*	*shouxu*		*hai*	*wei*	*ban-hao,*
	but because	some necessary	**sub**	procedure		still	**neg**	do complete
iii	*rengran*	*mei you*	*huode*	*qianzheng.*				
	still	**neg** have	obtain	visa				

He did, with some difficulty, get a passport, but because some of the necessary formalities had not yet been completed, he still has not obtained a visa.

f: expanding clause complex, in which participants and enhancing conjunctions are thematic:

(42)

	Theme		Rheme			
i	*Zhanggui*		*shi*	*yi fu*	*xiong*	*liankong,*
	boss		be	one **meas**	brutal	face
ii	*zhugu*		*ye*	*mei*	*hao shengqi,*	
	customer		also	not-exist	good humour	
iii	_____		*jiao*	*ren*	*huo-bu-de;*	
			make	person	live not can	
iv	*zhiyou*	*Kong Yiji*	*dao*	*dian,*		
	only-if	Kong Yiji	arrive	shop		
v	_____		*cai*	*keyi*	*xiao*	*ji*	*sheng*
			only-then	can	laugh	some	sound

vi *suoyi zhijin*   *hai   jide.*
   so to-present   still   remember

The boss had a brutal face, the customers were ill-humoured, making one miserable; it was only when Kong Yiji came to the shop that (we) could have a few laughs, and so today (I) still remember (him).

4.3 Patterns of thematic progression

From the examples above, we can identify a number of different patterns of thematic progression in the clause complex. These are summarised below in terms of the movement of information between Theme and Rheme (thematic progression proper), and the general logico-semantic relations (see Table 4) between the clauses in the clause complex.

a: Participant introduced in Theme *i*; progression from initial Theme maintained by ellipsis throughout. Note in representing the thematic progression here, *i -n* refer to the number of the clause in the relevant clause complex (see the numbering system in examples (37-41):

The clauses in clause complex (37i-v) are related through extension, whereas those in (39i-iv) are related through elaboration. In both cases a simple linear pattern of thematic progression obtains:

(37) Th *i*   Rh *i*   (39) Th *i*   Rh *i*
        Th *ii*   Rh *ii*   Th *ii*   Rh *ii*
        Th *iii* Rh *iii*   Th *iii* Rh *iii*
        Th *iv* Rh *iv*   Th *iv* Rh *iv*
        Th *v*   Rh *v*

b: In (40) the initial Theme of (40i) provides the setting; Rheme *i* of the complex introduces two participants; the Theme in (40ii) and (40iii) relate each to one of the two participants, extending them. The clauses of (40) are, thus, related by extension:

(40) Th *i* Rh *i* (participant 1)   Rh *i* (participant 2)
       Th *ii* Rh *ii*   Th *iii* Rh *iii*

c: In clause complex (38), there are two main participants; the first is introduced in the Theme of (38i). This participant is restated in the Theme of

(38iv). The second participant is introduced in Rheme of (38i); subsequently, it is the understood Theme of clauses (38ii-iii). Clauses (38i) and (38iv) are related by extension; clauses (38ii and 38iii) by enhancement:

(38) Th *i*   Rh *i*
      Th *ii*   Rh *ii*
      Th *iii*   Rh *iii*
   Th *iv*   Rh *iv*

d: Participants are introduced in the initial Theme of (41)-(42); some following Themes are realized by (enhancing) conjunctions; progression between Themes is by logical relation. The clauses of (41) are related by enhancement, while clauses (42i-iii) are related by addition and clauses (42iv-vi) by enhancement:

(41) Th *i*   Rh *i*
      Th *ii*   Rh *ii*
      Th *iii*   Rh *iii*
(42) Th *i*   Rh *i*
      Th *ii*   Rh *ii*
      Th *iii*   Rh *iii*
                     Th *iv*   Rh *iv*
                     Th *v*   Rh *v*
                     Th *vi*   Rh *vi*

An analysis of thematic progression through a complete text is given in Appendix 2, using the same text – Dreams – introduced for thematic analysis in Appendix 1. In both appendices, for ease of presentation, the text has been divided into 'paragraphs'. The use of this term is simply to suggest convenient segments of text; we have not attempted to give a rigorous definition of 'paragraph' here, since that would necessarily involve considerations of text structure that lie beyond the scope of the current paper. It may however be noted that a change in thematic progression is often used to divide paragraphs from each other.

5. Conclusion

We have shown how it is possible to use the textual function of the grammar to define and explain the ordering of elements within clauses and clause complexes, and have identified some of the characteristic patterns of thematic progression in text. It has only been possible in this brief study to set up a preliminary framework: we hope that further research will be able to put our findings on a firmer footing. There is a need to carry out a systemic functional analysis of a wide range of text types in order to gain a better understanding of textual organisation in Chinese.

Abbreviations:

asp aspect particle: perfective or imperfective (subtypes not indicated here)

Circ Circumstance

disp disposal marker: marks Goal as part of Given and moves it to front of clause

ext marks Circumstance of extent following Process

meas measure word (also known as classifier): obligatory for noun modified by numeral or demonstrative

mod modal particle: interrogative, exclamative, etc. (subtypes not shown here)

neg negation adverb: neutral, perfective or potential (subtypes not shown)

Pro Process

sub subordinating particle: makes preceding group/clause into modifier of following nominal group

text textual (pause) particle

Transcription

All Chinese examples and terms are given in the standard orthography of the People's Republic of China, Hanyu Pinyin; tone marks are omitted.

References

Chao, Yuenren. 1968. *A Grammar of Spoken Chinese*. Berkeley & Los Angeles: University of California Press.

Fang, Yan. 1989. A Contrastive Study of Theme and Rheme Structure in English and Chinese. Paper presented at the International Conference on Applied Linguistics, Xi'an Jiaotong University.

Fries, Peter H. 1981. On the status of Theme in English: Arguments from discourse. *Forum Linguisticum* 6.1, 1-38.

Fries, Peter H. 1992. The structuring of information in written English text. *Language Sciences* 14.4, 461-488.

Gao, Houkun. 1984. End focus in the information structure of English and Chinese. *Foreign Language Teaching and Research* 1, 7-13.

Halliday, M.A.K. 1967. Notes on transitivity and theme in English: Part 2. *Journal of Linguistics* 3, 199-244.

Halliday, M.A.K. 1978. *Language as Social Semiotic*. London: Edward Arnold.

Halliday, M.A.K. 1979. Modes of meaning and modes of expression: types of grammatical structure, and their determination by different semantic functions. *Function and Context in Linguistic Analysis*, edited by D.J. Allerton, Edward Carney and David Holdcroft, 57-79. Cambridge: Cambridge University Press.

Halliday, M.A.K. 1985. *An Introduction to Functional Grammar.* London: Edward Arnold

Halliday, M.A.K. and Ruqaiya Hasan. 1976. *Cohesion in English*. London: Longman.

Li, Charles N. and Sandra A. Thompson. 1978. Grammatical relations in languages without grammatical signals. *Proceedings of the Twelfth International Congress of Linguists*, edited by Wolfgang U. Dressler and Wolfgang Meid, 687-691. Innsbruck.

Li, Charles N. and Sandra A Thompson. 1981. *Mandarin Chinese: A functional reference grammar*. Berkeley: University of California Press.

Li, Ying-che. 1971. *An Investigation of Case in Chinese Grammar*. South Orange, N.J.: Seton Hall University Press.

Long, Rijin. 1981. *Transitivity in Chinese*. M.A. Dissertation. Sydney: University of Sydney.

McDonald, Edward. 1992. Outline of a functional grammar of Chinese for teaching purposes. *Language Sciences* 14.4, 435-458.

Ouyang, Xiaoqing. 1986. *Clause Complex in Chinese*. M.A. Dissertation. Sydney: Linguistics, University of Sydney.

Tam, Mo-shuet. 1979. *A Grammatical Description of Transitivity in Mandarin Chinese with Special Reference to the Correspondences with English Based on a Study of Texts in Translation*. Ph.D Dissertation. London: University of London.

Tang, Ting-chi Charles. 1972. *A Case Grammar of Spoken Chinese*. Taipei: Hai-Guo Book Company.

Teng, Shou-hsin. 1975. *A Semantic Study of Transitivity Relations in Chinese*. Berkeley: University of California Press. (Reprinted 1982 Taipei: Student Book Co.)

Tsao, Feng-fu. 1980. *A Functional Study of Topic in Chinese: the first step towards discourse analysis*. Taipei: Student Book Co. reprinted 1988.

Zhu, Dexi. 1981. *A Grammar Course*. Beijing: Commercial Press.

Appendix 1: The analysis of a complete text

The text, called Dreams, is presented through the analysis of Theme-Rheme at the rank of clause. Each ranking clause is numbered, and two columns are established, the left showing Theme, the right Rheme. The element New is shown by italicising the constituent which realizes that function.

	Theme	Rheme						
PARAGRAPH I								
1.	Dishang	mei	you	*gui,*				
	earth-on	**neg**	exist	ghost				
2.	gui	zai	*na'r?*					
	ghost	be-at	where					
3.	Gui	dou	zai	*renxin*	*litou.*			
	ghost	all	be-at	person-mind	inside			
PARAGRAPH II								
4.	Ni	bu	*xin?*					
	you	**neg**	believe					
5.	_____	Jiu	kan	*meng.*				
		then	look	dream				
PARAGRAPH III								
6.	Meng li	name	duo	ren	dou shi	*na'r lai*	*de?*	
	dream in	so	many	people	all be	where come	**sub**	
7.	_____	You	*ni*	*ba,*				
		exist	you	father				
8.	_____	you	*ni*	*ma,*				
		exist	you	mother				
9.	_____	you	*nide*	*laoshi*	*he*	*tongxue,*		
		exist	your	teacher	and	classmate		
10.	_____	you	he	ni	zai	yiqi	*shenghuo*	*guo* de	ren,
		exist	with	you	at	together	live	**asp** **sub**	person
11.	_____	ye	you	ni	zhi	*tingshuo guo*	*mingzi* de	ren,
		also	exist	you	only	hear **asp**	name	**sub**	person
12.	zhe	dou	*bu*	*kepa.*				
	this	all	**neg**	frightening				
PARAGRAPH IV								
13.	Kepa	de	shi	hai	you	ni	mei	*jian guo,*
	frightening **sub**		be	still	exist	you	neg	see asp
			mei	*ting guo,*	mei	*chi guo,* mei	*wen*	*guo,*
			neg	hear **asp**	**neg**	eat **asp** **neg**	smell	**asp**

		meng	dou	mei	*meng guo*	de	ren,
		dream	even	**neg**	dream **asp**	**sub**	person
14.	zhe yi hui	*bu-qing-zi-lai*			le.		
	this one time	**neg**-invite-self-come			asp		

PARAGRAPH V

15.	Ni	you	bu	neng *wen*:
	you	again	**neg**	can ask
16.	"Ni	zi	na'r	*lai?*"
	you	from	where	come
17.	_____	"Yao	dao	na'r	*qu?*"
		will	to	where	go
18.	_____	jiushi	*wen le*,
		just-be	ask **asp**
19.	ta	ye	bu	*shuo*.
	s/he	also	**neg**	say

PARAGRAPH VI

20.	_____	Zuo-wan	le	*shi*,
		do finish	**asp**	matter
21.	_____	hui	shen	jiu	*zou*,
		turn	body	then	leave
22.	na shi'r	ni	*dao*	*si*	ye	mei jian-guo.
	that matter	you	to	die	also	**neg** see **asp**

PARAGRAPH VII

23.	Ni	*shuo*
	you	say
24.	tamen	bu	shi	*gui*
	they	**neg**	be	ghost
25.	_____	shi	*shenme?*
		be	what

PARAGRAPH VIII

26.	Tian	na,	gui	jiu	zhu-zai	*women*	*shenti*	*li*,
	heaven	**text**	ghost	just	live at	we	body	in
27.	[xiang duo]	ye	duo-bu-kai.
	want escape	also	escape-**neg**-away

(If) on the earth there are no ghosts, (then) where are the ghosts? The ghosts are in people's minds. You don't believe (me)? Then take a look at dreams. In dreams, all those people come from where? There's your father, your mother, your teacher and classmates, there are people who have lived with you, there are also people you've only heard the names of, none of this is frightening. The frightening thing is there are also people you've never seen, never heard, never eaten, never smelt, never even dreamt of in dreams, this time they come without being asked. Nor can you ask (a ghost): "Where do you come from?" "Where are (you) going?" (You) just ask, and it doesn't say (anything). After (it) has finished doing something, it turns and leaves, that thing you'll never see in your whole life. (If) you say they're not ghosts, (then) what are (they)? My god, the ghosts live in our bodies, (if we) want to escape (them), (we) can't!

Appendix 2: Thematic Progression in Dreams

Note ellipsed Themes are enclosed in round brackets e.g. in (4).

Theme	New
PARAGRAPH I	
1. *dishang* 'on the earth'	*gui* 'ghosts'
2. *gui* 'the ghosts'	*na'r* 'where'
3. *gui* 'the ghosts'	*renxin litou* 'in people's minds'
PARAGRAPH II	
4. *ni* 'you'	*xin* 'believe'
5. (*ni*) 'you'	*meng* 'dream'
PARAGRAPH III	
6. *meng li* 'in dreams'	*na'r lai de* 'come from where'
7. (same as 6)	*ni ba* 'your dad'
8. (same as 6)	*ni ma* 'your mum'
9. (same as 6)	*nide laoshi he tongxue* 'your teacher and classmates'
10. (same as 6)	*shenghuo-guo (de ren)* '(people) lived (with)'
11. (same as 6)	*tingshuo-guo mingzi (de ren)* '(people whose) names (you)'ve heard'
12. *zhe* "this" (= 6-11)	(*bu*) *kepa* '(not) frightening'
PARAGRAPH IV	
13. *kepa de* 'the frightening thing' = 'what is frightening'	*jian guo (de ren)* '(people you)'ve seen'
	ting guo (de ren) '(people you)'ve heard'
	chi guo (de ren) '(people you)'ve eaten'
	wen guo (de ren) '(people you)'ve smelt'
	meng guo (de ren) '(people you)'ve dreamt of'
14. *zhe yi hui* 'this time' (contrast with clauses 7-11)	*bu-qing-zi-lai* 'come without being asked'
PARAGRAPH V	
15. *ni* 'you'	(*bu neng*) *wen* '(can't) ask'
16. *ni* 'you' (different from 15)	*lai* 'come'
17. (same as 16)	*qu* 'go'
18. (same as 15)	*wen* 'ask'
19. *ta* 'it' (coreferential to 16-17)	*shuo* 'say'

PARAGRAPH VI

20.   (same as 19)   *shi* 'thing, matter'
21.   (same as 19)   *zou* 'leave'
21.   *na shi'r* 'that thing'   *dao si* 'till death - all your life'

PARAGRAPH VII

23.   *ni* 'you' (coreferential to 15)   *shuo* 'say'
24.   *tamen* 'they'   *gui* 'ghosts'
25.   (same as 24)   *shenme* 'what'

PARAGRAPH VIII

26.   *tian na, gui* 'my god, the ghosts'   *women shenti li* 'in our bodies'
27.   [*xiang duo*] 'want to escape'   *duo-bu-kai* 'can't escape'

8

A Systemic Functional Approach to the Thematic Structure of the Old English Clause[*]

Michael Cummings
Glendon College
York University, Toronto

I. The problem

1.1 Motive for the study

Most of the current work in the area of theme/rheme refers to contemporary dialects, not historical dialects. One reason for this of course is the priority modern linguistics has given to synchronic studies, especially of spoken language, and the primary datum of historical linguistics is after all the written word. A second reason is the very theoretical nature of studies on theme/rheme. The basic concept of theme/rheme is defined very differently by different schools of linguistics, and even within a single linguistic tradition, a variety of approaches can be met.

It is natural to ask, however, whether the functional distinction between theme/rheme is restricted to recent historical dialects, or whether, in some language like English, it has been part of the linguistic repertoire in all extant stages of historical development. It would also be worth finding out which approaches to the identification of theme/rheme are helpful in the struggle to clarify meaning and to characterize styles in historical texts. It appears that the Prague school tradition has made the greatest contribution to studies of

* Earlier versions of several parts of this article were given as papers at the *2nd National Seminar on Systemic Linguistics*, University of Suzhou, Suzhou, People's Republic of China, July 16, 1991; at the *18th International Systemic-Functional Congress*, The International Christian University, Tokyo, Japan, July 30, 1991; and at the *19th International Systemic-Functional Congress*, Macquarie University, Sydney, Australia, July 17, 1992.

this kind to date (e.g., Svoboda 1981, Kohonen 1983), and the present study is intended to explore the appropriateness of extending the alternative systemic functional approach to the interpretation of theme and rheme in a remote historical dialect.[1]

1.2 The variety of approaches

It will be useful to begin by comparing the Prague school and systemic linguistics on the subject of theme/rheme. The Prague school of course is the context in which an interest in a functional distinction between theme/rheme originated. A contemporary proponent of the theory in this tradition is Jan Firbas, whose approach very clearly continues the Prague tradition that theme is to be associated with given information within the mutual development of text and context. Rheme therefore necessarily provides the locus for new information within the information flow of discourse. On this account, neither theme nor rheme can be precisely tied to the sequence order of clause elements (Firbas 1986).

The systemic approach, which is largely due to M.A.K. Halliday, offers instead a concept of theme/rheme which is primarily focused on the grammar of the clause rather than on the rhythm of the discourse. Theme/rheme is a different sort of distinction from that of given/new. Theme in clause is both a point of departure and a kind of topicalization[2] ("what the clause is going to be about" Halliday 1985:39), and rheme accordingly is a remainder. Given is the projection by the speaker that the information is recoverable by the hearer from the context. The functional distinction between given and new can be mapped together with that of theme/rheme in the generation of clauses, but each distinction retains its own functional identity. Theme is

1. I am indebted for my original interest in this question to the work of Prof. Martin Davies, University of Stirling, first encountered as his paper "Theme from 'Beowulf' to Shakespeare", delivered to the *16th International Systemic Functional Congress*, University of Helsinki, Helsinki, Finland, June 12, 1989, and forthcoming as "Theme until Shakespeare" in M. Berry, C. Butler and R. Fawcett, eds., *Meaning and Choice in Language: Studies for Michael Halliday. Vol. 3, Grammatical Structure: A Functional Interpretation* (Norwood, N.J.: Ablex).

2. On the question of the relation between Theme and Topic in the SF approach, see Fries, this volume. (Editors).

able to be associated with sequence order of elements in clauses in a way in which the given/new distinction cannot (Halliday 1967: 199 ff., esp. 211-223, 236-243; Berry 1975/77: I, 77-82, 161-66, 188-90).

Various systemicists, however, differ on various aspects of this approach. For Halliday, in declarative mood, the unmarked instance of a thematic clause element related to the interpersonal metafunction is the Subject. Marked instances occur as a Complement or circumstantial Adjunct preceding the grammatical Subject, which is then not thematic. Some systemicists have preferred to include this displaced Subject in the thematic stretch of elements all the same (Berry 1989:71; Downing 1990; 1991:125-128). A more radical difference is found in the approach of Michael Gregory. Whereas Halliday finds theme in clause complexes, i.e., sentences, usually limited to preposed subordinate clauses, Gregory finds that a number of Halliday's clausal thematic elements are regularly located within the structure of sentence (Gregory 1983: 2-8, 14; 1984: 315-318; 1988: 306).[3]

---

3. Halliday (1985: 192-193) and other systemicists (e.g. Berry 1975/77) take a view of the rank scale which makes sentence equivalent to clause complex, i.e., only clauses, singly or in a complex, can be the immediate constituents of sentence structure. Gregory (1983: 1-2) on the other hand sees the sentence as oriented as much to discourse as to lexico-grammar. His constituents of sentence realize the roles of various theme-related elements (link, topic, attitudinal, vocative), as well as that of the propositional element, which alone is normally realized morphosyntactically by clauses.

The link element is realized by a class of words which overlaps with Halliday's conjunctive Adjuncts (*however, nevertheless*, etc.) and continuatives (*oh, OK*). The topic element is distinguished from Halliday's topical theme in clause by being very markedly oriented to the pattern of the discourse, not susceptible to the marked/unmarked distinction and tending to be lexically and morphosyntactically bound (*in reference to the above, as for Mary*). The attitudinal element is realized by a class of words and phrases essentially the same as Halliday's modal Adjuncts (*unfortunately, surely*, etc.) and also by post-position groups and clauses which evaluate (*..., which was a good thing for us all!*). The vocative element is realized by the same words and groups as Halliday's clause element vocative (1983: 2-7).

A number of those elements therefore which are thematic in the structure of clause for Halliday (2.1 below) are thematic in the structure of sentence for Gregory, whereas other thematic elements properly belong to the structure of clause all the same, e.g., "clause theme" (1983: 4), which is essentially equivalent to Halliday's topical theme. It should be noted, however, that Halliday at one point (1985: 57-58) wavers between assigning to the structure of the main clause or to the structure of the clause complex thematic elements which precede a preposed β-dependent clause syntactically.

1.3 An approach

One of the most significant tests for a functional linguistic model is to determine whether or not the model yields useful information about texts. To illustrate the possibility of useful systemic functional theme/rheme analysis in historical dialect, it has seemed best to begin by accepting the assumptions and procedures of just one systemic approach, and applying them unreservedly to historical text until a point is reached where assumptions break down and procedures become irrelevant. We begin by accepting Halliday's framework as presented in *Introduction to Functional Grammar* (1985, hereafter *IFG*).[4] The notion of theme is there presented as a putative language universal; however the realizational statements (and the correlation of theme with initial position in the clause) are presented as a description of modern English only. It is therefore natural not only to ask if this model illuminates the structure of real texts, but also to ask if it can be applied usefully to texts in historical dialect.

The first object of this paper is to demonstrate an application of the Halliday model for theme/rheme to Old English prose texts, and to show how the analysis suggests a connection between the distribution of types of theme and the distribution of register in texts which move in and out of narrative register as they proceed (sections 2-8). The texts include a pair of sermons by Archbishop Wulfstan and the abbot Ælfric which tell the story of salvation history in stages separated by non-narrative digressions. Both sermons are sophisticated works of oratory, written near the end of one of the highest periods of pre-Conquest English literary culture, and their language is now almost one-thousand years old. The aspect of these sermons that makes them particularly interesting for text-related linguistic analysis is their regular shifting back and forth between narrative and non-narrative registers. These two sermons are also compared with an intensively narrative text, the *Anglo-Saxon Chronicle*. The information which results is seen to

---

4. Halliday's treatment of theme in *IFG* differs chiefly by omission and addition from his earliest published analysis (1967) and subsequent treatments. For example it does not explicitly refer to any of the networks for theme options discussed earlier, but organizes and expands the description of constituency and realization. On the other hand some changes in theory have occurred; for example, early treatment (1967: 220-221) rejected both the thematicity and clause constituency of coordinating conjunctions, which are regularly included in textual clause theme segments later (1985: 51-54, 64-66).

justify the approach; but at the same time, a number of questions are raised about the theoretical framework.

The second object is to relate the systemic functional analysis of Old English theme/rheme to more traditional philological approaches on the question of Old English clause order, in order to determine how the functional approach may clarify the issues (sections 9-14).

2. The resources

2.1 Coding theme/rheme in *IFG*

It is necessary at this point to characterize the framework for the analysis of Theme offered by Halliday in *IFG* (although omitting many details and qualifications which the reader must pursue in the references). The following summation of this framework observes an order from the more inclusive syntactic unit to the less inclusive, starting with the sentence (i.e., clause complex), and from the phenomena least central to our concern to those that are most central.

In the sentence, theme is realized by clauses. Halliday's treatment of theme realized as a clause assigns thematic status (a) to some kinds of main clause segment in indirect discourse construction (i.e., those which foreground the modality of the speaker, as illustrated in (1i) below; and (b) to hypotactic i.e. ß-dependent clauses when preposed to the main clause (Halliday 1985: 57-59); this is exemplified in (2i):

(1)   i   **I don't believe**
      ii this work is your very best.
(2)   i   **If this is your best work,**
      ii I'll eat my hat.

The treatment of theme within clauses distinguishes dependent and embedded clauses from independent. In the former types, nonfinite clauses, may have initial preposition and/or Subject as theme. This is exemplified in (3i) where both the preposition and the Subject are picked out in bold. Finite dependent clauses e.g. (4i) may have conjunction as structural Theme and Subject as the topical Theme (cf. 1985: 62-63), as shown in bold in example (4i):

(3)   i   **For work** to be your best
      ii it must be done with care.

(4)   i **If this** is your best work, ...

Within the category of independent clauses, minor clauses, i.e. clauses with neither mood nor transitivity e.g. (5), have no thematic structure, and elliptical clauses may have all or part of the thematic element omitted as shown by (6ii):

(5)   Waiter!
(6)   i   She did her best,
       ii **and** made us proud.

But major clauses articulate theme according to the choice of mood. Imperative clauses may show an unmarked theme in various ways: as the *you* Subject e.g. in (7), as the *do* or *let* auxiliary, or perhaps just as the Predicator. Indicative clauses, both declarative, as in example (8) and interrogative e.g. (9), articulate theme as textual, interpersonal and topical elements, usually in that order. Textual elements are continuatives, e.g. *oh*, structural (conjunctions), and conjunctives (conjunctive Adjuncts like *nevertheless*). Interpersonal elements are vocatives, modals (modal Adjuncts like *certainly*) and finites (as interrogative mood markers). Last in any theme segment is the topical theme, unmarked as Subject, but marked as Complement or circumstantial Adjunct or (rarely) a lexical verb (Halliday 1985: 44-56, 63-64).

(7)   **You** just do your best!
(8)   **Oh, but actually, Mary, in my opinion, we** deserve your best work.
(9)   **Well, but in any case, John, surely don't we** deserve your best work?

Additional types of Theme in indicative clauses (though of a lesser concern to the present question) are embedded clauses serving as nominalisations in psuedo-cleft sentences as illustrated in (10), and the main clause segment of cleft sentences as in example (11). (See Halliday 1985: 41-44, 59-61.)

(10)   **What I want from you** is just your very best.
(11)   **It is just your very best** that I want from you.

2.2 Late Old English prose

The body of late Old English prose from which the specimen texts are taken represents a long literary tradition in English. The earliest extant literary texts in English verse may stem from the mid-seventh century. By the end of the ninth century, the court of King Alfred had superintended the development of a vernacular prose for the purpose of translating Christian Latin classics. Two generations later, a redevelopment of Benedictine monasticism in England was in full flower; and by the end of the tenth century, this had produced two writers of ecclesiastical prose possessing stature: the abbot Ælfric and the archbishop Wulfstan.

3.   The first text

3.1 Manuscript and edition

Wulfstan was consecrated Archbishop of York in A.D. 1002, and it may be to this period that his sermon on salvation history belongs. It is preserved in several manuscripts of the eleventh century, of which one of the principals is MS Bodleian Hatton 113. This sermon has been most recently edited by Dorothy Bethurum (1957), who took the Hatton MS as the basis for her text (hereafter Bethurum homily VI; cf. 1957:1-4, 59-62, 103, 142 ff.).

3.2 Outline of the text

As archbishop of a diocese which had been profoundly Scandinavianized in the period of the Viking invasions, Wulfstan had to be concerned with renewing the very elements of Christian education (Bethurum 1957:69 ff.). This sermon is typical of that effort. It begins by reminding his subordinate clergy, both bishops and priests, that they have an obligation to try to teach the fundamental truths of religion. He then begins to recount the basic outline of salvation history, beginning with the creation of the universe, the creation of the angels and their fall, the creation of mankind, the temptation and fall of mankind, the story of Cain and Abel, and the Flood. It should be noted that these two initial parts of the sermon are first expository and then narrative respectively.

Another expository section follows, on the subject of the Devil as the corrupter of mankind. The narrative resumes with the stories of Abraham, the Jewish patriarchs, Moses and the receiving of the Law, the Babylonian captivity, the return of the Jews from exile, and the birth of Christ. This last occasions another expository section, a treatment of the theology of the two natures of Christ. Narrative resumes again with the stories of the childhood

of Christ, the choosing of the disciples, the teaching mission of Christ, then
the betrayal, passion, death, resurrection and ascension. A final, quasi-
narrative section covers eschatology: the future appearance of Antichrist, the
second coming of Christ, and the Day of Judgement, all of which are immi-
nent.

4.   The method

4.1 Preparation and coding of the text

The initial preparation of the texts for analysis owes a debt of thanks to the
Dictionary of Old English Project at the University of Toronto, for their
supplying an ASCII version of the Old English corpus. A PROLOG language
search-&-read program was used to abstract Bethurum homily VI and
selections from the *Anglo-Saxon Chronicle*. (The Ælfric homily was keyed
in.) The texts were then word-processed to produce worksheets for the
analysis of their different sections. This editing is very simple, and consists
mainly of separating graphological sentences into blocks, and separation of
clauses by lines. The logical subordination of clauses is marked by progressive indentation. Each successive worksheet represents the next alternation
between narrative and non-narrative sections. In the worksheet notation,
theme segments are separated from rheme segments with slants, and marked
topical themes are underlined.

4.2 Preliminary statistics

An elementary statistical profile of each section of the homilies is obtained
simply by counting instances. Clauses are distinguished as independent or
dependent. In each category, the number of clauses with marked topical
themes is measured against the total number of clauses to indicate the degree
of markedness in the section. Since each section is interpreted as narrative
or non-narrative, a correlation is determined between degree of markedness
and register type.

5. Some results

5.1 Similarities to modern English theme/rheme

The first result of the analysis is an impression that the IFG categories for thematic elements and its predictions for the sequencing of those elements work about as well for Old English as for modern English. The typical thematic element in declarative independent clauses and finite dependent clauses is the grammatical Subject. Foregrounding effects are achieved when the Complement or topical Adjunct precedes the Subject. Various kinds of repetition realized in successive topical thematic elements, whether marked or unmarked, are used to establish rhythm in sections of the discourse. Clause elements which can precede the topical thematic element and are therefore included in the theme segment are continuatives (e.g., *Hwæt,* 'Lo'), structural elements like coordinating conjunctions (*ond,* 'and'), and subordinating conjunctions (*þæt,* 'that'), conjunctive Adjuncts (*nu,* 'now'), vocatives (*Leofan men,* 'Dearly beloved'), modal Adjuncts (*ea,* 'ever') and perhaps finites (*wæs,* 'was') as well. Nothing in the Old English text examined suggests the sequence order possibilities for these elements are not permitted by the rules for modern English.

5.2 Some differences

It is also to be expected that the language of the year A.D. 1000 shows some differences from modern English in the realization of theme. One of the most striking differences is the frequent positioning of a Predicator element prior to any other element which is a carrier of ideational meaning in declarative clauses, i.e., the use of the Predicator element to realize topical theme in declarative clauses. Sometimes it is the whole Predicator, realized by a single finite verb word, which is thematized, but more frequently it is a finite auxiliary element. This observation is congruent with the nature of Old English auxiliaries, which for the most part are not really auxiliaries in the modern sense, but have a status intermediate between lexical verbs and auxiliary verbs. A question remains whether the thematized auxiliary is topical when it is realized by a form of *beon/wesan* ('to be'), since in this case it would not have lexical content. In the analysis of modern English offered by IFG, Predicator in declarative clauses is rarely a topical theme, and when it is, it is always lexical. The finite in itself always has the status of an interpersonal theme (Halliday 1985: 47-49, 54-56, 63).

The principles of *IFG* would dictate labelling a thematized Predicator in declarative mood "marked", insofar as it is a carrier of ideational meaning ordered prior to the grammatical Subject. That is the procedure followed here, but the construction is at the heart of a long-standing controversy, and will be dealt with in greater detail below (see sections 5.7 and 13.4) in order to come at the meaning of the term "marked" in this context.

It should also be noted that the text under examination does not show all possible realizations of theme itemized in *IFG*. Some of the relevant constructions absent from the homily are pseudo-cleft sentences (nominalizations), cleft sentences, non-finite clauses initiated by a preposition, and the imperative with 2nd-person pronoun Subject.

5.3 Part I, page I: non-narrative

To illustrate the method of working, and its results, the beginning of the first worksheet for Bethurum homily VI is reproduced in Figure I (see Appendix I for Figures I-8). The first worksheet actually covers the text from lines 3 to 23, a non-narrative section, but the Old English text reproduced in Figure I is limited to the first five graphological sentences. Each clause is located on a separate line. Each successive subordination (whether β-dependent or rankshifted) is indented further from the left. Three dots at the end of a clause signal the onset of subordination. Three dots at the beginning of a clause signal continuation of an interrupted independent clause or the onset of an independent clause preceded by a preposed subordinate clause. The boundary between theme and rheme is marked with a slant. A double slant is used to mark the boundary between a thematized preposed subordinate clause and its main clause. Marked topical themes whether in independent or subordinate clauses are italicised. Thus the first sentence begins with an independent clause whose Subject is realized by a following rankshifted dependency itself divided between a main segment and a β-dependency. The latter also consists of two segments, but these are parallel. Each of these segments, whether main or subordinate, is realized by a finite or semi-finite (subjunctive) clause. In the main clause, the thematic segment consists of an interpersonal theme, the vocative *Leofan men* ('Dearly beloved'), followed by a marked topical preposed Complement (*us,* 'to us'). The first two subordinate clauses start with a structural theme, the subordinating conjunction *þaet* ('that'), and the Subject. The last subordinate clause is elliptical, showing only the coordinating conjunction 7 ('and') in the thematic segment.

The most important aspect of these five sentences is that they contain only two marked topical themes, the second being the quasi-auxiliary *scealt* ('must') in the main clause of the fifth sentence. This lack of marked topicalization is characteristic of those parts of the homily which are in a non-narrative register.

5.4 Part 2, page I: narrative

The beginning of the second worksheet in Figure 2 shows in just four sentences a rather different pattern in the distribution of themes. This worksheet covers lines 24 to 76, the first narrative section of the homily, telling the story of Creation, the Fall, Cain and Abel, and the Flood. The first four sentences illustrate a feature which runs throughout the section: a relative abundance of marked topical themes (italicised). Of the ten main clauses in these sentences, eight have marked topical themes. Four of these consist of foregrounded Predicators (*wearð*, 'was made'; *þuhte*, 'seemed'; *hreas*, 'fell'; *gescop*, 'created') preceded in the thematic segment by a conjunctive Adjunct (*þa*, 'then' or *æfter þam*, 'after that'). The other marked topical themes consist of Complements (*An*, 'One'; *heom*, 'for them') and circumstantial Adjuncts (*on fruman*, 'in the beginning'; *of Adames anum ribbe*, 'from a single rib of Adam'). In the continuation of this pattern throughout the section, twenty-one out of a total of thirty-two main clauses (excluding elliptical clauses) show marked topical themes. The contrast with the pattern of the preceding section is extreme, and it is hard not to take the inference that the abundance of marking is part of Wulfstan's method of telling a story.

5.5 Table of thematic realizations

Another sort of result from the analysis is the identification of various means of realizing the non-topical multiple theme elements, some of which have already been itemized (5.1, 5.3, 5.4 above). Figure 3 is a table of realizations for non-topical thematic elements occurring in Bethurum homily VI. Of the textual thematic elements, continuatives, coordinating and subordinating conjunctions, and conjunctive Adjuncts are listed. Of the interpersonal thematic elements, modal Adjuncts and wh-elements are listed, omitting therefore relatives, vocatives and finites, which are never difficult to identify. It should be noted that some items are polyvalent. For example, *þonne* and *syððan* may be either subordinating conjunctions ('when', 'after') or conjunctive Adjuncts ('then', 'afterwards'). An inspection of the list of conjunctive Adjuncts will show that many of these items have the potential to realize circumstantial Adjuncts, and indeed there are many cases in which the distinction is hard to maintain.

5.6 Basic statistics and features

Sections 1, 3 and 5 of this homily are non-narrative; sections 2, 4, 6 and (to some degree) 7 are in a narrative register. Respective numerical and percent results are offered in Tables 1a and 1b. In subordinate clauses, the proportion of topical themes which are marked is so low in both register types, ranging from 0% to 11.5%, that they are disregarded. The elliptical clause is excluded from consideration because it has no grammatical Subject. In main clauses, the proportion of marked topical themes in the non-narrative sections is respectively (1) 29.4%, (3) 45.5% and (5) 52.6%. The proportion in successive narrative sections is respectively (2) 65.6%, (4) 58.3%, (6) 50.0%, and (7) 52.9%. These figures suggest that the strong initial contrast in the degree of marking between the two register types dwindles after the first four sections. For these four sections, however, the average proportion of marked topical themes in narrative is more than 75% higher than in non-narrative. The effect is as if the homilist discards contrast in markedness as a resource once he has established the pattern.

Table 1a: Non-narrative sections

Clause type		Section							
		1		3		5		totals	
		N	%	N	%	N	%	N	%
Independent	mrkd themes	5	29.4	5	45.5	10	52.6	20	42.6
	total clauses	17		11		19		47	
Subordinate	mrkd themes	0	0	1	7.7	1	4.3	2	3.6
	total clauses	19		13		23		55	
Elliptical		4		2		3		9	

Another interesting potential for marked topical themes in narrative is the formation of cohesion chains. For example, section 4 contains six successive main-clause marked topical themes in just four sentences. These are *of ðære mægðe* ('from that tribe'), *of ðam mæran Abrahame* ('from that glorious Abraham'), *of his mæran cynne* ('from his glorious kindred'), *ðam sylfan cynne* ('for that self-same kindred'), *of ðam sylfum Abrahames cynne* ('from that self-same kindred of Abraham' and *of his cynne* ('from his kindred'). Thus all these marked themes are chained together cohesively by both lexical and grammatical repetition.

Table 1b: Narrative sections

Clause type		Section									
		2		4		6		7		totals	
		N	%	N	%	N	%	N	%	N	%
Independent	marked themes	21	65.6	14	58.3	11	50.0	9	52.9	55	57.9
	total clauses	32		24		22		17		95	
Subordinate	marked themes	4	9.3	3	10.7	2	6.9	3	11.5	12	9.5
	total clauses	43		28		29		26		126	
Elliptical		10		5		2		2		8	

5.7 Problems and issues

The analysis of the thematic structure of Old English has provided a number of insights into the structure of the texts analyzed. However, it has also raised some unresolved questions. Figure 4 presents four sentences from Bethurum homily VI which illustrate these questions. The first and second of the sentences (lines 178 ff. and 96 ff.) represent a very common construction in Old English prose style: a preposed temporal subordinate clause initiated by *þa* or *þa þa* ('when') followed by a main clause initiated by *þa* ('then' if translatable) and the Predicator (or a Predicator auxiliary) followed by its Subject. On the principles of *IFG*, the preposed subordinate clause is taken to be thematic in the clause complex, and the Predicator is taken to be a marked topical theme in its own clause. Questions arise from the frequency of this construction: are the prepositionings of the subordinate clause and of the Predicator in the main clause mutually bound, and if so, does this affect the markedness of the thematic Predicator? It should be noted that prepositioning of the Predicator does not invariably occur in this construction.

Related to this construction is the simpler instance in which the sentence begins with an independent clause, itself initiated by *þa* or some other temporal conjunctive Adjunct followed by the finite Predicator or Predicator auxiliary (see Figure 2). In both of these cases the implication has often been taken that the prepositioning of the finite Predicator element is bound to that of the Adjunct. Statistical evidence overwhelmingly supports the notion that ordering the finite Predicator element immediately after an initial temporal or locative conjunctive Adjunct is a norm for Old English clauses (Bean 1983:60, 70 ff., 116-117, 136-137), so that 'marked' in this instance can hardly mean 'emphatic'. This dilemma, on systemic terms, corresponds to a long-standing controversy on philological terms, and will be pursued further below (section 13.4). It should also be recognized that initial *þa* in such cases has long been discussed as a marker for discourse structuring (e.g., Enkvist 1972), corresponding to the notion of narrative discourse as a sequence of actions or events (sections 5.4, and 6.3-6.5 below).

Another question which these two sentences generate also relates to the preposed subordinate clause. Here the preposed subordinate clauses are preceded by elements which *IFG* usually identifies as thematic elements in the main clause: *And, syððan, æfter þam, Leofan men* (but cf. 1985: 57-58). One wonders how the thematicity of these elements in the theme segment of the main clause relates to the supposed thematicity of the subordinate clause in the clause complex.

Still another question concerns an aspect of sentences two (96 ff.) and three (54 ff.). Sentence three shows the verb *wæs* ('was') from *beon/wesan* ('to be') used as a quasi-auxiliary and two shows it as an existential verb. In neither case can it have any lexical content, and the analysis of sentence three takes the Subject following to be the topical theme. The main clause of the second sentence accordingly has no theme/rheme structure at all. But if the *beon/wesan* finite in such constructions is not a marked topical theme, why is it put before the Subject like lexical Predicators or quasi-auxiliaries which are marked topical themes? Is it not possible that what is being thematized in all such instances is the past tense carried by the finite, as a marker of narrative register?

One final question worth raising has to do with the determination of the function of items which alternatively realize conjunctive Adjuncts or topical circumstantial Adjuncts. Sentence four (147 ff.) contains circumstantial Adjuncts – *Ær* ('previously') in the first clause, and *nu* ('now') in the third clause – which realize marked topical themes. However, the same word items are more frequently conjunctive Adjuncts. This raises the question of exactly where does the boundary between circumstantial and conjunctive Adjuncts lie?

5.8 Summary of results

It is proper that a theory of theme/rheme should raise more questions than it can answer, but at the same time yield useful information about a text. One of the more interesting conclusions that arises from an analysis of this homily is that there is a connection, at least in this text, between the frequency of marked topical themes and the narrative register. The difference in the relative frequency of this feature between narrative and non-narrative sections is at its most extreme when the difference in register is also at its most extreme. Thus in part one, which has no element of narrative, the percentage of main clauses with marked topical themes is 29.4% of the total number of main clauses. In part two, which establishes narrative as a pattern in the homily, the percentage rises to 65.6%. By contrast, the final part which discusses eschatology and is only a commuted form of narrative, shows a percentage of 52.9%.

Some other results of the study so far, however, are suggestions for extending or modifying the theory. Quite a number of the items which are enumerated in the table of realizations for Old English textual and interpersonal themes have equivalents in modern English not listed in *IFG*.[5] Although relative pronouns are probably always unmarked themes, that is, not markedly thematic when realizing Complement or circumstantial Adjunct, *IFG* does not assist in settling this question. Finally, the question previously

5. This is chiefly in the area of temporal conjunctive Adjuncts. To the items listed (1985:50), add *later, now, after that, afterwards, at once, then*, and to modal Adjuncts expressing usuality add *ever*.

raised about the relationship of a preposed subordinate clause to preceding thematic elements possibly belonging to the main clause in fact casts doubt on the situating of some textual and interpersonal themes within the structure of the clause unit. One alternative theory would be to view most such items as elements in sentence structure, along with the preposed subordinate clause and the main clause proper. Another approach would be to treat the thematic preposed subordinate clause as filling an element of structure (such as Adjunct or Complement) of the dominant clause.[6]

6. An Ælfric homily

6.1 The text

The sermon *De initio creaturæ* ('The beginning of creation') by the abbot Ælfric (Thorpe, ed. 1844-6: I, 8-28) was probably written about ten years previous to Wulfstan's homily (Godden, 1979: xciii), for which it may have been the model (Bethurum 1957: 293). In about 4000 words it covers the same narrative from the creation of the heavens and the earth down to the ascension of Christ and the coming end of the world. The difference between narrative and digression is handled with greater subtlety, however. The first section is an exposition on the power and nature of God: the creation of the heavens and the earth and all other creatures is embedded in it, as if an afterthought, within a non-restrictive relative clause. The creation of the angels is quite incidental to a discussion of their nature and variety. The first narrative section proper begins with the fall of the angels. Thus boundaries between narrative and non-narrative sections are often less abrupt than in Wulfstan. Partly because Ælfric uses long and frequent direct quotations, there are 17 alternating narrative and non-narrative sections, ranging in length from one sentence to three pages.

6. Each of these hypothetical approaches has been considered by Gregory. The former approximates his present position (1983: 1-9): see note 3 above. Thematic elements syntactically prior to the β-dependent clauses in the problem sentences discussed above (section 5.7) would be classified by Halliday as conjunction, conjunctive Adjuncts, and vocative: basically clause constituents. For Gregory, they would be conjunctive links and vocative: all sentence constituents, along with the clause complex itself, taken as a realization of the sentence constituent propositional.

6.2 Part 1, page 1: non-narrative

In Figure 5, the beginning of the worksheet for section 1 illustrates Ælfric's expository technique. The evocation of the language of the psalms is due both to overt lexical references and to grammatical parallelism. Marked topical themes are relatively infrequent, limited here to three of the last four independent clauses. Together with the absence of interpersonal themes and the minimal use of textual themes, the repetition of the unmarked topical theme *he* ('he') achieves a striking effect, part of the intertextuality. The insignificance of topical theme marking to the style persists through the whole section. In 23 main clauses, only 6 topical themes are marked (26.1%) and in the 11 dependent clauses, no marked topical themes occur.

6.3 Part 2, page 2: narrative

In Figure 6, the second page of the worksheet for the first narrative section shows a style which contrasts in several ways. Intensive parallelism of independent clauses has given way to multiple subordination. Textual themes abound in the form of conjunctions and conjunctive Adjuncts. Subject ellipsis has now appeared: nearly half of the independent clauses on this page and very nearly one-third of the independent clauses in the section show this effect. Excluding elliptical clauses, the proportion of independent clauses with marked topical themes has risen to 61.5%, more than double that of the preceding section. All but one of the marked topical themes in the section consists of a preposed Predicator element preceded by a temporal conjunctive Adjunct, thus forming a cohesive chain. The impression taken is that the story being told is a list of events, realized in the form of foregrounded past-time processes.

Table 2a: Non-narrative sections

Clause type		Sections					
		1, 3, 5, & 7		9, 11, 13, 15, & 17		totals	
		N	%	N	%	N	%
Independent	marked themes	23	26.4	11	29.7	34	27.4
	total clauses	87		37		124	
Subordinate	marked themes	2	3.3	4	12.1	6	6.4
	total clauses	61		33		94	
Elliptical		15		8		23	

Table 2b: Narrative sections

Clause type		Sections					
		2, 4, 6, & 8		10, 12, 14, & 16		totals	
		N	%	N	%	N	%
Independent	marked themes	24	53.3	38	49.4	62	50.8
	total clauses	45		77		122	
Subordinate	marked themes	1	2.9	4	6.2	5	5.0
	total clauses	35		65		100	
Elliptical		28		48		76	

6.4 Basic statistics and features

Since many of the separate sections are very short, section-by-section comparison is unprofitable. Tables 2a and 2b offer a token breakdown of the homily by halves. For the whole homily, the proportion of main clause topical themes which are marked in non-narrative sections is 27.4% whereas in narrative sections it is 50.8%, for a gain of more than 85%. As in Bethurum VI, the proportions for dependent clauses are so low (6.4% and 5.0% respectively) as not to seem significant. The longest non-narrative section consists of 45 clauses in 27 lines and has a proportion of 30.8%, while the longest narrative section, with 160 clauses in about 3 pages, has a proportion of 49.2%; this is roughly consistent with the proportions of the whole text.

The predominance of preposed Predicator elements realizing main clause marked topical themes noted in connection with the first narrative section persists throughout the other narrative sections. In 5 out of 8 narrative sections, the density and contiguity of preposed Predicators suggests a cohesive chain foregrounding the progression of events. Another common pattern is a sentence with several independent clauses, the first having a marked topical theme, and some or all of the rest having Subject ellipsis.

6.5 Comparison with Bethurum VI

Although the Wulfstan homily is half the length of its model, its narrative and non-narrative sections are much more closely proportioned in size than those of the Ælfric homily, which heightens the consistency of contrast between the two register types. In the choice of marked topical themes, the Wulfstan homily greatly prefers preposed Complements and circumstantial Adjuncts, whereas its model to an even greater degree shows preference for preposed Predicator elements. The Ælfric homily has proportionately almost twice as much Subject ellipsis as its counterpart. What both homilies have in common is a significant contrastive use of greater marked topicalization in the thematic segments of independent clauses in narrative register, and a capacity for forming successive marked topical themes into cohesion chains.

7. The Anglo-Saxon Chronicle

Begun in the reign of Ælfred to keep a record of contemporary or at least recent civic history, *The Anglo-Saxon Chronicle* is a very pure form of narrative, with only occasional digressions. Two passages selected more-or-less at random from the Parker MS make for an interesting comparison to the homilies. These are the entries for A.D. 920 and 921, and 1001 (Plummer, ed. 1892: I, 101-103, 132), comprising about 1000 words. The first part of the first worksheet is printed out in Figure 7 and shows an intensive use of marked topical themes which foreground temporal references. The first and last sentences on this page illustrate another technique important to the *Chronicle* style, the location of the marked topical in the first independent clause, and a series of Subject-elliptical independent clauses following. Within these entries, the proportion of topical themes which are marked in independent clauses is 75.0%, and in dependent clauses 8.3%, showing that marked topical themes are even more predominant in the independent clauses of this form of narrative, but again irrelevant in dependent clauses.

8. Results

8.1 Some conclusions

Halliday's own presentation of the theme/rheme model (1967, 1985 and elsewhere) leaves part of the argumentation to the reader. This paper has argued in support of the model on the grounds that its terms can be transferred without difficulty to a remote historical dialect, and that it shows within that dialect what an important stylistic resource is the contrast in markedness between the two main types of topical themes.

8.2 Further questions

At the same time, we have noticed that the materials studied raise some questions about details in the application of the model. In *IFG*, preposed finites in interrogative mood are interpersonal themes. We have noted that in Old English preposed finites appear frequently in declarative mood as marked topical themes, a status assignment supported by the lexicality of those finites which only in later English will have become true auxiliaries. However forms of *beon/wesan* ('to be') show the same potential for pre-positioning as other finites. Can they truly be considered topical themes, and if so, what is it in a finite which is being topicalized?

We have also noticed that the pre-positioning of Predicator elements in Old English main clauses is frequently associated with preceding temporal themes, both conjunctive Adjuncts and marked topicals, and with a preceding temporal subordinate clause. Is this to some degree a bound condition, and if so, does it bear on the thematic status of the preposed Predicators?

A final question relates to the clause complex. The tendency of *IFG* is to assign theme in clause complexes only to preposed subordinate clauses. However, both the Ælfric homily and the *Chronicle* text show marked topical themes in initial independent clauses whose semantic domain extends to following Subject-elliptical independent clauses. Would it not be more logical to assign these themes to the clause complex?

9. The philological tradition

This examination of Old English prose texts suggests that theme/rheme analysis along the lines formulated in *IFG* is applicable in English historical dialects, and that it can offer results significant to understanding discourse in historical dialects. However, the ordering of elements in Old English clauses has been described extensively in a long tradition of scholarship, and any attempt to view the question within a systemic functional perspective must eventually digest the results yielded by more traditional approaches. The philological tradition has long recognized the grammatical significance of the ordering of elements in the Old English clause, but the interpretation of that ordering has been various. The further purpose of this article is to characterize that tradition, and to suggest in what ways it might be clarified by a systemic functional approach. The first step will be to summarize three very well-known approaches to Old English clause order from the perspective of traditional grammar (see sections 10-12), the second step will be to suggest how to reinterpret the evidence from the systemic functional viewpoint (section 13), and last will be a further analysis of text to illustrate (section 14).

10. A text-editor's approach

At one time it was naively asserted that word order in Old English is 'free' because inflection obviates the need for identifying clause elements by syntactic means, and traces of this misconception persist even today. (A good summary of the development of the theory of Old English clause order can be found in Kohonen 1983: 10-19.) One early study to argue for the significance of Old English syntactic patterns was S.O. Andrew's *Syntax and Style in Old English* (1940).

10.1 Object and method

Andrew begins with the already well-known observation that among the myriad patterns of Old English clauses, three basic general orders can be distinguished (1-2). His 'common' order is simply SPCA, chiefly characteristic of principal clauses, and often varied by the preposing of the Complement for 'emphasis'. Another order is 'conjunctive', with telltale reversal of the common ordering of head after auxiliary in periphrastic verbal groups, and location of the Predicator towards the end of the clause [S + ... + V(v)]. This ordering is characteristic of both coordinate main clauses, and subordinate clauses. The third order is 'demonstrative', in which the initial element ('headword') of the clause is followed by the Predicator and then the Subject [initial + V + S . . .].

Andrew observes that many headwords in Old English clauses are grammatically ambiguous, e.g., initial *þa* is either a subordinating conjunction or a conjunctive Adjunct (either 'when' or 'then'). His purpose is to determine the correlation between the order of the clause and the function of the headword by comparison between translations and Latin originals. His final object is to rescue the correct division of sentences and clauses from both the misinterpretations of modern editors and the mistaken readings of medieval scribes, which have frequently resulted in the identification of a subordinate clause as a principal clause beginning the next clause complex, and vice-versa.

10.2 Some rules of syntax

Three ambiguous headwords can be grouped together, *þa*, *þær* and *þonne*. Each as headword may be either subordinating conjunction or else conjunctive Adjunct (respectively 'when' or 'then', 'where' or 'there', 'whenever' or 'then'). If any such headword is followed by clause elements in common or conjunctive orders, then the clause is subordinate. If the following order is demonstrative, then some ambiguity remains, although principal clause status is more likely – and certain if a line of verse shows the immediately following verb word not taking the strong stress, because it is the conjunction which is unstressed (pp. 3-30).

The rules are a little looser for a second set of ambiguous headwords, *ær*, *nu*, *forðam*, etc. (respectively 'before' or 'previously', 'now that' or 'now', 'because' or 'accordingly'). These headwords are subordinating conjunctions when followed by conjunctive order. The ambiguity remains in common order. Demonstrative order usually implies that the clause is principal, but significant exceptions will be found (pp. 31-34).

A similar ambiguity affects the negative word *ne*, which as a headword may be either the negative particle or a negative coordinating conjunction ('nor'). In demonstrative order, i.e., followed by the verb, *ne* is headword in a principal clause. When followed by conjunctive order, *ne* must head a clause which is extended. In other words, the rule for editors is that *ne* not followed immediately by the verb can't be headword in a principal clause (pp. 62-63).

The demonstrative *se* ('the'/'this'/'that') in whatever inflected form (other than the neuter *þæt* and some derived adverbs) cannot be functioning as a demonstrative pronoun when headword, but must be functioning as a relative pronoun in a subordinate relative clause, unless it is itself the antecedent of a relative clause. The latter case implies rules for order in the principal clause. If the antecedent demonstrative realizes Subject, then the order must be common (*Se ðe wyrcð mines Fæder willan se færð into heofonan rice*). If the antecedent demonstrative does not realize Subject, then the order will still be common if the Subject is realized by a pronoun, but demonstrative if the Subject is realized by a noun (*þone bær se ealda Symeon þe ealle ðing gewylt*; pp. 35-47).

11. A rhetorician's approach

A far more systematic and encompassing theory of Old English clause order is found in Paul Bacquet, *La structure de la phrase verbale à l'époque Alfrédienne* (1962). Bacquet includes in his sources the whole corpus of Old English translations of Latin classics originating in the court circle of King Alfred. He rejects statistical methods as misleading, and bases his categories on a case by case interpretation of the stylistic intent of each clause. The framework which he postulates rests on the contrast between basic order (*ordre de base*) and marked order (*ordre marqué*) for each type of clause. Marked order may be a characteristic of the whole clause (*marque de phrase, marque globale*) or of some individual elements within the clause (*marque individuelle*), with appropriately varying stylistic intention (Bacquet 1962: 13, 22-25, 64-65).

11.1 The three basic orders

The basic order for declarative mood main clauses with a simple Predicator is the same whether they are principal or coordinate with Subject: [(...) S (...) V (...)]. Before the Subject may occur a coordinating conjunction, between Subject and Predicator a pronominal object or adverb, and all other elements (*determinants*) follow the Predicator: nominal objects, Copular Complements, adverbs of manner, time or vector, nominal or prepositional circumstantial Adjuncts and propositions realized in subordinate clauses. A variation on this pattern is afforded by the periphrastic Predicator: [(...) S (...) v (...) V (...)]. The variation is that elements other than pronominal object or adverb, which come between the Subject and the finite auxiliary, are distributed on either side of the Predicator head: adverbs and nominal circumstantial Adjuncts must come before, propositions must come after, and the other elements are unrestricted (pp. 66 ff.).

The second basic order is for coordinate clauses without a Subject: [...V (v) (proposition)] (pp. 135 ff.). Similar to it is the third basic order, for subordinate clauses: [...S (...) V (v) (proposition)]. In the latter, the Subject is preceded by the subordinating conjunction, the relative, or the interrogative. All elements other than these and any subsequent proposition are to be found between the Subject and the Predicator (pp. 274 ff.). Negative versions of all these clauses show identical orders to the affirmative (pp. 127 ff., 178 ff., 366 ff., 502 ff.).

11.2 Three principal marked orders

The three principal types of marked orders in declarative main clauses are
Predicator-initial, Predicator second after *þa/þonne*, and Predicator-final.
Each of these orders is perceived as a marking of the whole clause, rather
than of any individual element. The first of these has an order: [(…) V S …]
in which the Predicator may be preceded only by a coordinating conjunction
or the negative particle, and all other elements come after the Subject. A
variation on this order is afforded by the periphrastic verbal group: [(…) v
S … V] in which the only difference is that the finite auxiliary comes before
the Subject, and the verbal head comes last. Bacquet insists that this marked
order is not in the least conditioned by a preceding subordinate clause, unlike
clauses in modern Germanic languages in which the Predicator must be
second after whatever element (pp. 585-596, 629-644).

The second marked order is seen to be a development of the first and
its periphrastic variant: [(…) *þa/þonne* V S…] or [(…) *þa/þonne* v S (…)
V (…)]. Needless to say, *þa* and *þonne* here realize adverbs (conjunctive
Adjuncts), not conjunctions. They may be preceded only by the negative
particle. After the verbal head in the periphrastic type may come nominal
objects, Copular Complements, prepositional phrases and any embedded
proposition – all other elements come between Subject and verbal head (pp.
596-617, 644-645). The third marked order is essentially identical to that of
basic order in subordinate and subjectless coordinate clauses: […V (v)], but
of course occurring in a main clause. Although each of these orders is a
marking of the whole clause, nevertheless, the marking of individual elements by displacement may also occur in any of them, just as in any of the
three basic orders (pp. 617-629, 645-646).

11.3 Additional marked orders

In declarative main clauses still another form of marked order has the
pattern: [(…) X V S…] or its periphrastic variant: [(…) X v S (…) V (…)].
In these patterns, the optional initial element is a coordinating conjunction.
The element ('x') before the Predicator or finite auxiliary may be a prepositional or nominal circumstantial Adjunct; a conjunctive Adjunct, either
adverbial (*þær, her, swa,* etc.) or other (*forðæm, ond eac, þeah, þæs,* etc.);
or an object, either nominal or pronominal. All the other clause elements

follow the Subject, or are distributed before and after the periphrastic verbal head in the usual fashion (pp. 647 ff.).

In coordinate clauses without a Subject, marked order is represented by reversal of the basic Predicator-final order, so as to put the non-Subject elements of the clause after the Predicator instead of before. In subordinate clauses, marked order comes close to the basic order of main clauses, having the patterns [(...) S V...] and [(...) S v (...) V]. In these, only the subordinating conjunction comes before the Subject, and all other clause elements follow the Predicator or the finite auxiliary respectively (pp. 688-690).

Within all of these clause orders, basic or marked, there still exists the possibility of foregrounding individual clause items by locating one or more of them in variant positions. For example, when the order of elements after initial *þa* or *þonne* in a declarative main clause is [S V], the function is the foregrounding of either the Subject or the Predicator element for whatever stylistic purpose (pp. 597-8). Very many of these foregroundings involve the removal of an element to either the pre-Subject position near the beginning of a clause, or to the post-verbal position at the end of the clause. Putting a non-verbal element before the Subject is a common means of foregrounding in the basic orders of declarative main clauses (pp. 695 ff.) and subordinate clauses (p. 688), and in the marked Predicator-final order of the declarative main clause (pp. 624-626; see section 11.2 above). Even a periphrastic verbal head can be preposed in a declarative main clause: [V v S...] (p. 679). Putting a Subject or some other non-verbal element into final position to foreground it can be found as a variation within the basic order of declarative coordinate and subordinate clauses, in the marked Predicator-initial and *þa/þonne*-initial clauses (Subject after non-Predicator elements), in the periphrastic version of ovs order which begins this section, [...v V S] (compare with [(...) X v S (...) V (...)] above), and within the marked order of periphrastic subordinate clauses (pp. 137-140, 164, 287-292, 592, 603-604, 678, 689).

12. A philologist's approach

Somewhat at variance with both Andrew and Bacquet is the approach taken by Bruce Mitchell, summarized in *Old English Syntax*, II (1985).

12.1 General principles

Mitchell's approach is positivist and descriptivist, by contrast with the implicit functionalism of his predecessors. His intent is not to offer a system of interpretation, but a factual description of a corpus which admittedly has not yet been definitively grasped. Statistical profiles are seen to be of more help than intuitions about stylistic intent. Andrew's rules for discerning the difference between main and subordinate clauses are seen to be too sweeping, and Bacquet's theory of complex stylistic contrast is seen to lead to many particular errors – for one, his conscious contradiction of statistical results.

12.2 Three basic orders and their variations

Mitchell's understanding of the basic orders comes close to those of Andrew with which we began (see 10.1). We may term them 'close', 'open' and 'inverted', all terms referring to the ordering of Subject and Predicator: respectively, SV, S...V, VS. Each of these orders has many particular manifestations, but none is more than loosely tied to a particular type of clause. Thus close order is to be associated with principal clauses, but may also be found after coordinating conjunctions and in subordinate clauses. Open order is frequent in the latter types of clause, but may also be found in principals. Inverted order may be found in all types of clause, and its absence after initial adverbs þa/þonne should not be taken as an absolute identifier of subordination. Mitchell's emphasis is on the identification of the order, and he does not speculate on the stylistic intent of any particular order in any particular type of clause (Mitchell 1958: II, pp. 963 ff.; 296-308).

Variations on close order may be divided between those with simple Predicator and those with periphrastic. In both types, the Subject may normally be preceded by conjunctions and various Adjuncts, realized both by adverbs and by prepositional phrases. Close order with simple Predicator typically shows the Subject and Predicator separated by dative or accusative object realized by pronoun, or by the negative particle, or by various kinds of Adjuncts. Close order with periphrastic Predicator shows Adjuncts, Copular Complements and objects of whatever case and realization between the finite auxiliary and the Predicator head. In both types, a great variety of non-Subject, non-verbal elements come after the Predicator. One variation that does indicate marked emphasis is the location of any kind of object, or of a Copular Complement, or of a periphrastic Predicator head before the Subject (pp. 964-967).

In open order, the periphrastic differs from the simple Predicator type only in that the finite auxiliary will come immediately after the Predicator head. Various non-Subject, non-verbal elements can come after the Predicator. Between the Subject and the Predicator come elements like Adjuncts, noun-realized objects, and Copular Complements realized by either nouns or adjectives (pp. 967-969).

Variations on inverted order are chiefly to be distinguished by the nature of the element, if any, which precedes the finite verb. That element may be an object or Copular Complement: [...C V S..., ...C v S V..., ...C v VS...]. Another variation is with initial adverbs *þær, þanon, þider, þa,* or *þonne,* perceived as the most frequent construction with vs order, and usually a principal clause. Again the preceding element may be the negative particle, an Adjunct, or a conjunction. Contrary to the theory of Bacquet, no instance of this order is perceived to be marked or emphatic (pp. 969-978).

13. A systemic functional approach

13.1 Sources of a systemic functional model

At its most general level, the systemic functional approach to ordering relationships in the English clause is the notion that the clause, like other syntactic stretches, has a beginning, a middle and an end. In light of their potential for contrast, the beginning is perceived as a carrier of 'focus' and the end as a carrier of 'prominence' (Gregory, 1988: 306, 311).[7] The focus of the clause is the informational point of departure, and the prominence of the clause is the point of greatest informational contrast. Thus 'theme' as a term within the structural analysis of clause represents the stretch of text which carries the focus, and 'new information' represents the stretch of text which carries the prominence. The nature of the rules for mapping theme and

7. I have adopted this terminology from Michael Gregory despite the potential for confusion with Halliday's phrase "focus of information" applied to elements carrying the tonic and serving to terminate the stretch of "new" information in clause (1985: 275ff.).

new information onto particular clause functions may vary among practicing systemicists (cf. sections 1.2 and 2.1 above), but for simplicity, the view adopted here is still that of *IFG*. The most salient points of that treatment for this discussion are that the thematic segment extends from the beginning of the clause through the first topical element, typically the Subject; and that the locus of new information embraces the clause element carrying the tonic prominence in spoken English, typically the last in the clause (Halliday 1985: 44-45, 53; 274-281).

13.2 Traditional and systemic functional analyses compared

Despite their differences in intention and in framework, the three traditional approaches we have reviewed have a lot in common. One such element is the reckoning of clause order from the Subject and verbal elements. Andrew and Mitchell are nearly alike in their definition of three basic orders founded on relative positions of Subject and Predicator, and Bacquet differs from them in this respect only in discerning a basic order for subjectless coordinate clauses and in finding all instances of inverted order to be marked. By contrast, the systemic functional approach views the question not as an ordering of elements to one another, but as an ordering of elements to the boundaries of the clause segment. In this framework, it is the extremeties of the clause which convey information, whereas in the traditional analysis, it is the central elements.

Another aspect of theory which separates the philologists from the systemicists is the mutual ordering of non-Subject, non-verbal elements. Since such an ordering typically occurs in the middle of the Old English clause, it is far from the concerns of theme/rheme analysis. But both Bacquet and Mitchell make good use of the traditional categorization of Old English clause elements by 'weight', which sees elements as 'heavier' or 'lighter', and gravitating in one direction or another (cf. esp. Reszkiewicz 1966). Thus pronominal object, nominal object and prepositional Adjunct is an ordering from lighter to heavier, and corresponds to the typical left-to-right ordering of such co-occuring elements in various clausal positions (Bacquet 1962: 67, 70; Mitchell 1985: 970). Since this is a typical ordering, a foregrounding effect can be achieved by fronting or ending an element which normally goes elsewhere in the chain, an effect much like theme marking.

Whereas the concepts of focus and prominence are fully developed in

the systemic functional approach to the clause as theme and new information, such a theory is only implicit in the traditional approach to the Old
English clause. Andrew, Bacquet and Mitchell alike recognize that some
elements made initial before Subject, e.g., objects and Copular Complements, have thus been foregrounded, achieving 'emphasis'. What is lacking
is a theory for this effect, which assigns the potential to achieve the effect
to the right elements, and which explains why the effect occurs. Similarly,
Bacquet recognizes that 'emphasis' can be achieved at the end of the clause
by transposing an element to that position which, within some one clause
type, would typically belong elsewhere. The explanation for the effect is
limited to the contrast with normal order, as defined by relation to Subject
and verb. Since a fully-developed theory of these effects is found in the
systemic functional framework, the task is now to reinterpret the evidence
on which traditional approaches are based within a systemic functional
perspective.

13.3 A systemic functional reinterpretation

A model for theme/rheme in Old English may proceed along the same lines
as that for modern English, but since nothing is known about intonation in
remote historical dialects of English, a theory of given/new information is
purely a theory of ordering elements into the segment of prominence.
Unmarked theme will therefore include all elements of the declarative main
clause from the beginning through Subject as the first topical element, and
unmarked new information will include the last lexical clause element
anticipated from the clause type. Unmarked theme is consonant with Bacquet's observation that elements preceding the Subject in unmarked clause
types include conjunctions and adverbial Adjuncts (for an expansion of these
possibilities, see sections 5.1, 5.5 above). Mitchell (1985: 964-965) implicitly adds Adjuncts realized by prepositional phrases. In subordinate clauses,
unmarked theme also includes interrogatives and relatives (which exclude
Subject from the thematic segment). Unmarked new information is factored
by the clause type. Bacquet's unmarked main clauses permit a variety of
unmarked non-Subject, non-verbal elements in final position. In subjectless
coordinate and in subordinate clauses, however, it is the lexical Predicator
which occupies the segment of prominence.

The general principle of marked theme is that any topical element preceding the Subject both terminates the thematic segment and represents a thematic foregrounding in place of the Subject. The general principle of marked prominence is that any element coming last in the clause in place of the element which normally occupies that position in a particular clause type (main, coordinate, subordinate) is prominent to a marked degree. The greatest variety of orders observed by the above three scholars belongs to the work of Bacquet, and systemic functional approach ought at least to account for the same data as he offers. Like that of Bacquet himself, this approach also offers an explanation for the variety of displacements within the fundamental orders as defined by Mitchell. The assignment of fore-grounding effects to the boundaries of the clause instead of to the relative disposition of Subject and Predicator offers an alternative explanation for most of the markedness effects observed by Bacquet (for discussion, see section 11 above), but one which is ultimately simpler, since it offers just two consistently applied principles by which to contrast marked orders with the basic. Thus it cuts across the categories of markedness offered by Bacquet, distinguishing only between marked and unmarked theme and prominence in three kinds of clauses. The distinction made by Bacquet, between a markedness of the whole clause (*marque de phrase*) and marked-ness of a single element (*marque individuelle*) is not to be lost, but should be seen as subsidiary to an assignment of markedness to individual elements within those clauses. Accordingly the order in which to view the specimens of markedness offered by Bacquet ought simply to be marked theme and marked prominence within declarative main, coordinate and subordinate clauses.

13.4 Coding marked theme and marked prominence

One important issue to dispose of is the status of thematized Predicator elements preceded by *þa* or some other temporal or even locative conjunc-tive Adjunct in declarative main clauses. Examination of texts from Wulf-stan, Ælfric and the *Chronicle* within a systemic linguistic perspective has raised questions about its degree of markedness (sections 5.2, 5.7 above), and it has been noted that the same issue on other terms has provoked disagreement within the more traditional approaches. The proposed solution on systemic terms is to recognize the thematicity of such Predicator elements as marked, but differing both in degree and kind from the markedness of thematized elements which are objects, Complements, topical Adjuncts or even Predicator elements not preceded by a conjunctive Adjunct. The argument for classifying such Predicators as marked lies in the nature of their functional contrast with unmarked theme. This contrast is like that provided by other marked themes in that it signals a registrational variation: in this case, the sequencing of events so characteristic of narrative. It is unlike other marked themes in that the Predicator element itself is not "emphasized" within its own clause type to achieve registrational variation, precisely because one expects the thematizing of the Predicator element to co-occur with the Adjunct.

Rules for coding markedness can now be summarized. In declarative main clauses, marked themes are realized as first topical elements in all instances of Predicator-initial clauses (a marked type for Bacquet, where only conjunctions, the negative particle and/or adverbs like *þa* or *þonne* normally precede a verbal element). These topical elements will include the simple Predicator itself, or else the finite auxiliary in a periphrastic Predicator (the preceding adverbial *þa*, *þonne* or the like is included in the thematic segment). Another form of marked theme is the topical element (thus other than adverbial *þa*, *þonne*, etc.), which precedes the Predicator-Subject sequence, including all forms of circumstantial Adjuncts and any sort of object. Yet another is provided by the initial periphrastic verbal head instead of the finite auxiliary which follows it before the Subject. However, the most obvious type of marked theme in a declarative main clause is provided by the preposing (after any conjunction) of a non-Subject topical element within basic order, any sort of object, Copular Complement or circumstantial Adjunct.

Marked prominence in a declarative main clause is to be observed in Bacquet's third principal marked order, with foregrounded Predicator, whether simple or periphrastic, at the end of the clause. It is also the property of a Subject put last in all the Predicator-initial clauses alluded to in the previous paragraph, and of a prepositional phrase following the verbal head in the periphrastic versions of the same type.

In subjectless coordinate clauses, theme will not occur at all, and marked prominence is exhibited when some element other than the Predicator is final. Subordinate clauses show marked theme simply by the preposing of a non-Subject topical element after the conjunction. Marked prominence may be exhibited by any non-verbal element coming last, or by the verbal head itself if last after the finite auxiliary.

14. Analysis of text

To illustrate a few of these marked and unmarked types, a familiar text is shown in Figure 8, annotated to indicate clause boundaries (//), foregrounding by thematicity and prominence (italic), and markedness (underlining). The elements itemized in the righthand column for each adjacent clause are just sufficient to enable each type of main or subordinate clause to be identified.

Appendix

(1) 3: Leofan men, *us* / is deope beboden...

    þæt we / geornlice mynegian 7 læran sculan...

        þæt manna gehwylc / to Gode buge

           7 / fram synnum gecyrre.

Beloved, to us it is sternly enjoined that we must exhort and instruct that each man should bend to God and turn from sin.

(2) 5: Se cwyde / is swyðe egeslic...

    þe / God þurh þone witegan be þam cwæð...

    þe / Godes folce bodian sculon,

    þæt / syndon biscopas 7 mæssepreostas.

That pronouncement is terrible indeed which God through the Prophet spoke concerning those who must preach to God's people, that is, bishops and priests.

(3) 7: He / cwæð be þam:

    Clama, ne cesses /;

    quasi tuba / exalta uocem tuam, et reliqua.

He spoke concerning those: Cry out, cease not; like the trumpet, raise up your voice, etc.

(4) 8: Clypa / hlude

    7 ahefe up / ðine stemne

    7 gecyð / minum folce...

    þæt hit / georne fram synnum gecyrre.

Cry out aloud and raise up your voice and instruct my people that it should zealously turn away from sin.

(5) 10: Gyf ðu / þonne þæt ne dest

    ac / forsuwast hit

    7 / nelt folce his þearfe gecyðan,

  //...þonne *scealt* / þu ealra þæra sawla
on domesdæg gescead agyldan...

    þe / þurh þæt losiað,...

        þe / hy nabbað þa lare 7 ða mynegunge...

           þe / hy beðorfton.

If you then don't do this, but are silent about it, and are unwilling to make known to the people its need, then must you pay the reckoning at Doomsday for all those souls who perish through this, that they have not the teaching and the exhortation that they needed.

Figure 1: Bethurum homily VI, part 1

(1) 24: *An* / is ece God...

   þe / gesceop heofonas 7 eorðan 7 ealle gesceafta,

   7 *on fruman* / he gelogode on þære heofonlican
   gesceafte, ...

      þæt / is, on heofona rice,

   ...engla weredu mycle 7 mære.

One is the eternal God who created the heavens and the earth and all creatures, and in the beginning he placed in the celestial creation, that is, in heaven, hosts of angels, great and glorious.

---

(2) 27: ða *wearð* / þær an þæra engla swa scinende 7 swa
   beorht 7 swa wlitig...

      þæt se / wæs Lucifer genemned.

Then was made there one of those angels so shining and so bright and so beautiful that he was named Lucifer.

---

(3) 29: þa *þuhte* / him...

   þæt he / mihte beon þæs efengelica...

      ðe / hine gescop 7 geworhte;

   and...

      sona swa he / þurh ofermodignysse þæt geðohte,

   //...þa *hreas* / he of heofonum 7 eall...

      þæt / him hyrde,

   7 hy / gewurðan of englum to deoflum gewordene,

   7 *heom* / wearð hyll gegearwod,

   7 hi / ðær wuniað on ecan forwyrde.

Then seemed it to him that he could be the equal of him who formed and created him; and as soon as he through pride conceived of that, then fell he from heaven and all who obeyed him,

and they became changed from angels to devils, and for them was hell prepared, and they remain there in eternal ruin.

---

(4) 34: Æfter þam *gescop* / God ælmihtig ænne man of
   eorðan, ...

      þæt / wæs Adam,

   7 *of Adames anum ribbe* / he gescop him wif to
   gemacan,...

      seo / wæs Eua genamod.

After that God almighty created one man from earth, who was Adam,

and from a single rib of Adam he created for him a wife as a companion, who was named Eve.

Figure 2: Bethurum homily VI, part 2

Continuatives	Coordinating Conjunctions	Subordinating Conjunctions	Conjunctive Adjuncts	Modal Adjuncts	WH-?
Hwæt	ond	þæt	nu	ea	hu
La	ac	gyf	þa	hwilum	þær
Eala	butan	þonne	æfter þam	foroft	
		swa swa	syððan	witod	
		sona swa	ðonne		
		swa	sona		
		swa...swa	swa þeah		
		swa...þæt	hwæðere		
		syððan	eft		
		ealswa	eac		
		þe ma þe			
		hwæþer			
		þe			
		hwæþer þe			
		forðam			
		forðam þe			
		butan			
		þa			
		þa þe			
		þæs ðe			
		ær			
		lange ær			
		oð			
		swylc			
		swylc... swylc			

Figure 3: Thematic realizations

(1) 178:   And syððan æfter þam...

       þa se tima / com...

          þæt he / for eall manncynn þrowian wolde,

    //...þa *sæde* / he his ðegnum fore...

      eal / hu hit gewurðan scolde,

    7 hit / sona æfter þam ealswa aeode.

And later after that, when the time came when he for all mankind wished to suffer,

then he predicted to his disciples beforehand altogether how it had to turn out, and right after that it came to pass just so.

(2) 96:   Leofan men, ...

      þa þa þæt / wæs...

         þæt deofol / folc swa mistlice dwelede, ...

        swa ic / eow ær rehte,

    //...þa wæs þeah an mægð...

     ðe / æfre weorðode þone soðan Godd,

    7 seo / asprang of Seme...

     se / wæs Noes yldesta sunu.

Beloved, when it was that the devil was deceiving the people in so many ways, as I related to you previously,

then was there nevertheless a nation which ever had worshipped the true God, and it derived from Sem, who was Noah's eldest son.

(3) 54:   He / ofsloh Abel, his agenne broðor,

    7 ða wæs Godes yrre / þurh ða dæde ofer eorðan yfele geniwod.

He slew Abel, his own brother, and then was God's wrath through that deed over the earth disastrously renewed.

(4) 147:   Ær / he wæs soð Godd on godcundnesse

    7 / næs na mann,

    ac nu / he is ægðer ge soð Godd ge soð mann.

Previously he was true God in divinity and was not human, but now he is both true God and true man.

Figure 4: Problems and issues

(1) 24a: AN ANGIN / is ealra þinga,...

      þæt / is God Ælmihtig.

There is one beginning for all things, which is God Almighty.

---

(2) 24b: He / is ordfruma and ende:

    he / is ordfruma,...

      forði þe he / wæs æfre;

    he / is ende butan ælcere geendunge,...

      forðan þe he / bið æfre ungeendod.

He is the beginning and the end. He is the beginning because he always was. He is the end without any ending because he is always unending.

---

(3) 27: He / is ealra cyninga Cyning, and ealra hlaforda Hlaford.

He is the King of all kings, and the Lord of all lords.

---

(4) 28: He / hylt mid his mihte heofonas and eorðan, and ealle gesceafta butan geswince,

    and he / besceawað þa niwelnyssa...

      þe / under þyssere eorðan sind.

He holds in his power the heavens and the earth and all creatures without effort, and he beholds the depths which are under this earth.

---

(5) 30: He / awecð ealle duna (10) mid anre handa,

    and *ne mæg* / nan þing his willan wiðstandan.

He raises all the mountains with one hand, and nothing may withstand his will.

---

(6) 2: *Ne mæg* / nan gesceaft fulfremedlice smeagan ne understandan ymbe god.

Nor may any creature fully comprehend or learn about God.

---

(7) 3: *Maran cyððe* / habbað englas to Gode þonne men,

    and þeah-hweðere hi / ne magon fulfremedlice understandan ymbe God.

Greater affinity have the angels to God than men (do), and nevertheless they may not fully learn about God.

Figure 5: De initio creaturae, part 1

(1) 31: And *swiðe rihtlice* / him swa getimode, ...

    þaða he / wolde mid modignysse beon betera...

      þonne he / gesceapen wæs,

      and / cwæð, ...

        þæt he/mihte beon þam Ælmihtigum Gode gelic.

And very rightfully it befell him so, since he desired in pride to be better than he was created, and said that he might be equal to the Almighty God.

---

(2) 34: Þa *wearð* / he and ealle his geferan forcuþran and wyrsan þonne ænig oðer gesceaft;

  and...

    þa (12) hwile þe he / smeade...

      hu / he mihte dælan rice wið God,

  //...þa hwile *gearcode* / se Ælmihtiga Scyppend him and his geferum helle wite,

  and / hi ealle adræfde of heofenan rices myrhðe,

  and / let befeallan on þæt ece fyr, ...

    þe / him gegearcod wæs for heora ofermettum.

Then became he and all his companions more foul and more evil than any other creature; and while he was considering how he might share power with God, all that time the Almighty Creator was preparing for him and his companions the punishment of hell, and he drove them all from the bliss of the kingdom of heaven and let them fall into that eternal fire, which was prepared for their pride.

---

(3) 5: Þa sona þa nigon werod /, ...

    þe / ðær to lafe wæron,

    ...bugon to heora Scyppende mid ealre eaðmodnesse,

    and / betæhton heora ræd to his willan.

Then at once the nine hosts which then remained submitted to their Creator with all humility, and conformed their thought to his will.

---

(4) 7: Þa *getrymde*/se Ælmihtiga God þa nigon engla werod, and gestaþelfæste...

    swa þæt hi / næfre ne mihton ne noldon syððan fram his willan gebugan;

Then straightened and strengthened the Almighty God the nine hosts of angels, so that they never might nor afterwards would wish to deviate from his will...

Figure 6: De initio creaturae, part 2

(1) 920.1: *Her on þys gere foran to middum sumera* / for
Eadweard cyning to Mældune,

7 / getimbrede þa burg

7 / gestaðolode...

ær he / þonon fore;

This year before mid-summer, King Edward travelled to Maldon and built the fortifications and garrisoned them before he went away again;

(2) .3: 7 *þy ilcan geare* / for Þurcytel eorl ofer sæ on
Froncland. mid þam mannum...

þe / him gelæstan woldon.

...mid Eadweardes cynges friþe 7 fultume.

and the same year jarl Thurkytel travelled over the sea to France, accompanied by those who wished to follow him, with King Edward's protection and assistance.

(3) 921.1: *Her on þysum gere foran to Eastron* /
Eadweard cyning het...

gefaran / þa burg æt Tofeceastre.

7 hie / getimbran;

This year before Easter King Edward ordered occupied the fortress at Towcester, and that it be fortified;

(4) .3: 7 þa eft æfter þam *on þam ilcan geare to
gangdagum* / he het...

atimbran / þa burg æt Wiginga mere;

and then later after that in the same year at Rogationtide, he ordered built the fortress at Wigingamere;

(5) .5: *Þy ilcan sumera betwix hlafmæssan 7 middum
sumera* / se here bræc þone friþ of Hamtune, 7 of
Ligeraceastre, 7 þonan norþan,

7 / foron to Tofeceastre,

7 / fuhton on þa burg ealnedæg,

7 / þohton...

þæt hie / hie sceolden abrecen;

that same summer between Lammas and midsummer, the host from Northampton and Leicester and north from there broke the peace and proceeded to Towcester, and assaulted the fortress the length of the day, and thought that they should penetrate it...

Figure 7: The Anglo-Saxon Chronicle

Nu ic þe hate,   hæleþ min se leofa, //   ...S C:pro V...
Now I enjoin upon you, my beloved champion,

þæt þu þas gesihþe   secge mannum; //   ...S C:n V...
that you reveal this vision to men;

onwreoh wordum//   þæt hit is wuldres beam, //   V...
make known with words that it is the tree of glory   ...S V...

se-þe ælmihtig God   on þrowode   ...S A V...
that Almighty God suffered on

for mann-cynnes   manigum synnum
for mankind's many sins

and Adames   eald-gewyrhtum.//
and Adam's deeds of old.

Deaþ he þær bierigde;//   hwæðre eft Dryhten aras   ...S A V
Death he tasted there; yet afterwards the Lord arose   ...S V...

mid his miclan meahte   mannum to helpe.//
with his great power for the rescue of mankind.

He þa on heofonas astag.//   Hider eft fundaþ   S A A V
He then ascended into heaven. Hither will he come   A A V...S...

on þisne middan-geard//   mann-cynn secan//   C:n V
again into this world to seek out mankind

on dom-dæge   Dryhten selfa,
on Judgement Day, the Lord Himself,

ælmihtig God   and his englas mid, //
Almighty God, and his angels with him,

þæt he þonne wile deman, //   se ag domes geweald, //   ...S A v V...
when he will judge – he who rules over judgement –   S V C:n

anra gehwelcum, //   swa he him æror her   ...S C:p...V
each man, accordingly as he previously merits

on þissum lænan   life ge-earnaþ.
here in this transitory life.

Figure 8: Dream of the Rood, 95-109 (adopted from Pope 1981: 13)

References

Andrew, S.O. 1940. *Syntax and Style in Old English*. Cambridge: Cambridge University Press. Reprinted New York: Russell & Russell, 1966.

Bacquet, Paul. 1962. *La structure de la phrase verbale à l'époque Alfrédienne*. (=*Publications de la Faculté des Lettres de l'Université de Strasbourg*, f. 145). Paris: Société d'Editions: Les Belles Lettres.

Bean, Marion C. 1983. *The Development of Word Order Patterns in Old English*. London: Croom Helm.

Benson, J.D., M.J. Cummings and Wm. S. Greaves. (eds.) 1988. *Linguistics in a Systemic Perspective*. Amsterdam: John Benjamins.

Berry, Margaret. 1975/77. *An Introduction to Systemic Linguistics*. 2 vols. London: B.T. Batsford.

Berry, Margaret. 1989. Thematic options and success in writing. *Language & Literature – Theory & Practice: A tribute to Walter Grauberg*, edited by Christopher Butler, Richard Caudwell & Joanna Channell. Nottingham: University of Nottingham.

Bethurum, Dorothy, ed. 1957. *The Homilies of Wulfstan*. Oxford: Clarendon Press.

Davies, Martin. 1989. Theme from 'Beowulf' to Shakespeare. Paper presented to the 16th International Systemic Functional Congress, University of Helsinki, Helsinki, Finland.

Davies, Martin. Forthcoming. Theme until Shakespeare. To appear in *Meaning and Choice in Language: Studies for Michael Halliday. Vol. 3, Grammatical structure: A functional interpretation*, edited by M. Berry, C. Butler and R. Fawcett. Norwood, N.J.: Ablex.

Downing, Angela. 1990. On topical theme in English. Paper presented to the 17th International Systemic Congress, University of Sterling, Sterling, Scotland.

Downing, Angela. 1991. An alternative approach to theme: A systemic functional perspective. *Word* 42.2, 119-143.

Enkvist, Nils Erik. 1972. Old English adverbial ÞA – An action marker? *Neuphilologische Mitteilungen* 73, 90-96.

Firbas, Jan. 1986. On the dynamics of written communication in the light of the theory of functional sentence perspective. *Studying Writing*, edited by C.R. Cooper and S. Greenbaum. London: Sage.

Godden, Malcolm, ed. 1979. *Ælfric's Catholic Homilies: the Second Series, Text*. (=*Early English Text Society*, ss. 5). London: Oxford University Press.

Gregory, Michael. 1983. *Outline of English morphosyntax, descriptive categories: clauses & sentences, Part II: Notes on communication linguistics*. York University: Toronto. Mimeo.

Gregory, Michael. 1984. Propositional and predicational analysis in discourse description. *The Tenth LACUS Forum 1983*, edited by Alan Manning, Pierre Martin and Kim McCalla, 315-322. Columbia, S.C.: Hornbeam Press.

Gregory, Michael. 1988. Generic situation and register: A functional view of communication. Benson, Cummings and Greaves, (eds.) 1988, 301-329.

Halliday, M.A.K. 1967. Notes on transitivity and theme in English, Part 2. *Journal of Linguistics* 3, 199-244.

Halliday, M.A.K. 1985. *An Introduction to Functional Grammar.* London: Edward Arnold.

Kohonen, Viljo. 1983. *On the Development of English Word Order in Religious Prose around 1000 and 1200 A.D.: A quantitative study of word order in context.* Abo: Research Institute of the Abo Akademi Foundation.

Mitchell, Bruce. 1985. *Old English Syntax.* 2 vols. Oxford: Clarendon Press.

Plummer, Charles, (ed.) 1892. *Two of the Saxon Chronicles Parallel.* 2 vols. Oxford: Clarendon Press.

Pope, John C., (ed.) 1981. *Seven Old English Poems.* 2nd ed. New York: W.W. Norton.

Reszkiewicz, Alfred. 1966. *Ordering of Elements in Late Old English Prose in Terms of their Size and Structural Complexity.* Wroclaw: Polskiej Akademii Nauk.

Svoboda, Ales. 1981. *Diatheme: A Study in Thematic Elements, their Contextual Ties, Thematic Progressions and Scene Progressions Based on a Text from Ælfric.* Brno: Univerzita J.E. Purkyne.

Thorpe, Benjamin, (ed.) 1844-6. *The Homilies of the Anglo-Saxon Church. The First Part, Containing the Sermones Catholici or Homilies of Ælfric.* 2 vols. London.

9

Themes, Methods of Development, and Texts[*]

Peter H. Fries
*Central Michigan University
and Hangzhou University*

1. Introduction

This paper explores the notion of Theme as it is conceptualized in the systemic functional model. The notion of Theme was clearly articulated by Mathesius as early as 1939 and has been developed by members of the Prague school since then. In the 1960's, M.A.K. Halliday, influenced by work within the Prague school, integrated a similar notion (which he called Theme) into the systemic functional model. Fries (1981) discussed the similarities and differences between the Prague school notion of Theme and the concept of Theme which was used in systemic functional theory. Much has been written since the sixties either supporting or disputing the various claims associated with Theme in systemic functional grammar. A large body of work uses Theme as part of the descriptive apparatus (Martin 1992, Ragan 1987, Rothery 1990, Plum 1988, Vande Kopple 1991 etc.). At the same time, a number of authors are quite critical of Theme. (See Brown and Yule 1981; Chafe 1976; Gundel 1977; Hudson 1986; Huddleston 1988, 1991, 1992 for examples.) Clearly, the concept of Theme stands in need of clarification and of further exploration. I intend to explore Theme in this paper by examining four hypotheses which concern the relation between Themes and texts[1].

[*] This paper was written while on sabbatical leave from Central Michigan University. I would like to thank Ruqaiya Hasan for detailed comments on an earlier version of this paper.

1. One issue concerning Theme is the relation between Theme and Subject. Such a discussion is outside the scope of this paper.

2. Review of previous work

Systemic grammarians generally base their descriptions of Theme on the classic descriptions provided by Halliday (e.g. 1967, 1970 and 1985). In these works Halliday described the Theme of the clause in the following terms:

> The theme is what is being talked about, the point of departure for the clause as a message ... (1967:212)

> The theme is the element which serves as the point of departure of the message; it is that with which the clause is concerned. (1985:38)

> The English clause consists of a 'theme' and a 'rheme' ... [the theme] is as it were the peg on which the message is hung, ... The theme of the clause is the element which, in English, is put in first position; ... [1970:161]

These passages define Theme as the 'point of departure of the message', the 'peg on which the message is hung' or 'what the message is about', and they say that Theme can be recognized in English by the fact that it occurs first. Elsewhere, Halliday has said that the element of structure Theme may exist at several ranks, including group rank and the clause complex, in addition to the clause rank. A number of works (e.g. Bäcklund 1990, Fries 1981, *in press a*) have examined Themes in T-units[2]. Halliday's wording 'what the clause is about' has often been assumed to equate Theme in systemic functional grammar with what others called topic, and a number of articles have devoted considerable space to demonstrating that what occurs first in clauses is often not the topic. (See Gundel 1977; Downing 1991; and Huddleston 1988 for examples of this interpretation.) I also showed (Fries 1981, *in press b*) that Theme is not topic (or given or even necessarily nominal). Rather, Theme functions as an orienter to the message. It orients the listener/reader to the message that is about to be perceived and provides a framework for the interpretation of that message[3].

In his early presentations, Halliday generally discussed isolated sen-

---

2. A T-unit is a clause complex which contains one main independent clause together with all the hypotactic clauses which are dependent on it. For an early description of T-units, see Hunt (1965).

3. See Bäcklund (1989) and Winter (1977:475) for similar wordings.

tences as examples. I found that his descriptions were persuasive, but felt that his case could be made stronger by considering the thematic contribution to texts considered as wholes. If Theme is a meaningful element on the level of clause or clause complex, then we should find that the kinds of meanings that are made thematic would vary depending on the purposes of the writers. Further, we should be able to manipulate reader's and listener's reactions to texts by changing the content of the Themes of those texts in much the same way that we can manipulate reader and listener reactions to texts by changing the words of the text (e.g. by changing *and* to *but* in certain places). With this end in view, I investigated a number of short (one and two paragraph) texts to see whether thematic content within these texts related to the purposes of the authors and the perceptions of readers. The results of that study were presented in Fries (1981).

In that paper, I hypothesized that:

(i)   different patterns of Thematic progression correlate with different genres, i.e. patterns of thematic progression do not occur randomly but are sensitive to genre; and

(ii) the experiential content of Themes correlates with what is perceived to be the method of development of a text or text segment [4].

Since Fries (1981), two additional hypotheses have been articulated:

(iii) the experiential content of Themes correlates with different genres, and

(iv) the experiential content of the Themes of a text correlates with different generic elements of structure within a text.

Clearly all four hypotheses mentioned here concern the relation between some aspect of the information which is used as Theme in a text and some aspect of the text as a whole. However these hypotheses relate thematic content to slightly different aspects of texts. The work published on Theme since my initial paper has generally supported the four hypotheses listed above. However this work has also shown that the picture is complicated. Things are not as simple as the above wording of the hypotheses would lead one to believe.

---

4. A closely related hypothesis presented in Fries (1981) is indirectly relevant to this paper: information which is perceived to constitute the point of a text or text segment is regularly found within the Rhemes. In other words, information which is perceived to present the point of a text segment would **not** be found in the Themes.

2.1 Hypothesis 1

The first hypothesis concerns the relation of different thematic progressions to different genres. The notion of thematic progression, derived from the work of Daneš (1974) and others, concerns the ways that texts develop the ideas they present. More specifically thematic progression concerns where Themes come from – how they relate to other Themes and Rhemes of the text. Patterns of thematic progression are formed by a systematic relation between the Theme-Rheme selections and experiential selections in a text. Thematic progression may be investigated by exploring the cohesive ties which occur within the various Themes within a text and the locations of the items the cohesive ties presume. Thus, given a Theme, what are the cohesive items within that Theme and where are those cohesive items resolved? Daneš described a number of typical Thematic progressions, including the three diagrammed in Figure 1.

The first type of Thematic progression in Figure 1 could be called 'linear thematic progression'. In linear thematic progression, the content of the Theme of a second sentence (Theme 2) derives from the content of the previous Rheme (Rheme 1), the content of Theme 3 derives from Rheme 2 etc. The second type of thematic progression could be called 'Theme iteration'. In Theme iteration, the same Theme enters into relation with a number of different Rhemes. The result of this type of Thematic progression is that the Themes in the text constitute a chain of (typically) co-referential items which extends through a sequence of sentences or clauses. The third type of thematic progression might be called a progression with derived Themes. In this case, the passage as a whole concerns a single general notion, and the Themes of the various constituent clauses all derive from that general notion, but are not identical to one another.[5] Thus, an obituary might use Themes which refer to the person who died, services, the funeral, burial, etc. Clearly these items are not coreferential, but they can all be seen to relate to the situation as a whole.

Subsequent work on Thematic progression has only weakly supported hypothesis 1. For example, Gill Francis (1989, 1990) examined articles

---

5. Cloran (this volume) points out that one must also consider patterns of progression in the Rheme, adding at least Rheme → Rheme progressions. See also her characterisation of the thematic progression patterns.

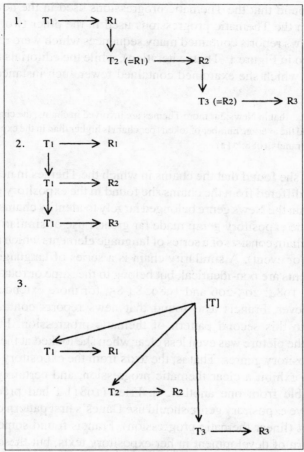

Figure 1: Three patterns of Thematic progression according to Daneš

which were found in three contexts in two newspapers. She examined the clause Themes of front-page news reports, editorial comments, and letters to the editor which expressed some sort of complaint. She took the different placement in the newspapers to indicate that the articles belonged to different genres, and assigned news reports to the news report genre, editorials to analytical exposition ('persuading that'), and letters of complaint to the genre of hortatory exposition ('persuading to'). Her results supported hypothesis 1 in that she found that the Thematic progressions used in the news reports differed from the Thematic progressions used in the other two genres. In particular, news reports contained many sequences which were reminiscent of pattern two in Figure 1 (Theme iteration), while the editorials and letters to the editor which she examined contained fewer such instances. As she said:

> It is clear ... that in News, far more Themes are involved in chains, the chains are longer, and the average number of tokens per chain is higher than in the expository genres. (Francis 1988: 212)

Further, she found that the chains in which the Themes in news reports participated differed from the chains she found in the expository genre. The Themes within the News genre belonged largely to identity chains, while the Themes of the expository genre made far greater use of similarity chains[6]. An identity chain consists of a series of language elements which refer to the same thing (or event). A similarity chain is a series of language elements whose referents are non-identical, but belong to the same or related classes. (See Hasan, 1984: 205-206 and 1989: 84-85, for more extended descriptions.) However, Francis also found that news reports contained many exceptions to this second pattern of thematic progression. Further, she reports that the picture was even less clear when she looked at the texts from the two expository genres. That is, the texts from the expository genres did not seem to exhibit a clear thematic progression, and certainly were not distinguishable from one another. In Fries (1981) I had predicted that argumentative expository genre should use Daneš's first pattern of thematic development (linear thematic progression). Francis found some examples of this pattern of development in her expository texts, but these texts also contained many unexplainable exceptions to this pattern. The exceptions were so varied that she was unable to discover any general pattern of thematic progression in her expository texts. She described the situation in the following terms:

> There is an extraordinary diversity here and it is difficult to see a Theme-Rheme pattern emerging, even at paragraph level. (Francis 1989: 215)

6. Of course identity chains and similarity chains may be found within any part of a clause or sentence (Theme or Rheme). For the purposes here, Francis explored only those chains which contained at least one member which occurred within the Theme of a clause.

Bäcklund's (1990) discussion of eight telephone conversations from the London-Lund Corpus makes a similar point. While Bäcklund finds 61 instances of Theme iteration (Daneš's second pattern) most of these instances are found in sequences of two or three identical Themes. She finds 40 instances of Daneš's first pattern, but all of these instances consist of minimal chains of two links. In other words, both Francis and Bäcklund find at least some genre which seem not to have a clear pattern of thematic progression. Both Francis and Bäcklund seem to be looking for uninterrupted thematic progressions and make the point (in different ways) that one needs to explore chains which are interrupted by other material. However, it seems unreasonable to expect that every Theme of a text, particularly a long text, should fit into a single pattern of thematic progression. Most texts achieve several purposes, and one should expect the grammatical structures used in these texts (including choice of Themes) to change as one or another purpose is addressed. Francis suggests that even chains with relatively few tokens may range over large portions of text in news reports, forming one device which news writers use to maintain coherence over long stretches of text. Hypothesis 4 suggests that the intermittent recurrence of specific information as Theme (e.g. as described in Francis) might signal some aspect of text structure. (This topic will be discussed again later.)

It is clear that in its present form, hypothesis 1 does not account for all the data. It is possible that it may be improved by integrating a view of text structure (or invoking the notion of information types, following Longacre 1981, 1989, 1990).

2.2 Hypothesis 2

The second hypothesis concerns the relation between the experiential content of the Themes of a text and readers' and listeners' interpretations of that text. Two texts may say roughly the same thing but develop their ideas in different ways. The way in which a text develops its ideas can be called the method of development of the text. The method of development of a text affects the reactions of its listeners and readers. There is no requirement that a good text develop its ideas in a single self-consistent manner. However, some texts do so. The second hypothesis claims that if a text is perceived to have a single simple method of development, then the Themes of the clauses and clause complexes of the text will be seen to express meanings which relate to that method of development. Most typically, texts which are perceived to develop their ideas in a single simple way (i.e. which are perceived to use a single simple method of development) base that development on just a few experiential meanings being presented in the text. Hypothesis 2 predicts that the texts which take that approach will use the experiential content of the Themes to construct that development. A corollary of this hypothesis is that if we change the experiential content of the Themes of a text, we will change readers' perceptions of how the ideas in that text are developed. Thus, this aspect of hypothesis 2 should be testable using standard psychological testing techniques measuring readers' interpretations of texts. However, no one has yet carried out such an experiment systematically.

I should point out that the notion of method of development is not a structural idea but a semantic one. Different texts may be perceived to express single methods of development to varying degrees. Or, to put it another way, some texts develop their ideas in simple ways, while others develop their ideas in quite complicated ways. Hypothesis 2 predicts that the perceived simplicity or complexity of the development of the ideas in a text will correlate with the degree to which the experiential content of the Themes of the text may be seen to be derived from a limited set of semantic fields. Some studies, such as Thompson (1985) and Francis (1989, 1990), do not find texts with long series of Themes which derive from a single semantic field. This finding in itself does not contradict the hypothesis, since it focuses only on the formal characteristic of the texts. Such a finding would only contradict this hypothesis if the texts were also perceived (by listeners or readers) to have a single simple method of development. While Thompson and Francis do not discuss the semantic impression conveyed by the texts being analyzed, the examples which they provide show that not only is it the case that the experiential content of the Themes of the component clauses and clause complexes does not derive from a single semantic field, but also these texts develop their ideas in relatively complex ways. Hence these studies may in fact be taken to partially support hypothesis 2.

Further partial support for hypothesis 2 is supplied by the many studies of individual texts or small groups of texts in which the experiential content of the Themes of the clauses of the text is examined and tied to the interpretation of the passage. These studies (For example Benson, Greaves, and Stillar 1992, Halliday 1993, Martin 1986, 1989, and 1992, and Ragan 1987), report a correlation between the experiential content of the Themes of the clauses and the impression produced by the texts examined. Ragan, for example, studied directions written by native and nonnative speakers, and found that sets of directions contained three major elements of structure: one, which was obligatory, described the procedure to be done, a second (optional) element of structure oriented the reader to the task, while the third (again optional) element of structure recapitulated and concluded what was said earlier. The descriptions of the procedure to be done always used the processes to be done (the actions) as method of development. This correlated with the fact that the Themes of the descriptions of the procedures regularly contained simple Themes which referred to processes. Thus, for example, the procedure portion of the text produced by student MPIAV-3 contained 14 non-embedded clauses. The Topical Themes of 11 of these clauses referred to processes.

Similarly, Benson et al compared two critical reviews of a film which conveyed radically different impressions. They found that, among other things, the methods of development of the two texts differed. One review seemed to develop its point very simply, focusing on the film as a product, and that simple development correlated with the fact that six of eight topical Themes refer to the film itself, while the remaining two Themes refer to characters portrayed in the film. The second review took a more complex approach to the task and presented the film as a process in which many people participated. This complexity in impression correlated with more complex semantic patterning in the experiential content of the Themes of the clauses of the text. Only one of 18 clause Themes referred to the film as a whole, and even this Theme also included the director's name. Other clause Themes referred to the script and script writer, characters other than romantic leads, actors, and costumes. Celebrities of the period represented in the film are separated from their portrayal in the film in several Themes, etc. In other words, Benson et al's results follow the predictions of the second hypothesis.

2.3 Hypothesis 3

The third hypothesis predicts that the experiential content of the Themes in a text is sensitive to different genres. At one level, this may appear quite self-evident. For example, we expect tour guides to contain many references to spatial location. Therefore, even if these references to spatial location were to occur randomly in the clauses and sentences of a tour guide, we would

still expect a relatively larger number of references to spatial location in the
clause and sentence Themes of such texts. However, this hypothesis predicts
that meanings are not randomly distributed in different positions in the
sentences and clauses of a text. A basic purpose of tour guide texts is to
present and explain the various sights to the reader. References to spatial
location are typically present to orient the reader to the location of these
sights. Therefore, because of the purposes of tour guide texts, references to
spatial location will play an orienting role. This orienting role will lead
authors of tour guide texts to place a greater proportion of their references
to spatial location within the Themes of the text. On the other hand, in
narratives, references to spatial location in clauses which refer to event line
processes[7] typically play a much more focal role. Due to this different textual
role, references to spatial location in event-line processes will be less likely
to occur thematically. Thus, this hypothesis cannot be explored with simple
raw counts of how many Themes refer to spatial location. Rather, when
comparing texts we must examine all references to a type of meaning (such
as spatial location) in the texts and then compare the proportions of thematic
versus non-thematic occurrences.

   The third hypothesis has been explored in greater detail than the second.
Indeed, several papers over the last few years (e.g. Berry 1987, Bäcklund,
1990, Francis 1989 and 1990, and Wang Ling 1991 and 1992) have focused
on exactly this issue. It is of interest to find that the results have varied
depending on which genres were explored. Francis's (1989 and 1990)
comparison of Themes in news reports, editorials and letters of complaint
found that the Themes used in the news reports differed from the Themes
used in the other two genres. She found that "The typical and most predominant Themes in News are material and verbal, while far fewer relational
participants/processes are selected as point of departure for the message"
(1990: 53). (I believe this result could be paraphrased as 'the Themes of the
clauses in news reports referred much more often to verbal and material
processes or to participants in verbal and material processes than they did
to relational process or participants in relational processes.' More simply put,
News contained far more material or verbal processes than relational processes, and as a result references in the clause Themes to portions of these

---

7. The term 'event-line processes' refers to the description of events in a story line. (See
Longacre 1981, 1989, 1990.)

processes (the participants), or to the processes themselves were more frequent than references to relational processes or to participants in relational processes.) By contrast, "Editorials and Letters *both* thematize fewer material processes, very few verbal processes and a much higher percentage of relational processes." (Francis 1990:53)

Francis also investigated the sorts of information which were thematized in the three genres. She investigated the distributions of four basic semantic categories of Theme:

> 1) people/groups/institutions i.e. all humans individually and collectively; 2) concrete things such as *aeroplane* and *dress*; 3) abstractions, which includes both nominalized processes like *inquiry* , *proposal*, *refusal*, etc., and the more 'domesticated' abstract nouns like *job, percentage*, and *law*; and 4) time expressions. (Francis 1990: 55).

A fifth category called 'other' consisted of processes or non-lexical Themes. The distributions of these information types is given in Table 1 (adapted from Francis Figure 3).

Table 1: Distribution of typical lexis of Theme in Francis' data

Information type	News	Editorials	Letters
1) people etc.	107 (=53%)	32 (=22%)	52 (=28%)
2) concrete things	18 (=9%)	13 (=9%)	12 (=7%)
3) abstractions	43 (=21%)	61 (=41%)	62 (=34%)
4) time	10	7	10
5) other	23	30	47
Total Themes	201	143	183
1) + 2)	125 (= 62%)	45 (= 31%)	64 (= 35%)

Clearly News contains far more people and 'thing' Themes than the other two genres. By the same token, the two expository genres use abstractions as Theme much more often than News does.

Francis also investigated the distribution of thematic equatives (*What the Duke gave to my aunt* was that teapot.), predicated Themes (*It was John who wanted us to go.*) or Embedded (rankshifted) clausal Themes (*That Caesar was dead was obvious to all.*) and modifying clausal Themes (*Far from your leader (June 5) containing misstatements of fact and misunderstandings, as Mr Bailey alleged,* it was, in my view, very accurate). (Themes in these examples are indicated in bold). The Themes of Editorials and Letters contained more examples of these constructions than did the Themes of News. Table 2 (her Figure 5) presents the results of her analysis of her data.)

Table 2: Distribution of clausal Themes in Francis' data

	News	Editorials	Letters
embedded clausal Themes	0	2	2
thematic equatives	1	3	1
predicated Themes	1	3	2
modifying clausal Themes	4	9	11
Total	6	17	16

Of course the structures just listed may be regarded as simply grammatical constructions. However, these grammatical constructions have semantic consequences. Embedded clauses are means by which processes may be made into participants. As a result they provide an index of the range of phenomena which may serve as Theme. Does this range include or not include processes and facts, etc.? Thematic equatives and predicated Themes involve markedness. Typically this markedness is a markedness of focus or of Theme (or both). In either case, "this sort of markedness is associated with degrees of intervention of the writer." (Francis 1990: 60) As a result, thematic equatives and predicated Themes provide an index of how often writers use some sort of marked textual structure. Since news reporting is presented as objective while letters of complaint and editorials involve overt authorial intervention, we should expect grammatical structures which overtly encode marked focus to occur more frequently in letters of complaint and in editorials than in News[8].

8. While Francis describes the relative frequencies of those embedded clauses, nominalizations, etc. which occur thematically in her data, she does not indicate what proportion of all nominalizations etc. are found thematic in her texts. As a result we cannot determine if the frequencies which she reports arise directly from the overall frequencies of these constructions in the three genres or whether the constructions are being used in different ways in the three text types. For example, it is possible that the differences between News and the other genres arises because of the differences in overall frequencies of these constructions in the three genres. News may simply use many fewer nominalizations, etc., and therefore fewer of these constructions are found thematic within the clauses of News.

Finally, it is a feature of the News reports which Francis studied that the clause Themes of news reports contained a high proportion of lexical items. Francis refers to this index as an index of lexical density (see also Ure 1971 and Halliday 1989 Chapter 5) and finds that Themes in editorials have an over all average lexical density of 2.0, Themes in News reports 1.7 and Themes in letters of complaint 1.5. Much of the high lexical density in News reports was achieved through the use of apposition within the various Themes. Such use of apposition was not characteristic of either letters to the editor or of editorials.

In summary, Francis' results supported hypothesis 3 only partially. The Themes used in news reports differed clearly in content from the Themes of the two expository genres. However, when Francis compared the Themes of the Letters with those of the Editorials, she found that the overall averages for each of the two genre did not differ very much. Further, the variation between individual texts within each of the two expository genres was so great that the differences in the averages which she found did not seem significant. This finding conflicted with the results that Martin (1986, 1989) reported in which he found very marked differences between the experiential content of the clause Themes of hortatory and analytical exposition. In commenting on the differences between her results and Martin's, Francis (1990: 54) focuses on the small size of the samples being examined, concluding that "The variability from one text to another suggests that the size of the sample is a major factor in determining one's findings." Clearly she is correct in this. Studies based on three or four instances of a genre can be taken as suggestive at best. I would like to add, however, that the criteria which are used to gather and make an initial sort of the data are also critical. It is dangerous to assume too close an association of physical position (e.g. in a news paper) with genre characteristics. While, for example, it may be reasonable to assume that editorials differ in regular ways from news reports, is it reasonable to assume that all editorials (or news reports) belong to the same genre and that they are therefore uniform? Francis' results would seem to argue a negative answer. (See Hasan in press for a discussion of the constitutive role of language in social interactions.)

In contrast to Francis's study, a number of other researchers have found the experiential content of the clause Themes to correlate fairly strongly with genre type. In a study of the use of place names in texts from four genres, viz. a guide book, a travel brochure, a transcript of a coffee party, and a transcript of a committee meeting, Berry (1987) provided evidence which suggests that place names have different distributions in the four genres. She examined the first 25 place names which occurred in each text and found the distributions presented in Tables 3 and 4 (= Berry's Tables 2 and 3).

Table 3: Occurrences of place names in Subject, Object, Complement, Adverbial

	Coffee party	Committee meeting	Travel Brochure	Guide book
Subject	0	3	12	16
Object	3	5	1	4
Complement	1	2	1	0
Adverbial	21	15	11	5

Table 4: Occurrences of place-names in Theme with comparative figures for Subject

	Coffee party	Committee meeting	Travel Brochure	Guide book
Theme	2	3	10	14
Subject	0	3	12	16
Themes which are not Subjects	2	0	4	0
Subjects which are not Themes	0	0	6	2

The guide book and travel brochure clearly use place names as Subject and as Theme much more often than the other two texts. In examining Table 3 it is important to remember that all Berry's texts had 25 instances of place names. Thus, in the coffee party text, 23 of the 25 occurrences of place names were neither Theme nor Subject. Similarly, 22 of the place names used in the committee meeting functioned neither as Theme nor as Subject. On the other hand, 10 of the 25 place names in the travel brochure and 14 of the 25 place names in the guide book functioned as Theme. While the numbers in this study are small, they are supported by related projects my students have done. For example, a class project by Nie (1991) studied the choice of Themes in a portion of a guide book to Hangzhou and found that six of 14 clause Themes referred to spatial location. Examples of such Themes included *At the top of Jade Emperor Hill, half way up, From this point on the road*, etc. Another group of six Themes contained names of places or portions of the sites, e.g. *the well of the site, Phoenix Hill, the three sitting Buddhas*, etc. Since each of these refers to portions of sites, we may think of these six Themes as at least implying spatial orientation. Thus, twelve of the fourteen Themes in this section of the guide book provided either direct or implied spatial orientation.

In a study which is part of her Masters Thesis at Peking University, Wang Ling (1991) examined five-page sections of six plays by Sam Sheppard, and compared the language of the text which is to be spoken by the actors (the line text) with the text which provides stage directions and descriptions, etc. (the scene text). She found that the Themes in the scene text differed from the Themes of the line text. Scene text used a far higher percentage of simple Themes than did line text. (e.g. *Buried Child* showed a ratio of 28/29 =96%, vs. 74/163 = 45%). In other words, scene text uses the experiential metafunction as the source for thematic material practically exclusively. Within the simple Themes, scene text used a higher percentage of marked Themes than did Line text. (Again, *Buried Child* showed the following ratios 6/28 = 21% vs. 4/74 = 5%). While Wang Ling did not describe the semantic nature of the marked Themes in scene text, her examples include:

(1) *In the dark*, the light of the lamp and the TV slowly brighten in the black space.

(2) *Up right* is an old, dark green sofa with the stuffing coming out in spots.

Clearly spatial location constitutes an important point of departure for scene text. Further, the Themes of the scene text contained very little variation in construction or in meanings when compared to Themes used in the line text. Wang Ling found very few instances of clauses used as Themes, and no instances of predicated Themes in the scene text. She does not give figures for the occurrence of these constructions in the line text, but does say that the line text contained many examples of these constructions.

The last study I report on here examined eight sample conversations from the London Lund Corpus of Spoken English. In this study, Bäcklund found that in fully 51% of her data (216 T-units) "the ideational Theme refers to one of the speakers (*I, you*) or to a group including one of the speakers or both (*we, you*)[9]." Further, all but 19 of the 419 T-units have the Subject as ideational Theme. Of the 19 marked Themes, 15 are Adverbial clauses, 3 are temporal *now*, and one is *from then*. None of the texts studied in the works reported on here show such a heavy concentration of Themes which refer to participants in the conversation. However, a comment in Berry (1987: 84) suggests that speakers in the coffee party text which she analyzed used personal Themes more than absolutely necessary.

Table 5 summarizes several features of the works which have just been described and one which will be discussed in Section 2.4. Since the studies were performed by different workers who measured different features, the numbers are not all comparable. For example, only one of the five authors (Xiao) enquired into the effect of the generic structure on the phenomena examined. Text lengths were described using word count (Francis) clause count (Wang and Xiao) and T-unit count (Bäcklund and Nie). Luckily Francis also mentioned the number of Themes she examined, and this number provides at least a minimum count of the clauses in her data. Table 5 is divided into two parts, Table 5A and 5B. Table 5A focuses on general descriptions of the texts and on the grammatical structures which function as Theme. Table 5B provides information on the use of different types of meanings in the Themes of the various texts. 'Yes' in the column for line text under Wang indicates that Wang reports the occurrence of embedded clausal Themes and predicated Themes, but provides no counts of her data. Since Wang provides no specific information on the use of different types of meanings in the Themes of scene text and line text, no column is provided for her work in Table 5B. Berry's work was sufficiently different from the others as to make it impossible to place it in Table 5 at all. Dashes in the columns for the texts studied by Francis (see bottom of Table 5B) indicate that Francis did not separate out locational meanings as a separate category, and so these meanings may be included in the figures for her 'Other' category.

---

9. This result is supported by other researchers as well. Givón suggests that humans tend to make humans the topic of their conversations. Berry (1987: 84) reported that in the casual conversation she analyzed "... speakers have actually avoided assigning place-names to grammatical subject even where this would have been topically appropriate."

Table 5A: Summary of properties of Themes reported in Francis, Wang, Bäcklund, Xiao, and Nie

Genre type:	Francis News Reports	Francis Editorials	Francis Letters to Eds	Wang (Buried Child) Scene Text	Wang (Buried Child) Line Text	Bäcklund Conversation	Xiao Recipes Intro	Xiao Recipes Procedure	Xiao Fables	Nie Guide book
Generic Elements							Intro	Procedure		
Length of Text	2500 wds 201 Themes	2500 wds 143 Themes	2500 wds 183 Themes	29 cls	163 cls	419 T-units	8 cls	38 cls	39 cls	14 T-units
Grammatical Structures in Themes:										
Simple Themes				28 (96%)	74 (45%)	182 (43%)	8 (100%)	35 (92%)	32 (82%)	14 (100%)
Marked Themes				6 (21%)	4 (5%)	19 (5%)	0	6 (16%)	5 (13%)	8 (57%)
Embedded Clausal Themes	0	2	2	0	0		0	0	0	0
Thematic Equatives	1	3	1	0	yes		0	0	0	0
Predicated Themes	1	3	2	0	yes		0	0	0	0

Table 5B: Experiential content of Themes reported in Francis, Bäcklund, Xiao and Nie

	Francis			Bäcklund	Xiao			Nie
					Recipes		Fables	
Genre type:	News reports	Editorials	Letters	Conversation	Intro	Procedure		Guide book
Generic Structure:								
Retrospective Text References	few	freq	freq		0	0	0	0
Speaker/Hearer				216 (51%)	0	0	0	0
Major Text Participant	107 (53%)	32 (22%)	52 (28%)		6 (75%)	5 (13%)	26 (67%)	
Concrete things	19 (9%)	13 (9%)	12 (7%)				3 (7.7%)	6 (43%)
Abstract concept	43 (21%)	61 (41%)	62 (34%)				5 (13%)	
Process						27 (71%)		
Time	10	7	10		1 (13%)		3 (7.7%)	1 (7%)
Location	–	–	–					6 (43%)
Other	23	30	47		1 (13%)	6 (16%)	3 (7.7%)	1 (7%)

2.4 Hypothesis 4

The fourth hypothesis concerns the relation between the experiential content of the Themes of a text and the different elements of structure within that text. This hypothesis has two forms. The first version of hypothesis 4 (henceforth hypothesis 4A) assumes that as a text moves from one element of structure to the next, the purposes to be accomplished will change. As a result, the meanings expressed in each element of structure of the text will change and therefore the language used in each will change. The differences which are found in the Themes of the clauses of the different elements of structure are simply part of the differences in language which are generally encountered. (This version of hypothesis 4 can be regarded as a more sensitive version of hypothesis 3.) Plum (1988 vol. 1: 283) put it this way:

> … we would expect a predominant realisation of Theme in a way which allows for the potential realisation of 'character', i.e. by Themes which are potentially co-referential, to correlate not only with narrative-type genres generally but also specifically with the crisis stages in narrative. Similarly, we would expect other stages, such as an end stage, to correlate with a choice of Theme which is not at all concerned with the realisation of character but instead by a Theme which foregrounds its metatextual function by making anaphoric reference to events already related in the text, i.e. by either extended or text reference, since it is part of the meaning of an end stage to 'wrap up' the text.

Hypothesis 4A can in fact be made more specific. As we saw above, the element of structure Theme has been described in terms such as 'point of departure', 'peg on which the message is hung', 'framework for the interpretation of the message' and 'orienter'. By contrast, Rheme has been described as the unmarked location of New information[10] – information which is 'newsworthy' and to which the listener should pay attention. Since the descriptions of the meanings of Theme and New differ in important ways, we can predict that while both Themes and Rhemes will change as a text progresses through its various elements of structure the two will respond to different forces and will contain different sorts of information. In a study of written English, Fries (*in press a*) coined the term N-Rheme (for New/Rheme) for the last constituent of a clause – the constituent which

10. See Halliday (1967: 201-202; 1985: 274), and Chafe (1984: 437).

is the unmarked location of New information, and made the following hypothesis:

> As we examine the text, we should keep in mind that the N-Rheme is the news-worthy part of the clause, that is, the part of the clause that the writer wants the reader to remember. As a result we should expect the content of the N-Rheme to correlate with the goals of the text as a whole, the goals of the text segment within those larger goals, and the goals of the sentence and the clause as well. On the other hand, the Theme is the orienter to the message conveyed by the clause. It tells the reader how to understand the news conveyed by the clause. As a result, we should expect the choice of Thematic content usually to reflect local concerns. For example, if we are examining a text which has a problem – solution structure, we should expect the meanings to change as the text moves from the description of the problem to the description of the solution. Both the Thematic content and the N-Rhematic content should change. However, the content of the N-Rhemes should be more obviously connected with the goals of each text portion. For example, in the section which describes the problem, the N-Rhemes should have an obvious connection with what is wrong, while in the section which describes the solution, the N-Rhemes should have an obvious connection with what was done to solve the problem. The Themes of the problem section, on the other hand, might well concern different aspects of the item which is causing the problem (say an engine which is not functioning properly), while the Themes of the solution section might concern notions such as the relative temporal order of the actions taken in solving the problem[11].

Fries found a relation between the purposes of texts and the information found in the Themes and the N-Rhemes of written advertisements (1992, 1993) and of a fundraising letter (*in press a*). However Fries' work does not relate the experiential content of the Themes and the N-Rhemes to the generic structures of the texts examined. While the specific hypotheses relating the information in the Themes and the N-Rhemes to generic structure suggested in Hypothesis 4A have not been seriously investigated, a number of studies support the general trends predicted by hypothesis 4A. Ragan

---

11. The relationship which holds between the hypothesis described here and the discussion of the functions of Theme → Rheme and Rheme → Rheme progressions found in Cloran (this volume) needs to be explored. Clearly the claims are similar in that they focus on the importance of considering the information placed in the Rheme. They differ in that one focuses on the experiential content of the Rheme and the role of that content in the text, while the other focuses on the ties between the various Rhemes of a text and their relation to the structure of the text. As a result of this difference, it remains to be seen whether they make compatible predictions.

(1987) reports that the instruction genre which he studied contained three elements of structure: an optional orientation element, an obligatory procedure element, and an optional recapitulation element. A very high proportion of the clause Themes of the procedure element referred to processes in his data, while the clause Themes of the other two elements of structure rarely referred to processes. For example in one of his texts, 12 of 15 clauses in the procedure element of structure referred to processes. By contrast, 6 of 9 clause Themes of the recapitulation referred to the design as a whole, and only two clause Themes (one of which is in a branched clause which has no overt subject) refer to processes.

A class project by my student Qun Xiao finds similar trends. She examined Thematic choices in recipes with thematic choices in fables. She found that the recipes had four elements of structure, an introduction, a list of ingredients (not analyzed in her project, since the lists consisted exclusively of nominal groups), a description of the procedure, and a summary. In the introductions, 6 of 8 Themes mentioned the dish as a whole. In the descriptions of the procedure, 27 of 33 Themes referred to actions involved in preparing the food. Another 5 Themes referred to instruments involved in the preparation, and 1 Theme expressed a Circumstance of Manner for the process. The five Themes of the Summaries were all implicit and referred to the dish as a whole. By comparison two thirds of the Themes which occurred in the fables (26 of 39 = 67%) referred to major characters in the fables. Five Themes referred to abstract concepts. All the references to abstract concepts occurred in the expression of the moral, a portion which clearly constituted a separate element of structure in the tales.

In a much larger study, Plum (1988) found a correlation between clause Themes and generic structure. He divided the topical Themes in the narratives he examined into (potentially) participant chaining Themes and non-participant chaining Themes, and found that roughly 90% of the clause Themes in elements of structure such as Incident and Crisis used participant chaining Themes, while less than 60% of the clause Themes in elements of structure such as Reorientation, Interpretation and Abstract used participant chaining Themes[12].

A second version of hypothesis 4 (henceforth hypothesis 4B) claims that

---

12. Plum (1988) also found that the textual themes of the clauses of the different elements of structure of his texts differed as well.

as one moves from one element of structure within a text to the next, that move will be signaled in the Themes of the clauses and clause complexes[13]. More specifically, the Theme of the first clause of the new element of structure of the text will indicate that a new element of structure has begun. This hypothesis is too strong as worded here, since it is quite easy to locate specific examples where the move to a new element of structure of a text is not signaled in the Theme of the first clause or clause complex in any obvious manner. However, if we consider this statement to describe a statistical tendency, then it may be more acceptable. I do not know of much empirical work which explores this hypothesis. Prideaux and Hogan (1993) provide some suggestive information that initial placement of subordinate clauses may have a discourse marking function. They gathered oral and written narratives in controlled conditions, made a structural analysis of these narratives (focusing on locating the boundaries of episodes in those narratives). They then examined all instances of subordinate clauses in the narratives, and compared the placement in episodes of sentences which began with the subordinate clauses (SC + MC) with the placement of sentences which began with the main clause (MC + SC). They found that 35 of 37 instances of the order MC + SC in the oral narratives occurred after the episode had been initiated (i.e. not as the first sentence of the episode). By contrast 23 of 34 instances of the order SC + MC in the oral narratives occurred as the first sentence of a new episode. Further, the 11 instances of the SC + MC ordering which did not occur initially within their episode (a) referred back to the first mention of the episode, (b) signaled the end of an episode, or (c) signaled an especially important or salient event. (1993: 405) They found similar trends in their written narratives. Clearly this evidence suggests that something special happens at the boundaries of new discourse elements. Of course, while this evidence is suggestive, it does not directly address the issue of whether the experiential content of the clause complex

---

13. Another related hypothesis which needs to be explored is that the move from one element of structure in a text to the next will be signaled in the first sentence of the new element of the structure, but not necessarily in the Theme of the first sentence. This hypothesis seems to imply that the element of text structure is itself a unit which may have an analog to thematic structure on the levels of clause and clause complex. Martin (1992: 437 ff. and 1993 in Halliday and Martin 1993: 244-257) makes clear use of this notion when he discusses Macrotheme and Hypertheme. I, however, do not know of any empirical study of the use (or non-use) of Macrotheme and Hypertheme in randomly selected texts.

Themes is part of the signaling. (One possible interpretation of their results is that the presence of the order SC + MC itself (regardless of the content of the SC – the Theme of the clause complex) was sufficient to signal a discourse boundary.) As a result, this experiment only suggests that hypothesis 4B is worth exploring.

2.5 Summary

In summary, while previous work has made considerable progress in exploring the four hypotheses, we need considerable expansion of the data which are used to test them. Even the most robust of the studies mentioned above, those of Bäcklund, Francis, and Plum, use limited data. The other studies are based on data so restricted as to be of limited value except as support for trends found in other studies. For example, the two class projects by students clearly could not stand on their own because of the exceedingly small size of the samples used. Further, we need considerably more careful description of factors which can help explain the nature of the texts used as data. Bäcklund's study suffers from the fact that no major effort is made to describe the contexts in which the conversations are being held in anything more than the most general terms. Francis attempts to deal with three different genres, but simply uses location within the newspaper as the sole criterion for membership in a genre. Her data show a great deal of variation within each of her genres, and we are therefore not sure whether her criterion is sufficient to isolate uniform text types. We need much more data taken from a range of more carefully defined genres and generic structures to use as a basis for our conclusions. With this aim in view, in the next Section I shall describe some details of an investigation into the thematic patterning found in certain text types.

3. Theme in discourse: A further study

As a step toward increasing the breadth of data on which to base our conclusions concerning the relation between the experiential content of Themes and the organisation of text, and as a means of exploring the complexities of assigning particular texts to particular genres, I examined the Themes in a number of short texts which involved narration. I have chosen varieties of narration so that all texts would be seen to have some comparable features.

However, while each text involved narration, each was also produced in special conditions which imposed special constraints on it.

3.1 The Data

The texts examined fall into four major groups which might be loosely called 'super-genre'. The first group – obituaries – consists of three subgroups which I will call 'texts'. I analyzed five obituaries from *Time Magazine*, two from *the New York Times*, and four from *The Morning Sun* (the local newspaper in Mount Pleasant, Michigan). The second group consists of a single text, a program note which described the performer at a concert which I attended. The third group consists of narratives and includes a fairy tale, namely *Little Red Riding Hood*, the first chapter of *A Farewell to Arms* by Ernest Hemingway, and two short historical accounts – one an account of Napoleon's invasion of Russia, and the second *The Bathtub Navy*. Finally, the fourth group consists of one expository text, called *Balloons and Air Cushion the Fall*, which is a report of a new invention. Since I am contrasting the five obituaries which were found in *Time Magazine* with other texts as a group, I will sometimes refer to the *Time* obituaries as if they constituted a single text. Similarly, for the same reason, I will often refer to the two obituaries from the *New York Times* and the four obituaries found in *The Morning Sun* as if each group constituted one text. It is important, however, to remember that these three 'texts' are actually groups of short texts and so will exhibit special properties.

We must be careful to notice that while all the texts in the data involve narration, they do not constitute a single genre, even though they share certain characteristics. For example we might be tempted to classify all obituaries as Recounts (Martin and Rothery 1986). But these Recounts are produced under different conditions which affect the language used. At a very general level, texts written under strong space constraints typically have a very high lexical density. Thus, the obituaries from *Time Magazine* use many grammatical devices (such as appositives) which increase the information conveyed per clause, and they contain relatively many clauses per sentence. The obituaries found in *The Morning Sun* do not contain many instances of such 'condensing' devices. By the same token, we might think that all obituaries have the same structure. However, the ones I examined were found in three importantly different contexts and contained three different structures. The ones taken from *Time Magazine* were from a section labeled "Milestones". Milestones include more than simply deaths: one can be *Released, Married, Divorced* etc. As a result the first word of each text indicates which milestone has been 'passed'. All the obituaries taken from *Time Magazine* begin with the bolded word DIED (the Theme of the first clause), and then in smaller bold print give the name of the person who has died. Finally the first sentences typically concluded by describing the circumstances under which the death occurred and the location of the death. By contrast all the other obituaries were taken from sections of the newspapers where the heading of the section made it clear that the **entire** section dealt with deaths. In these cases, the Theme of the first clause indicated who had died. However, these obituaries also fell into two groups, depending on their source. *The Morning Sun* is a local newspaper. The obituaries are of interest to area inhabitants and so, tend to mention information relevant to the potential actions of the readers. Thus, one finds information about how the family can be contacted, where the services will be held, who will officiate, etc. The people described in these obituaries are usually not prominent, but merely local residents. These obituaries seem to focus on when and where things happened; thus we may have comments such as *Mr. Baumgardner was born August 1, 1921 in Macomb IL, to...* and *Moving to Mount Pleasant in 1951, he...* By contrast, *The New York Times*, while serving a local community, is at the same time a national newspaper and is distributed nationally, and it prints local, national and international news. One finds only prominent people mentioned in its obituary section. The actions typically described are ones that have affected many people. The *New York Times* obituaries typically do not include references to where and how the family may be contacted, where the memorial services will be held, etc.

The program note resembles the obituary from the *New York Times* in that it attempts to present aspects of the expertise of the performer. Of course there is the obvious difference from an obituary in that the program note focuses on the **present** credentials and abilities of the performer. (This focus is most easily noticed in the verb forms of the text.)

Within the group of texts I have labeled 'Narratives' *Little Red Riding Hood* is a fairy tale told to children. As a result, we can infer that the structure will be relatively simple and straight forward. By contrast, the other three texts I have labeled narratives are written for adults and we can expect them to be more complex, particularly in their interpersonal stance. Again, calling these three texts 'narratives' conceals some significant differences. The Napoleon text and *the Bathtub Navy* are both accounts of historical events. *The Bathtub Navy* was published in the *Readers Digest* as a complete account. The Napoleon text is a short excerpt from a longer text and more closely resembles a recount. The Hemingway text is the first chapter from a novel. Of course, the entire **novel** constitutes the narrative. This chapter merely sets the scene for the narrative. Indeed, it is very difficult to find any real events in which a single participant (or small group of participants) did anything in this chapter. In other words this chapter is not itself what one would typically call a narrative. Finally, *Balloons and Air* describes an invention by a company which solves a problem. This text involves narration in that it describes a set of events. However it is not a simple narrative. It is clearly structured in a Situation – Problem – Solution – Evaluation structure. More to the point, this text clearly focuses on the problem and its solution rather than on the people who found the solution. (Compare this aspect of this text with *The Bath Tub Navy*, which has a similar structure, but which focuses on the participants involved to a much greater degree.) As a result, the *Balloons and Air* narrative is best treated as a type of expository text. As a final comment on these texts, I should mention that all of these texts show strong evidence of having been carefully edited. Indeed the obituaries from *Time* and *The Morning Sun* seem to have been written according to formula.

3.2 Hypothesis 3 revisited

How are these aspects of the context reflected in the language of the texts and particularly in the experiential content of the clause Themes? The search for efficient ways of expressing what is said which is typical of national news media is evident in the number of hypotactic clause relations used in news, and also in the amount of ellipsis – particularly the ellipsis of Subjects in branched clauses. The amount of hypotaxis and Subject ellipsis in a text can be measured by finding the ratio of non-embedded clauses per T-unit. The texts found in *Time* and *The New York Times* contained 1.9 non-embedded clauses and 1.8 non-embedded clauses per T-unit, respectively. Except for *Little Red Riding Hood*, the other texts had significantly fewer non embedded clauses per T-unit, ranging from 1.2 to 1.5 clauses per T-unit. *Little Red Riding Hood* had 1.8 non-embedded clauses per T-unit – a relatively high number. Much of this number came from the 22 quotations and the 10 branched clauses with Subject ellipsis which occurred in the text. These features – particularly the quotations – were rarely found in the other texts in my data. If these clauses are excluded from the ratio, the text would show a ratio of 1.24 clauses per T-unit, a ratio that matches the other non-newspaper narratives.

Let me now move to the grammatical properties of the Themes in the texts I investigated. The texts in my data made relatively little use of marked experiential Themes in clauses. Percentages ranged from 2% for the obituaries in *The Morning Sun* to 36% marked Themes in the clauses of the Napoleon extract. None of the texts in my data use embedded clausal Themes, thematic equatives, or predicated Themes. Few texts in my data used nominalizations as Theme. Three texts use one thematic nominalization each. One set of texts, the *Morning Sun* obituaries contains nine nominalizations, but they are closely associated with the schema which is invoked by the situation. (**Burial** *will be in Riverside Cemetery,* ... and **Memorials** *may be made to* ...) The texts in my data therefore do not encode author intervention through the thematic use of embedded clause Themes, thematic equatives, predicated Themes or nominalizations as Theme. These results should be compared with the figures Francis presents for her data in which she finds several embedded clause Themes, thematic equatives, predicated Themes and nominalizations as Themes in her hortatory and analytical exposition texts, but she finds few of these structures in the news reports she examined.

Again, like the studies summarized in section 1, I found many more simple Themes than I did multiple Themes. As many as 89% of the clause Themes from *the Morning Sun* obituaries were simple. The lowest percentage of simple Themes was found in Chapter 1 of Hemingway *A Farewell to Arms*, where simple Themes made up only 47% of the total Themes. When multiple Themes occurred in the texts, they were typically combinations of textual and experiential Themes. The Hemingway chapter contained the highest percentage of textual Themes. 49 % of the clauses from the Hemingway text contained textual Themes. Most of the textual Themes in the texts consisted of markers of addition, contrast, or of sequence.

Only 11 interpersonal Themes occurred in the data. Five of those 11 occurred in the conversations in *Little Red Riding Hood*. The remaining 6 were found in *the Bathtub Navy*, *Farewell to Arms*, and *Balloons and Air*. These texts have relatively complicated interpersonal stances. The compli-

Table 6A: Summary of grammatical properties of Themes in various texts involving narration

		Genre									
		Obituaries			Program	Narratives				Expos	
		Time	NY Times	Morn Sun	Blurb	LRRH	Napoleon	BT Navy	Farewell	Ballns	Total
Length of Text	Clauses	39	44	57	20	98	22	19	49	19	367
	T-units	21	24	46	15	53	18	13	40	13	243
Density	Cl/r-unit	1.86	1.83	1.24	1.33	1.85	1.22	1.46	1.23	1.46	1.51
Grammatical properties of overt Themes	Simple Themes	20 (51%)	34 (77%)	51 (89%)	17 (85%)	68 (69%)	14 (64%)	13 (68%)	23 (47%)	14 (74%)	254 (69%)
	Mult. Themes	9 (23%)	10 (23%)	5 (9%)	3 (15%)	27 (28%)	8 (36%)	6 (32%)	24 (49%)	5 (26%)	97 (26%)
Marked themes	CL	8 (21%)	4 (9%)	1 (2%)	6 (30%)	5 (5%)	8 (36%)	5 (26%)	14 (29%)	2 (11%)	53 (14%)
	T-UN	4 (19%)	1 (4%)	1 (2%)	2 (13%)	5 (9%)	8 (44%)	5 (38%)	14 (35%)	2 (15%)	42 (17%)
Embdded clause Themes		0	0	0	0	0	0	0	0	0	0
Thematic Equatives		0	0	0	0	0	0	0	0	0	0
Predicated Themes		0	0	0	0	0	0	0	0	0	0
Nominalizations as Theme		2 (5%)	0 (0%)	0 (0%)	0 (0%)	3 (3%)	2 (9%)	2 (11%)	4 (8%)	1 (5%)	14 (4%)
Interprsonl Theme		0 (0%)	0 (0%)	0 (0%)	0 (0%)	2 (2%)	1 (5%)	2 (11%)	2 (4%)	2 (11%)	11 (3%)
Textual Theme		9 (23%)	8 (18%)	5 (9%)	3 (15%)	25 (26%)	10 (45%)	5 (26%)	24 (49%)	4 (21%)	93 (25%)
addition/sequence (and, but, then)		6 (15%)	7 (16%)	4 (7%)	1 (5%)	22 (22%)	9 (41%)	2 (11%)	22 (45%)	2 (11%)	75 (20%)

Table 6B: Summary of semantic properties of Themes in various texts involving narration

	Obituaries			Program		Narratives				Expos	
	Time	NY Times	Morn Sun	LRRH	Blurb	Napoleon	BT	Navy	Farewell	Ballns	Total
Ideational content of Themes:											
Retrospective Text References	0	0	0			0	0	0	0	1	1
Speaker/Hearer	0	0	0	9						0	9
Major Text Participant	16 (41%)	13 (30%)	39 (16%)	30 (31%)	7 (35%)	13 (59%)	7 (37%)	1 (5%)		0 (0%)	126 (34%)
Abstract concept	0 (0%)	3 (7%)	9 (16%)	6 (6%)			3 (16%)	1 (5%)	1 (2%)	4 (21%)	21 (6%)
Process:											
a: total	11 (28%)	5 (11%)	3 (5%)	27 (28%)	3 (15%)	0 (0%)	3 (16%)	3 (16%)	1 (2%)	2 (11%)	55 (15%)
b: non-fi hypotactic clause	6 (15%)	4 (9%)	4 (9%)	6 (6%)	3 (15%)	0 (0%)	3 (16%)	0 (0%)	0 (0%)	2 (11%)	27 (7%)
c: verbal process	0	0	0	19	15	0	0	0	0	0	
Temporal location:											
a: Clause theme	4 (10%)	1 (2%)	1 (2%)	3 (3%)	6 (30%)	4 (18%)	2 (11%)	4 (8%)		0	25 (7%)
b: T-unit theme	7 (33%)	1 (2%)	4 (4%)	5 (9%)	6 (47%)	5 (28%)	4 (31%)	4 (10%)	2 (9%)	0	36 (15%)
Spatial location	0 (0%)	0 (0%)	0 (0%)	0 (0%)	0 (0%)	1 (5%)	3 (16%)	3 (16%)	6 (12%)	1 (5%)	14 (4%)
Subject ellipses	6 (15%)	10 (23%)	4 (7%)	6 (15%)	0 (0%)	0 (0%)	3 (16%)	0 (0%)	1 (2%)	0 (0%)	33 (9%)
Other	1	3	0	0	0	0	1	0	1	1	1

cated interpersonal stances might be expected to increase the use of interpersonal elements as Theme. For example, the only interpersonal Theme which is also a T-unit Theme in the *Balloons and Air* text is found at a point where the author evaluates a portion of the situation as a problem.

Tables 6A and 6B summarize the results discussed in this section. The four major 'super genres' are separated into groups of columns. The individual texts are given abbreviated names and figures for each text are placed within individual columns. Table 6A presents grammatical features of Themes in the data, while Table 6B summarizes semantic features. The percentages indicate the percent of clauses (or T-units) in a text which exhibit some feature. For example, the *Time* obituaries contain 9 textual Themes. Since these obituaries contain 39 clauses, 23% of the clauses of the *Time* obituaries contained a textual Theme. Only overt (i.e. non-elliptical) Themes have been taken into account, hence percentages comparing the occurrence of simple and multiple Themes do not always total 100%. The rows labeled Marked Themes provide the occurrence of marked experiential Themes in clauses and in T-units. The percentage below the number of marked clause Themes is the percent of clauses which have marked Themes. The number given in the row for marked T-unit Themes gives the number of hypotactic clauses which function as Theme for their T-units. (Hypotactic clauses would not be considered Themes of clauses.) Since in these data all the marked clause Themes are also marked T-unit Themes, it is necessary to total the number of marked clause Themes with the number of marked T-unit Themes to obtain the percentage of T-units which contain a marked Theme of some sort. The percentages beside the figures Marked T-unit Themes give the percentage of T-units which have marked Themes.

3.3 Hypotheses 2 and 3 revisited

We have said earlier that the experiential content of the Themes contributes to what I have called 'the method of development' of a text. This is the place where hard counts of data are weakest. As a first approximation to this issue Table 6B classifies various meanings which were used as experiential Themes in the texts. Clearly the major text participants (for example references to Little Red Riding Hood and to the wolf) accounted for many experiential Themes in the data. The two major exceptions to this trend, *Farewell to Arms* and *Balloons and Air*, were expected to depart from this trend since they differ seriously from normal narrative. The *Balloons and Air* text did not have an obvious major participant; the text concerned a problem and how the problem is being solved. While the Hemingway text is from a narrative which has recognizable major participants, the section of the text which I analyzed never really got to the story. As mentioned above, the chapter I examined simply presents the setting for the story. In all the other texts, references to the major characters account for at least 31% of the Themes (in *Little Red Riding Hood*) and accounts for over 40% of the Themes in four texts (the three groups of obituaries, and Napoleon).

Since all of the texts in my data involve narration, we might expect that references to temporal and/or spatial locations would be used to move the texts along. With the exception of the expository text *Balloons and Air* (the text we would expect to be least likely to foreground these meanings) all texts in the data contain at least one thematic reference to temporal or spatial location. However, the number of references to temporal and spatial location clearly does not constitute a 'single method of development' in any of these texts in the sense that I intended this term in my early work. Further, temporal and spatial location are foregrounded to different degrees in the texts and in different ways in the texts. None of the texts in my data even approaches the thematic use of spatial location that Nie found in his travel guide for Hangzhou, and the travel brochures which Margaret Berry studied also used spatial location significantly more as Themes of clauses than any of my texts. Table 7 summarizes every non-embedded reference to temporal or spatial location which occurred in the clauses of my data. (For ease of comparison I have included at the bottom of Table 7 the comparable figures for Berry's study and Nie's study.) A non-embedded reference is one which is not a part of a larger group or phrase. The bold portions of Examples 1-4 below are non-embedded references to temporal or spatial location, while the italicized portions of the examples are embedded references to temporal and spatial locations and were not counted. These are reproduced below:

(i)   Mr. Brand, who was born **in Kewanee IL**, joined the Army and served as a platoon sergeant **in World War II**, ...

(ii)   Moving **to Hollywood**, he made his film debut **in 1950** as a hoodlum ...

(iii)   His first attempt at acting was in a *1946* Army Signal Corps movie

(iv)   As the *morning* sun lighted the beaches *of Dunkirk*, the first of hundreds of small boats pulled **onto the shore**.

Table 7: References to spatial and temporal location

Meaning Choice: Location / Genre type & source	Theme Temp	Theme Spa	Theme =Role	Other Temp	Other Spa	Other =Role	N-Rheme Temp	N-Rheme Spa	N-Rheme =Role	Total Temp	Total Spa	Total =Role
Time	2	0		1	4		6	7		9	11	
Obituary: NY Times	0	0		2		3	11	8	3	13		7
Obituary: Morn Sun	1	0		16	7		8	25		25	32	
Program Note	4			4	7		6	9		10		
Stories: LRRHood	3	3		0	2		4	23		7		
Stories: Napoleon	3	3		0	0		3	7		3	8	
Stories: BT Navy	3	3		0	0		3	6			10	
Stories: Hemingway	4	4		2	3		7	13			20	
Exposition: Balloons & Air	0			1	0		1	1	1		25	
Exposition: Coffee Party		2									25	
Exposition: Committee Meeting		3									25	
Berry Texts: Travel Brochure		10									25	
Berry Texts: Guide book		14									25	
Nie Long Text: Hzo Guide book	1			0	3		10	5		10	14	

I divided each clause in my data into three sections: Theme, N-Rheme, and Other. The Theme of a clause is the initial constituent of that clause and provides a framework for the interpretation of the message expressed by the clause. The N-Rheme of a clause is the final constituent of the clause, and is of interest because it is the location of the unmarked placement of New information. Since clauses usually contain more than two constituents (and so the combination of Theme and N-Rheme typically does not always exhaust the clause), I added an 'Other' category for material which was neither Theme nor N-Rheme.

The *Morning Sun* obituaries and *Little Red Riding Hood* resemble Berry's Coffee Party and Committee meeting texts in that none of these texts uses Spatial Location very often within the clause Themes. This is not to say that these texts do not refer to Spatial Locations, rather the spatial references typically form part of the focus of the messages and therefore occur regularly in the N-Rhemes of the clauses. The Hemingway text, with its focus on description of a scene, vaguely resembles a guidebook in its orientation to spatial location and this fact is reflected in its somewhat greater use of Spatial Location as Theme. However, Hemingway's writing is still very far from the guidebook genre which Berry and Nie found.

The texts I examined contained a number of thematic references to processes (up to 28 percent of the clauses of some texts referred to processes in the Themes.) The major source of these thematic references to process consisted of non-finite clauses beginning with verbs (e.g. the bolded clause in *Mr. Baumgardner worked for Federal Mogul for 35 years, **retiring in 1978**.*). Of course, the imperatives in *Little Red Riding Hood* also added to the number of verb initial clauses, and, finally, *Little Red Riding Hood* contained 15 instances of quoting verbs which began their clauses. (e.g. *"And where does your grandmother live?" **asked** the wolf politely.*) This ordering of verbal process and Sayer seems strongly associated with fairy tale language[14]. It is useful to note, however, that this inversion of Verbal process and Sayer was not found at the beginnings of the stories I have looked at. Rather, it began once the story was under way. In the case of *Little Red Riding Hood*, once the story was begun and the first Subject – Predicator

14. Of course inversion of Subject and predicator in quotatives is not limited to fairy tales. News reports often contain instances of this sort of inversion.

inversion was found, 15 of 18 quotative clauses used the Verbal Process as Theme[15].

3.4 Hypothesis I revisited

Finally, let us examine the evidence for the relation between thematic progression and genre type. One factor involved in thematic progression concerns the chain relations in which the various Themes of a text participate. As a means of exploring this issue I examined nominal groups which were found as part of the Themes of the clauses of the texts in my data and asked whether these nominal groups participated in chains. If the answer was *yes*, I then located the most recent previous member of the chain. Specifically, was the most recent previous member of the chain located in the Theme, Other, or N-Rheme portion of the earlier clause? Text I provides some examples of how I counted the data.

Text 1: A Farewell to Arms

1.   In the late summer of that year we lived in a house in a village that looked across *the river* and *the plain* to the mountains.

2a.   In **the bed of the river** there were pebbles and boulders, dry and white in the sun,

2b.   and **the water** was clear and swiftly moving and blue in the channels.

3a.   *Troops* went by the house and down the road,

3b.   and the dust they raised powdered *the leaves of the trees*.

4a.   **The trunks of the trees** too were dusty

4b.   and **the leaves** fell early that year

4c.   and we saw the troops marching along the road ...

5a.   **The plain** was rich with crops,

Each punctuated sentence in Text 1 is given a number and begins a new line. If a sentence contains more than one non-embedded clause, then each

---

15. In all cases of inversion of verbal process and Sayer, at least part of the quotation preceded the quoting clause. As a result, the general nature of the process in the quotative was not at issue. It was clear from the context that it would be some sort of verbal process. What was at issue was the specific identity of the Sayer. In other words, one important factor in the use of these inversions seems to be the placement of Sayer in a position of focus relative to the process. (A further factor relevant to the analysis of these constructions is that the quotatives would probably be read as a minor tone group (Tone 3 in a 1-3 combination).

non-embedded clause is given a letter and begins a new line.

Obvious members of chains are *the leaves* (Theme of 4b) which forms part of an identity chain which has *the leaves of the trees* in the N-Rheme of 3b as its last previous occurrence, and *the plain* (Theme of 5a) which forms part of an identity chain which has *the plain* in the N-Rheme of 1 as its last previous occurrence. Slightly less obvious is *the bed of the river* (Theme of 2a) which forms part of a similarity chain which has *the river* in the N-Rheme of 1 as its last previous occurrence. *The water* (the Theme of 2b) is the next member of the same similarity chain. In the case of 2b (*the water*), the last previous member of the similarity chain is in the Theme of 2a. The Theme of 4a, (*the trunks of the trees*) also belongs to a similarity chain. The last previous mention of the chain is found in the N-Rheme of 3b (*the leaves of the trees*). If we now focus on the coding of the data, the Theme of 2a (*in the bed of the river*) contains an item which belongs to a chain which has as its last previous member an item which has been mentioned in the N-Rheme of a clause in the previous sentence. It was therefore coded as N-Rheme of the previous sentence (= Prev s). The Theme of 5a (*the plain*) belongs to a chain whose last member occurred in the N-Rheme of the clause in sentence 1. Three sentences intervene between Sentence 1 and Sentence 5, hence this item was coded as N-Rheme, Skip 3. Some items belonged both to similarity chains (e.g. *the leaves* in 4b can be seen as part of a similarity chain with *the trunks of the trees* in 4a) and to identity chains (*the leaves* in 4b can be seen as part of an identity chain with *the leaves of the trees* in 3b). In these cases, the identity chain relation was counted, not the similarity chain relation.

Tables 8A, B, and C summarize the results of the counts of thematic progression by major text group.

Clearly the obituaries display a strong tendency to use a Theme iteration (Theme → Theme) progression. Exceptions to this pattern are concentrated in the Time Magazine obituaries. These exceptions result from the requirement that every obituary in *Time Magazine* begin with the Theme *Died*. Because of this requirement, all the remainder of the first sentence is either N-Rheme or Other. Since the second sentence of each of these obituaries elaborates on the person who died (not on the nature of the death), the second sentence in every obituary exemplifies either an N-Rheme → Theme progression or an Other → Theme progression (two variants of Linear thematic progression). The effect of this formula for writing obituaries in

Table 8A: Last Previous mention of Nominal Themes: Obituaries

	Same s Prev Cl	Prev s	Skip 1	Skip 2	Skip 3	Skip >3	Total
Theme							
Morning Sun		30	1	4	3	1	39
Time	2	8					10
N.Y. Times	1	9					10
Total	3	47	1	4	3	1	59
Other							
Morning Sun							0
Time		3					3
N.Y. Times		2	1				3
Total		5	1				6
N-Rheme							
Morning Sun							0
Time	1	3					4
N.Y. Times		1					1
Total	1	4					5

Time is increased by the fact that all the *Time Magazine* obituaries are very short. The longest *Time* obituary in my data contains only six sentences. Most contain only three sentences. A further consequence of the brevity of the *Time* obituaries is that it was rarely possible to have chains which skipped more than two sentences in these texts.

Little Red Riding Hood (LRRH) shows a similar pattern of theme iteration progression, though 14 (a significant minority) of the clause Themes in that story relate most recently to the N-Rheme of some previous clause. Three of these 14 N-Rheme → Theme sequences result when the most recent previous mention of a Theme is found in a quotative segment which has undergone Subject – Predicate inversion, and three others are found when the most recent mention of a Theme is found in a vocative at the end of a previous quotation. Both of these situations constitute special factors which affect this text but not the others in my data. The Napoleon text and *The Bath*

Tub Navy (BT Navy) also show a predominance of Theme iteration progressions, however the Hemingway chapter exhibits a strong trend towards a linear (N-Rheme → Theme) progression. However, I have already pointed out that this chapter is not truly a narrative, but rather the setting of the scene for a narrative.

In summary, then, the narratives reported on here show a general progression from a Theme iteration (Theme → Theme) progression in the story written for children toward a greater use of a linear (N-Rheme → Theme) progression in stories written for adults. The difference in Thematic progression results from the fact that the stories written for adults achieve a variety of tasks other than simple narration. If one looks at Text 1 taken from the Hemingway chapter we see that significant portions of this chapter can be viewed as elaborations of several basic sentences. For example, clauses 2A, 2B and 5A in Text 1 above can be seen to elaborate parts of clause 1, and the Themes of these three clauses direct the reader's attention back to the points of elaboration. The points being elaborated are located in the N-Rheme of clause 1. Roughly similar factors contribute to the use of

Table 8B: Last previous mention of nominal Themes: Stories

	Same S Prev Cl	Prev S	Skip 1	Skip 2	Skip 3	Skip >3	Total
Theme							
LRRH	3	16	7	1			27
Napoleon	4	3					7
BT Navy		1	2	2	1	2	8
Farewell	7	4				3	14
Other							
LRRH		2	1				3
Napoleon	2			1	1		4
BT Navy		2					2
Farewell				1			1
N-Rheme							
LRRH	2	7	3	1	1		14
Napoleon	3		1				4
BT Navy	1	1					2
Farewell	3	7			1	3	14

Table 8C: last previous mention of nominal Themes: program note and 'Balloons and Air'

	Same S Prev Cl	Prev S	Skip 1	Skip 2	Skip 3	Skip >3	Total
Theme							
Prog. Note	1	4					5
Balloons	1	1		1			3
Other							
Prog. Note		2					2
Balloons		1					1
N-Rheme							
Prog. Note		2					2
Balloons	1	2	1				4

N-Rheme → Theme and Other → Theme progressions in the other narrative texts. Thus, three of the seven instances of these patterns in the Napoleon text occur in descriptions of the situation which obtained at the time being described.

Finally, *Balloons and Air*, the sole example of expository writing, shows a tendency to use linear (N-Rheme → Theme) progressions. In three out of the four instances of this pattern, the second member of the pair elaborates a portion of the first member, and the cohesive tie in which the Theme participates indicates what is being elaborated.

4. Conclusion

This paper has explored hypotheses 1 and 3. A serious examination of hypothesis 2 would require an investigation of reader/listener responses to texts, which is beyond the scope of this study. Similarly, hypothesis 4, the relation of the experiential content of the Theme to the generic structure of texts, has not been systematically explored. The data discussed in this paper and in the works summarized in section 1 make it quite clear that hypotheses 1 and 3 are worth exploring carefully. Thematic progressions and the experiential content of the Themes do not occur randomly in these texts. In my data, the frequencies of the various thematic progressions vary with genre type, the experiential content of the Themes varies with genre type, and the proportions of times that certain meanings are expressed thematically also varies with genre type. Further, while my data did not support a careful investigation of the relation of these features to the generic structure of texts[16], the data did suggest that such a study would be profitable[17]. Having said that the thematic progressions and the experiential content of Themes in a text do not occur randomly, the problem remains of describing the patterns of occurrence in a positive way. These patterns are complicated. Many of the complications derive from the particular purposes of the text at a given point. It is not reasonable that we should expect an entire text to do only one thing. Stories not only must recount events, they must evaluate, they often tell what could have occurred but did not, and so forth. As the author changes task and responds to different pressures, the Themes of the clauses of the text will reflect and encode those changes. The texts I have chosen are all narrative in some sense and so may be assumed to encode some basic similarity of purpose. I have taken pains in the choice of my data, however, to demonstrate that what may appear at first glance to be instances of similar purposes may involve important differences in actual situation to which the participants respond. These differences are encoded in the language of the texts. Thus, while *Farewell to Arms* is a narrative, that portion of the novel which I analyzed will be seen as a very strange narrative unless we notice that at that point it is **not** a narrative, it sets the scene. We should expect this fact to affect the Thematic choices made in the text at this place. Because of the nature of the texts I used as data, I have focused on the presence of elaboration as a source of deviation from ordinary patterns of thematic progression. It is easy to show that the presence or absence of elaboration correlates with the contextual construct in my data – the obituaries and *Little Red Riding Hood* (a story which is told to children) have little elaboration while the other texts use elaboration more often. It is also easy

16. In the original conception of this paper, I wished to use a categorization of verb types such as the one proposed by Longacre (1983 and 1989) as a means of indicating the different functions which clauses might play in a text. It seemed clear to me that such a categorization would correlate with different thematic content. It was not possible to explore these issues in the present paper, however, because I did not choose data which exhibited sufficient variation in internal structure or in information types to make it worth exploring.

17. See Cloran this volume for some interesting suggestions.

to see that the presence of elaboration correlates with a certain type of experiential content of the clause Themes and thematic progression. Thus, in the data discussed in section 2 of this paper, many of the exceptions to the general patterns of thematic progression and the patterns in the experiential content of the Themes are related to genre types.

References

Bäcklund, Ingegerd. 1989. To sum up: Initial infinitives as cues to the reader. Paper presented at the Sixteenth International Systemic Congress. June 12-16, 1989. Helsinki, Finland.

Bäcklund, Ingegerd. 1990. Theme in English telephone conversation. Paper delivered at the 17th International Systemic Congress, Stirling, Scotland. June 1990.

Benson, James D., William S. Greaves, and Glen Stillar. 1992. Motivating text and construing context in two film reviews. Paper presented to the 19th International Systemic Functional Congress, July 13-18, 1992.

Berry, Margaret. 1987. The functions of place names. *Leeds Studies in English, New Series* XVIII: Studies in honour of Kenneth Cameron, edited by Thorlac Turville-Petre and Margaret Gelling, 71-88. Leeds: School of English, University of Leeds.

Brown, Gillian, and George Yule. 1983. *Discourse Analysis*. Cambridge: Cambridge University press.

Chafe, Wallace. 1976. Givenness, contrastiveness, definiteness, subjects, topics, and point of view. *Subject and Topic*, edited by Charles Li, 27-55. New York: Academic Press.

Chafe, W.L. 1984. How people use adverbial clauses. *Proceedings of the tenth annual meeting of the Berkeley Linguistics Society* Berkeley: Berkeley Linguistics Society, 437-449.

Daneš, Frantisek. 1974. Functional sentence perspective and the organisation of the text. *Papers on Functional Sentence Perspective*, edited by Frantisek Daneš, 106-128. The Hague: Mouton.

Downing, Angela. 1991. An alternative approach to Theme: A systemic functional perspective. *Word* 42.2, 119-143.

Francis, Gill. 1989. Thematic selection and distribution in written discourse. *Word* 40, 201-221.

Francis, Gill. 1990. Theme in the daily press. *Occasional Papers in Systemic Linguistics* 4, 51-87.

Fries, Peter H. 1981. On the status of Theme: Arguments from discourse. *Forum Linguisticum* 6(1), 1-38.

Fries, Peter H. 1992. The structuring of written English text. *Current Research in Functional Grammar, Discourse, and Computational Linguistics with a Foundation in Systemic Theory*, edited by M.A.K. Halliday and F.C.C. Peng. Special Issue of *Language Sciences* 14.4, 1-28.

Fries. Peter H. 1993. Information flow in written advertising. *Language, Communication and Social Meaning*, edited by James Alatis, 336-352. Georgetown University Round Table on Languages and Linguistics, 1992. Washington DC: Georgetown University Press.

Fries, Peter H. *in press a*. On Theme, Rheme and discourse goals. *Advances in Written Text Analysis*, edited by Malcolm Coulthard, 229-249. London: Routledge and Kegan Paul.

Fries, Peter H. *in press b*. Patterns of information in initial position in English. *Discourse and Meaning in Society: Functional perspectives* edited by Peter H. Fries and Michael Gregory. Norwood NJ: Ablex Publishers.

Gundel, Jeanette. 1977. The role of topic and comment in linguistic theory. Bloomington, IN: Indiana Linguistics Club.

Halliday, M.A.K. 1967. Notes on transitivity and theme in English: Part 2. *Journal of Linguistics* 3.2, 199-244.

Halliday, M.A.K. 1970. Language structure and language function. *New Horizons in Linguistics*, edited by John Lyons, 140-164. Harmondsworth: Penguin.

Halliday, M.A.K. 1985. *An Introduction to Functional Grammar.* London: Edward Arnold.

Halliday, M.A.K. 1989. *Spoken and Written Language.* London: Oxford University Press.

Halliday, M.A.K. 1993. The construction of knowledge and value in the grammar of scientific discourse: Charles Darwin's *The Origin of Species.* M.A.K. Halliday and J. R. Martin, 1993, 86-105.

Halliday, M.A.K. and James R. Martin, 1993. *Writing Science: Literacy and discursive power.* London: Falmer Press.

Hasan, Ruqaiya. 1984. Coherence and cohesive harmony. *Understanding Reading Comprehension*, edited by James Flood, 181-219. Newark DE: International Reading Association.

Hasan, Ruqiaya. 1985. The texture of a text. In *Language, Context and Text: Aspects of language in a siocial semiotic perspective*, by M.A.K Halliday and Ruqaiya Hasan, 76-96. Geelong, Victoria: Deakin University Press.

Hasan, Ruqaiya. *in press*. The conception of context in texts. *Discourse in Society: Functional perspectives*, edited by Peter H. Fries and Michael Gregory. Norwood, NJ: Ablex Publishers.

Huddleston, Rodney. 1988. Constituency, multifunctionality and grammaticalization in Halliday's functional grammar. *Journal of Linguistics* 24, 137-174.

Huddleston, Rodney. 1991. Further remarks on Halliday's functional grammar: A reply to Matthiessen and Martin. *Occasional Papers in Systemic Linguistics* 5, 75-129.

Huddleston, Rodney. 1992. On Halliday's functional grammar: A reply to Martin and to Martin and Matthiessen. *Occasional Papers in Systemic Linguistics* 6, 197-212.

Hudson, Richard. 1986. Systemic grammar. Review article. *Linguistics* 24, 791-815.

Hunt, Kellogg. 1965. *Grammatical Structures Written at Three Grade Levels*. Champaign, IL: NCTE.

Longacre, Robert E. 1981. A spectrum and profile approach to discourse analysis. *Text* 1.4, 337-359.

Longacre, Robert. 1983. Vertical threads of cohesion in discourse. *Papers in Textlinguistics* 38, 99-111.

Longacre, Robert. 1989. Two hypotheses regarding text generation and analysis. *Discourse Processes* 12, 413-460.

Longacre, Robert E. 1990. *Storyline Concerns and Word Order Typology*. Los Angeles, CA: Department of Linguistics, University of California at Los Angeles. (Introduction)

Martin, James. R. 1986. Grammaticalising ecology: the politics of baby seals and kangaroos. *Language, Semiotics, Ideology*, edited by T. Threadgold, E.A. Grosz, G. Kress & M.A.K. Halliday, 225-268. Sydney: Sydney Association for Studies in Society and Culture (Sydney Studies in Society and Culture 3).

Martin, James R. 1989. *Factual Writing: Exploring and challenging social reality*. London: Oxford University Press. Second edition.

Martin, James. 1992. *English Text: System and structure*. Amsterdam: John Benjamins

Martin, James R. and Joan Rothery. 1986. What a functional approach to the writing task can show teachers about 'good writing'. *Functional Approaches to Writing: Research perspectives*, edited by Barbara Couture, 241-265. Norwood, NJ: Ablex.

Mathesius, V. 1939. O tak zvaném aktuálním cleneni vetném [On the so-called Functional Sentence Perspective]. *Slovo a Slovestnost* 5, 171-174.

Nie, Long. 1991. An analysis of texts of different genres in terms of thematic selections and process types. Unpublished Manuscript.

Plum, Gunther. 1988. Textual and contextual conditioning in spoken English: A genre-based approach. Ph. D. Dissertation. Sydney: University of Sydney.

Prideaux, Gary D. and John T. Hogan. 1993. Markedness as a discourse management device. *Word* 344, 397-411.

Ragan, Peter. 1987. Meaning in the communication of a set of instructions. Ph.D. Dissertation, National University of Singapore.

Rothery, J. 1990. *Story Writing in Primary School: assessing narrative type genres.* Ph.D. Thesis. Department of Linguistics, University of Sydney.

Thompson, Sandra A. 1985. Initial vs final purpose clauses in written English discourse. *Text* 5 1-2, 55-84.

Ure, Jean. 1971. Lexical density and register differentiation. *Applications of Linguistics* edited by G.E. Perrin and J.L.M. Trim, 443-452. Cambridge: Cambridge University Press.

Vande Kopple, W.J. 1991 Themes, thematic progressions, and some implications for understanding discourse. *Written Communication* 8, 311-347.

Wang, Ling. 1991. Analysis of thematic variations in *Buried Child* Paper delivered to the First Biennial Conference on Discourse. Hangzhou Peoples Republic of China. June 7-9, 1991.

Wang, Ling. 1992. The theory of Theme and its application to drama analysis. MA Thesis, Department of English Language and Literature, Peking University.

Winter, Eugene O. 1977. *Replacement as a Function of Repetition: A study of some of its principal features in the clause relations of contemporary English.* #77-70,036, Ann Arbor MI: University Microfilms.

Xiao, Qun. 1991. Toward thematic selection in different genre: Fables and recipies. Unpublished manuscript.

10

Defining and Relating Text Segments:
Subject and Theme in Discourse[*]

Carmel Cloran
Macquarie University

1. Introduction

In this paper I will attempt to demonstrate, via the analysis of extended
extracts of text, the semantic functions of the elements of mood structure,
Subject and Finite; I will also consider the function of thematic structure in
relating 'chunks' of text. It will be claimed that the semantic functions of
Subject and Finite define and delimit segments of text. However, in order
to support this interpretation, these structural elements – Subject and Finite
– must be considered from the point of view of the semantic nature of the
units that actualise them rather than from their ordering vis-a-vis each other,
which happens to be the usual perspective on these structural elements, at
least so far as the grammatical discussion of these elements is concerned.

1.1 Text in the systemic functional model

Text is a semantic unit (Halliday 1977a: 195) so that, in the identification and
delimitation of 'chunks' of text the relevant stratum of language is the
semantic stratum. This is not to suggest that the lexicogrammatical stratum
is irrelevant. On the contrary, it is via wording that linguistic meaning is
construed; it is only via wording that linguistic meaning is accessible. The
lexicogrammatical stratum of language has been comprehensively described
in terms of its constituent units, classes, structures and systems. One of the

---

* The analysis presented in this paper is based on research undertaken for my doctoral
dissertation. While the dissertation has been successfully submitted, the research itself is very
much in progress, and far from complete.

issues yet to be addressed, at least in systemic functional linguistics, is the possibility of describing the semantic stratum in such terms. Pioneering work has already been undertaken in this area, notably by Hasan (e.g. 1983; 1989). Hasan proposes that the basic constituent unit of text is the message. She characterises the relationship between text and message as follows: a message is the smallest unit which is capable of realising an element of the generic structure of a text (Hasan 1991: 81). A message is realised by the lexicogrammatical unit clause, though the realisational relationship is not a one-to-one affair. Thus, according to Hasan, a message is typically realised by a clause which, in order to serve this function, must have at least two characteristics: (i) it must be ranking, i.e. non- embedded, and (ii) it must be non-projecting. The latter condition implies that a lexicogrammatical unit made up of a projecting and a projected clause is considered to construe just one single message.

The text extracts used throughout this chapter have been segmented into messages on the basis of Hasan's definition. Each extract is taken from dialogues which occurred during everyday routine interaction between mothers and their preschool-age children. Extract 1 represents a part of one such dialogue. The extract has been divided into two segments within each of which a number of 'chunks' are identified. These 'chunks' are termed rhetorical activity. Each segment of the extract will be discussed in terms of the kinds of rhetorical activities identified. After this informal analysis of extract 1, I will address the questions: what are the criteria by which these rhetorical activities may be recognised and in what relationship do they stand to one another? Finally I will attempt to locate the category 'rhetorical activity' within the overall framework of Halliday's systemic functional model of language.

1.2 An informal analysis

Consider extract 1, where Stephen (aged 3.5 years) and his mother talk while having lunch. Transcription conventions[1] are given at the end of this paper.

---

1. The extracts used in this paper have been taken from research directed by Ruqaiya Hasan at Macquarie University. I thank her for permission to use this data.

Extract 1: Segment 1

208	Stephen	This is a boat that flies
209	Mother	A boat that flies?
210	Stephen	yes
211	Mother	Is it a hydroplane?
212	Stephen	Yes
213	Mother	A hydroplane is a plane that can land on the water
214	Stephen	Yes
215	Mother	Or is it a hydrofoil?
216	Stephen	No
217		It's a hydroplane …
218		This is – that's the water
219		and it saves people
220	Mother	Does it?
221	Stephen	Yes
222		Every person that's um that's got drowned
223	Mother	Oh .. There's a helicopter that goes up and down the beaches in summer watching out for people
224		It's called a rescue helicopter
225	Stephen	Oh that's [? mine] (= THAT'S WHAT MINE IS)
226	Mother	I think it mainly watches um for sharks
227		but it might also rescue people
228		if they're a long way out from the beach and in trouble
229		It's a good idea isn't it?
230	Stephen	Is it – this is one of them
231	Mother	That's a rescue helicopter, is it?
232	Stephen	Yes
233	Mother	Where's the pilot?
234	Stephen	Um this man
235	Mother	Which?

In message 208 of this extract, Stephen initiates the exchange by making an observation about the inherent characteristics of an object that is co-present in the immediate material situation, referring to it exophorically as *this*. Though we do not have any means of ascertaining the identity of the object it seems fairly safe to assume that it is not, in reality, *a boat that flies*. Rather, Stephen is drawing his mother's attention to either a representation of such an object in the form of a toy or is imaginatively assigning these characteristics to some object which does not inherently possess them, e.g. some food item that is to hand. This latter interpretation would be consistent with the kind of imaginative play that children of his age frequently engage in.

The talk centres around this situationally identified object for about 24 messages (up to message 233) with, however, some sidetracking initiated by the mother. Thus, in message 213, she provides a generalisation which serves to define the signifier she has suggested in message 211 for the object around which Stephen's observation is centred, namely, *hydroplane*. The talk returns to the situational object and Stephen expands on its function.

In messages 223-229 the mother introduces an account of the existence of an indefinite object – *a helicopter* – which serves the kind of function Stephen has identified for his object, i.e. that of saving people. The mother's account is interrupted by Stephen (message 225) who observes that his object is a member of the class of objects named by the mother as a rescue helicopter. In other words, message 225 *That's mine* is interpreted as 'that's what mine is'.

At the end of her account, the mother makes an evaluative comment on the existence and function of the rescue helicopter – *It's a good idea, isn't it?* – but the child returns to his own observations about his situational object. The mother enters into his observation by expanding it to include a commentary on the whereabouts of a related entity – *Where's the pilot?*

In segment 1, the main entity around which the talk centres is referred to exophorically by the demonstrative *this*; it is this situationally identified entity, whose inherent characteristics (208) and habitual function (219) are described by the child. The rhetorical, ie linguistic activity being undertaken by the interactants may be called *observation*. Informally speaking, the rhetorical activity of *observation* consists in making linguistic observations about an entity that is perceptually observable in the here and now of the talk, as the referent of *this* (208) is in extract 1; furthermore, for the linguistic activity to have the status of *observation*, this situationally present entity must be described in terms of some inherent attributes, which are, therefore, construed as being timeless or characteristic. Within this *observation* are enclosed three other rhetorical activities: (i) generalisation; (ii) account; and (iii) commentary. Each of these is discussed briefly below.

(i) **Generalisation:** This rhetorical activity consists in making class exhaustive reference to whatever class of entity is mentioned irrespective of its taxonomic location. Such class exhaustive entities are described in terms of characteristic (i.e. timeless) attributes. In extract 1, message 213 constitutes the type of activity where some inherent attributes are ascribed to a non-specific entity representing the entire class of entity *hydroplane*. Message 213, thus, represents the activity of **generalisation.**

(ii) **Account:** This type of rhetorical activity consists in giving a linguistic account of a non-co-present (i.e. situationally absent) non-class-exhaustive entity in terms of inherent attributes or characteristic functions. Messages 223- 228 give an account of the existence and habitual function of an entity – *a helicopter*. Note that this entity is neither present in the here and now of talk, nor does it represent an entire class. The *account* constituted by messages 223-228 is interrupted by an interpolation by the child in his message 225. This is a return to the original *observation* concerning an inherent attribute of the perceptually observable (though imaginary) entity; it does not form part of either the *generalisation* or the *account*.

(iii) **Commentary** is the third type of rhetorical activity identified in extract 1. This class of rhetorical activity is defined as one where a speaker comments on an event or state of affairs in which a co-present (and therefore perceptually identifiable) entity is engaged at the time of speaking. Thus messages 233-235 in extract 1 initiate an undeveloped *commentary* on the non-habitual concurrent state of a co-present entity *the pilot. Commentary* differs from *observation* in terms of the non-habitual nature of the event in which the co-present entity is involved.

Message 229 is an *observation* but, unlike the earlier *observation* that began with 208, the *observation* in 229 refers to textual rather than situational phenomena. Thus, in message 229, the item *It* refers to the previous messages (226-228) assigning the content of these a positive evaluation. To distinguish this type of *observation* from the other type, I will refer to it as textual *observation,* using the abbreviated form *t-observation*, for short.

The 28 messages constituting this part of the extract may be schematically represented as shown in Figure 1.

Figure 1 shows the relation among the rhetorical activities identified for segment 1 of extract 1. Where a rhetorical activity is enclosed, or embedded

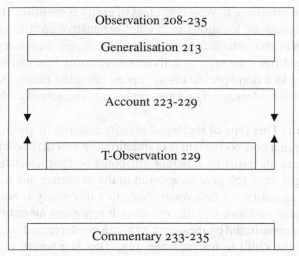

Figure 1: Schematic representation of extract 1, segment 1

(to use a grammatical analogy) within another rhetorical activity, this relationship is shown by boxing the embedded activity within the matrix one. Where an embedded rhetorical activity is temporarily suspended, suspension and subsequent resumption is indicated by arrows. Thus in Figure 1, the *generalisation, account and commentary* are considered to be embedded within the *observation*, and the *account*, which is temporarily suspended at message 225 due to the resumption of the *observation* in this message, has embedded within it a *t-observation*.

   The precise way in which the relation of embedding is established will be discussed presently. Suffice to say at this point that Figure 1 illustrates in a concrete way that the *observation* initiated by the child in message 208 is the context for the mother's *generalisation, account and commentary*; and that the immediate context for the *t-observation* (message 229) is the foregoing *account* constituted by messages 223-228. The structure of segment 1, in terms of its constituent units, may be represented, again by analogy with grammatical phenomena, as shown below:

observation[generalisation][account[observation]][commentary]

1.2.1 *Summary of the analysis of segment 1*

Within the span of the 28 messages of Segment 1, four kinds of rhetorical activity have been identified – *observation, generalisation, account* and *commentary*. An *observation* is defined as the kind of rhetorical activity which involves the characteristic states or activities of co-present objects or persons other than the interactants. A *commentary*, by contrast, is defined as the kind of rhetorical activity involving the non-habitual (punctiliar) states or activities of co-present objects or persons, including the interactants. An *account* is the kind of rhetorical activity which construes the typical states or activities of particular absent persons or objects. Finally, a *generalisation* is said to be a rhetorical activity that expresses the characteristic states or activities of classes of objects or persons.

Hopefully, this brief recapitulation makes it clear that certain linguistic features are being used to provide the criteria for the recognition of the categories identified. Thus the orientation of events has been described, so far, in terms of usuality – whether or not habitual states or activities are being expressed. Further, the experiential identification of entities has been described in terms of their co-presence or absence in the immediate material environment of the speech event, and more delicate distinctions have been made within these broad categories. Two specific linguistic phenomena stand out as crucial: the temporal orientation of the messages, and the attributes of the entity around which the linguistic activity revolves. This being the case, where a message contains more than one entity the question naturally arises: is there any motivated way of determining which entity is the crucial one? This question will be addressed in section 2, but before this I will return to other segments of extract 1, in order to informally identify other cases of the types of rhetorical activities already brought to attention, as well as to identify certain other new ones, which have so far not been mentioned.

1.2.2 *Segment 2*

Extract 1 is part of a lengthy dialogue between Stephen and his mother. The next segment is constituted by messages 236-291. However, since this segment is itself fairly lengthy, it will be divided into two parts – segment 2a and segment 2b – to ensure easier discussion. Segment 2a consists of messages 236-264, segment 2b, of messages 265-291.

Extract 1: Segment 2a

236	Stephen	What does pilots do?
237	Mother	Drive aeroplanes and helicopters
238		They're really drivers ..
239	Stephen	Are the captains are?
240	Mother	Captains? Um I think the captain is the pilot that's in charge
241		Sometimes aeroplanes have more than one pilot
242		because the very big aeroplanes that can fly for a long time..they need more than one pilot
243		so the captain is the man in charge
244		and he's in charge of the people that come and offer you drinks and dinner and things too
245		He's in charge of everybody, the captain
246	Stephen	Even the – even the people that um fly the aeroplane?
247	Mother	Well I think the captain -
248		Yes he's in charge of the other people that drive the aeroplane
249		and I think the captain drives the aeroplane sometimes
250	Stephen	Yeah …
251		[?]
252	Mother	I can't hear what you said
253		because you filled your mouth full of peanut butter sandwich
254		It's hard talking to you <255> isn't it?
255		when you've got your mouth full
256		It's a bit rough I think
257	Stephen	Is the captain in charge of the um ..the um – the trees Mummy?
258	Mother	No, the captain's not in charge of the trees
259		He's in charge of all the people on – that work on the aeroplane
260	Stephen	Oh
261	Mother	The stewards and the stewardesses and the other-
262	Stephen	Stewart!
263	Mother	Stewards, not Stewart, steward
264		The steward is the man that offers you drinks, coffee, tea

The *commentary* of messages 233-235 (segment 1) ends rather abruptly as the child, ignoring the mother's question in message 235 and apparently losing interest in the fantasy, initiates a *generalisation* concerning the habitual activities of the class of entity that the mother had introduced, i.e.

pilots. The talk centres around this entity and lexically related generic entities – (the) captain(s), the steward – up to and including message 264. The **generalisation** constituted by these messages is, however, interrupted by messages 252-256, where the talk centres around the interactants and the verbal activity itself. This segment arises as a result of the nature of the non-linguistic activity of eating that is taking place at the same time as the linguistic one: the former impinges on the latter causing transmission difficulties. Thus the mother recounts the effect of the child's non-linguistic behaviour on her, and presents her negative evaluation of the behaviour in an **observation** (see messages 254-256).

Channel difficulties overcome, the talk continues as before until message 262-264 at which point some confusion arises as a result of the near identity of the signifiers *steward* and *Stewart*. In response to his mother's identification of the referent of the signifier *steward* (message 264), Stephen identifies the referent of the signifier *Stewart* (message 265). *Stewart* subsequently becomes the entity around which the talk centres, leading us into segment 2b.

Extract 1: Segment 2b

265	Stephen	And the – Stewart is um is um Joanne's Mum – I mean Dad
266	Mother	That's right
267		Stewart is Joanne's Dad ..
268	Stephen	Is he a printer?
269	Mother	Yes, he is a printer ..
270	Stephen	Is he a captain?
271	Mother	No he doesn't go in an aeroplane
272	Stephen	Well why?
273	Mother	Because he's a printer
274		He ah works in a place where they print magazines and things
275	Stephen	Does he work in a plane where they print things?
276	Mother	No, no a place
277		He works in a place, not a plane
278		He doesn't work in an aeroplane
279	Stephen	But Mummy when he doesn't go to work sometimes
280		does he um does he go on a aeroplane?
281	Mother	Yes, Stewart's been on an aeroplane
282		Helen and Stewart went to America
283	Stephen	Oh

284	Mother	They came to visit us last time we were in America
285		when you were in Mummy's tummy
286	Stephen	Oh
287	Mother	They went in an aeroplane
288		and then they caught an aeroplane back home
289	Stephen	Oh did Joanne come with them?
290	Mother	No
291		Joanne hadn't been born then ..

In segment 2b, in response to Stephen's probings, the mother provides an account of the personal and professional role held by Stewart – a unique and, therefore, non-class-exhaustive non-co-present entity. The account is elaborated when the mother, in response to Stephen's determination to locate Stewart within the semantic domain of aeroplane crew covered in the previous generalisation, recounts a previous event in which Stewart travelled by aeroplane. This recount centres again around Stewart but also includes Helen who, being conjoined with Stewart as the relevant entity, is presumably Stewart's wife. In message 289 Joanne, Stewart's daughter (see messages 265-267) displaces Stewart as the entity at the centre of the recount.

In this segment there are then two rhetorical activities – an *account* and a *recount*. The *recount* is considered to be embedded within the *account* which is itself embedded within the *generalisation* constituted by the messages of the previously discussed segment. In other words, the *generalisation* of messages 236-264 provides the context of the *account* which in turn provides the context of the *recount*. A schematic representation of these relationships is presented in Figure 2 which incorporates the information from Figure 1 as well in order to show the relationship between the two segments of the extract.

As was the case in Figure 1, in Figure 2 wherever a rhetorical activity is enclosed by a solid line within another activity the relationship between the two is one of embedding. Where a rhetorical activity is bounded by a dotted horizontal line, (e.g. at the *generalisation* beginning at message 236) the relation between this activity and the prior activity is considered to be one of expansion, to continue the grammatical analogy. In other words, the *generalisation* is considered to expand the previous *observation* with its embedded activities. Note that *recount-1* which interrupts the *generalisation* is, nevertheless, included within it. This is because *recount-1* (with its

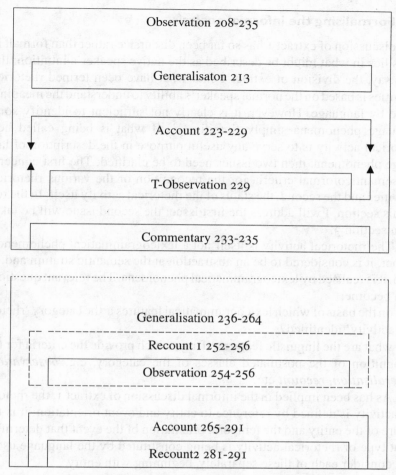

**Figure 2: Schematic representation of extract 1
(messages 208-291)**

embedded *observation*) has a function within the context of the *generalisation*: it serves to facilitate it. This included activity is bounded by broken rather than solid lines, so as to distinguish it from the embedded ones.

These relations of embedding, expansion and inclusion and the basis on which they are distinguished will be discussed in section 3, after the formal criteria for identifying the crucial entity have been discussed.

2. Formalising the informal analysis

The discussion of extract I has so far been discursive rather than formal. Its basis lies in what might be described as the native speaker's intuition; that is to say, the division of extract I into what have been termed rhetorical activities is based on the normal speaker's ability to understand the meanings made by language. However, it is clearly not sufficient to identify some language phenomena simply 'intuitively'. If what is being called here rhetorical activity is to serve any useful purpose in the description of language phenomena, then two issues need to be clarified. The first concerns the semanticoformal criteria for the recognition of the various rhetorical activities and the second, the status of the rhetorical activity itself. In the rest of this section, I will address the first issue; the second issue will be taken up in section 3.

The rhetorical activity is itself not a lexicogrammatical phenomenon. Rather, it is considered to be an abstraction at the semantic stratum and, as such, it is realised by lexicogrammatical phenomena. The relevant questions then become:

(i)   on the basis of which lexicogrammatical features is the category 'rhetorical activity' identified?

(ii) what are the linguistic features, if any, which provide the criteria for the recognition of the postulated classes of the category, e.g. *observation, generalisation, recount* etc?

As has been implied in the informal discussion of extract I, the rhetorical activity is defined by reference to entity and event orientation; it is the nature of the entity and the temporal orientation of the event that determine what type of rhetorical activity is being constituted by the language use. I will consider each of these separately, beginning with entity.

2.1 Entity

It is important to note that entity is a semantic notion; its lexicogrammatical realisation is effected through the selection of some nominal group having a functional role in the clause. Halliday (1985: 159ff) characterises the experiential structure of the nominal group in terms of the specification of its "semantic core" – the Thing. Thus the Thing may be described with varying degrees of specificity in terms of its membership of a set, its number, quality and class by a Deictic, Numerative, Epithet and Classifier respectively. The nominal group as a whole may thus be broadly characterised as expressing the description of an object. Entities usually do occur within any object description though this is not necessarily the case, for example there is not a single entity in *It's hot outside*, despite the nominal group *it*. The absence of entities is discussed in section 2.3.

2.1.1 Central entity

Since a message may potentially contain more than one entity, I will refer to that entity which enters into a configuration with event orientation as the **central entity** (hereafter CE). The crucial question then becomes: given the presence in a message of a number of entities, which of these entities may be identified as the entity on the basis of which the identification of rhetorical activity is made? To answer this question, we need to examine those instances of rhetorical activities where an entity was considered central in the identification of the rhetorical activity as an instance of some specific type. As the informal discussion of Segments 1-2 shows this is the case with, for example, *commentary, observation* and *account:* in identifying each of these activities, the concept of central entity was crucial. However, instead of going back to the earlier examples, I will use the case of *commentary* exemplified in extract 2:

Extract 2:

269	Mother	Come on .. eat your dinner
270	Karen	Oh
271	Mother	Now
272	Karen	I can't eat it now
273		'cause it's already dirty
274	Mother	Well finish your sandwich
275	Karen	Is it, Mum?
276	Mother	Mm

Here, the *commentary* is constituted by messages 272-273 and continued in messages 275-276. The entity around which the talk centres – the CE – in message 272 is considered to be *I*, while in messages 273 and 275, the role of CE is played by *it* (= Karen's dinner). It was suggested in section 1.2 that to be treated as CE in a *commentary*, an entity must possess specific attributes. It is these attributes that act as one of the criteria in the recognition of messages as constitutive of **commentary**: the CE must either play the role of interactant (expressed lexicogrammatically by 1st or 2nd person pronouns *I, you, we*) or it must be an entity that is co-present with the interactants in the material situation (referred to by (a) 3rd person pronouns *he, she, it, they,* or (b) demonstratives *this, that,* or (c) a nominal group premodified by the specific determiner, e.g. *the x* where *x* refers to some co-present person or object.) However, it is possible for a message to contain two object descriptions, both of which refer to the interactant(s), and/or to some co-present object, as for example in message 272 of extract 2 *I can't eat it now*. This implies the need for some further criterion to determine which of the (possible) entities should be taken as CE; for example, in 272, should it be *I*, referring to Karen as an interactant or *it*, referring to Karen's dinner, a co-present object. One such promising criterion is the location of entities in the message.

It has already been pointed out that the entities at the centre of the talk in extract 2 – its CEs – are *I* in 272 and *it* in 273 and 275; that both expressions refer either to an interactant or to something co-present in the material situation; note also now the difference between the *it* of 272 as compared with the *it* of 273 and 275. Only the latter instances of *it* – those in 273 and 275 – have the same location in the message as *I* does in 272: all occur within the point of departure of the message. The *it* of 272 is different: it is not located in the point of departure. (The term 'point of departure' refers to the semantic value construed by the lexicogrammatical element Theme; for discussion, see section 3.2.2).

The observation that all the expressions acting as CE in the extract 2 **commentary** occur within the message's point of departure suggests a hypothesis regarding the crucial criterion for the identification of a CE: the CE is that entity which occurs within the scope of the message's point of departure. Consider, however, extract 3:

Extract 3: Account
152 Mother   What does Claudia do at school Stephen?
[messages 153-156 are omitted as irrelevant to the topic of Claudia's activities]
157 Stephen She does what I do
158 Mother   Does she? ..
159   Drawing?
160 Stephen Yes

161	Mother	Painting?
162	Stephen	Yes
163	Mother	Cutting?
164	Stephen	Yes
165	Mother	Sticking?
166	Stephen	Yes
167	Mother	Gluing?
168	Stephen	Yes ..
169		Everything she does

The messages of this extract constitute an *account* which, as pointed out in section 1.2, is the type of rhetorical activity that concerns the habitual activities or states of a particular but absent object or person, i.e. a particular entity that is not co-present in the speech situation. In extract 3 it is the habitual activities of the absent entity, Claudia around which the talk centres. Note that message 169 contains two entities – *everything* and *she* (Claudia). If the CE were always that entity which occurs in the message's point of departure, then the candidate for CE in message 169 is *everything*. If *everything* is considered to be the CE of message 169 then this message cannot be considered to be part of the same *account* since, as previously stated, a property of any entity capable of functioning as CE in an *account* is that it should refer to a particular absent entity. Clearly, *everything,* not being particular, would not qualify on that ground; rather, a message having *everything* as CE would constitute a *generalisation* since the criterial property of the CE in this type of activity is class-exhaustiveness. However, the analysis of message 169 as a *generalisation* is less than satisfactory. Intuitively, this message does seem to construe the same kind of activity as the previous messages, i.e. to be part of the *account* of what Claudia does. If message 169 is to be considered part of the *account*, then the only entity that could be seen as central from this point of view is *she*. But *she* does not occur within the message's point of departure. It follows, then, that the simple hypothesis put forward above must be abandoned. An entity does not attain the status of CE simply by virtue of occurring within the message's point of departure.

Is there, then, no connection between these two concepts - CE and message point of departure? To answer this question, the cases on the basis of which the hypothesis was put forward must be examined more closely.

A survey of the rhetorical activities under discussion will show that the CE in all cases, except message 169 of extract 3, does indeed occur within the message's point of departure. The problem is resolved when closer inspection reveals that, with the exception of message 169 in extract 3, all messages constituting rhetorical activities are realised by clauses with unmarked Theme; message 169 in which the realising clause has a marked Theme is the only exception to this general rule. This implies that the entity considered central in the rhetorical activities under focus here possesses two attributes in all cases except message 169 of extract 3: the CE occurs within the message's point of departure and, in addition, it is 'modally responsible' in the sense that it is lexicogrammatically realised by Subject. A CE is therefore **typically** that entity which carries modal responsibility, being realised by Subject. The fact that it also typically occurs within the message's point of departure can be attributed (i) to the higher probability of the occurrence of declarative over other MOOD types, and (ii) to the higher probability of the selection of unmarked Theme rather than marked Theme (Halliday 1985).

2.1.2 Subject as central entity

It is pertinent to ask: why should the CE be realised as Subject? Here we may appeal to Halliday's claim that Subject is the modally responsible nominal (1977a:183). His semantic gloss for Subject is the entity in which is vested responsibility for the validity of the proposition, the entity "by reference to which the proposition can be affirmed or denied …. in respect of which the assertion is claimed to have validity" (Halliday, 1985: 76). The modal responsibility of the Subject is well exemplified in extract 4:

Extract 4:

300	Mother	Don't swing on that chair please
301	Karen	This not the – this chair's swinging 'round by itself
302	Mother	It doesn't swing by itself
303		You push it around
304	Karen	No I'm not
305	Mother	It doesn't swing by itself Karen
306	Karen	Yes it does
307	Mother	It doesn't

In message 301 and 302 the argument centres around the actions of the

Subject as manifested by the entity fulfilling this role and instantiated as *this/that chair*. The point of reference in the argument shifts in messages 303 and 304 where actions of the child (*you*) are affirmed (303) and denied (304). In messages 305-307 the resting point of the argument returns to the entity *this chair:* it is the action of this entity realised by Subject that is denied and affirmed.

Note that I closed section 2.1.1, with the suggestion that the CE is **typically** an entity functioning in the Subject role. This formulation suggests that such is not invariably the case, implying that exceptions to this general state of affairs need to be outlined. This will be done briefly in section 2.3.

2.2 Event orientation

Let us turn now to the second of the two semantic functions involved in the identification of rhetorical activity – that of **event orientation**. The event orientation categories considered relevant to the identification of types of rhetorical activity concern the temporal reference of the event spoken about, i.e. simultaneous with, preceding or following the moment of speaking, as well as the spoken about event's frequency, possibility, necessity and hypotheticality. For present purposes, little more needs to be added to the description of event orientation beyond a brief outline of the formal means of its realisation.

Broadly speaking, the temporal orientation of the event is realised by the tense Finite in the clause realising the message. However, there are other lexicogrammatical phenomena, e.g. adjuncts or conjoined dependent clauses which are capable of expressing the event's temporal orientation.

The role of the Finite is evident in extract 4: the argument is grounded, in message 301, in the ongoing non-habitual state of affairs as manifested by the temporal orientation realised by the Finite element of the verbal group. These temporal grounds shift, in message 302 and 303, to the habitual behaviour of the entity *chair* in message 302 (and again in messages 305-307), and that of the child (*you*) in message 303.

2.3 Central entity and Subject

Is central entity invariably realised by Subject? Indeed, does every message contain a central entity? The answer to both questions is, in a word, no. A

message may contain no central entity as happens when the clause realising
a message has as Subject the non-referential meteorological *it* as in:

(1)   It's raining

Here, the Subject *it* is of the type that is often referred to as a 'dummy'
Subject; no referring expression capable of realising a central entity exists
in clauses such as this. Compare the non-referential *it* of example (1) with
the referential *it* in clauses realising messages (2-3):

(2) It's lucky that we left early
(3) It's July that is the coldest month

Message (2) is realised by a postposed subject type of construction. In this
construction, thematic *It* refers cataphorically to *that we left early* which is
evaluated by the thematic segment realising the point of departure of the
message. This evaluative segment may also be expressed by such evaluative
adjuncts as *Luckily*. Therefore, in the analysis developed here, the evaluative
segment *It's lucky* is considered to be an interpersonal type of theme in the
clause realising the message. The implication of such an analysis is that the
rhetorical configuration which identifies the type of rhetorical activity
constituted by messages such as that in example (2) is considered to be
located in the evaluated segment of the message, i.e. *that we left early*.

Message (3) is by contrast not evaluated but the CE is, again, anticipated
by cataphorically referring *It*. Here, the CE is considered to be the entity to
which *It* refers, i.e. July. Thus, in messages realised by theme predicated
clauses such as (3) above, the CE is realised, not by the entity actualising the
Subject role but by the entity actualising the role of Complement. This
analysis implies that the CE in messages realised by theme predicated clauses
is the same as that in the non-theme predicated equivalents. For example, the
CE in the non-theme predicated equivalent of (3) – *July is the coldest month*
– is also *July*.

The CE is also realised by the entity actualising the Complement role in
the type of clauses introduced by non-referential *there* as in example (4):

(4) There aren't many passionfruit out there at the moment

Unlike the clause realising the message in example (1) above, the message
in example (4) does contain an entity that is capable of realising the role of
CE, namely, *many passionfruit*. That this entity does not actualise the Subject

role may be due to the fact that it is indefinite and is introduced into the discourse for the first time. Huddleston (1984: 467) notes that it is entities of this type that occur in post-verbal position in such existential constructions. This interpretation of the entity functioning in the role of Complement as the realisation of the CE in existential *there* type of constructions is consistent with the view taken in traditional grammars (cited in Huddleston 1984: 70) that the Subject in such constructions is the post-verbal nominal group.

In summary, then it may be stated that although the CE is typically realised by the entity actualising the lexicogrammatical role of Subject this is by no means invariably the case. Thus for example, where the Subject of a clause is actualised by a non-referring expression, the CE is realised by Complement if this role is actualised by an entity. If there is no entity present in a message then clearly that message has no CE.

The fact that lexicogrammatical phenomena other than Subject may realise CE (and, for that matter, that the temporal orientation of an event may be realised by means other than the Finite) does not invalidate the model put forward here. Rather, it is a manifestation of the fact that there is not a one-to-one relation between the strata of lexicogrammar and semantics. In Hasan's (in press) terms the relation between strata is a non-conformal one: the facts of one stratum do not conform exactly to the facts of the other. Hasan makes the point that this kind of relation is necessary in a multi-stratal model.

Before turning to the second of the two points raised in section 2, one further type of message needs to be discussed, i.e. those messages which are prefaced, for such messages contain two rhetorical configurations.

2.4 Rhetorical configuration in prefaced messages

As was mentioned in the definition of the message given in section 1.1, a projecting clause and the clause which it projects are not distinguished as realising separate messages. Rather, a projecting clause is said to realise the preface of a message. However, since a preface is realised by a clause it has its own configuration of entity and temporal reference realised by Subject and Finite roles. Thus within prefaced messages there are two rhetorical configurations; for example, in the message – *Daddy said you have to have a sleep this afternoon* – the preface, ie *Daddy said* has its own rhetorical configuration as does the remainder of the message realised by the projected clause – *you have to have a sleep this afternoon*. The question then arises: which of the two rhetorical configurations in a prefaced message identifies the class of rhetorical unit to which the message belongs? When the two rhetorical configurations are similar there is no problem. In extract 5, messages 139, 145 and 146 are prefaced (The prefaces are shown in bold) but it is only in the latter message, ie 146, that the rhetorical configurations of the preface and the prefaced parts of the message differ significantly:

Extract 5:

128	Stephen	Do they eat people?
129	Mother	Water snakes?
130	Stephen	Yeah
131	Mother	Do they eat people?
132	Stephen	Yeah
133	Mother	I don't think any snakes eat people
134	Stephen	No um .. no, the aborigines
135	Mother	Do the aborigines eat people?
136	Stephen	Yes
137	Mother	No
138	Stephen	Why?
139	Mother	Well **they know** that you just don't eat other people darling
140	Stephen	Oh
141	Mother	It's not very nice, is it?
142	Stephen	They eat -
143	Mother	There used to be some people in New Guinea
144	Stephen	Oh
145	Mother	**Some people said** that they ate people
146		but **I don't know** whether they really did or not.

The messages of this extract construe a *generalisation* within which is embedded a *recount* (messages 143-146) and a *reflection* (message 146). *Reflection* is the type of rhetorical activity which involves the habitual states or activities of the interactant(s) themselves. The two rhetorical configurations in message 139 – *they know* and *you* (i.e. people) *don't eat other people* – both construe a *generalisation*; similarly, the two rhetorical configurations in message 145 – *some people said* and *they ate people* – both construe a *recount*. In message 146, by contrast, the two rhetorical configurations construe different kinds of rhetorical activity: *I don't know* construes a *reflection*, and *they (some people in New Guinea) did (eat)* is a continuation of the **recount** of the previous message. Message 146 is taken to construe a **reflection** for it is the rhetorical configuration located in the preface that is considered criterial to the recognition of the rhetorical activity type constituted by this message. There are two arguments in favour of considering as criterial the rhetorical configuration in the preface of a prefaced message: first, it is the rhetorical configuration of the preface that is picked up in a message tag, e.g. *Daddy said you have to have a sleep this afternoon, didn't he?* Secondly, such an analysis is consistent with the typical location of the CE within the scope of the message's point of departure as discussed previously.

3. The status of rhetorical activity

It is clear from the discussion in section 2 that, typically, it is the lexicogrammatical structural function Subject that expresses the CE of a message and that attributes of the CE in configuration with the orientation of the event identify classes of rhetorical activity. What, however, is the status of the rhetorical activity? This question, the second of the two issues raised at the beginning of section 2.0, is perhaps best broached by first considering the relations of embedding and expansion that may exist between activities and the means by which these relations may be established.

3.1 Relating rhetorical activities

In the analysis of extract 1, embedded and non-embedded related rhetorical activities were distinguished mainly by their function in the context of the activities to which they were related. The question is: are there any means by which the distinction between embedded and non-embedded related activities can be made by reference to formal criteria?

It may be claimed in answer that such means are, indeed, available and that they are to be found by reference to two components of the textual metafunction – theme and cohesion. A re-examination of the discussion will reveal that the latter system has been implicitly consulted in the analysis given above, for example, in the tracking of the CEs throughout the messages making up a particular rhetorical activity. It is considered that the relations between rhetorical activities are determined by patterns of thematic progression, i.e. by the location of cohesive items within the theme-rheme structure of the clauses realising the initial message(s) of a rhetorical activity. The realisation of the relations between rhetorical activities is, thus, the lexico-grammatical responsibility of systems of the textual metafunction.

3.2 The textual metafunction

Halliday (1977a: 181) refers to the textual metafunction as the text-forming component of the semantic system. He points out that, although all meta-functions are active in the production of a text, the textual metafunction

> is the component whose function is specifically that of creating text, of making
> the difference between language in the abstract and language in use. In other
> words, it is through the semantic options of the textual component that language
> comes to be relevant to its environment ... (ibid)

According to Halliday the textual metafunction has an enabling role in that it enables ideational and interpersonal meanings to "take on relevance to some real context" (Halliday 1979: 60). Because it enables ideational and interpersonal meanings to be presented as text in context, this metafunction is said to be "instrumental and not autonomous" (Halliday 1974: 48) and oriented towards second order or symbolic reality – the reality brought into existence by language itself. The other two metafunctions, by contrast, are concerned with first order reality: the ideational, with the representation of external and internal reality; and the interpersonal, with personal or social reality.

In his discussion of the structural expression of the textual metafunction – thematic structure – Halliday (1977b) traces the notion of theme and rheme back to the ideas about language held by the ancient Greeks. However, he also acknowledges his more immediate debt to the Prague School linguists, in particular to their founder Vilém Mathesius (1928), for his conceptualisa-tion of theme and information structures. As is well known, Halliday's interpretation varies from that of the Prague School: whereas Prague School scholars combine the concept of theme as point of departure with informa-tion focus, Halliday separates these two functions. He reserves the term theme for the first concept, ie the point of departure from which a speaker or writer proceeds in the enunciation of the message; information, by contrast, is what is known or given. The two elements – theme and informa-tion – are, according to Halliday, the output of two distinct systems, each construing a distinct semantic choice for the speaker, and each being realised in different ways. The separation of the Theme Rheme structure from the Given New one is therefore justified both by lexicogrammatical evidence as well as by their separate functions.

For present purposes it is the system of THEME rather than of INFORMA-TION FOCUS that is most relevant. It is argued that THEME, in combination with the non-structural textual resource of cohesion, is involved in the specification of the relationship between rhetorical activities.

3.2.1 Theme as the point of departure of messages

The semantic gloss for the lexicogrammatical element Theme, given by both Mathesius and Halliday is that it is the point of departure of a speaker's message indicating what is psychologically uppermost for the speaker. In the following, the gloss – point of departure (hereafter POD) – will be technica-lised and used as the semantic label which is realised by the lexicogram-matical element Theme. The lexicogrammatical feature that realises the point of departure of the message typically indicates its speech function so that in commands and offers, which are concerned with getting someone to do something and offering to do something for someone, respectively, the doing that is to be done is the typical POD. The meaning of the POD of such mes-sages is 'I want you to do...' (commands) or 'I want to do .. for you' (of-fers). In questions, on the other hand, the typical POD is the question-ness of the message. Where what is sought is a missing piece of information, an item representing the piece of information that is sought – *who, what, when, where, why* etc. – functions as Theme in the interrogative clause realising the message. Halliday (1985: 47) points out that the meaning of such elements as Theme is "I want you to tell me the person, thing, time, manner, etc." By contrast, polarity is thematised where what is sought is confirmation (rea-lised by polar interrogatives), the meaning of the Theme in such interrogative clauses being "I want you to tell me whether or not." (ibid). The semantic principle underlying theme selection – start by relating to the speaker in the context of the speech event (Halliday 1985: 166) – is thus embodied in the structural make-up of interrogatives and imperatives (op. cit.: 47-48). In these cases when the typical option, i.e. unmarked theme, is chosen, the actualisation of theme in the clause is fully decided by virtue of choices in the mood system.

In declaratives, where the Theme is typically conflated with the Subject, the meaning is "I want to tell you about something". Given that the semantic role of Subject as discussed above is that of modal nominal – the entity in whom is vested the success or failure of a proposition or proposal – the typical conflation of Subject with theme would seem to mean something like: "I want to tell you about something in respect of which we can argue."

However, there are cases of declaratives with a marked Theme choice, where Theme is conflated with some element other than Subject. In extract 3 (section 2.1.1) an instance of non-Subject as Theme in a clause realising a statement (message 169 *everything she does*) was noted. Extract 6 provides a further instance of such a marked theme in the clause realising a statement message. In this extract, Stephen's mother explains why she has refused to comply with Stephen's request to be given a vitamin C tablet; the marked theme (message 57) is shown in bold:

Extract 6:

55	Mother	Well they're very big tablets, sweetie
56		Very big tablets
57		**500 milligrams** there are in those
58		That's twice as much as any other tablets ..
59		so you really had two tablets this morning

In this extract, the marked Theme, *500 milligrams* in message 57, specifies more precisely what is meant by the attribute *very big* in messages 55 and 56. While it has the grammatical status of Complement/Theme in message 57, it becomes Subject/Theme in message 58 and thus the entity with reference to which the assertion can be affirmed or denied.

Further discussion of markedness of theme will be deferred until after the discussion of thematic progression. The reason for this is implied in the above discussion: it is only when a sequence of messages is examined that the reason for choosing marked theme can be determined.

3.2.2 Interpreting Theme in clause complexes

At the lexicogrammatical stratum, the first clause of a clause complex is said to function as Theme (Halliday 1985: 57). This is the case both in projection as well as in expansion. A projecting clause, as noted in section 2.4, realises the preface of a prefaced message; such a clause is typically thematic so that the POD of a prefaced message is usually the preface, serving to signal explicitly that the prefaced part of the message is a particular point of view. Clauses related by expansion, unlike those related by projection, realise separate messages. An expanding clause might potentially realise a message which serves to specify certain circumstances pertaining to related messages. Thus a basic message (i.e. one realised by a primary clause) may be expanded by certain kinds of supplementary messages (i.e. those realised by hypotactic dependent clauses of expansion). When such supplementary messages occur initially in a complex then the point of departure of the basic message is, for example, time, place, reason, manner, condition etc. This point may be clarified by a consideration of extract 7, which is again taken from a dialogue between Stephen and his mother:

Extract 7

70	Mother	Do you think we should plant a passionfruit vine at our new house?
71	Stephen	Yes .. yes
72	Mother	I think that would be a good idea
73	Stephen	Me too ..
74	Mother	All gone ..
75		It usually takes a couple of years
76		before you get many passionfruit on your vine
77		When you're six ..
78		we'll have lots of passionfruit

In message 77 of this extract the mother, by referring to the child's age, makes concrete her estimate of the time it will take for the planned passionfruit vine to bear fruit. In other words, the time reference in message 77 – *when you're six* – is treated here as the point of departure of message 78 – *we'll have lots of passionfruit* . Thus 77 is interpreted as an attempt to make concrete for the child the *generalisation* constituted by messages 75-76: the passage of time between planting passionfruit vines and harvesting the fruit. This extract is analysed in Figure 3 in terms of its rhetorical activities.

In messages 70 and 71 the interactants plan a possible future course of action and evaluate this *plan* in messages 72-73. Message 74, *All gone* ('All the passionfruit is gone'), has been ignored for the moment since it bears no direct relation to the rhetorical activity construed by the immediately contiguous messages; rather, it is related to the preceding text segment (messages 63-69).

In messages 75-76 the mother generalises about the time lag between planting and harvesting. This *generalisation* constitutes a rhetorical activity

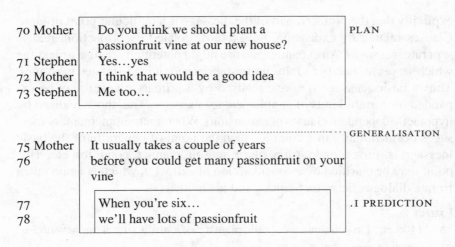

Figure 3: Analysis of extract 7, messages 70-78

that is related to but not embedded in the *plan* of messages 70-73; it is considered to expand the *plan* rather than to serve some function within it. Messages 77-78 constitute a *prediction* which, like *plan*, is a type of rhetorical activity involving future events or states. Note that *plan* and *prediction* are considered distinct rhetorical activities, the basis of the distinction being (a) the identity of the CE - speaker or other person or object; and (b) where the CE is the speaker, whether the event is volitionally undertaken. A *plan* must have, as CE, the speaker, realised lexicogrammatically as 1st person pronoun, whether singular *I* or plural *we*, and the future event must be volitional. A (set of) message(s) is recognised as *prediction* under one of the following two conditions: (a) the CE is the speaker and the future event is non-volitional; OR (b) the CE is an entity other than the speaker and the event is forecast to occur in the future.

Returning to the instance of *prediction* being considered here (messages 77-78): it was previously pointed out that this *prediction* serves to pin down or make concrete the previous *generalisation*. Because the *prediction* serves this function with respect to the *generalisation*, it is considered to be embedded within it.

The decision to consider the relation between the *plan* and *generalisation* to be one of expansion, and the relation between the *generalisation* and *prediction* to be one of embedding is supported by linguistic evidence. This evidence is provided by patterns of thematic progression.

3.3 Thematic progression and cohesion

Patterns of thematic progression indicate whether a rhetorical activity is embedded within, related to or unrelated to a preceding activity. The concept of thematic progression inherently involves the concept of cohesion. Before demonstrating the basis of the claim that patterns of thematic progression determine the existence and type of relationship between rhetorical activities, the concept of thematic progression will be briefly reviewed. Familiarity with the concept of cohesion will, however, be assumed and little will be said about it except to state that it is the influential work of Halliday and Hasan (1976) and Hasan's extensions (Hasan, 1984a; 1984b; 1985) which inform the analysis to be presented.

3.3.1 Thematic progression

The notion of thematic progression was introduced by the Prague linguist, Daneš, in order to conceptualise the role of Theme in text organisation and construction. Daneš (1974: 109) points out that the choice of themes of individual messages in a text is not a matter of chance – is not random and without structural connection to the text. Rather the choice of themes is patterned. Indeed one would intuitively expect that some kind of regularity or pattern would govern the progression of the presentation of subject-matter.

Daneš identifies 3 main types of thematic progression (hereafter TP) maintaining that these 3 basic patterns may be used in various combinations in any one text. Oversimplifying somewhat, these patterns are as follows:

(i) **Simple linear TP** is a pattern of progression with a linear thematisation of rhemes, where each rheme becomes the theme of the next utterance. This most basic, elementary TP pattern may be shown as Rheme > Theme.

(ii) **Continuous theme TP** is a pattern where the same theme appears in a series of utterances but the Rheme for each is different; this may be symbolised as Theme > Theme.

(iii) **Derived theme TP** is the pattern formed by deriving particular utterance themes from a "hypertheme" e.g. the theme of a paragraph.

Daneš's model is based on the Prague School's combining approach to the definition and realisation of theme. Fries (1981) has applied the notion of thematic progression using Halliday's separating approach. Fries argues that thematic progression correlates with the structure of a text and thematic content with a text's method of development. In other words, texts having a particular type of generic structure are likely to have a particular type of thematic progression; and where there is a common semantic thread running through thematic content of component sentences, this thematic content will be perceived as the text's method of development.

The argument, then, is that there is a patterned rather than random interaction between cohesive items forming the lexical strings and reference chains which contain the theme selections of the clauses or sentences realising the text. The concern of both Daneš and Fries is with thematic content. For this reason they do not consider other possible patterns of thematic progression, e.g. Theme > Rheme and Rheme > Rheme patterns, i.e. the patterns in which the second of two items standing in a cohesive relation occurs in the Rheme of the respective message. These patterns, as well as Daneš's patterns (i) and (ii) are of particular importance in the present analysis, as will be seen in the discussion of embedding and expansion. That analysis seeks to account for these relations between rhetorical activities, and it is the formation of cohesive ties through componential and organic means that is relevant together with the location of these ties within or not within a message's POD.

3.4 Relating rhetorical units

Two kinds of relations between rhetorical activities have been identified: first, a relation of embedding; and, secondly, that of expansion. A third kind of relationship may be identified, namely, that where no relationship exists between rhetorical activities but where there has been no indication of "conversational disengagement", in terms of Grice (1975). In section 3.4.1 below, each of these relationships will be exemplified and their identification will be elucidated.

3.4.1 Embedding and expansion

As previously stated, the relations between rhetorical activities are established primarily through patterns of thematic progression and componential and organic cohesive ties. Some specialisation of these patterns vis-a-vis the relationships of embedding and expansion is to be noted and will be discussed first by reference to Figure 4. Note that in this Figure a dotted line runs between messages 69 and 70. The reader will recognise the dialogue below this line as Extract 7, used earlier (see section 3.2.3). Extract 7 is in fact a continuation of the same dialogue where the messages in the first half of Figure 4 occur. I will refer to the whole extract analysed in Figure 4 as Extract 7a. The analysis of extract 7a in Figure 4 should in part resemble that provided in Figure 3, which presented the analysis of extract 7.

Before discussing the relations between the rhetorical activities of the messages of extract 7a, attention is drawn to the fact that in this extract there is one rhetorical activity that has not previously been identified, that of *action*. This is the type of rhetorical activity that is constituted by messages expressing the exchange of goods and services. The central entities of such messages are the interactants themselves. The temporal orientation of the message events is to the immediate future and, furthermore, these events may be circumscribed in terms of obligation or inclination.

With regard to the relationship of embedding: Figure 4 shows that there are two separate instances of embedding. One of these occurs within the *action* activity (messages 63-69 and 74), and the other within the *generalisation* (messages 75-78). Note that the *action* activity is temporarily discontinued at message 69 and resumed at message 74. This aspect of the unfolding of the rhetorical activities will be discussed more fully in section 3.4.1.1 below. Embedded within the rhetorical activity of *action* are four activities, namely, *observation, recount, generalisation* and *commentary*. Further, the *recount* is embedded within the *observation* and the *generalisation* within the *recount*. Using SF structural notation and using dots to indicate discontinuity, the relationships here may be represented as:

Action[Observation[Recount[Generalisation]]]..[Commentary]

The item which cohesively links each of these rhetorical activities occurs within the POD of the initial message of each activity. Thus in message 64 *It* is coreferential with *the rest* (= of the passionfruit) of message 63; in message 66 *it* refers to *this passionfruit* of messages 64-65; in message 67 *they* is related to *it* (= this passionfruit) of message 66 by co-classification; and in message 74 *All* is co-referential with *the passionfruit* which is the interpretative source of *the rest* in message 63.

In clauses realising the initial messages of each of the four embedded activities the cohesive link is thematic. The TP pattern is Rheme > Theme (messages 63-64 and messages 65-66), Theme > Theme (messages 66-67) and Rheme > Theme (messages 63 and 74).

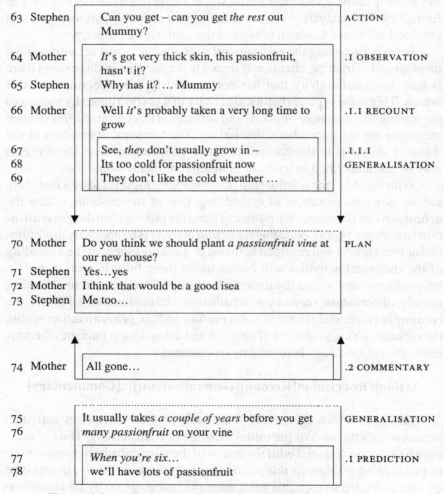

63	Stephen	Can you get – can you get *the rest* out Mummy?	ACTION
64	Mother	*It*'s got very thick skin, this passionfruit, hasn't it?	.1 OBSERVATION
65	Stephen	Why has it? … Mummy	
66	Mother	Well *it*'s probably taken a very long time to grow	.1.1 RECOUNT
67		See, *they* don't usually grow in –	.1.1.1
68		Its too cold for passionfruit now	GENERALISATION
69		They don't like the cold wheather …	
70	Mother	Do you think we should plant *a passionfruit vine* at our new house?	PLAN
71	Stephen	Yes…yes	
72	Mother	I think that would be a good isea	
73	Stephen	Me too…	
74	Mother	All gone…	.2 COMMENTARY
75		It usually takes *a couple of years* before you get	GENERALISATION
76		*many passionfruit* on your vine	
77		*When you're six…*	.1 PREDICTION
78		we'll have lots of passionfruit	

Figure 4: Relations between rhetorical activities of extract 7a

In the second instance of embedding where the *prediction* (messages 77-78) is embedded within the *generalisation*, the TP pattern between the two activities is also Theme > Theme. However, the cohesive link is formed not by componential cohesion but by expressions of time realised by clauses. Thus what links the *prediction* to the previous *generalisation* is the supplementary message (77) expressing time. This expression of time – *when you're six* – is cohesively linked to an expression of time in message 75 – *a couple of years* – and is thematic in the clause complex realising the messages 77-78. It is tempting to say that *a couple of years* and *when you're six* are in actual fact co-referential in that, in this particular text the time interval represented by the latter when *you're six* instantiates the former *a couple of years*. However, this would perhaps be an unwarranted extension of the use of the metalanguage since co-reference is usually viewed as a componential cohesive device. The embedded status of rhetorical activities will be further exemplified after the relations of expansion found in Figure 4 have been discussed.

The relationship of expansion is indicated in Figure 4 as usual by dotted horizontal lines. Figure 4 shows that there are two rhetorical activities standing in an expanding relationship: *plan* (messages 70-73), and the *generalisation* together with its embedded rhetorical activity of *prediction* (messages 75-78). The *plan* is related by expansion to the previous *action*, together with the activities that are embedded therein. As with the embedding, this relation of expansion is given by the existence and location of the cohesive link between the two activities, *action* and *plan*. This cohesive link is formed by *passionfruit:* more specifically, the cohesive reference item *they* ('passionfruit') in message 69 forms a cohesive tie with *a passionfruit vine* in message 70, the initial message of the *plan*. Note, however, the location of the second member of the cohesive tie, i.e. *a passionfruit vine*. It occurs in the Rheme of the clause realising message 70, thus giving a TP pattern Theme > Rheme between messages 69 and 70.

A similar situation occurs in the second instance of the expanding relation – messages 75-79 constituting a *generalisation* in which is embedded a *prediction*. There is an explicit cohesive link between *plan* and *generalisation* with its embedded *prediction*: *many passionfruit* in message 76 is cohesively linked to *a passionfruit* of message 70-73. Note that the message in which the second member of the cohesive tie – *many passionfruit* – occurs is realised by the sequent clause in a clause complex; in terms of thematic structure it forms the Rheme of the clause complex. Thus the TP pattern of Rheme > Rheme occurs between the *plan* (messages 70-73) and the *generalisation* containing the embedded *prediction* (messages 75-79). Because there does exist a cohesive relation between these two activities and because the cohesive link is in the Rheme (message 76) of the messages introducing the second activity of *generalisation*, this activity is considered to be related to the *plan* by expansion.

By these steps, all the relations between the various rhetorical activities of extract 7a have been described – all except for one: the *commentary* of message 74. Is this activity related in any way to the immediately previous activity of *plan*? If so, how? It was claimed above that the *commentary* is related by embedding to the non-contiguous *action* activity since the item cohesively linking the *commentary* with *action* is located within the POD of message 74 (cf *All* 'all the passionfruit'), such a location of the cohesive link indicating an embedding relationship even though the two activities are not contiguous. The direct relation between the *action* with its embedded activities and *commentary* is indicated in Figure 4 by the arrows in the outer-most frame. The *commentary* is related to the contiguous activity, *plan*, only indirectly, if at all, through the relation of this activity to *action*, i.e. via the expanding relation between *plan* and *action* with its embedded activities, one of which is the *commentary* under focus. Table 1 summarises the cohesive links and TP patterns between the rhetorical activities of extract 7a.

Hopefully, it is clear from the above discussion of the relationships of embedding and expansion that the determination of each of these relations is achieved primarily through the existence and location of cohesive links within thematic structure. Thus it was suggested that the embedded status of a rhetorical activity is typically indicated by a TP pattern of Theme > Theme or, alternatively Rheme > Theme; in other words the cohesive item linking activity-B with activity-A is to be found within the POD of the message introducing activity-B. By contrast, the cohesive link between activities that stand in a relation of expansion is not found within the POD of the initial message of activity-B.

We are, thus, exploring four logical possibilities in TP: (i) Theme > Theme; (ii) Theme > Rheme; (iii) Rheme > Theme; and (iv) Rheme > Rheme. If, in the relationship of expansion, the POD of activity-A is not cohesively linked to activity-B, then it follows that only patterns (ii) and (iv)

Table 1: Cohesive links and TP patterns between rhetorical activities of extract 7a

Embedding relations

64 *It* co-refers to *the rest* (=of the passion fruit) (63)   = Rheme → Theme

66 *it* co-refers to *this passionfruit* (64-65)   = Rheme → Theme

67 *they* co-classifies with *it* (=this passionfruit) (66)   = Theme → Theme

74 *all* co-refers to 'the passionfruit' (63)   = Rheme → Theme

77 *when you're six* instantiates *a couple of years* (75)   = Theme → Theme

Expanding relations

70 *passionfruit vine* co-extends with *(this) passionfruit* (63ff):   Theme → Rheme

76 *many passionfruit* co-classifies with *passionfruit vine* (70):   Rheme → Rheme

---

can occur between expanded and expanding activities, i.e. the TP patterns for an expansion relation is Theme of activity-A > Rheme of activity-B or Rheme of activityA > Rheme of activity-B. In the embedding relation, on the other hand, the pattern must be (i) or (iii), i.e. Theme of matrix activity > Theme of embedded activity or Rheme of matrix activity > Theme of embedded activity.

It would seem that an embedded activity usually serves some function within the context of the activity in which it is embedded. This fact has been implicit in the discussion of the analyses of extracts 1 and 7. In extract 7, for example, attention was drawn to the function of the embedded *prediction* of messages 77-78: it serves to clarify and make concrete for the child the meaning of the expression *a couple of years* referred to in message 75. However, it would seem that either function or cohesive links alone may be adequate under certain circumstances. Thus in extract 7a the *observation* constituted by 64-65 appears to serve no identifiable function within the context of the previous *action* though there is a cohesive relationship which is located in the POD of message 65. Note that the cohesive item is a pronominal (*It*) the referent of which is clarified at the end of the message, i.e. *this passionfruit*.

By contrast with this instance of embedding where a cohesive link exists within the POD of the message though the message seems to serve no function other than that of maintaining conversational contact, in extract 1, segment I, there is a rhetorical activity which is considered to be embedded despite the fact that the cohesive link is not within the scope of the POD of the initial basic unsupplemented message of the activity i.e. message 223. The relevant messages of this segment of extract I are reproduced below (note that a lexical rendering of these messages would identify *a hydroplane* as the item with which *a helicopter* in message 223 is cohesively linked):

216 Stephen No
217   It's a hydroplane ...
218   This is – that's the water
219   and it saves people
220 Mother Does it?
221 Stephen Yes ..
222   Every person that's um that's got drowned
223 Mother Oh .. There's a helicopter that goes up and down the beaches in summer watching out for people
224   It's called a rescue helicopter

Message 223 was previously identified as the beginning of an embedded *account*. Its function in the context of the *observation* of the previous messages would seem to be to provide additional information in elaboration of that provided by Stephen. However, the location in message 223 of the cohesive link *a helicopter* is not within the POD of the message. This would suggest that the *account* introduced by messages 223 is in fact an expanding activity rather than an embedded one. Note, however, that the lexicogrammatical realisation of message 223 is problematic in terms of its Theme-Rheme structure: existential *there* has no function in transitivity structure and, as 'dummy' Subject, is analysed as interpersonal theme. The first element to have a function in the transitivity structure of the clause is the lexical verb instantiated as *'s*. This element, then, is analysed as topical Theme and the rest of the clause – in this case, consisting of the element Existent – is the Rheme. In other words, and in the unmarked case, the only possible location for a potentially cohesive nominal element in such existential constructions is in the Rheme. In such cases, i.e. where a Rhematic nominal expressing the CE in a message that is realised by existential 'there' clauses is cohesively tied to a prior nominal element, the rhetorical activity introduced by such messages is considered to be embedded.

Generally speaking, a rhetorical activity is considered to be embedded

in an immediately prior activity if the item which cohesively links the activities is located within the POD of the initial message(s) of the embedded
rhetorical activity and if it serves some function within the context of the activity in which it is considered to be embedded. The exceptions to this general rule are specifiable (For a more detailed discussion see Cloran 1994.)

3.4.1.1 Interrupting rhetorical activities   It was shown in Figure 4 that a
rhetorical activity may be temporarily suspended and later resumed. In
extract 7a (shown in Figure 4) the rhetorical activity *action* with its embedded activities (messages 63-69 and 74) exemplifies this phenomenon. The
type of temporary suspension and resumption exemplified here is associated
with the fact that some non-verbal activity may co-occur with some unrelated verbal activity. In other words, the talk may pertain to what is happen-
ing non-verbally or it may be totally unrelated to the non-verbal activity. In
extract 7a, the *action* activity is directly related to the co-occurring non-
verbal activity of eating. Within this activity, a progressive detachment of
the verbal activity from the non-verbal activity occurs until there is a complete detachment between the two. The verbal activity, having become
detached from the immediate material situation is free to range and this
occurs in the form of a *plan*. The *plan*, however, is not totally unrelated to
the prior *action* with its embedded activities since it takes up and expands
an item previously introduced. In the meantime the non-verbal activity
continues and the potential remains for the verbal and non-verbal activity to
once more coincide. This, indeed, occurs at message 74 but immediately
after this the two types of activity – the verbal and non-verbal – are again
completely detached.

   A rhetorical activity may be temporarily suspended and later resumed,
being interrupted by an activity which has some function in the context of
the activity it interrupts but not being cohesively linked to the interrupted
activity in the way that activities need to be linked in order to be considered
embedded, i.e. Theme or Rheme > Theme. This state of affairs occurred in
Extract 1 Segment 2a when Stephen's message 251 was unintelligible
because of his difficulty in carrying on the verbal and non-verbal activities
simultaneously. His mother interrupted the *generalisation* being construed
by messages 236ff in order to draw his attention to this fact. The activity
construed by the mother at this point thus interrupts the *generalisation* which
is, however, resumed when, presumably, Stephen has swallowed his food.

Unlike the interrupting activities discussed above, this interrupting activity construed by the mother in extract 1, segment 2a – *recount [Observation]* – is considered to be an included text, i.e. included within the *generalisation* that it interrupts, since it functions to facilitate this activity. The included nature of this interrupting activity is indicated in Figure 2 by the broken horizontal and vertical lines which signal its boundaries.

3.4.2 Unrelated rhetorical activities

That a dialogue may consist of more than a single text is shown in the analysis of extract 8 in Figure 5.

The *commentary* of message 207 is unrelated to the previous *commentary* with its embedded activities. Similarly the *observation* of message 208-

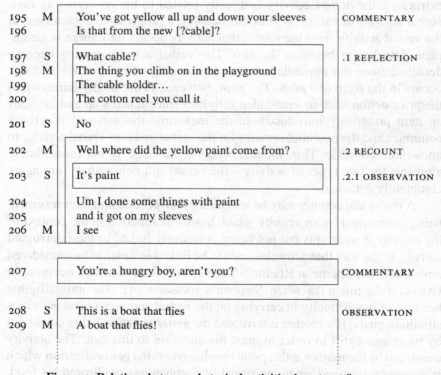

195	M	You've got yellow all up and down your sleeves	COMMENTARY
196		Is that from the new [?cable]?	
197	S	What cable?	.1 REFLECTION
198	M	The thing you climb on in the playground	
199		The cable holder…	
200		The cotton reel you call it	
201	S	No	
202	M	Well where did the yellow paint come from?	.2 RECOUNT
203	S	It's paint	.2.1 OBSERVATION
204		Um I done some things with paint	
205		and it got on my sleeves	
206	M	I see	
207		You're a hungry boy, aren't you?	COMMENTARY
208	S	This is a boat that flies	OBSERVATION
209	M	A boat that flies!	

Figure 5: Relations between rhetorical activities in extract 8

209ff is unrelated to the *commentary* of message 207 (the dots in Figure 5 indicate that this activity continues). To say that there is no relation between each of these rhetorical activities and the immediately preceding activity is simply to say that: (i) each lacks any function in the context of the activity preceding it; and (ii) there exists between them no cohesive relation except that constituted by the cohesive link between the items which refer to the interactants themselves, i.e. *I* and *you*, in messages 205-206 and 207. The *commentary* of messages 207, nevertheless, seems totally unrelated to the preceding *commentary* with its embedded activities. This suggests that when the cohesive link is provided by an item referring to the interactants themselves then this link by itself is not sufficient to relate rhetorical activities. This is in keeping with Hasan's (1985: 84-85) claim that co-reference chains referring to the interactants themselves are text-dependent and cannot be used to define text boundaries; rather text boundaries, however defined, delimit the extent of the interactant co-reference chains. The lack of relation between these rhetorical activities is shown by the solid line (it will be recalled that a dotted line is indicative of expansion, while a solid boxing shows embedding.)

With regard to the rhetorical activity constituted by messages 195-206 of extract 8 in Figure 5, this may be regarded as a complete text having the immediate constituent structure:

Commentary[Reflection][Recount[Observation]]

If this *commentary, reflection, recount* and *observation* are called A, B, C, and D respectively then the structural relation between these rhetorical activities can be schematically represented as A[B][C[D]]. Thus A is the matrix term into which are embedded [B] as a simple term and [C[D]] as a complex term. There is no direct relation between [B] and [C[D]], unlike the relation between C and D; instead [B] and [C[D]] are indirectly related through their common relation to A.

At this point, digressing somewhat but nevertheless continuing the discussion of the role of theme and cohesion in discourse, attention is drawn to a phenomenon briefly discussed earlier (section 3.2.2) i.e. the function of marked Theme. In this segment of the extract the function of marked Theme is exemplified by the marked Theme in the clause realising message 200 in extract 8. Using the notion of topic in the sense of subject-matter, in message

195 a fresh topic was introduced in the Complement/Rheme of the clause realising the message. This fresh topic becomes Subject/Theme in the clause realising message 196. This kind of progression seems to be quite typical for topic continuation in certain types of discourse: a fresh topic is introduced within the clause segment which realises the conflated functions of Complement/Rheme; thereafter the topic is maintained within conflated Subject/Theme position. In extract 8 the continuation is short-lived since a clarification is sought regarding *the new cable* – a potentially fresh topic introduced via Rheme/Complement of 196. Messages 197-199 are treated here as elliptical. When this ellipsis is expanded, it becomes obvious that each clause realising these messages consists only of Complement as evidenced by the bold segments in the following expansions:

197 Stephen **What cable** do you mean?
198 Mother   I mean **the thing you climb on in the playground**;
199   I mean **the cable holder**.

The clarification is not completed at message 199; message 200 is part of this clarification, and it is not surprising that the element Complement is retained as Theme since the segment functioning as Theme/Complement, i.e. *the cotton reel* in fact names the very object referred to by the Complement of 197-199. At the same time, the function New is also realised by this same segment so that all three functions – Theme/Complement/New – are conflated. In Halliday's (1977a: 181) terms, this is a case in which theme and information choices are "locally unmarked"; in other words, the meaning of Theme in message 200 is "I want to tell you about what we have been talking about". From this point of view, topic continuation is effected via the cohesive properties of the Complement throughout these messages.

What is it that the markedness of Theme achieves in message 200? I suggest that the markedness of the Theme in this message in combination with the markedness of New is a means of indicating that additional facts are being supplied within the context of a topic that is continued. In other words, the conflation of the functions Theme/Complement/New would seem to be a means of indicating that the speaker is on about new information on an old topic.

The rhetorical activity analysis of messages 195-201 seems to support the interpretation given above. It was previously suggested that these messages constitute a ***commentary*** in which is embedded a ***reflection***. The *reflection* of messages 197-200 is considered to be embedded because (i) it is functional within the context of the commentary, serving to clarify an item introduced there; (ii) the initial message of the *reflection*, message 197, is cohesively related to the preceding message; and (iii) the items entering in this cohesive relation in 197 are located within its POD.

3.5 Summary

The analysis and discussion above have, hopefully, demonstrated how it is that the structural and non-structural resources of the textual metafunction interact to form the various patterns of thematic progression. I have suggested that these text-forming resources of the linguistic system – both the structural resource of theme-rheme and the non-structural resource of cohesion – establish the status of a 'chunk' of text, identified here as rhetorical activity, as embedded, related or unrelated to a preceding rhetorical activity. Having observed the semantic forms, functions of and relations between rhetorical activities, it is now possible to consider the theoretical status of the category 'rhetorical activity'.

4. Rhetorical activities: a unit of text

At this point it should be clear that the concept of rhetorical activity as used here refers to an abstraction at the semantic level. It is not, however, the same kind of semantic abstraction as, say POD or central entity; rather, it is more like the semantic abstraction, message; indeed, it has been implied in the preceding discussion though not explicitly stated that a rhetorical activity may consist of one or more than one message. If there is a 'consists of' relationship between rhetorical activity and message, and if the message is a semantic unit as suggested by Hasan (e.g. 1983) and Halliday (1985), then the text 'chunk' called rhetorical activity into whose structure messages enter must be a unit at the level of semantics in the way that text and its constituent message are semantic units. To be more precise, it is suggested that, at the semantic level, there exists a rank scale with at least three well-defined units: text, 'rhetorical activity' and message: messages are constituents of 'rhetorical activity' and 'rhetorical activities' are constituents of text. This intermediate semantic unit is, then, the rhetorical unit and its various classes, some of which have been briefly discussed in this paper.

4.1 Rhetorical unit classes and context

The lexicogrammatical realisations of the semantic features criterial to the recognition of the classes of rhetorical unit have not been fully specified in the above discussion due to space limitations. Such specification, however, is entirely possible and considers the relation of the classes of rhetorical unit from the stratum below that at which the unit is located, i.e. it addresses the question of construal – the lexicogrammatical means of the recognition/ realisation of the classes of the category rhetorical unit. An equally important consideration, however, is the relation of the classes of this unit to the stratum above, i.e. that of context, so that the question becomes: what activates the classes: what is it that these classes express? It is considered that the classes of rhetorical unit are the expression of the contextual category known as the role of language in the social process, which, within the systemic functional framework, is an aspect of the contextual variable Mode of discourse. Hasan (e.g. 1985: 58) conceptualises the role of language in the social process as a continuum. At one end of the continuum language is an ancillary of other activities and, at the opposite end, language constitutes the activity. The classes of rhetorical unit identified in the extracts throughout this paper – *action, commentary, observation, account, generalisation, prediction* and *recount* – together with others not found in the extracts analysed here, may be represented as ranging along this continuum. At the ancillary end of the continuum is located language use that is based, to a greater or lesser degree, in the material here-and-now; the rhetorical unit classes *action, commentary* and *observation* represent realisations of such language use. At the opposite end, language use is based in the symbolic relations created by language itself; such constitutive language use is realised by the classes *account, prediction, recount* and *generalisation* among others that I have not had the occasion to discuss here.

5. Concluding remarks

The analysis presented in this paper has attempted to show the semantic role of the elements of mood structure – Subject and Finite – in the realisation of an intermediate unit of text, the rhetorical unit. It has been suggested that the lexicogrammatical function Subject, when manifested by certain specifiable types of nominal element, realises the central entity of a message, while the Finite is the primary means of expressing the temporal orientation of the event of a message. It has further been suggested that the configuration of these two semantic functions – central entity and event orientation – construes the rhetorical unit.

The role of theme in the construal of text has also been highlighted in the analysis presented here. It has been shown that the existence and types of relationships between rhetorical units are given by patterns of thematic progression. The analysis shows clearly the role of theme in determining the relevance of a message to its textual environment, how it is that "language comes to be relevant to its environment" (Halliday, 1977a:181).

The analysis supports a constituency-based model of text proposed by Hasan. The idea of a constituency based analysis of discourse is of course not new: Sinclair and Coulthard (1975) proposed a model containing four ranks of unit. Theirs is, however, a model, which despite its developments by others (Berry 1987; Martin 1992) remains limited to dialogic discourse; further, the relation of its units to the lexicogrammar remains a vexed question. The constituents being proposed here – text, rhetorical unit, and message – have been shown to be competent in the analysis of both dialogic and monologic discourse (Cloran 1994). As to the relation of the rhetorical unit to the lexicogrammar, this paper has attempted to show how the intermediate constituent – rhetorical unit – was operationalised first in terms of the semantic features which distinguish its classes and how these in turn were realisationally related by patterns at the lexicogrammatical stratum. In this way, I have tried to keep both the perspective of activation i.e. the relation of the stratum of context to the rhetorical unit, and the perspective of construal, i.e. the relation of the rhetorical units to the formal resources of language.

Transcription conventions

[?]	= unintelligible item
[? item]	= uncertain transcription of item
–	= message not completed
..	= pause in conversation
(IN CAPITALS)	= transcription commentary
abc ?*	= speaker does not allow time for addressee to answer a question
abc-	= interrupted speech, e.g. 158 M *I think you–*
<7>	= Elaborating message interrupts basic message

         e.g. 6 M *It gives you a pain <7> doesn't it?*

             7   *when it's going down*

References

Berry, Margaret. 1987. Is teacher an unanalysed concept? *New Developments in Systemic Linguistics. Volume 1: Theory and description*, edited by M.A.K. Halliday & Robin P. Fawcett. London: Francis Pinter.

Cloran, Carmel. *1994. Rhetorical Units and Decontextualisation: An enquiry into some relations of context, meaning and grammar. Monographs in Systemic Linguistics*. Nottingham: Nottingham University.

Daneš, F. 1974. Functional sentence perspective and the organisation of the text. *Papers on Functional Sentence Perspective*, edited by F. Daneš, 43-53. The Hague: Mouton.

Fries, P. 1981. On the status of theme in English: arguments from discourse. *Forum Linguisticum*, 6.1, 1-38.

Grice, H. 1975. Logic and conversation. *Syntax and Semantics. Vol 3: Speech acts*, edited by Peter Cole & Jerry L. Morgan, 41-58. New York: Academic Press.

Halliday, M.A.K. 1974. The place of 'functional sentence perspective' in the system of linguistic description. *Papers on Functional Sentence Perspective*, edited by F. Daneš, 43-53. The Hague: Mouton.

Halliday, M.A.K. 1977a. Text as semantic choice in social contexts. *Grammars and Descriptions*, edited by Teun A. Van Dijk & J.S. Petöfi, 176-225. Berlin: de Gruyter

Halliday, M.A.K. 1977b. Ideas about language. *Aims and Perspectives in Linguistics*, 32-49. Sydney: Applied Linguistics Association of Australia, Occasional Papers Number 1.

Halliday, M.A.K. 1979. Modes of meaning and modes of expression: types of grammatical structure and their determination by different semantic functions. *Function and Context in Linguistic Analysis*, edited by D.J. Allerton, E. Carney & D. Holdcroft, 57-79. Cambridge: Cambridge University Press.

Halliday, M.A.K. 1985. *Introduction to Functional Grammar*. London: Edward Arnold.

Halliday, M.A.K. & Hasan, Ruqaiya. 1976. *Cohesion in English*. London: Longman.

Halliday, M.A.K. & Hasan, Ruqaiya. 1985. *Language, Context, and Text: Aspects of language in a Social-semiotic perspective*. Deakin University, Victoria: Deakin University Press. (Re-issued: London: Oxford University Press 1989).

Hasan, Ruqaiya. 1983. *A Semantic Network for the Analysis of Messages in Everyday Talk between Mothers and their Children*. Mimeo. Macquarie University: School of English & Linguistics.

Hasan, Ruqaiya. 1984a. Coherence and cohesive harmony. *Understanding Reading Comprehension*, edited by J. Flood, 181-219. Newark, Delaware: International Reading Association.

Hasan, Ruqaiya. 1984b. Ways of saying: ways of meaning. *The Semiotics of Culture and Language, Volume 1: language as social semiotic*, edited by Robin P. Fawcett, M.A.K. Halliday, Sydney M. Lamb & Adam Makkai, 105-162. London: Frances Pinter.

Hasan, Ruqaiya. 1985. The texture of a text. Halliday & Hasan 1985.

Hasan, Ruqaiya. 1989. Semantic variation and sociolinguistics. *Australian Journal of Linguistics*, 9, 221-275.

Hasan, Ruqaiya. 1991. Questions as a mode of learning in everyday talk. *Language Education: Interaction and development*, edited by Thao Le & M. McCausland, 70-119. Launceston: University of Tasmania.

Hasan, Ruqaiya. in press. The conception of context in text. To appear in *Discourse in Society: Systemic functional perspectives*, edited by Peter H. Fries & Michael Gregory. Norwood, NJ: Ablex.

Huddleston, R. 1984. *Introduction to the Grammar of English*. Cambridge: Cambridge University Press.

Martin, J. R. 1992. *English Text: System and structure*. Amsterdam: John Benjamins.

Mathesius, Vilém. 1928. On linguistic characterology with illustrations fom modern English. Reprinted (1964) in *A Prague School Reader in Linguistics*, edited and translated by J. Vachek (ed. & Tr.), 59-67. Bloomington: Indiana University Press.

Sinclair, J. McH. & Coulthard, R.M. 1975. *Towards an Analysis of Discourse: The English used by teachers and pupils*. London: Oxford University Press.

Index

In the CURRENT ISSUES IN LINGUISTIC THEORY (CILT) series (edited by: E.F. Konrad Koerner, University of Ottawa) the following volumes have been published thus far or are scheduled to appear in the course of 1995:

1.   KOERNER, Konrad (ed.): *The Transformational-Generative Paradigm and Modern Linguistic Theory.* 1975.
2.   WEIDERT, Alfons: *Componential Analysis of Lushai Phonology.* 1975.
3.   MAHER, J. Peter: *Papers on Language Theory and History I: Creation and Tradition in Language.* Foreword by Raimo Anttila. 1979.
4.   HOPPER, Paul J. (ed.): *Studies in Descriptive and Historical Linguistics. Festschrift for Winfred P. Lehmann.* 1977.
5.   ITKONEN, Esa: *Grammatical Theory and Metascience: A critical investigation into the methodological and philosophical foundations of 'autonomous' linguistics.* 1978.
6.   ANTTILA, Raimo: *Historical and Comparative Linguistics.* 1989.
7.   MEISEL, Jürgen M. & Martin D. PAM (eds): *Linear Order and Generative Theory.* 1979.
8.   WILBUR, Terence H.: *Prolegomena to a Grammar of Basque.* 1979.
9.   HOLLIEN, Harry & Patricia (eds): *Current Issues in the Phonetic Sciences. Proceedings of the IPS-77 Congress, Miami Beach, Florida, 17-19 December 1977.* 1979.
10. PRIDEAUX, Gary D. (ed.): *Perspectives in Experimental Linguistics. Papers from the University of Alberta Conference on Experimental Linguistics, Edmonton, 13-14 Oct. 1978.* 1979.
11. BROGYANYI, Bela (ed.): *Studies in Diachronic, Synchronic, and Typological Linguistics: Festschrift for Oswald Szemérenyi on the Occasion of his 65th Birthday.* 1979.
12. FISIAK, Jacek (ed.): *Theoretical Issues in Contrastive Linguistics.* 1981.   Out of print
13. MAHER, J. Peter, Allan R. BOMHARD & Konrad KOERNER (eds): *Papers from the Third International Conference on Historical Linguistics, Hamburg, August 22-26 1977.* 1982.
14. TRAUGOTT, Elizabeth C., Rebecca LaBRUM & Susan SHEPHERD (eds): *Papers from the Fourth International Conference on Historical Linguistics, Stanford, March 26-30 1979.* 1980.
15. ANDERSON, John (ed.): *Language Form and Linguistic Variation. Papers dedicated to Angus McIntosh.* 1982.
16. ARBEITMAN, Yoël L. & Allan R. BOMHARD (eds): *Bono Homini Donum: Essays in Historical Linguistics, in Memory of J.Alexander Kerns.* 1981.
17. LIEB, Hans-Heinrich: *Integrational Linguistics. 6 volumes. Vol. II-VI n.y.p.* 1984/93.
18. IZZO, Herbert J. (ed.): *Italic and Romance. Linguistic Studies in Honor of Ernst Pulgram.* 1980.
19. RAMAT, Paolo et al. (eds): *Linguistic Reconstruction and Indo-European Syntax. Proceedings of the Colloquium of the 'Indogermanischhe Gesellschaft'. University of Pavia, 6-7 September 1979.* 1980.
20. NORRICK, Neal R.: *Semiotic Principles in Semantic Theory.* 1981.
21. AHLQVIST, Anders (ed.): *Papers from the Fifth International Conference on Historical Linguistics, Galway, April 6-10 1981.* 1982.
22. UNTERMANN, Jürgen & Bela BROGYANYI (eds): *Das Germanische und die Rekonstruktion der Indogermanischen Grundsprache. Akten des Freiburger Kolloquiums der Indogermanischen Gesellschaft, Freiburg, 26-27 Februar 1981.* 1984.
23. DANIELSEN, Niels: *Papers in Theoretical Linguistics. Edited by Per Baerentzen.* 1992.
24. LEHMANN, Winfred P. & Yakov MALKIEL (eds): *Perspectives on Historical Linguistics. Papers from a conference held at the meeting of the Language Theory Division, Modern Language Assn., San Francisco, 27-30 December 1979.* 1982.
25. ANDERSEN, Paul Kent: *Word Order Typology and Comparative Constructions.* 1983.

26. BALDI, Philip (ed.): *Papers from the XIIth Linguistic Symposium on Romance Languages, Univ. Park, April 1-3, 1982*. 1984.

27. BOMHARD, Alan R.: *Toward Proto-Nostratic. A New Approach to the Comparison of Proto-Indo-European and Proto-Afroasiatic. Foreword by Paul J. Hopper*. 1984.

28. BYNON, James (ed.): *Current Progress in Afro-Asiatic Linguistics: Papers of the Third International Hamito-Semitic Congress, London, 1978*. 1984.

29. PAPROTTÉ, Wolf & René DIRVEN (eds): *The Ubiquity of Metaphor: Metaphor in language and thought*. 1985 (publ. 1986).

30. HALL, Robert A. Jr.: *Proto-Romance Morphology. = Comparative Romance Grammar, vol. III*. 1984.

31. GUILLAUME, Gustave: *Foundations for a Science of Language*.

32. COPELAND, James E. (ed.): *New Directions in Linguistics and Semiotics*. Co-edition with Rice University Press who hold exclusive rights for US and Canada. 1984.

33. VERSTEEGH, Kees: *Pidginization and Creolization. The Case of Arabic*. 1984.

34. FISIAK, Jacek (ed.): *Papers from the VIth International Conference on Historical Linguistics, Poznan, 22-26 August. 1983*. 1985.

35. COLLINGE, N.E.: *The Laws of Indo-European*. 1985.

36. KING, Larry D. & Catherine A. MALEY (eds): *Selected papers from the XIIIth Linguistic Symposium on Romance Languages, Chapel Hill, N.C., 24-26 March 1983*. 1985.

37. GRIFFEN, T.D.: *Aspects of Dynamic Phonology*. 1985.

38. BROGYANYI, Bela & Thomas KRÖMMELBEIN (eds): *Germanic Dialects:Linguistic and Philological Investigations*. 1986.

39. BENSON, James D., Michael J. CUMMINGS, & William S. GREAVES (eds): *Linguistics in a Systemic Perspective*. 1988.

40. FRIES, Peter Howard (ed.) in collaboration with Nancy M. Fries: *Toward an Understanding of Language: Charles C. Fries in Perspective*. 1985.

41. EATON, Roger, et al. (eds): *Papers from the 4th International Conference on English Historical Linguistics, April 10-13, 1985*. 1985.

42. MAKKAI, Adam & Alan K. MELBY (eds): *Linguistics and Philosophy. Festschrift for Rulon S. Wells*. 1985 (publ. 1986).

43. AKAMATSU, Tsutomu: *The Theory of Neutralization and the Archiphoneme in Functional Phonology*. 1988.

44. JUNGRAITHMAYR, Herrmann & Walter W. MUELLER (eds): *Proceedings of the Fourth International Hamito-Semitic Congress*. 1987.

45. KOOPMAN, W.F., F.C. Van der LEEK , O. FISCHER & R. EATON (eds): *Explanation and Linguistic Change*. 1986

46. PRIDEAUX, Gary D. & William J. BAKER: *Strategies and Structures: The processing of relative clauses*. 1987.

47. LEHMANN, Winfred P. (ed.): *Language Typology 1985. Papers from the Linguistic Typology Symposium, Moscow, 9-13 Dec. 1985*. 1986.

48. RAMAT, Anna G., Onofrio CARRUBA and Giuliano BERNINI (eds): *Papers from the 7th International Conference on Historical Linguistics*. 1987.

49. WAUGH, Linda R. and Stephen RUDY (eds): *New Vistas in Grammar: Invariance and Variation. Proceedings of the Second International Roman Jakobson Conference, New York University, Nov.5-8, 1985*. 1991.

50. RUDZKA-OSTYN, Brygida (ed.): *Topics in Cognitive Linguistics*. 1988.

51. CHATTERJEE, Ranjit: *Aspect and Meaning in Slavic and Indic. With a foreword by Paul Friedrich*. 1989.

52. FASOLD, Ralph W. & Deborah SCHIFFRIN (eds): *Language Change and Variation*. 1989.

53. SANKOFF, David: *Diversity and Diachrony*. 1986.

54. WEIDERT, Alfons: *Tibeto-Burman Tonology. A comparative analysis.* 1987
55. HALL, Robert A. Jr.: *Linguistics and Pseudo-Linguistics.* 1987.
56. HOCKETT, Charles F.: *Refurbishing our Foundations. Elementary linguistics from an advanced point of view.* 1987.
57. BUBENIK, Vít: *Hellenistic and Roman Greece as a Sociolinguistic Area.* 1989.
58. ARBEITMAN, Yoël. L. (ed.): *Fucus: A Semitic/Afrasian Gathering in Remembrance of Albert Ehrman.* 1988.
59. VAN VOORST, Jan: *Event Structure.* 1988.
60. KIRSCHNER, Carl & Janet DECESARIS (eds): *Studies in Romance Linguistics. Selected Proceedings from the XVII Linguistic Symposium on Romance Languages.* 1989.
61. CORRIGAN, Roberta L., Fred ECKMAN & Michael NOONAN (eds): *Linguistic Categorization. Proceedings of an International Symposium in Milwaukee, Wisconsin, April 10-11, 1987.* 1989.
62. FRAJZYNGIER, Zygmunt (ed.): *Current Progress in Chadic Linguistics. Proceedings of the International Symposium on Chadic Linguistics, Boulder, Colorado, 1-2 May 1987.* 1989.
63. EID, Mushira (ed.): *Perspectives on Arabic Linguistics I. Papers from the First Annual Symposium on Arabic Linguistics.* 1990.
64. BROGYANYI, Bela (ed.): *Prehistory, History and Historiography of Language, Speech, and Linguistic Theory. Papers in honor of Oswald Szemérenyi I.* 1992.
65. ADAMSON, Sylvia, Vivien A. LAW, Nigel VINCENT and Susan WRIGHT (eds): *Papers from the 5th International Conference on English Historical Linguistics.* 1990.
66. ANDERSEN, Henning and Konrad KOERNER (eds): *Historical Linguistics 1987. Papers from the 8th International Conference on Historical Linguistics, Lille, August 30-Sept., 1987.* 1990.
67. LEHMANN, Winfred P. (ed.): *Language Typology 1987. Systematic Balance in Language. Papers from the Linguistic Typology Symposium, Berkeley, 1-3 Dec 1987.* 1990.
68. BALL, Martin, James FIFE, Erich POPPE &Jenny ROWLAND (eds): *Celtic Linguistics/ Ieithyddiaeth Geltaidd. Readings in the Brythonic Languages. Festschrift for T. Arwyn Watkins.* 1990.
69. WANNER, Dieter and Douglas A. KIBBEE (eds): *New Analyses in Romance Linguistics. Selected papers from the Linguistic Symposium on Romance Languages XVIIII, Urbana-Champaign, April 7-9, 1988.* 1991.
70. JENSEN, John T.: *Morphology. Word structure in generative grammar.* 1990.
71. O'GRADY, William: *Categories and Case. The sentence structure of Korean.* 1991.
72. EID, Mushira and John MCCARTHY (eds): *Perspectives on Arabic Linguistics II. Papers from the Second Annual Symposium on Arabic Linguistics.* 1990.
73. STAMENOV, Maxim (ed.): *Current Advances in Semantic Theory.* 1991.
74. LAEUFER, Christiane and Terrell A. MORGAN (eds): *Theoretical Analyses in Romance Linguistics.* 1991.
75. DROSTE, Flip G. and John E. JOSEPH (eds): *Linguistic Theory and Grammatical Description. Nine Current Approaches.* 1991.
76. WICKENS, Mark A.: *Grammatical Number in English Nouns. An empirical and theoretical account.* 1992.
77. BOLTZ, William G. and Michael C. SHAPIRO (eds): *Studies in the Historical Phonology of Asian Languages.* 1991.
78. KAC, Michael: *Grammars and Grammaticality.* 1992.
79. ANTONSEN, Elmer H. and Hans Henrich HOCK (eds): *STAEF-CRAEFT: Studies in Germanic Linguistics. Select papers from the First and Second Symposium on Germanic Linguistics, University of Chicago, 24 April 1985, and Univ. of Illinois at Urbana-Champaign, 3-4 Oct. 1986.* 1991.

80. COMRIE, Bernard and Mushira EID (eds): *Perspectives on Arabic Linguistics III. Papers from the Third Annual Symposium on Arabic Linguistics*. 1991.

81. LEHMANN, Winfred P. and H.J. HEWITT (eds): *Language Typology 1988. Typological Models in the Service of Reconstruction*. 1991.

82. VAN VALIN, Robert D. (ed.): *Advances in Role and Reference Grammar*. 1992.

83. FIFE, James and Erich POPPE (eds): *Studies in Brythonic Word Order*. 1991.

84. DAVIS, Garry W. and Gregory K. IVERSON (eds): *Explanation in Historical Linguistics*. 1992.

85. BROSELOW, Ellen, Mushira EID and John McCARTHY (eds): *Perspectives on Arabic Linguistics IV. Papers from the Annual Symposium on Arabic Linguistics*. 1992.

86. KESS, Joseph F.: *Psycholinguistics. Psychology, linguistics, and the study of natural language*. 1992.

87. BROGYANYI, Bela and Reiner LIPP (eds): *Historical Philology: Greek, Latin, and Romance. Papers in honor of Oswald Szemerényi II*. 1992.

88. SHIELDS, Kenneth: *A History of Indo-European Verb Morphology*. 1992.

89. BURRIDGE, Kate: *Syntactic Change in Germanic. A study of some aspects of language change in Germanic with particular reference to Middle Dutch*. 1992.

90. KING, Larry D.: *The Semantic Structure of Spanish. Meaning and grammatical form*. 1992.

91. HIRSCHBÜHLER, Paul and Konrad KOERNER (eds): *Romance Languages and Modern Linguistic Theory. Selected papers from the XX Linguistic Symposium on Romance Languages, University of Ottawa, April 10-14, 1990*. 1992.

92. POYATOS, Fernando: *Paralanguage: A linguistic and interdisciplinary approach to interactive speech and sounds*. 1992.

93. LIPPI-GREEN, Rosina (ed.): *Recent Developments in Germanic Linguistics*. 1992.

94. HAGÈGE, Claude: *The Language Builder. An essay on the human signature in linguistic morphogenesis*. 1992.

95. MILLER, D. Gary: *Complex Verb Formation*. 1992.

96. LIEB, Hans-Heinrich (ed.): *Prospects for a New Structuralism*. 1992.

97. BROGYANYI, Bela & Reiner LIPP (eds): *Comparative-Historical Linguistics: Indo-European and Finno-Ugric. Papers in honor of Oswald Szemerényi III*. 1992.

98. EID, Mushira & Gregory K. IVERSON: *Principles and Prediction: The analysis of natural language*. 1993.

99. JENSEN, John T.: *English Phonology*. 1993.

100. MUFWENE, Salikoko S. and Lioba MOSHI (eds): *Topics in African Linguistics. Papers from the XXI Annual Conference on African Linguistics, University of Georgia, April 1990*. 1993.

101. EID, Mushira & Clive HOLES (eds): *Perspectives on Arabic Linguistics V. Papers from the Fifth Annual Symposium on Arabic Linguistics*. 1993.

102. GARGOV, Georg and Petko STAYNOV (eds) : *Explorations in Language and Cognition. Selcted Papers from the workshop : The notion of cognitive in linguistics, September 1989*. n.y.p.

103. ASHBY, William J., Marianne MITHUN, Giorgio PERISSINOTTO and Eduardo RAPOSO: *Linguistic Perspectives on Romance Languages. Selected papers from the XXI Linguistic Symposium on Romance Languages, Santa Barbara, February 21-24, 1991*. 1993.

104. KURZOVÁ, Helena: *From Indo-European to Latin. The evolution of a morphosyntactic type*. 1993.

105. HUALDE, José Ignacio and Jon ORTIZ DE URBANA (eds): *Generative Studies in Basque Linguistics*. 1993.

106. AERTSEN, Henk and Robert J. JEFFERS (eds): *Historical Linguistics 1989. Papers from the 9th International Conference on Historical Linguistics, New Brunswick, 14-18 August 1989*. 1993.

107. MARLE, Jaap van (ed.): *Historical Linguistics 1991. Papers from the 10th International Conference on Historical Linguistics, Amsterdam, August 12-16, 1991.* 1993.

108. LIEB, Hans-Heinrich: *Linguistic Variables. Towards a unified theory of linguistic variation.* 1993.

109. PAGLIUCA, William (ed.): *Perspectives on Grammaticalization.* 1994.

110. SIMONE, Raffaele (ed.): *Iconicity in Language.* 1995.

111. TOBIN, Yishai: *Invariance, Markedness and Distinctive Feature Analysis. A contrastive study of sign systems in English and Hebrew.* 1994.

112. CULIOLI, Antoine: *Cognition and Representation in Linguistic Theory. Translated, edited and introduced by Michel Liddle.* 1995.

113. FERNÁNDEZ, Francisco, Miguel FUSTER and Juan Jose CALVO (eds): *English Historical Linguistics 1992. Papers from the 7th International Conference on English Historical Linguistics, Valencia, 22-26 September 1992.*1994.

114. EGLI, U., P. PAUSE, Chr. SCHWARZE, A. von STECHOW, G. WIENOLD (eds): *Lexical Knowledge in the Organisation of Language.* 1995.

115. EID, Mushira, Vincente CANTARINO and Keith WALTERS (eds): *Perspectives on Arabic Linguistics. Vol. VI. Papers from the Sixth Annual Symposium on Arabic Linguistics.* 1994.

116. MILLER, D. Gary: *Ancient Scripts and Phonological Knowledge.* 1994.

117. PHILIPPAKI-WARBURTON, I., K. NICOLAIDIS and M. SIFIANOU (eds): *Themes in Greek Linguistics. Papers from the first International Conference on Greek Linguistics, Reading, September 1993.* 1994.

118. HASAN, Ruqaiya and Peter H. FRIES (eds): *On Subject and Theme. A discourse functional perspective.* 1995.

119. LIPPI-GREEN, Rosina: *Language Ideology and Language Change in Early Modern German. A sociolinguistic study of the consonantal system of Nuremberg.* 1994.

120. STONHAM, John T. : *Combinatorial Morphology.* 1994.

121. HASAN, Ruqaiya, Carmel CLORAN and David BUTT (eds): *Functional Descriptions. Transitivity and the construction of experience.* 1995.

122. SMITH, John Charles and Martin MAIDEN (eds): *Linguistic Theory and the Romance Languages.* 1995.

123. AMASTAE, Jon, Grant GOODALL, Mario MONTALBETTI and Marianne PHINNEY: *Contemporary Research in Romance Linguistics. Papers from the XXII Linguistic Symposium on Romance Languages, El Paso//Juárez, February 22-24, 1994.* 1995.

124. ANDERSEN, Henning: *Historical Linguistics 1993. Selected papers from the 11th International Conference on Historical Linguistics, Los Angeles, 16-20 August 1993.* 1995.

125. SINGH, Rajendra (ed.): *Towards a Critical Sociolinguistics.* n.y.p.

126. MATRAS, Yaron (ed.): *Romani in Contact. The history, structure and sociology of a language.* 1995.

127. GUY, Gregory R., John BAUGH, Deborah SCHIFFRIN and Crawford FEAGIN (eds): *Towards a Social Science of Language. Papers in honor of William Labov. Volume 1: Variation and change in language and society.* n.y.p.

128. GUY, Gregory R., John BAUGH, Deborah SCHIFFRIN and Crawford FEAGIN (eds): *Towards a Social Science of Language. Papers in honor of William Labov. Volume 2: Social interaction and discourse structures.* n.y.p.

129. LEVIN, Saul: *Semitic and Indo-European: The Principal Etymologies. With observations on Afro-Asiatic.* 1995.

130. EID, Mushira (ed.) *Perspectives on Arabic Linguistics. Vol. VII. Papers from the Seventh Annual Symposium on Arabic Linguistics.* 1995.

131. HUALDE, Jose Ignacio, Joseba A. LAKARRA and R.L. Trask (eds): *Towards a History of the Basque Language.* n.y.p.